Complete Old English

Complete
Old English

Mark Atherton

First published in Great Britain in 2006 by Hodder Education. An Hachette UK company.

This edition published in 2019 by John Murray Learning.

Copyright © Mark Atherton 2006, 2010, 2019

The right of Mark Atherton to be identified as the Author of the Work has been asserted by him in accordance with the Copyright, Designs and Patents Act 1988.

Database right Hodder & Stoughton (makers)

The *Teach Yourself* name is a registered trademark of Hachette UK.

British Library Cataloguing in Publication Data: a catalogue record for this title is available from the British Library.

Library of Congress Catalog Card Number: on file.

ISBN: 9781473627925

1

The publisher has used its best endeavours to ensure that any website addresses referred to in this book are correct and active at the time of going to press. However, the publisher and the author have no responsibility for the websites and can make no guarantee that a site will remain live or that the content will remain relevant, decent or appropriate.

The publisher has made every effort to mark as such all words which it believes to be trademarks. The publisher should also like to make it clear that the presence of a word in the book, whether marked or unmarked, in no way affects its legal status as a trademark.

Every reasonable effort has been made by the publisher to trace the copyright holders of material in this book. Any errors or omissions should be notified in writing to the publisher, who will endeavour to rectify the situation for any reprints and future editions.

Typeset by Cenveo Publisher Services.

Printed and bound in Great Britain by CPI Group (UK) Ltd., Croydon, CR0 4YY.

John Murray Learning policy is to use papers that are natural, renewable and recyclable products and made from wood grown in sustainable forests. The logging and manufacturing processes are expected to conform to the environmental regulations of the country of origin.

Carmelite House
50 Victoria Embankment
London EC4Y 0DZ
www.hodder.co.uk

Contents

Acknowledgements

I would like to thank the following people in particular for their encouragement or helpful comments on sections of this book: Julie Dyson, who kindly read through sections of this book in draft, Catherine A.M. Clarke, who provided a second voice for the audio recording, Andy Orchard, who advised on the text for the Beowulf in unit 23, Susannah Jayes, who researched the illustrations, Michelle Armstrong, Stephen Baxter, Jenny Campbell, Ginny Catmur, Vincent Gillespie, Emma Green, Tony Harris, Peter Jackson, Kazutomo Karasawa, Francis Leneghan, Anne MacDonald, Rafael Pascual, who advised on metre, Barbara Raw, Victoria Roddam, Fritz Stieleke, Daniel Thomas, Christina Wood; colleagues and students at Regent's Park College, and the very many students who participated in the Old English language classes and lectures at the English Faculty, University of Oxford, and at the Department of Medieval English Literature at the Heinrich-Heine-University, Düsseldorf.

About the author

Mark Atherton began teaching Old English in 1997 after completing a DPhil in linguistics and medieval studies at the University of York. He now teaches and lectures at the University of Oxford; he is Senior College Lecturer in Old and Middle English at Regent's Park College and Lecturer in English Language at Mansfield College. He recently spent a year as Visiting Professor in Medieval English Literature at the Heinrich-Heine-University, Düsseldorf, Germany. He is the author of *The Making of England: A New History of the Anglo-Saxon World* (London, 2017).

Introduction

Old English (Anglo-Saxon)

Old English, or Anglo-Saxon, as it is sometimes called, was the language spoken and written in England until the twelfth century. Its rich literature ranges from the epic *Beowulf* to the visionary poem *The Dream of the Rood* to the varied prose writings of archbishop Wulfstan and the *Anglo-Saxon Chronicle*. As the language of historical record, Old English opens an invaluable window on the early history of England: on the political events that shaped the land, on the culture and spirituality of the writers of the time, on landscape history and the layout of towns and villages, on the history of institutions. Through the study of their language these documents can be made to speak with their own voices and express their concerns. All languages have their own phrases and modes of expression, and by learning Old English you can appreciate how the men and women of the time actually thought and felt.

Beginning as a set of dialects spoken in the provinces and petty kingdoms of southern Britain, Old English eventually became the standard written language used by the rulers of England from Alfred the Great to king Harold. In many respects, this language is with us today, in the very names of the towns and villages in which we live. These place-names reflect the shape of the land and relate how it was used: Longridge and Revidge (i.e. Rough Edge) near the dark or shining stream of Blackburn; Swindon, the hill where the pigs were grazed; Oxford, the river crossing suitable for oxen; Bury St Edmunds, the borough or town with a monastery church dedicated to St Edmund, patron and defender of its rights. It is significant that Old English had a core vocabulary that we still use in our everyday speech and writing. *Head and heart, hands and feet, sticks and stones*, all go back to Old English in a different spelling; *sun, moon and stars*, or *thunder and lightning* are originally Old English words, as are *love and hate, strength and weakness*. The basic grammar of present-day English has older roots: the way we talk about the past by ringing the changes in the vowels of *sing, sang, sung* or *choose, chose, chosen*; the way we express moods of volition and obligation with auxiliary verbs such as *will–would, may–might, shall–should*; the way we refer intimately to ourselves and others with personal pronouns such as *me and you, his and hers*, or even *I and thou*.

In his poem 'Bone Dreams' from his book *North*, the Irish poet Seamus Heaney pictures the history of the English language as a kind of archaeological dig; the excavator explores the many layers or accretions that the language has gathered over the centuries. Digging down from the present time through the colonial periods the archaeologist uncovers layer after layer of influences that affected the English lexicon:

Colonialism	Asian, American, African words come into English
Enlightenment	Latin and Greek scientific terms
Renaissance	Latinate learned words
Middle ages	French literary and cultural influences
Norman	French administration
Old Norse	everyday words especially in the north and east
Old English – the foundation	

At the base of his trench, the poet archaeologist finds **ban-hus** (pronounced '*bahn-hoos*'); this is the poetic compound *bone-house*, a kenning or metaphor from *Beowulf* that signifies the body, where the spirit lives. For Heaney, as translator of *Beowulf*, this is one of the attractions of the Old English poetic line, the compression of its imagery. Other modern poets and writers have felt similarly drawn: W.H. Auden and Ted Hughes to its strength and craftedness, Gerard Manley Hopkins to the lilt of its alliterative rhythms, J.R.R. Tolkien to its strong contrasts of light and dark and its myth-making power.

The aim of this book is to help you to gain an efficient reading knowledge of Old English. It offers a graded progressive course in Old English based on authentic texts selected from the rich archive of poems, prose and historical documents that have survived from the libraries of early medieval England. Passages from famous poems such as *Beowulf* and *The Battle of Maldon* will be presented, but there are also extracts from the writings of great prose writers such as archbishop Wulfstan of York, and whole texts from the administrative records of the period, chosen for their cultural and historical interest. The passages are presented with minimal adaptation, so that you may, if you wish, go back to the original editions and read them with confidence. In reading these texts, you will at the same time also explore the political, cultural and literary contexts in which they were written.

How the book works

In *Complete Old English* you will explore a range of texts and documents from Anglo-Saxon England, focussing on the reigns of Æthelred the Unready (reigned 978–1016) and his son Edward the Confessor (1042–1066) and in particular on the intervening period of Anglo-Danish rule under Cnut the Great (1016–1035). Study texts include chronicle, riddle, treatise, declaration, royal writ, marriage agreement, charter bounds, biblical narrative, saint's life, heroic poem, epic, elegy, and romance. You begin with the account of Edward the Confessor's coronation in 1043 from the *Anglo-Saxon Chronicle*. By the end you will be in a position to read with fluency the coronation oath that Edward performed at that ceremony, as well as explore the language and style of *The Battle of Maldon* and *Beowulf*.

The book has the following features.

▶ **What you will learn** identifies what you should be able to do in Old English by the end of the unit.

▶ **Vocabulary builder** presents a theme-based way of recording and learning the words and phrases of the language in which keywords from the study texts are arranged into appropriate sense groups and semantic fields. Sometimes the connection with modern English will be made explicit: you will be shown how words in Old English are related in form or meaning to their modern English equivalents. Above all, you will also study the meaning and connotations of words against the social and intellectual background of the period.

▶ **Old–modern connections** give insights into the ways in which Old English is still connected with the language of the present day.

▶ **Pronunciation** of the texts is important for appreciating the literature, whether poems or prose documents, and for recreating their dramatic and rhetorical effects. It also makes the language easier to learn and helps you to make clear the correspondences between Old English and modern English. A reference guide to spelling and pronunciation is provided at the beginning of the book. It will help if you refer to this frequently, especially at first, and listen to the recordings. Further guidance is given in the early units of the book, and an approximate pronunciation based on modern English spelling is given in inverted commas.

▶ **Study texts** form the basis of each unit, with help and guidance on vocabulary, cultural background, and grammar. Usually the study text will be accompanied by supplementary reading. All texts appearing in the audio recording are marked with an icon.

▶ **Grammar** sections will explain three or four points of language usage. In the earlier units, these explanations will be in non-technical terms, with the main focus on increasing your ability to read the study texts in the original. Later units give further grammatical information, using more traditional tables and paradigms to sum up what has already been learned, and to fill in any gaps.

▶ **Language discovery** encourages you to read the study text and work out the language patterns for yourself.

▶ **Practice** offers a variety of exercises, including comprehension, gap-fill and listening, to give you a chance to see and understand words and phrases in context.

▶ **Reading** sections in each unit are intended to supplement the study texts with passages of verse and prose selected for similarity of theme or vocabulary. These are accompanied by a parallel translation but without a vocabulary list. The aim is to encourage a lighter, more extensive kind of reading where you read for gist or general understanding, and so improve your knowledge of the language.

▶ **Language and style** in later units will provide you with insights into the different techniques used by Old English writers, whether they are writing prose or poetry. Information will be given on choice of word or phrase, the use of rhythm and metre, the frequent use of alliteration (e.g. light and life). By studying such devices, along with sentence structure, word order and rhetoric, you will begin to recognize the style of a particular author, for example the distinctive 'voice' heard in the writings of archbishop Wulfstan, and to make connections with other texts you have read.

▶ **Test yourself** is a short exercise allowing you to assess what you have learned in the unit.

▶ **Self-check** reviews what you can do in Old English after completing each unit.

▶ The **Answer** key at the back of the book allows you to check your progress by providing answers to the various exercises in the main units.

▶ The **Word index** at the back of the book lists all the words and phrases that appear in the study texts and practice exercises, with cross-references to the unit(s) where the word is explained or discussed. At first, in order to give as much primary assistance as possible, words are given exactly as spelt in the texts themselves, as well as in the base form with which they would appear in a dictionary. To encourage passive learning, the vocabulary in the reading sections is not given specific listings in the index at the back, since the parallel translations should provide all the help that is needed for extensive reading for general understanding.

▶ The focus, then, is on the study text. In the units you can read or listen to the texts, learn the meanings of their vocabulary and grammar and explore their literary, historical and cultural contexts. After completing units 1–24 you will be ready to proceed with advanced study of Old English. The select bibliography provides general reading and particular recommendations for the topics covered in the individual units.

Learning to learn

This book aims to provide material for as many different interests, and as many different kinds of learner, as possible. Some learners like systematic grammar, others prefer to assimilate linguistic patterns gradually as they appear in the texts; some like to start reading and thinking in the language immediately, others like to translate; some develop systematic techniques for learning vocabulary, others like to listen to audio recordings, to acquire the natural rhythms of the language and learn 'chunks' and naturally occurring phrases. In this book, you are encouraged to try out all these various approaches, and extend your own repertoire of language learning techniques into territory with which you are not yet familiar. It is recommended that you work at the language in regular short intervals: half an hour a day over a period of five days is preferable to three hours in a block once a week.

People and places

The study of Old English opens a window on the past and illuminates the history and the literature. Through the texts we gain glimpses of the people of the time and hear snatches of their talk. You will see the flood tide ebb in the Blackwater estuary as the men of Essex prepared to face the Vikings in the poem *The Battle of Maldon*. You will read texts that were composed for or used by such historic figures as king Æthelred the Unready, and Byrhtnoth, the leading man of Æthelred's early reign and the tragic hero of the fight at Maldon in the year 991. Various units will explore documents and prose texts from the career of the writer and statesman Wulfstan, who served as archbishop of York from 1002 to 1023, and the king he influenced, Cnut, the former Viking who ruled England from 1016 to 1035. Five units will use study texts taken from the *Story of Joseph* in the remarkable illustrated Old English *Hexateuch*. This biblical paraphrase is a literary text in its own right but also reflects the cultural and political life of the eleventh-century audience for which it was intended. Everyday life is not forgotten, and various units include sections on the place-names of England, predominantly Old English in origin, which reflect the precise and meaningful ways in which ordinary people interacted with the land on which they lived.

In one historical document, to give a longer example, we see the social strength and influence of women at the time: a lawsuit takes place between a man and a woman over a piece of land. The woman calls on the aid of the queen herself, and a whole group of women attend the assembly of the shire court to support her (see unit 19). The assembly meets at Cwichelm's Barrow, an ancient mound at the junction of the old Ridgeway and the road to West Hendred in Berkshire. Now partly obscured by trees and damaged by a pre-twentieth-century archaeological dig, the mound is still accessible; it is possible to stand on the site where those people met to argue their case, as recorded on a slip of parchment a thousand years ago.

In another lawsuit, heard by the shire court in Herefordshire, a woman was sued by her own son. In this instance no women attended the hearing, and perhaps they were prevented, but the indignant mother sent a message to the assembly, and the case was ratified by the men present (see unit 20). Then the presiding official, Thorkell the White, husband of the woman's kinswoman, rode to Hereford and had her exact words recorded in a blank space of a Latin gospel book at the cathedral, where it remains to this day. Here is a tangible material connection between the present and the past. Such explorations can bring many rewards: a renewed sense of past connections, new social and historical insights, even new ways of seeing the English language and its literature.

Some linguistic terms used in the book

Adjective: a word that describes or qualifies a noun (*fearful*, *green*, *happy*)

Adverb: a word that qualifies a verb (*swam quickly*) or modifies an adjective (*extremely easy*); expresses the time, manner, place of an action (*then*, *quickly*, *here* etc.)

Article: either the definite article *the* or the indefinite article *a*, *an*

Cognate: a related word in languages (English two is cognate with German 'zwei' because they both descend from a common ancestor in primitive Germanic)

Determiner: an article such as *the* or a pronoun like *my* used before the noun (or before adjective + noun) in a noun phrase, e.g. *the sun*, *the bright sun*, *my lord*, *my good lord*

Noun: a word referring to a person, thing or idea (*man*, *tree*, *friendship*)

Preposition: a short connecting word, such as *to*, *for*, *by*, *with*, *from*

Verb: a word denoting an action in time (*swim*, *arrived*, *sang*) or a state of being, mind, or emotion (*be*, *have*, *believe*, *loved*)

Prefix: a meaningful syllable or short word affixed to the beginning of a word; the prefix changes the meaning of the root word, e.g. *mis-take*, *be-come*, *under-stand*

Suffix: a similar affix added to the end of a word, e.g. *good-ness*, *holi-ness*, *lord-ship*, *lady-ship*

Pronunciation

SHORT INTRODUCTION

The pronunciation of Old English has been carefully worked out by a process of historical and comparative research. In the overview here, many linguistic facts have been omitted, but further distinctions and fine tunings will be made in the course of the book. For those interested in phonetics, some further reading on the sounds of the language will be given at the end of the book.

The following is a quick guide to sounding broadly correct. It is important to learn the basic sounds of the language, so that the texts and poems can be read fluently and with their original rhythmical effects. In addition, once the basic sounds are learnt the connections with modern English become much clearer and the language is much easier to learn.

In the vocabularies, the Old English is given in bold, the meaning in italics, and where appropriate a rough pronunciation based on modern English orthography is indicated by inverted commas: e.g. **rice** *kingdom* 'ree-cheh'.

LANGUAGE INSIGHT

The basic rule is to pronounce every letter as written, including **-e** on the end of words. The letters **þ** and **ð** were pronounced as modern 'th'; **g** adjacent to **e** or **i** becomes a 'yuh' sound and **ic** is 'itch'. Vowels sound very like those in modern English: **pat**, **pet**, **pit**, **pot**, **put**, or like continental European vowels when lengthened; **ea** is a one-syllable 'e-a' as in the vowel in '*air*' in southern British English (without any sounding of the consonant '*r*').

Pronunciation guide for later study

Further details on pronunciation are given below and these are pages to which you should return frequently for reference purposes. However, it is suggested that you cover at least the first three units of the book before you study the information below in greater detail.

Many consonants sounded as in modern English: *b, p, t, d, l, r, w, m, n, x.*

The consonants **f**, **s**, and **þ** have two pronunciations:

1 Initially and finally they sound like 'f' and 's' and the 'th' in 'thin'.

2 When they appear in the middle of a word between vowels, they take on the voiced pronunciation 'v' and 'z'. Thus **heofon** and **freosan** sound more like their modern equivalents *heaven* and *freeze* than they might appear at first sight and the medial **-þ-** will sound like 'th' in 'bathing', not like the voiceless 'th' in 'mathematics'.

The letter **c** represents 'k' in **cyning** *king* and **candel** *candle*, but when adjacent to the vowels **e** and **i** in **ceap** *goods*, **cild** *child* and **cirice** *church* or names ending in **-ric** like **Ælfric** and **Godric**, it had the modern 'ch' sound of 'rich'. Similarly **g** is 'g' in **gōd** *good* but becomes a 'y' sound in **gif** *if* 'yif' and **geong** *young* 'yeong' and **dæg** *day* 'dæy'. In the middle of words, such as **boga** *bow*, **g** later came to be pronounced 'w', but in the Old English period it was pronounced like a Dutch 'g' or a German voiced 'ach' sound heard in north German 'sagen Sie'. The letter combination **cg** is equivalent to the modern spelling 'dge'; thus **ecg** and **brycg** sound very like modern 'edge' and 'bridge'. Similarly, **sc** is the digraph for 'sh' as in **scip** *ship*, pronounced 'ship'.

In the middle of words **h** sounded like the medial '-ch-' in German 'Sicht' while in final position it sounded like the '-ch' in Scottish 'Loch Ness'.

The letter **a** represents a back vowel like 'a' in 'psalm'. It contrasts with the front vowel spelt **æ**, pronounced as in southern British English or standard American 'man'. There are two diphthongs, written **ea** and **eo**. Again, each letter should be pronounced, but the tongue should glide quickly from one vowel to the next so that the diphthong remains one syllable.

Each vowel and diphthong has a short and long sound. The long vowel has the same quality of sound as the short vowel; the difference is basically one of extension: the short vowel is drawled out to make it long. Listen carefully for long vowels in the recordings. In Old English, the word **is** with a short vowel (pronounced roughly as 'iss') means *is*, whereas **īs** with a long vowel (pronounced 'ees') means *ice*. Similarly, note the difference between the short vowels in **man** *person*, **full** *full* and **god** *god* compared with the long vowels in **mān** *evil*, **fūl** *foul* and **gōd** *good*, pronounced 'mahn', 'fool' and 'goad' respectively.

Sometimes the scribes marked length with an accent, e.g. **ís** and **gód**, but this was done only occasionally and often inconsistently. Especially for poetic texts, many modern textbooks of Old English employ a macron over the long vowel, e.g. **stān**, **īs** and **gōd** (meaning *stone, ice* and *good* respectively).

In keeping with the aim of this book to present texts unencumbered and with minimal adaptation, macrons will not be used in the actual study texts. In explanations, however, occasional use of the macron will mark the long vowels of words like **īs** and **gōd**. Attention to long vowels helps to make connections with modern English, and will be useful when reading the poetry, where precise distinctions of length are necessary for the correct study of the metre of the poems.

> **LEARNING INSIGHT**
>
> Most traditional textbooks of Old English are arranged as a systematic grammar, covering pronouns, adjectives, nouns, verbs, sentence structure separately. All this is in a set order: in verbs, for instance, the full rules of the present tense are taught before those of the past tense, regular verbs are given first before irregular, and so on. There is a rationale to this, but as one nineteenth-century educationalist put it, 'Would you teach dancing by giving rules for dancing and keeping the learner fixed in his seat?' (Joseph Payne, *Monthly Journal of Education*, 1874: 306). Language learning is a skill or integrated set of skills, and even though each element can and should, to a certain extent, be taught separately, in the actual experience of say, reading a text, all the elements of a language, from its sounds and spellings to its pronouns, verbs and case-endings to its vocabulary and phraseology are present simultaneously. Keeping this in mind, you will see that each unit in this book takes as a basis a certain type of text or genre such as a chronicle entry, a riddle, a king's declaration etc. and teaches some essentials for reading that particular text in context. The aim is to provide an integrated approach to the learning of the language.

1 *Her wæs Eadward gehalgod to cinge*
Here Edward was consecrated as king

In this unit you will learn about:
- ▶ *Old English words, prefixes, and endings*
- ▶ *basic spelling and pronunciation rules*
- ▶ *dithematic (two-part) personal names*
- ▶ *common place-names*

You will read:
- ▶ *The Coronation of Edward the Confessor, from the* **Anglo-Saxon Chronicle** *AD 1043*

 01.00

Her wæs Eadward gehalgod to cinge
Here Edward was consecrated as king

Vocabulary builder

STATUS AND POSITION

cing	*king*
æþeling	*prince*
ealdorman	*high-ranking nobleman*
arcebisceop	*archbishop*
bisceop	*bishop*
preost	*priest*
folc	*people*

VERBS

wæs	*was*
wæron	*were*

The use of English

In 1040, Edward the atheling – prince and heir to the throne – returned to England after twenty-four years of exile on the Continent. Two years later he succeeded to the throne of England and, in the following year, the *Anglo-Saxon Chronicle* reports that Edward was consecrated king with great honour.

Edward the Confessor, as he came to be called by his successors, ruled a stable and prosperous England for twenty-four years. Yet during his lifetime (c.1005–1066), the country became subject to a bewildering variety of cultural influences: from Norse and Anglo-Danish to Norman and French. One constant in all this period of change was the large and central role played by the Old English language in the political, literary and spiritual life of the country. Unlike most of Europe at this time, where Latin was the only written language in use, England had developed a considerable literature in the vernacular, and much of its everyday administration was also conducted through the medium of written English.

VERSION C OF THE *ANGLO-SAXON CHRONICLE*

It so happened that a new version of the *Anglo-Saxon Chronicle* was started around the time of Edward's accession. The *Chronicle* was a year-by-year record of the nation's affairs probably begun in the time of king Alfred in the ninth century. The new recension of the 1040s, known as version C, was made perhaps at Abingdon Abbey or at an ecclesiastical centre in Mercia, the Midland region of Anglo-Saxon England. The compiler copied the earlier *Chronicle* up to his own day and then began entering new records in the annual list of events. By adding his own stories, he was essentially acting as a contemporary observer of political events. The following short Old English text is his own, typically brief, account of the coronation of 1043.

The *Anglo-Saxon Chronicle:* the year 1043

 01.01 As you read or listen, note the spellings of the personal names in the passage. How many people are named in the text? What expressions are used to say when and where Edward was consecrated as king?

1043 Her wæs Eadward gehalgod to cinge on Wincestre on forman Easterdæig mid myccelum wyrðscype, and ða wæron Eastron .iii. Nonas Aprelis. Eadsige arcebisceop hine halgade, and toforan eallum þam folce hine wel lærde, and to his agenre neode and ealles folces wel manude. And Stigant preost wæs gebletsad to bisceope to Eastenglum.

AD 1043 Here Edward was consecrated as king at Winchester on the first Easter Day with great honour, and that year Easter fell on the third of the nones of April. Archbishop Eadsige consecrated him, and before all the people instructed him well, and for his own need and that of all the people admonished him well. And the priest, Stigand, was blessed as bishop to the East Angles.

● OLD–MODERN CORRESPONDENCES

The phrase **mid myccelum wyrðscype** meaning *with great honour* is much closer to modern English than it might first appear. Remember that the letter ð (called 'eth') represents a modern 'th' and that **sc** is modern 'sh'. The last word is therefore the compound *worth-ship*, the origin of the modern word *worship*, which originally had the more general meaning of *honour*.

 01.02 Listen to the account of Edward's coronation, and compare it with the translation above.

 Language discovery

STRATEGIES FOR READING OLD ENGLISH

1 The first strategy to employ when tackling a text written in an inflected language like Old English is to mark up the inflections with hyphens or by underlining, i.e. all the endings which the language uses to mark grammatical meanings in the text. It is also useful to highlight the root or stem of each word by marking any prefixes: an example of an ending is **-e** on **cing** *king*, a prefix **ge-** occurs before **halgod** *hallowed, consecrated*; in the same word, the ending **-od** corresponds to the modern *-ed*.

2 Try doing a literal word-for-word translation of the text. This helps to understand the structure of the language.

 3 01.03 Next, listen to the text being read out loud on the recording (or by someone familiar with the language); this will help with comprehension. Many words (e.g. **Easterdæig**) become instantly recognizable once they are heard and the connections between Old and modern English start to emerge. Using the guide to pronunciation (in the introduction), you can also try reading out loud on your own; it is possible to learn to pronounce the basics of Old English surprisingly quickly. At first, remember that ð, þ represent the modern 'th' sound in 'thorn'. Next, careful attention should be paid to the letter-to-sound correspondences of **æ**, **g**, **c**, **cg** and **sc**.

 4 01.04 Listen again and start observing the patterns of the language: its frequent meaningful endings, its word order, its typical modes of expression and idioms. When reading texts from the *Chronicle*, for instance, you will soon find that a typical word-order is *Here was Edward… Here commanded the king…, Here came Cnut…* etc. As you gradually acquire more knowledge of the rules of grammar, this may seem less necessary, but, in fact, a good habit of observation is always essential: it will strengthen your grasp of the language and enrich your knowledge of its resources.

5 One further option is to experiment with transcribing the text in a slightly modernized spelling, in order to become familiar with the form and shape of the words. An example would be transcribing **Wincestre** as *Winchestre*.

READING STRATEGIES IN PRACTICE

Taking a sentence at a time, we can apply the above strategies to our text from the *Anglo-Saxon Chronicle*.

1 Highlight inflections and prefixes

Her wæs Eadward ge-halg-od to cing-e on Wincestr-e on forma-n Easterdæig mid myccel-um wyrð-scype.

2 Do a literal translation

Here was Edward hallowed to king on Winchester on former Easterday with mickle (i.e. great) worthship.

The literal translation can then be turned into natural modern English:

Here Edward was consecrated as king at Winchester on the first Easter Day with great honour.

3 Pronounce out loud

Pronounce every letter and syllable. For finer points, use the pronunciation guide in the introduction; the following are some hints:

her: pronounce 'hayr' with a long, close vowel like French 'été'. The long vowel points to its later modern form *here*.

wæs: the letter **æ** represents a medium-low front vowel like **-a-** in standard English *cat*.

Eadward: 'Aed-ward'.

ge-halgod: pronounce 'yuhHALgod' (note that the capital letters represent the stressed syllable); make the **a** a long back vowel. The **g** was a guttural or fricative like in Dutch, but a later pronunciation was **w**, which perhaps makes the connection with modern English *hallowed* more obvious.

to: rhymes roughly with modern English 'tow' not with 'too'.

dæig: 'dæi' (glide from the 'æ' to the 'ih' sound). To British ears this may sound rather like an Australian 'G'day!'.

myccelum: 'MÜTCH-eh-lum' (pronounce **y** as French 'u' or German 'ü').

wyrðscype: 'WÜRTH-shih-peh' (**sc** sounds like modern English 'sh').

4 Observe linguistic patterns

Note the word order: *here was Edward hallowed…* In present-day English, the natural sequence is to place Edward before the verb *was consecrated*, but Old English often placed the verb in second position with the subject following. Observe also the use of the prepositions **to**, **on**, **mid**. In Old English it was natural to say that someone *was hallowed to king* rather than *as king;* the preposition still makes perfect sense in modern English, but the idiom is no longer used. From the evidence of this sentence, note also the use of **on** + location in the phrase *on Winchester*, as well as **on** + time in *on Easter Day*.

5 Experiment with modernized spellings

Try modernizing the spelling, replacing **þ** and **ð** with *th*, soft **c** with *ch*, soft **g** with *y* or *i*, and medial guttural **g** with *w*:

Her wæs Edward i-halwod to kinge on Winchestre on forman Easterdæi mid michelum weorthshipe.

If you transcribe the text on these principles, it begins to 'look like' English, or at the very least like a kind of Middle English, and the exercise helps you to become familiar with the orthography or spelling system of Old English.

The words **biscop** *bishop* and **preost** *priest* are originally Greek 'epi-skopos' (literally *over-seer*) and 'presbuteros' (*elder*) borrowed into the Church Latin of Rome as 'episcopus' and 'presbyter' and then into the older Germanic languages when these came into contact with the late Roman empire. As the example of bishop shows, there is a pattern here: the earlier a word is borrowed into English (i.e. taken into the language), the more thoroughly it is assimilated, and takes on a new phonetic identity, so that the connection between 'episcopus' and *bishop* is not immediately obvious.

Practice 1

Using the instructions as a guide, apply some of the reading strategies outlined above to the remaining two sentences from the text below. Some suggested answers for the exercise can be found in the key at the back of the book.

1 **Eadsige arcebisceop hine halgade, and toforan eallum þam folce hine wel lærde, and to his agenre neode and ealles folces wel manude.**

2 **And Stigant preost wæs gebletsad to bisceope to Eastenglum.**

Tasks:

   a do a very literal translation first

   b next, retranslate into idiomatic, natural-sounding English

   c identify potential pronunciation difficulties involving **þ**, **ð**, **æ**, **c**, **g**, **cg** and **sc**

   d make a note of any patterns you can observe in the language of the text, such as use of prepositions (e.g. to, for), or frequent endings on words, or word order

   e transcribe the first sentence with a modernized spelling; omit any endings wherever you can.

Edward's earlier career

In contrast to the relative peace and stability of his period of rule, Edward the Confessor's earlier life had been far from secure. Born in about 1005 at Islip near Oxford on an estate later owned by his mother, Emma of Normandy, he grew up in a country devastated by Viking wars and divided by the alleged misrule of his father Æthelred 'the Unready'. In 1009, for instance, Oxford, an important trading port on the old border of Wessex and Mercia, was burned to the ground. In 1013–14 the Danes seized power and the royal family fled abroad. The following year the situation was reversed and, though still a young boy, Edward was sent back to England on a mission to negotiate with the Council for his father's return to power. But in 1016 Æthelred died and the throne was taken by the Danish warrior Cnut (whose reign will feature in several of the texts in this book). As the new Anglo-Danish dynasty consolidated its power Edward again fled the country for refuge with his Norman relatives.

As a modern biographer and historian has pointed out, Edward was probably resigned to the life of an exile and may never have expected to succeed to the throne when he did. There are some hints about this in our source text. The Chronicle text for the year 1043 suggests that archbishop Eadsige made a special point of instructing the king in his royal duties.

Perhaps he thought that Edward was unprepared for the greatness that had been thrust upon him, and possibly the archbishop was concerned about Edward's reputation as a son of Æthelred the Unready.

> **CULTURAL INSIGHT**
>
> Edward's father is known to history as Ethelred the Unready (reigned 978–1016): this is a modernization of the personal name Æþelræd and the negative byname Unræd given him by others (though presumably not in the presence of the king himself). The word **ræd** means *advice* or *counsel* and **æþel** means *noble*, whereas **un-** is the negative prefix. So Æþelræd Unræd is a pun; it is a later, negative assessment of the reign of Æthelred the ill-advised.

It would be intriguing to know the content of archbishop Eadsige's speech at the coronation before the king and people. One text that we can be fairly certain was used at the ceremony was the Old English coronation oath, the same oath that Edward's father Æthelred had sworn many years before, in AD 978 (for the text, see unit 24). It is possible that the king repeated the words of the oath after the archbishop. But Eadsige probably had more to say than simply this. The Chronicler's choice of the past tense verbs **lærde** and **manude** (*instructed* and *admonished*) is reminiscent of opening formulas from sermons. It is likely that the archbishop preached a set-piece sermon on that solemn occasion. The most influential writer of political sermons in this period was archbishop Wulfstan, a prominent churchman and administrator of the previous generation. His writings were in widespread circulation through the eleventh century and it is perhaps one of these that Eadsige used for his sermon. An ideal text for his purposes would have been archbishop Wulfstan's so-called Institutes of Polity, a treatise on the duties of all the ranks of society, with a recommendation that the king should be a shepherd of the people and carefully keep God's commands and frequently seek out wisdom with the Council (a pointed critique of Æthelred, one is tempted to think). (For a full translation of this passage from the *Institutes of Polity*, see Michael Swanton, *Anglo-Saxon Prose*, in the Bibliography.)

Reading 1

In the reading section of each unit you are invited to read and browse through some passages supplementary to the main study text of the unit. While the study text is the main focus of the unit, the reading texts are chosen for similarity of theme, outlook or vocabulary, but it is not necessary to understand every word or phrase in them. To keep progressing at a steady pace, read these reading texts more quickly and cursorily for their meaning.

THE OPENING WORDS OF AN ELEVENTH-CENTURY SERMON

Leofan men, ure Drihten, ælmihtig God, us þus singallice manað and læreð þurh his ða halgan bec þæt we riht and soð don her on worulde in urum life.

Beloved people, our Lord, almighty God, thus continually admonishes and instructs us through his holy books that we should do right and truth here in this world in our life.

Old English personal names

In the early middle ages, most men and women simply had one name. This meant that many people tended to have the same name, with obvious potential for confusion, although bynames or even nicknames were used to distinguish them. Sometimes a set of related names tended to run in an important family. This is certainly true of the West Saxon royal dynasty, in which a recurrent name element is **Ead-** (modern English *Ed-*), meaning *bliss* and *prosperity*, found in names of the tenth-century kings **Eadmund**, **Eadred**, **Eadwig**, **Eadgar**, **Eadward**.

Dithematic (two-part) names

The common type of Old English personal name is referred to as dithematic because, like a compound, it is made up of two meaningful words put together. Thus the name **Eadward** consists of two elements **ead** *blessed* + **weard** *guardian*, an apt name for a man intended to be a shepherd of the people. A typical woman's name **Godgifu** pronounced 'GOD-yi-vuh' (later spelling Godiva) consists of **god** *God* + **gifu** *gift*. In the following table, most of the elements can be combined productively to give common Old English names.

Practice 2
MAKING NAMES

Match first and second elements to create Old English names. Find five famous men and five famous women. Check your results in the key at the back of the book. For help, consult the *Blackwell Encyclopedia of Anglo-Saxon England* or Stenton (1998).

Men's names

first element	second element	
ælf *elf*	**gar** *spear*	**sige** *victory*
æþel *noble*	**heah** *high*	**stan** *stone*
ead *blessed*	**ræd** *advice*	**weard** *guardian*
eald *old*	**ric** *powerful*	**wine** *friend*
god *God*		
leof *dear*		

[As either first or second element: **beorht** *bright*, **os** *god*, **wig** *battle*, **wulf** *wolf*]

Women's names

first element	second element
ælf *elf*	**flæd** *beauty* (used only in names)
æþel *noble*	**gifu** *gift*
ead *blessed*	**þryþ** *power*
god *God*	**gyð** *battle*
wyn *joy*	

Reading 2

Here is a passage from version D of the *Anglo-Saxon Chronicle* describing the coronation in 973 of King Edgar the Peaceable, who was Edward the Confessor's grandfather. Edgar had succeeded to the throne in 959, but this second coronation was considered to be a special ceremony:

Her wæs Eadgar æþeling gehalgod to cyninge on Pentecostenes mæssedæg on .v. Idus Mai, þy .xiii. geare þe he on rice feng, æt Hatabaþum, and he wæs þa ane wana .xxx. wintre. And sona æfter þam se cyning gelædde ealle his scipfyrde to Leiceastre, and þær him comon ongean .vi. cyningas, and ealle wið hine getreowsodon þæt hi woldon efenwyrhtan beon on sæ and on lande.

Here Prince Edgar was consecrated as king on the Feast of Pentecost on the fifth of the Ides of May in the thirteenth year since he succeeded to the kingdom, **æt Hatabaþum** *'at the Hot Baths'. And he was just thirty winters. And immediately thereafter he led his fleet to Chester and there six kings came to him, and they all pledged him that they would be his allies by sea and by land.*

Old English place-names

The former Roman city of Bath, site of Edgar's coronation, had at least three names, one of which, **æt Hatabaþum**, *At the Hot Baths*, was purely English (see unit 10 for a possible allusion to this name in the poem *The Ruin*). The alternative name **Baþanceaster** meaning *City of the Baths* uses the element 'ceaster' *chester*, a loan word from Latin betraying the Roman origin of the city. Also attested is **Akemannesceaster**, which connects the name with that of **Akemannesstræt**, the Roman road 'Akeman Street', which led to **Lunden** (Latin 'Londinium'), otherwise known as **Lundenburh** or (in the dative case) **Lundenbyrig**. After his coronation, Edgar seems to have proceeded to Chester, one of the large former Roman cities in the north of his kingdom, where he again staged an elaborate ceremony.

Old English ceaster

Old English	Modern English	Etymology
Leiceaster	*Chester*	army camp (Latin 'castra')
Wintanceaster	*Winchester*	unknown (Latin 'Venta')
Wigoraceaster	*Worcester*	city of the Wigora tribe

While **ceaster** names derive from Latin 'castra', the alternative **burh** indicates a *fortified settlement* or *walled town* and derives from the Old English verb **beorgan** *to protect*. Similarly the *-ton* endings originate in Old English **tun**, which must originally have meant *enclosure* (cf. Dutch 'tuin' *garden*, German 'Zaun', *fence*). In Old English place-names **tun** came to mean *farm* or *estate*.

---

1 *Her wæs Eadward gehalgod to cinge* Here Edward was consecrated as king

Old English **burh**

Old English	Modern English	Etymology
Bebbanburh	*Bamburgh*	*Bebba's fortress*
Burh	*(Peter)borough*	*fortified town*
Ealdelmesbyrig	*Malmesbury*	*Aldhelm's town*

Old English **tun**

Old English	Modern English	Etymology
Hamtun	*(South) Hampton*	*home farm*
Middeltun	*Milton*	*middle estate*
Æppeltun	*Appleton*	*farm with apple orchard*

Practice 3

THE ORIGIN OF PLACE-NAMES

Use the Old English–English word index at the back of the book to work out the derivation of the following place-names. What original Old English words lie behind these names?

- **a** Kingston
- **b** Somerton
- **c** Norton
- **d** Sutton
- **e** Acton
- **f** Merton
- **g** Shipton
- **h** Oxford
- **i** Hereford
- **j** Hertford
- **k** Newbridge

? Test yourself

1 Match the words with their meaning:

a	**mycel**	1	*day*
b	**ælf**	2	*was*
c	**wæs**	3	*friend*
d	**forma**	4	*great*
e	**ræd**	5	*first*
f	**dæg**	6	*elf*
g	**wine**	7	*advice*

2 Complete the phrases with words from the box.

cynge	halgade	forman	biscope

a on _____ Easterdæg

b Eadsige arcebisop hine _____

c gebletsod to _____

d gehalgod to _____

SELF-CHECK

I CAN ...
recognize words, prefixes, and endings
apply basic spelling and pronunciation rules
understand how dithematic personal names work
understand the origin of some common place-names
read and pronounce a short text from the *Anglo-Saxon Chronicle*

2 Cyning sceal rice healdan
A king must hold a kingdom

In this unit you will learn about:
- ▸ *more rules of spelling and pronunciation*
- ▸ *the form and use of the infinitive*
- ▸ *the meanings of the auxiliary verb* sceal
- ▸ *the meaning and use of case endings*
- ▸ *rhythm and alliteration in Old English verse*

You will read:
- ▸ *extracts from the poem* Maxims II

Vocabulary builder

Where do you imagine these subjects would be located? Match the following subjects with their usual or expected locations, then read and study the passages from the study text, the poem *Maxims II*, **below.**

SUBJECTS		LOCATIONS	
beorh	*mound*	**ætsomne**	*together*
bera	*bear*	**of dune**	*from hill*
cyning	*king*	**on eorle**	*in nobleman*
ea	*river*	**on eorþan**	*on earth*
fyrd	*army*	**on foldan**	*on land*
God	*God*	**on hæðe**	*on heath*
treow	*loyalty*	**on healle**	*in hall*
wisdom	*wisdom*	**on heofenum**	*in (the) heavens*
wudu	*wood*	**on were**	*in man*

The opening lines of the poem *Maxims II*

🎧 02.00

Cyning sceal rice healdan

A king must hold a kingdom

cyning	*king* 'KÜ-ning'
sceal	*must* a one-syllable 'SHÉal'
rice	*kingdom* 'REE cheh'
healdan	*rule, hold* 'HÉal-dan'

THE GENRE OF *MAXIMS II*

Cyning sceal rice healdan is the first verse of *Maxims II*, a collection of proverbial sayings arranged into a poem to form a series of reflections on the order of the natural world and human society. Generically, maxims are proverbs, a traditional form of oral literature, their purpose being to preserve for posterity the cherished beliefs and wisdom of a society. In the poem *Maxims II* you can find key aspects of Anglo-Saxon material culture, the social hierarchies, traditions and customs, views of the natural world and religious and historical attitudes.

THE MANUSCRIPT

Maxims II is known to us only from one manuscript – in the mid-eleventh century a scribe copied the text at the beginning of version C of the *Anglo-Saxon Chronicle*, along with another poem (called *Menologium*) that briefly records and celebrates the festivals of the Church calendar. As we saw in unit 1, Version C was written around the time of Edward the Confessor's accession to the throne in 1042 and coronation in 1043. Since the Chronicle was the main annual record of political events in the kingdom, it looks as if the two poems serve as a preface: a set of moral reflections which introduce the chronicle of England that then follows. The manuscript itself is now preserved in London, in the Cotton Collection of the British Library (shelfmark Cotton, Tiberius B. i); the text of *Maxims II* is located on folio 115r. For some more texts from the same chronicle, see unit 4.

THE KING'S PLACE IN SOCIETY

The king was the mainstay of Old English society. Later shortened to **cyng** or **cing**, the word **cyning** in its original meaning is connected with the idea of *kin, kindred*, Old English **cynn**. In very early Anglo-Saxon times, the king was the leader of a small group of people who were familiar to him, like the chief of a clan. The traditional role of the king, therefore, was to form a strong bond of loyalty between himself and his followers. The verb **sceal** expresses necessity, and can usually be translated *must*, but in some contexts also *will* or *shall* or even *belong*, since proverbs express the idea of where something naturally must belong in the right order of things.

THE KING'S ROLE IN THE WORLD

To understand the maxim *a king must rule a country* we need to see the larger context of the poem in which it occurs. Here is a translation of the opening section:

The king must rule over a realm. Cities are conspicuous from afar, those which there are on this earth, the ingenious constructions of giants, ornate fortresses of dressed stones. The wind in the sky is the swiftest thing and thunder in its seasons is the loudest. The powers of Christ are great: Providence is the most compelling thing (translation by S.A.J. Bradley).

The chain of associations continues through the later lines of the poem. We hear talk of the seasons and the fruits of the year, the clarity or fickleness of truth, the value of gold, wisdom and the clouds flitting by. The poet then explores the necessary qualities of a young nobleman before exploring people and things in their requisite locations. This is a poem about the rightful place of smaller things in the wider whole, the spear held in the hand, the jewel on the ring, the mast on the ship, the sword on the lap, the dragon in its cave, the fish in the water.

> **LANGUAGE INSIGHT**
>
> In **cyning sceal rice healdan,** the word **healdan** *to hold* is classed as an infinitive and is identified by the ending **-an**. In many languages, infinitives are marked by an ending: compare French 'ten-ir' or German 'halt-en' with Old English **heald-an**. This is one advantage of an inflected language, i.e. a language that marks most of its words with inflectional endings: the function and meaning of a word is shown by its shape.

Language discovery

SPELLING AND PRONUNCIATION

 02.01 Listen to the audio recording and practise the pronunciation of the first maxim cyning sceal rice healdan. Remember the general principle of Old English spelling that every letter represents a sound.

▶ Exceptionally, the combination of two letters **sc** in **sceal** is pronounced as one sound, like *sh* in modern English *shall*.

▶ The letter **c** is pronounced *k* in **cyning** (sometimes spelt **kyning**). But in **rice** the letter **c** sounds like the *ch* of modern English *rich* or *chair*. Avoid pronouncing **c** like the *s* sound that it often takes in modern English.

▶ **Rice** itself is a two-syllable word **ri-ce** sounding rather like 'REE cheh' (i.e. with stress on the first syllable). **Healdan** is also two syllables, **heal-** and **-dan**.

▶ The combination **ea** is a falling diphthong, in which the tongue glides quickly from the prominent vowel 'e' to the weaker vowel 'a'; accordingly **heald-** sounds rather like 'HAYald' or 'HÉald' run together as one syllable. Other examples of one-syllable diphthongs occur in **beag, eald** and **eorl**.

> ● **OLD–MODERN CONNECTIONS**
>
> The noun **rice** *kingdom* or *kingship* is connected with the ending **-ric** in present-day English *bishopric*. It is also cognate with the Old English adjective **rice** *powerful*, which gradually took on the meaning *rich and powerful* and then simply *rich*. Under later Norman influence, the change in meaning was reinforced by French 'riche'.

MAXIMS II, LINES 28B–36B

The king in hall

 02.02 After the lines associating the phenomena of the dragon in the cave and the fish in the water, the poem *Maxims II* (lines 28b–31a) continues with the king in hall. As you read or listen, make notes.

1 What two further subjects or phenomena are placed in parallel with this king?

_____

2 What is described as flood-grey?

_____

> [...]   **Cyning sceal on healle**
> **beagas dælan.**   **Bera sceal on hæðe,**
> **eald and egesfull.**   **Ea of dune sceal**
>   **flodgræg feran.**

heall	*hall* one-syllable '**HÉal**'; **on healle** *in a hall* '**HÉal-leh**'
beag	*ring* one-syllable '**BÉag**'; **beagas** *rings* '**BÉa-gas**' (plural)
dælan	*to share out, apportion* '**DÆ-lan**' (pronounce the long **æ** here like the open sound in modern British English *air*; when short, **æ** is like the *a* in *cat*)
bera	*bear* 'berra'
on hæðe	*on [the] heath* (**hæð** is also written **hæþ** – pronounce **þ** and **ð** like modern English *th*, voiced between vowels in **hæðe** and voiceless at the end of the word in **hæð**)
eald	*old* a one-syllable 'Éald'
egesfull	*terrible* 'EH-yes-full'
ea	*river* 'éa'
dun	*hill* 'doon' (see unit 21 on the name **Mæl-dun** Maldon); **of dune** *from the hill* 'off DOO-neh'
flod-græg	*flood-grey* 'fload-græy'
feran	*to go, travel* 'FÉ-ran'

CULTURAL INSIGHT

The **heall**, *hall*, was the central meeting place of the town or settlement, the seat of government, the place of feasting and festival; in literature it becomes a symbol of right living in the world. In a poem such as *Beowulf*, **beag** (also spelt **beah**) means *a ring* in the sense of *treasure, wealth* given by a **beah-gifa**, *the ring-giver or king*; it perhaps refers to large rings of precious metal that could be looped onto the pommel of a sword. In later Old English, the word is used for *an armlet* or *arm-ring*, normally made of silver and often of considerable weight. It was used by the king to reward loyalty and must have been equivalent to a large sum of money.

The army rides together

 02.03 Read and listen to the next section of *Maxims II* (lines 31b–36b).

1 How does the poem further describe the army?

_____

2 Where are the wood and the mountain located?

_____

3 What attributes of God are presented in the text?

_____

[...]	**Fyrd sceal ætsomne,**
tirfæstra getrum.	**Wudu sceal on foldan**
blædum blowan.	**Beorh sceal on eorþan**
grene standan.	**God sceal on heofenum,**
dæda demend.	

fyrd	*army, militia* 'fürd'
ætsomne	*together*
getrum	*troop* 'yuh-TRUM'
tirfæstra	*of the glorious* (**tir** *glory* + **fæst**)
wudu	*wood*
folde	*land, earth* (a more poetic synonym for **eorþe** *earth*)
blædum	*with fruits* (dative plural of **blæd**, *fruit*)
blowan	*flourish*
beorh, beorg	*mountain* (cf. iceberg)
grene	*green* 'GRÉ-neh'
on heofenum	*in the heavens* (dative plural of **heofenas** *heavens*, from **heofon** *heaven*)
dæda	*of deeds*
demend	*judge* 'DÉ-mend'

> **CULTURAL INSIGHT**
>
> The noun **fyrd**, also spelt **fierd**, means literally *expedition*, and in texts of the 10th or 11th century it refers to *a standing army*, which could be called out on expedition to deal with *an invading army*, which was known as a **here**. This is the situation at the beginning of the poem *The Battle of Maldon* (for a long extract, see unit 21).

Grammar

1 THE INFINITIVE

Old English is an inflected language. This means it uses inflections, i.e. endings added to the main stem, to indicate the meaning and role of a word in the sentence. The base form of the verb (as listed in dictionaries) is the infinitive, in modern English *hold* or more often *to hold*. In Old English the infinitive is indicated by the ending **-an**.

Verb	Meaning	Stem	Ending	Pronunciation
healdan	(to) hold	**heald-**	**-an**	'HÉal-dan'
dælan	(to) share	**dæl-**	**-an**	'DÆ-lan'
feran	(to) travel	**fer-**	**-an**	'FÉ-ran'

Other infinitives include: **biddan** *to pray*, **bringan** *to bring*, **cyðan** *to proclaim*, **gretan** *to greet*, **niman** *to take*, **scinan** *to shine*, **standan** *to stand*, **wyrcean** or **wyrcan** 'wür-chan' *to work, create*; an exceptional form is **beon** *to be*.

The grammatical term infinitive indicates a non-finite, i.e. time-less or non-tensed form of the verb. For example in **grene standan** *stand green*, the infinitive *stand* is non-temporal in meaning. In that phrase, **standan** could refer to past, present or future, whereas in other contexts the form **stynt** *stands* can only be present tense, and **stod** *stood* has to be past tense.

2 THE AUXILIARY

Because it normally takes an infinitive, **sceal** is known as an auxiliary (i.e. a 'helping' verb). Examples of auxiliaries in modern English are *can, may, must, shall, will* – these are followed immediately by the infinitive: *a king must rule, a bear shall dwell on a heath, a wood will blossom*. Old English auxiliaries include:

sceal *must*   **mæg** *can*   **mot** *is allowed*   **wile** *will, wants*

3 WORD ORDER WITH AUXILIARY AND INFINITIVE

Unlike in modern English, the infinitive can come much later in the Old English sentence, as seen in the sentence structure (syntax) of the proverbs in *Maxims II*:

subject	auxiliary	adverbial	object	infinitive
Cyning	sceal	on healle	beagas	dælan

subject	auxiliary	adverbial	complement	infinitive
Beorh	sceal	on eorþan	grene	standan

In the above scheme, the subject is the doer of the action expressed by the verb; the object is the person or thing directly affected by the action of that verb. An adverbial qualifies the verb in some way giving information about time, manner, or place of the action. The complement in this sentence refers back to the subject.

In brief, as the two example sentences show, the auxiliary often sends the infinitive to a position at or near the end of the sentence. Having the infinitive at the end of the sentence may seem strange at first, but you may have come across this word order in German, and it is quite common that the reader or listener anticipates what the infinitive is going to be before they hear it. This phenomenon of anticipation means that in some cases the infinitive can be omitted by ellipsis, because it is 'understood'.

4 ELLIPSIS (OMISSION) OF THE VERB

Ellipsis usually happens when the expected verb after **sceal** is a form of *to be* (**beon** or **wesan**), or a related idea such as *to remain* or *to dwell* (**gewunian**):

Treow sceal on eorle, wisdom on were.

Treow	*loyalty*
on	*on, in*
on eorle	*in an earl* (from **eorl** *nobleman, earl*)
on were	*in a man* (from **wer** *man*)

2 Cyning sceal rice healdan A king must hold a kingdom   **17**

In these cases, **sceal** can be translated in various ways:

Loyalty must be in a warrior, wisdom in a man.

Loyalty belongs in an earl, wisdom in a man.

Loyalty will remain in a warrior, wisdom in a man.

5 INTRODUCTION TO CASE ENDINGS

Note again the endings on the noun in the following phrases:

of dun-e	*from the hill*
on eorl-e	*in a man*
on glof-e	*on a glove* (e.g. a falcon)
on hæð-e	*on the heath*
on wer-e	*in a man*
on heofen-um	*in the heavens*

All these nouns have a dative ending attached to them. To explain this idea, we will need to consider the phenomenon of a case ending.

Nouns and adjectives decline, i.e. take endings, to show their meaning and role in the sentence. There are some basic distinctions to be made, and more will be given on the uses of cases in later units. The nominative is the base form of the word and the subject of the sentence, while the accusative is usually the recipient of the action (see units 5 and 6 for more details). The genitive case expresses a general idea of possession and can usually be translated as *of* (see unit 7). For example, in the phrase **dæd-a demend** *judge of deeds*, the ending **-a** in **dæd-a** marks the genitive plural meaning *of deeds*.

The dative case has several uses. In the phrase **on eorl-e** the ending **-e** marks the dative, which is used here after the preposition **on**. Prepositions (short relational words such as *for, of, on*) force the following noun to take a case ending, usually the dative:

on + singular **hæð** *heath*	= **on hæð-e** *on [the] heath*
on + plural **heofenas** *heavens*	= **on heofen-um** *in [the] heavens*

Another meaning of the dative is *to* or *with*, as in **blæd-um blowan** *to flourish with fruits;* further meanings will be discussed in unit 8.

Reading

The Old English poem *Beowulf* is arguably the most famous surviving English poem. Its opening scene is set in Zealand in Denmark and tells the legend of Scyld Scefing (whose name means *Shield Sheafson*). Scyld comes of mysterious origins from across the sea and founds a new line of Danish kings who become overlords of the whole region. The poet narrrator clearly approves of the prowess and authority of this dynasty as he praises Scyld's son Beow, who flourishes and prospers even in his father's own lifetime, *for this is how a young man* **sceal** *should be* (lines 20–25):

20　　**Swa sceal geong guma　　gode gewyrcean,**
　　　fromum feohgiftum　　on fæder bearme,
　　　þæt hine on ylde　　eft gewunigen
　　　wilgesiþas,　　þonne wig cume,
　　　leode gelæsten.　　Lofdædum sceal
25　　**in mægþa gehwære　　man geþeon.**

So should a young man bring it about, by good action and

by splendid gifts of wealth while still in his father's protection,

that in his maturity there will remain with him

willing companions, when war comes,

who support their leader. By praiseworthy deeds

a man should prosper in every nation.

Language and style

RHYTHM AND ALLITERATION IN OLD ENGLISH

Old English writers loved rhythmical phrases in which the sounds echoed each other; modern examples include *sticks and stones, to have and to hold, light and life, life and liberty*. These are found in Old English writings of all kinds from charters to sermons to poems. Such alliteration – the repetition of word-initial consonants or initial vowels, combined with a four-beat rhythm – was the mainstay of Old English poetry. The basic metre is as follows. Each line of poetry is divided by a gap – the caesura – into two verses or half-lines connected by alliteration. And each verse contains two beats or, as they are usually called, lifts. More information on rhythm will be covered in units 11 and 14, and the technical details of the alliterative style will be given in units 21 and 22, which cover longer extracts from *The Battle of Maldon* and *Beowulf*. But it is fundamental to Old English, and at this stage you should start to acquire the rudiments of rhythm and alliteration.

Practice

02.04 Listen to a reading of the extract from the poem *Maxims II* (lines 28b–35a) and note the emphatic words in each line that alliterate e.g. **beagas** and **bera,** or **eald** and **ea**.

　　[…]　　　　　Cyning sceal on healle
　　beagas dælan.　　Bera sceal on hæðe,
　　eald and egesfull.　　Ea of dune sceal
　　flodgræg feran.　　Fyrd sceal ætsomne,
　　tirfæstra getrum.　　Treow sceal on eorle,
　　wisdom on were.　　Wudu sceal on foldan
　　blædum blowan.　　Beorh sceal on eorþan
　　grene standan.　　God sceal on heofenum,
　　dæda demend.

? Test yourself

Translate the proverbs into Old English.

a A bear belongs on a heath, old and terrible.

_____

b A river must flow, flood-grey from the mountain.

_____

c A wood belongs on the earth, flourishing with leaves.

_____

d A hill must stand green upon the earth.

_____

SELF-CHECK

I CAN ...
apply more spelling and pronunciation rules
recognize the form and use of the infinitive
understand the meanings of the auxiliary verb **sceal**
interpret some uses of case endings
recognize basic patterns of rhythm and alliteration in Old English verse
read and pronounce extracts from the poem _Maxims II_

3 *Saga hwæt ic hatte*
Say what I am called

In this unit you will learn about:
▶ *Bishop Leofric and the* Exeter Book
▶ *connections between Old and modern English vocabulary*
▶ *poetic words and phrases*
▶ *the personal pronoun* you
▶ *countries and people*
▶ *the endings of the present tense*
▶ *rhythm and alliteration*

You will read:
▶ *Riddle 66 from the* Exeter Book

 03.00

Saga hwæt ic hatte
Say what I am called

V Vocabulary builder 1

Old English has many synonyms and poetic expressions for the earth, sea and sky.
Fill in the missing modern English words in the list below:

eorþe	_____
folde	*earth* (used only in poetry)
middangeard	*world* (literally the middle-enclosure)
eard	*land*
eþel	*homeland*
sæ	*sea*
mere	*sea*
heofon	_____
swegl	_____
sunne	*sun*
mona	_____
steorra	_____
tungol	*luminary* (*star* or *planet*)

The *Exeter Book*

LEOFRIC, BISHOP OF EXETER

Edward the Confessor's succession to the throne in 1042 was, naturally enough, accompanied by a number of changes. After his long years of exile in Normandy he brought with him a number of Continental friends and supporters and he appointed some of these to work as chaplains and clerks in the royal household. When posts became available, these men were promoted, and in 1044 Leofric, a man of English descent from Lotharingia (Lorraine), was appointed bishop of Devon and Cornwall. In 1050, he moved the see of the bishopric to Exeter. Anxious to use English in his pastoral work, he collected a large set of books, listed in the record of his donations to the cathedral in 1069–72. One of them is described as follows:

mycel englisc boc be gehwilcum þingum on leoðwisan geworht

a large English book on various matters made in verse

Clearly this is a description of the late tenth-century *Exeter Book*, which, through Leofric's gift to the cathedral, was preserved for posterity.

RIDDLES FROM THE *EXETER BOOK*

The *Exeter Book* anthology owned by bishop Leofric contains a number of famous Old English poems: a set of religious lyrics exploring the season of Advent and the life of Christ known as *The Advent Lyrics*, poems on the hermit Guthlac, an elegiac search for wisdom in the famous poem *The Wanderer*, the poem of exile and pilgrimage known as *The Seafarer*, and two thematically connected lyrics of loss and reconciliation called *The Wife's Lament* and *The Husband's Message*. As well as these, there are ninety-five riddling poems that describe many aspects of the human and natural world, in a spirit sometimes of playful humour but usually also of wonder and exploration.

RIDDLE 66

ic eom mare þonne þes middangeard

I am more than this middle earth

The ten-line poem below is Riddle 66 from the *Exeter Book*. Take a moment to read through the Old English text, remembering the basic pronunciation rule that every letter counts, that the letters **þ** (**thorn**) and **ð** (**eth**) represent a *th* sound, that **ge-** is pronounced 'yuh-', that **c** is normally *k* but changes to a *ch* sound in words like **ræce**, *reach*, 'RÆ-cheh'.

 03.01 Listen to track 1: **saga hwæt ic hatte**. How many of the words of this poem have survived into modern English? What possible solution could be given to the final demand of Riddle 66: say what I am called?

> **Ic eom mare   þonne þes middangeard,**
> **læsse þonne hondwyrm,   leohtre þonne mona,**
> **swiftre þonne sunne.**
> *I am more than this middle world,*

less than a mite, lighter than the moon,

swifter than the sun.

 03.02

> [...]   **Sæs me sind ealle**
>
> **flodas on fæðmum   ond þes foldan bearm,**
>
> **grene wongas.**
>
> *[...]   The seas to me are all*
>
> *floods in my embrace, and this earth's lap,*
>
> *the green plains.*

> [...]   **Grundum ic hrine,**
>
> **helle underhnige,   heofonas oferstige,**
>
> **wuldres eþel,**
>
> *To the depths I touch*
>
> *hell I sink below, heavens I soar above,*
>
> *the glory land,*

Lines 7b–10

> [...]   **wide ræce**
>
> **ofer engla eard,   eorþan gefylle,**
>
> **ealne middangeard   ond merestreamas**
>
> **side mid me sylfum.   Saga hwæt ic hatte.**
>
> *[...]   widely I reach*
>
> *over the angels' land; the earth I fill*
>
> *– all the world and the ocean streams –*
>
> *widely with myself. Say what I am called.*

LEARNING INSIGHT

Modernizing the spelling assists the learning process. Compare the following transcription of the beginning of the text: **Ich eom mare thonne thes middan-yeard, læsse thonne hondwyrm, leoghtre thonne mona, swiftre thonne sunne.**

Language discovery

CONNECTIONS BETWEEN OLD AND MODERN ENGLISH

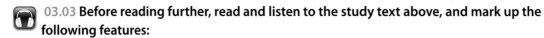 **03.03 Before reading further, read and listen to the study text above, and mark up the following features:**

a **Underline all words (or parts of words) that remind you of modern English. You should be able to recognize a good many words, either by their spelling or their sound. See notes 1–9 in this section for further explanations.**

b **Underline words in a different colour which alliterate, i.e. begin with the same letter. For more information, go to the section on Rhythm and alliteration further on in this unit.**

1 Although written in an ancient form of verse, the poem uses a good number of words that still belong to the core vocabulary of the English language:

grammar words: *am, and, less, me, more, on, than, this, what*

content words: *all, angel, earth, fathom, fill, flood, green, ground, hand, heaven, hell, mere, mid, moon, over, reach, under, say, self, stream, sun, wide.*

2 Some words are recognizable when the variable endings are highlighted:

sæ-s *sea-s*, **flod-as** *flood-s*, **swift-re** *swift-er*.

3 From what was said in the previous unit, you may recognize the dative ending in **-um** after prepositions **on** and **mid**:

line 4 **on fæðm-um** *in my embrace, in my encircling arms* and line 10 **mid me sylf-um** *with myself*, while **grund-um ic hrine** means literally *I touch to the depths*.

4 There are other word endings that do not survive in modern English: **midd-an** *middle*, **gren-e** *green*.

5 The perfective prefix **ge-** (pronounced 'yuh-') should be removed to get at the root of the word: **ge-fyll-e** *fill*.

6 There are similar pronunciations: some OE words may sound broadly similar to their present-day equivalents but have a different modern spelling: **geard** *yard, enclosure* (pronounced 'YÉard'), **ofer** *over* (pronounced as 'over'), **hwæt** *what* (pronounce each letter; rhymes with 'cat').

7 Occasionally a word may still exist in English, but its meaning will have changed over centuries of use. This is true of *yard* just quoted, and in **fæðm** *embrace*. There are connections with modern English *fathom*, which originally meant *to stretch out the arms wide* and so make a measurement. Such semantic change – developments in meaning over time – may be explored by consulting the word in the multi-volume or online version of the *Oxford English Dictionary*.

8 There are derivatives: the verb **stige** (pronounced 'STEE-yuh') in **ofer-stige** *climb over* connects with the noun **stigel** (pronounced 'STEE-yul') meaning *stile*, i.e. the wooden steps for climbing over farm walls and fences.

9 There are similar words – or cognates – in sister languages: often German, Dutch or Scandinavian languages provide parallels. For instance in line 6, the verb **hnige** comes from **hnigan** cognate with German 'neigen' *to incline*, while Old English **stigan** parallels German 'steigen' *to climb* and **ic hatte** *I am called* is like German 'ich heiße…' *I am called…*, i.e. my name is…

Language and style

POETIC VOCABULARY

1 Compounds

These were widely used in Old English writing. A compound can be defined as a combination of two words to form a new idea:
> line 1: **middangeard** = **middan** *middle* + **geard** *enclosure* = *the world*
> line 2: **hondwyrm** = **hond** *hand* + **wyrm** *worm, reptile* = *mite* or *insect*

2 Poetic words and expressions

Some nouns and phrases are found mostly or even exclusively in poetic texts:
> line 4: **foldan** from **folde** *earth*
> line 5: **wong-as** plural of **wong** *field, plain*
> line 7: **þes wuldres eþel** *this land of glory* (**wuldor** *glory* + **eþel** *homeland*)
> line 8: **engla eard** *region of angels*

3 Riddle formulas

Old English has a verb **hatan**, which means *to call* or *to be called*. The sentence formula **saga hwæt ic hatte** *say what I am called*, usually at the end of the poem, is a challenge to the listener to guess the name of the speaker and so arrive at the solution of the riddle. In this case the consensus solution is *creation*, Old English **gesceaft**. Another common formula, often at the beginning of the riddle, is **ic wiht geseah** *I saw a creature* (**wiht** *creature, wight*; **geseah** *saw*).

Grammar

THE PERSONAL PRONOUN *YOU*

1   Different languages find different ways of doing personal pronouns and it is worth remembering that the modern English system of interpersonal address is not the only one possible. There were more personal pronouns in Old English than in modern English, chiefly because there were three words for *you*. In fact, these are different ways of conceiving of the concept *you*: **þu** and **ge**, pronounced 'thoo' and 'yay' correspond to **thou** (the singular *you*) and **ye** (the plural *you*). There was also a dual pronoun **git**, pronounced 'yit', *you-two* and **wit** to refer to *we-two*:

	Singular		Dual		Plural	
1st person:	**ic**	*I*	**wit**	*we-two*	**we**	*we*
2nd person:	**þu**	*thou*	**git**	*you-two*	**ge**	*you*
3rd person:	**he**	*he*			**hi**, **hig**	*they*
	heo	*she*				
	hit	*it*				

2 In the *Story of Joseph* in Genesis, for example, two Egyptian officials are thrown into prison with Joseph; eventually they tell him, '**Wit gesawon swefn** (*We-both saw a dream*)', to which Joseph replies, '**Secgaþ me hwæt git gesawon** (*Tell me what you-both saw*)' (further extracts from this story are given in units 6, 9, 13, 14. For another example of the use of this dual pronoun, to address the king and queen together, see archbishop Wulfstan's letter in unit 18.)

3 On pronunciation, note that the combination of letters in **-ig** was always pronounced 'ee' and corresponds to the modern *-y* ending in *bloody*, *greedy* etc. (Old English **blodig**, **grædig**). Thus the word for *they* was pronounced 'hee' whether it was spelt **hi** or **hig**. The pronoun **ic** was pronounced 'itch' and later written **ich** (note that it did not have or need an initial capital letter). The pronoun **heo** *she* was occasionally spelt **hio**.

4 In the following extract from Shakespeare's *King Lear* (Act IV, scene 6) Edgar, disguised as a peasant and leading the blind, outlawed Gloucester by the arm, affects a rustic dialect as he is challenged by Oswald.

Which personal pronouns in the passage show vestiges of Old English?

Oswald: *Wherefore bold peasant*

dar'st thou support a publish'd traitor? Hence;

lest that th' infection of his fortune take

like hold on thee. Let go his arm.

Edgar: *Chill not let go, zir, without vurther 'casion.*

Oswald: *Let go, slave, or thou di'st.*

Edgar: *Good gentleman, go your gait, and let poor volk pass.*

In Shakespeare's time, *thou* and *ye* were clearly still current; but less obviously *ich* was also in limited use: the pronoun survived in dialect as the contracted form *chill* (= *ich will*) and *chould* (= *ich would*). The equivalent of *thou dar'st* in Old English was **þu dearst**, with the same **-st** ending on the verb. For the forms *me*, *thee*, *you*, *his* and *him*, which change according to case, i.e. their role or function in the sentence, see especially units 8 and 18.

> **LANGUAGE INSIGHT**
> The pronoun **þu** *thou* is simply the standard word for singular *you* in Old English. Only later in the middle ages did it become a marker of informal address, on the model of French 'tu', cf. German 'du', or Italian and Spanish 'tu/tú' (in these languages the word is singular and familiar or informal).

Countries and people

Regions or countries tended to be named after the people who lived there: accordingly **West-Seaxe** meant *West Saxons* but was used for the region Wessex. Other names are similar: **Suð-Seaxe** *South Saxons* for *Sussex*, **East-Seaxe**, *East Saxons* for *Essex*, **Eastengle**, *East Angles* for *East Anglia*. In the north of the country was **Norðhymbre**, another plural noun meaning primarily *Northumbrians* and hence *Northumbria*. In writings from the time of king Alfred the various regions came to be called collectively **Angelcynn**, the *Angle kindred*, as opposed to the **Wealhcynn** or **Wealas**, *the Welsh*. The neighbours of the Welsh, in what is now central England were the **Mierce** (pronounced 'Meer-cheh') meaning *Borderers*, hence **Mercia**, i.e. the March or Border Land (for map see Appendix II).

By a process of phonetic change, the term **Angle**, *the Angles* became **Engle**, *the English*, who spoke the language **englisc**. The older term **Angelcynn** still had an ethnic meaning when Cnut raised a tax for **eal Angelcynn** in the D version of the *Anglo-Saxon Chronicle* for the year 1017, but it was not by that time the name for the whole country. Instead, the process of political change that brought about the nation state in the tenth century gave rise to a new name: **Engla-land**, *Land of the English*.

Further afield are the following names: **Scottas**, *the Scots*, **Scotland**, *Scotland*; **Francland**, *Frank-Land* i.e. *France*; **Ealdseaxe**, *Old Saxons* i.e. *Saxony*; **Dene**, *the Danes*, **Denemearc**, *the Dane March* i.e. *Denmark*; **Norðweg**, *North Way* i.e. *Norway*, sometimes occurring as a plural noun e.g. the phrase **into Norðwegon**, *into the Northways*, the name partly retaining its literal, topographical sense.

CULTURAL INSIGHT

In the geography of this period, the island of Britain (**Brytene igland**) was located at the edge of the world, in the encircling ocean (**garsecg**). At the centre of the world was Jerusalem (**Hierusalem**), and the Mediterranean was known as the **Wendelsæ**.

Grammar

THE ENDINGS OF THE PRESENT TENSE

Verb	Translation	Pronunciation
ic ræce	*I reach*	'ich RAEchuh'
þu ræcst	*you (sing.) reach*	'thoo RAEchst'
he, heo ræcþ	*he, she reaches*	'hay, héo RAEchth'
we, ge, hig ræcaþ	*we, you, they reach*	'way, yay, hee RAEchath'

PRESENT TENSE OF THE VERB *TO BE (I AM, YOU ARE, SHE IS...)*

There were two forms of the verb *to be*: **wesan** and **beon**. They form their present tense as follows:

sg.	1	**ic**	**eom**	**beo**	*am*
	2	**þu**	**eart**	**bist**	*are*
	3	**he, heo, hit**	**is**	**bið**	*is*
pl.	1–3	**we, ge, git, hi**	**sind**	**beoð**	*are*

There is room for variation in the above. Just as the two ways of representing the 'th' sound can alternate, so do the vowels **i** and **y**, so that we also find **ys**, **byð**. Similarly, instead of **sind**, other writers use **synt**, **sindon**, or even **sindan**. To remember the form **beoð**, it may be helpful to visualize it as the verb *be* with the present tense ending *-eth* as found in Shakespearean English, e.g. *maketh*. The *be*-forms of the present tense sometimes also had a future meaning.

Rhythm and alliteration

 03.04 Listen again to a reading of the whole of Riddle 66, paying attention to the letters highlighted by underlining in each line. There are four lifts (accents or beats) to the line, and their varying patterns set the rhythm and metre of the poem. By modern editorial convention, each line is divided by a space in the middle, the caesura, into its two half-lines, known as the on-verse and the of-verse, connected by alliteration:

> **Ic** eom **ma**re   þonne þes **mid**dangeard,
>
> **læs**se þonne **hond**wyrm,   **leoh**tre þonne **mo**na,
>
> **swif**tre þonne **sun**ne.   **Sæs** me sind **eal**le
>
> **flo**das on **fæð**mum   ond þes **fol**dan **bearm**,
>
> 5   **gre**ne **won**gas.   **Grun**dum ic **hri**ne,
>
> **hel**le under**hni**ge,   **heo**fonas ofer**sti**ge,
>
> **wul**dres e**þel**,   **wi**de **ræ**ce
>
> ofer **en**gla **eard**,   **eor**þan ge**fyl**le,
>
> **eal**ne **mid**dangeard   ond **me**re**strea**mas
>
> 10   **si**de mid me **syl**fum.   **Sa**ga hwæt ic **hat**te.

Alliteration is an important stylistic device in Old English writing, far more important than rhyme. Because it is associated with traditional poetry and song, it was also used for rhetorical effect by prose writers in charters, chronicles, laws, saints' lives etc.

LANGUAGE INSIGHT

Alliteration in Old English texts, especially in the poems, is governed by rules of style and metre. The only significant alliteration falls on the lift, i.e. the heavy syllable of content words: semantically important nouns *sun*, *sea*, *flood*, *fathom*, adjectives *more*, *less*, *light*, *swift*, and infinitives of verbs (more rarely on finite verbs). Alliteration is not normally used with lightly stressed, grammatical words: connectives like *and* or *than*, determiners like *the* or *this*, pronouns such as *I* or *me*, and prepositions such as *on* or *over* (for more details see units 21 and 22).

MORE RIDDLES

 03.05 As you read and listen to these riddles selected from the *Exeter Book*, practise the pronunciation, particularly of consonants c, g, h, ð and þ and vowels æ, e, ea and eo.

What are the solutions? For suggested answers, see the key at the back of the book.

a Riddle 69

Wundor wearð on wege: wæter wearð to bane.

A wonder happened on the wave: water turned to bone.

b Riddle 75

Ic swiftne geseah on swaþe feran.

I saw a swift one travel on the track.

c Riddle 76

Ic ane geseah idese sittan.

I saw a lady sit alone.

? Test yourself

1 Translate these words and phrases into Old English.

   a thou art _____

   b thou dar'st _____

   c moon and sun _____

   d the English, the Welsh and the Scots _____

   e you two _____

   f sea _____

   g ocean _____

2 Fill in the missing gaps with the appropriate word from the box.

leohtre	ic	wiht	wearð

   a wæter _____ **to bane**

   b ic eom _____ **þonne mona**

   c saga hwæt _____**hatte**

   d ic _____ **geseah**

SELF-CHECK

I CAN ...

○	make connections between Old and modern English vocabulary
○	identify some poetic words and phrases
○	understand the three forms of the pronoun you: **þu, git, ge**
○	name countries and people
○	distinguish the endings of the present tense
○	hear the effects of rhythm and alliteration
○	read and pronounce Riddle 66 from the *Exeter Book*

4 Her on þissum geare
Here in this year

In this unit you will learn about:
- ▶ *the reign of king Cnut (1016–1035)*
- ▶ *titles and by-names of prominent people*
- ▶ **ealdorman** *and* **eorl**
- ▶ *the two kinds of past tense*
- ▶ *the prefix* ge- *('yuh')*
- ▶ *Roman dates as used in Old English writings*

You will read:
- ▶ *Annals 1019–1031 from version C of the* **Anglo-Saxon Chronicle**

04.00

Her on þissum geare
Here in this year

The *Anglo-Saxon Chronicle*

The *Anglo-Saxon Chronicle* is a unique contemporary record of early English history. Written by monks at important ecclesiastical centres like the New Minster Winchester or Christ Church Canterbury, its immediate purpose was commemorative – to record major events such as the succession of a new king or bishop, the marriage of a king and queen, the arrival of a comet, journeys, battles, harvests, famines. It was unique at this time because most chronicles in western Europe were written in Latin. In appearance a typical page of the *Chronicle* has a list of Roman numerals down the left margin signifying the years; the scribe selects any significant or eventful year and writes a short text or **annal** beside it on the page. The beginning of each annal is marked with the formulaic **her**, *here*, sometimes extended to **her on þissum geare**, *here in this year*.

The year 1019

04.01 Read and listen to the following entry from version C of the Chronicle. Where did king Cnut spend the winter of 1019–1020? Why was this necessary?

1019 Her gewende Cnut cyng to Denemearcon and ðær wunode ealne þone winter.

MOVEMENT

for	*went*
com eft	*came back*
gewende	*went*
wunode	*remained*
ferde	*departed*
nam	*took*
onfeng	*received*

RANK AND STATUS

cyng	*king*
cwen	*queen*
hlaford	*lord*
hlæfdige	*lady*
eorl	*nobleman*
ceorl	*peasant*
ealdorman	*ruler, governor, prince*

Language discovery

TALKING ABOUT THE PAST

What is a tense? The word came into English from French in the later middle ages and means *time* (cf. modern French 'temps', which developed from Latin 'tempus' *time*). In Old English, the word for a tense is **tid** ('teed'), which also means *time* or *hour*. In traditional grammar, a tense is a verb that changes its shape or form in order to indicate a specific time.

The following is an exercise in discovering your own grammar: the language that you know and use every day. Think of a few verbs in modern English. When talking about the past, how do you alter the shape of the verb to add the idea of 'pastness' to it? For further discussion, see the Grammar section.

Cnut's early reign

As a young Danish Viking, Cnut came to the throne after the long Anglo-Danish wars, which intensified in the 990's during the reign of Æthelred the Unready and culminated in the Danish victory in 1016 at Assandun (possibly Ashdon in north Essex near Saffron Waldon). A peace ceremony followed **æt Olanige wið Deorhyrste**, *at the island of Olney on the river*

Severn, near the town of Deerhurst (Gloucestershire), where an Anglo-Saxon church still stands to this day. At first Cnut was king in the north only while Æthelred's son, king Edmund Ironside (Eadmund Irensid), ruled in the traditional heartlands of Wessex. But Edmund was short-lived, and in 1017 Cnut **feng … to eall Englalandes rice** *succeeded to all the kingdom of England*. Rivals to the throne like Edmund's half-brother the young Edward (the Confessor) fled into exile, and Cnut married Æthelred's royal widow Emma of Normandy. In 1018 he imposed a large tax on **eall Angelcynn**, *all the English nation*, paid off the Danish fleet, and brought about an Anglo-Danish agreement **æt Oxnaforda**, *at Oxford*. His power and influence were growing, and from 1019, when he inherited the Scandinavian empire from his brother, Cnut had to divide his time and attention between the two kingdoms of England and Denmark.

The year 1020

 04.02 What were King Cnut's main concerns on his return to England in 1020?

1020 Her on þissum geare forðferde Lyfing arcebisceop.

And Cnut cyning com eft to Englalande, and þa on Eastron wæs mycel gemot æt Cyringceastre, þa geutlagode man Æþelweard ealdorman and Eadwig 'ceorla cyngc'.

And on ðisum geare se cyng for to Assandune, and Wulfstan arcebisceop and Þurkil eorl and manega bisceopas mid heom, and gehalgodan þæt mynster æt Assandune.

on þissum geare	*in this year* 'on THI-sum yéar-reh' (dative case)
forðferde	*departed, passed away*
Lyfing	pronounced 'Lüving' (also known as archbishop Ælfstan)
com	*came* 'cohm'
eft	*again, afterwards*
þa … þa	*when … then*
ge-mot	*meeting, assembly* 'yuh-MOAT'
ge-utlagode man	*they outlawed* 'yuh-OOT-lagoduh'
ealdor-man	*nobleman*
ceorl	*free peasant* 'CHÉorl'
ceorla cyncg	*king of peasants* (a nickname)
for	*went*
manega	*many*
mid heom	*with them*
ge-halgodan	*(they) consecrated* (from the adjective **halig** *holy*)
þæt	*the* (neuter)
mynster	*church, minster*

Personal names

TITLES

It was normal Old English practice when stating a person's title to give the name first, followed by the rank:

Cnut cyning	*king Cnut*
Lyfing arcebisceop	*archbishop Lyfing* (of Canterbury)
Wulfstan arcebisceop	*archbishop Wulfstan* (of York)
Æþelweard ealdorman	*ealdorman Æthelweard*
Þurkil eorl	*earl Thorkell*

BY-NAMES

This pattern of name + descriptor was also true of the nicknames that apportioned praise or blame, and of the many by-names, which were useful for distinguishing between people of the same name:

Æþelræd Unræd	*Æthelred the ill-advised*
Eadmund Irensid	*Edmund Ironside*
Æþelstan Healfcyning	*Æthelstan Half-king*
Eadwig ceorla cyng	*Eadwy king of the peasants*
Þurkil Hwita	*Thorkell the White*
Ælfgyfu seo hlæfdige	*Ælfgyfu the Lady* (Emma's adopted English name since the time of her marriage to Æthelred)
Ælfgyfu seo Hamtunisca	*Ælfgyfu of Northampton* (literally *the Northamptonian*)

Another Thorkell appears later in the reign of Cnut; his name is always given distinctively as **Þurkil Hwita** *Thorkell the White* (see unit 20). Cnut's first wife happened to have the same English name as his royal wife Emma of Normandy. This was the noble name Ælfgyfu ('ÆLF-yi-vuh'). To distinguish them the chroniclers called the first wife **Ælfgyfu of Northampton** or simply **seo oðre Ælfgyfu** *the other Ælfgyfu*, while the honorific title **seo hlæfdige** ('HLÆF-di-yuh') was reserved for **Ælfgyfu Imme** i.e. Ælfgyfu Emma.

EALDORMAN AND EORL

There was some difference between the old rank of **ealdorman** held by the exiled Æthelweard and the new rank of **eorl** as held by earl Thorkell, a former commander of the Danish army. While there had been around a dozen **ealdormanries** earlier in the tenth century, the earldoms were fewer in number at the beginning of Cnut's reign, just the four great provinces of Wessex, East Anglia, Mercia, and Northumbria. The rank of earl, then, was higher than the normal ealdorman, because he governed a larger territory. This situation had arisen once before in the early tenth century, when the powerful super-ealdorman was known as **Æþelstan healfcyning** *Æthelstan Half-king*. The term **eorl**, which originally meant *brave man*, *noble warrior* in the poetry, gained popularity because it sounded like **jarl**, the cognate word in Cnut's mother tongue Old Norse. In fact the two languages were similar enough for some mutual comprehension (for more discussion, see unit 20).

The years 1021 to 1027

In the following text it will be seen that the compiler of Chronicle C writes annals for the years up to 1023, but not for 1024–7; he thus emphasizes the period when Cnut was proving his credentials as an English king. Highlighted in this account is Cnut's honouring of the English martyr saint Ælfheah, or St Alphege as he came to be called, the courageous archbishop of Canterbury during the years 1006 to 1012.

04.03 Read and listen to the text, then answer the questions.

1 What happened to Thorkel on the Feast of St Martin in 1021? _____

2 What reasons could you suggest for the travels of king Cnut and archbishop Athelnoth in the year 1022? _____

3 Why did the king take Thorkel's son back with him to England? _____

4 What happened to the relics of St Alphege? _____

1021 Her on ðissum geare to Martines mæssan Cnut kyning geutlagode Þurkil eorl.

1022 Her Cnut kyningc for ut mid his scipon to Wiht, and Æþelnoð arcebisceop for to Rome.

1023 Her Cnut cyning com eft to Englalande, and Þurcil and he wæran anræde. And he betæhte Þurcille Denemearcan and his sunu to healdenne, and se cyning nam Þurciles sunu mid him to Englalande. And he let ferian syððan Sancte Ælfeges reliquias of Lundene to Cantwarabyrig.

1024 - [the scribe left a space but wrote nothing]

1025 -

1026 -

1027 -

1022:

1023:

ut *out* 'oot' (sometimes written **út**; pronounced with a long vowel) **for ut** *travelled out, sailed out to sea*; **mid his scipon** *with his ships* (dative plural after **mid**); **Wiht** *Isle of Wight* **wæran** *were*; **an-ræd** *of single counsel*, i.e. reconciled (pronounce both vowels long); **betæhte** *entrusted* 'be-TÆHte' (pronounce with a fricative 'h'); **to healdenne** *to hold, rule*; **se** *the* (masculine); **nam** *took*; **let** *ordered* 'late' (pronounce with a long close 'é' sound); **ferian** *carry, convey*; **syððan** *afterwards*; **reliquias** *relics*

Grammar

1 THE PAST TENSE

Some of the basics of the present tense of verbs have already been touched on in units 2 and 3, and more will be explained in unit 5, but by definition, of course, a chronicle deals with past events. There are two basic ways of forming a past tense in English. One is to add a consonant -*d* as an ending -*ed* to the stem of the verb:

I play   >   *I played*

the other is to change the vowel in the stem of the verb:

I drink   >   *I drank*

Both these means of forming the past tense go back to the early stages of the language. Their Old English equivalents are as follows:

ic plegie   >   **ic plegode**, adding **-ode** to the stem **pleg**

ic drince   >   **ic dranc** changing the vowel in the stem **drinc**

Verbs of the first type are known as consonantal, or 'weak verbs', while the others are vocalic (i.e. vowel-changing), or 'strong verbs'. Further examples of weak verbs you will meet are **feran** *depart* **ferde** *departed*, and **ahnian** *own* **ahnode** *owned*. Two strong verbs are **healdan** *hold* **heold** *held*, and **adrifan** *drive out* **adraf** *drove out*. Although numerically there are far more of the first type, so many, in fact, that they are termed the 'regular' verbs in modern English, nevertheless many common verbs, which you will come across frequently, belong to the vocalic type.

Some other past tenses already seen are:

weak verbs:	**heo hæfð** *she has*	>	**heo hæfde** *she had*
strong verbs:	**ic seo** *I see*	>	**ic seah** *I saw*
	hit wyrð *it becomes*	>	**hit wearð** *it became*
	hig sittað *they sit*	>	**hig sæton** *they sat.*

> **LANGUAGE INSIGHT**
>
> Every verb consists of two parts: stem + inflection. The stem is the base form of the word and when spoken it is stressed, i.e. pronounced with greater prominence. (In this book either underlining or capital letters are used to indicate stress.) The inflection is a variable ending (it is weakly stressed); it shows the use and meaning of the verb in the context of the sentence: 'WUN-ian' *to remain*, 'WUN-ode' *he remained*. In strong verbs, the stem vowel changes to form the past tense but an ending marks the plural.

2 THE PREFIX GE- ('YUH-')

For the past tense many Old English writers liked to attach an optional **ge-** prefix to the verb. This is pronounced 'yuh-' and is weakly stressed: the emphasis falls on the stem of the word, e.g. **ge-wende** is pronounced 'yuh-WENde'. As far as its meaning is concerned the **ge-** is a perfective prefix which conveys the idea of result or completeness; often it is prefixed to the past tense merely to emphasize the idea of a completed action in the past:

ic seah	and	**ic geseah**	both mean	*I saw*
ic nam	and	**ic genam**	both mean	*I took*

With some verbs, however, the perfective prefix adds to the meaning:

ahnian *to own*	**geahnian** *to take possession, prove ownership*
ascian *to ask*	**geascian** *to discover*
ridan *to ride*	**geridan** *to occupy*, i.e. ride round and occupy
sittan *to sit*	**gesittan** *to settle, inhabit*

In modern dictionaries of Old English, it is usual to ignore the prefix for reference purposes and to look up a word such as **sittan** or **gesittan** under the letter 'S'.

3 THE PREFIX GE- ('YUH') BEFORE NOUNS

The prefix **ge-** is also used with nouns derived from verbs, again to indicate a completed action, such as **ge-sceaft** (derived from **scieppan** *to create*), which means *that which has been created*, i.e. *creation*, or in the plural as **þa feower gesceaftas** *the four elements* (for which see unit 5).

Before other nouns **ge-** conveys an idea of grouping together or association:

ge-mot	*assembly* (cf. mod. Eng. folk moot or shire moot)
ge-trum	*troop*
ge-fera	*comrade, travelling companion* (from **feran** *to travel*).

On the same pattern, the singular **broðor** *brother* has the simple plural **broðru** *brothers*, but the plural with prefix **gebroðru** indicates *a group of brothers* hence also *co-religionists* or *monks*.

● OLD–MODERN CONNECTIONS

Sometimes the perfective **ge-** was used with adjectives. From the twelfth century Old English **genog** or **genug** was written with an initial **i-** prefix replacing the **ge-**, to give forms in Middle English such as **inug, genug, ynough**. The adjective *enough* is one of the few modern words to preserve the old **ge-** prefix. Another example is *handiwork*, Old English **handgeweorc**.

4 IRREGULAR PAST TENSES

As well as the two basic types of verb, the weak and strong conjugations, there are also a good number of verbs that do not fit the standard pattern. Some are common verbs such as *be, do, go,* or *know*. As in many languages, these occur so frequently in people's speech that they take on irregular forms in present and past tenses:

is	*is*	'iss'	>	**wæs**	*was*
deð	*does*	'day-th'	>	**dyde**	*did* 'dü-deh'
gæð	*goes*	'ga-th'	>	**eode**	*went* 'éo-deh'
wat	*knows*	'wah-t'	>	**wiste**	knew.

5 THE VERB *TO BE*

Compare the present and past tenses of *to be:*

Present						Past	
sg.	1	ic	eom	beo	*am*	**wæs**	*was*
	2	þu	eart	bist	*are*	**wære**	*were*
	3	he, heo, hit	is	bið	*is*	**wæs**	*was*
pl.	1–3	we, ge, git, hi	sind	beoð	*are*	**wæron**	*were*

6 THE PLURAL IN THE PAST TENSE

Marking the plural

In modern English, we distinguish singular *was* and plural *were* but not a singular *did* from a plural *did*, since with most verbs the form does not change. But in Old English the distinction **wæs/wæron** is invariably made with other verbs too: **dyde/dydon**, **eode/eodon**, **wiste/ wiston**. A simple rule is this: in the past tense, the plural takes the ending **-on**:

wiste = *he/she knew*   **wiston** = *they knew*

As can be seen from the study texts, however, the scribes sometimes write **-an**, because in late Old English the **-on** ending was pronounced as in modern English '*button*', and so the earlier distinction between **-an** and **-on** could no longer be heard.

Practice

COMPARING DIFFERENT VERSIONS OF THE *ANGLO-SAXON CHRONICLE*

Although based on a common core, the various versions of the *Chronicle* (versions A to G) have different agendas and emphases: they often select different details for inclusion.

1 The following annals from the D chronicle (which do not appear in C) reveal an interest in contacts with Rome and journeys to the papal court. Translate them using the grammar notes in this unit and the word index at the back of the book.

D 1026 Her for Ælfric biscop to Rome, and onfeng pallium æt Iohanne papan on .ii. Idus Nouembris. […]

D 1031 Her for Cnut cyng to Rome. And sona swa he ham com, þa for he to Scotlande, and Scotta cyng eode him on hand, and wearð his man, ac he þæt lytle hwile heold.

_____

_____

_____

_____

2 Two versions offer a different take on the story of the Norwegian king Olaf. Compare and contrast the annals for 1028–30 in manuscripts C and D of the *Chronicle*. What differences can be seen in the two versions of the narrative?

Version C

C 1028 Her Cnut cing for to Norwegon mid fiftig scipum.

C 1030 Her wæs Olaf cing ofslagen on Norwegon of his agenum folce, and wæs syððan halig. And þæs geres ær ðam forferde Hacun se dohtiga eorl on sæ.

Version D

D 1028 Her for Cnut cyng of Englalande mid fiftig scypum to Norwegum, and adraf Olaf cyng of þam lande, and geahnade him eall þæt land.

D 1029 Her com Cnut cyng eft ham to Englalande.

D 1030 Her com Olaf cyng eft into Norðwegon, and þæt folc gegaderade him togeanes and wið him fuhton, and he wearð þær ofslægen.

_____

_____

_____

_____

LANGUAGE INSIGHT

The adverb here
The first word of a typical annal, **her**, is pronounced 'hay-r' with a long close vowel like French 'é' and means literally *here* i.e. now at this point in the series of annals marked by the list of numbers in the left margin of the manuscript page. The same demonstrative adverb **her** is used in the Old English titles written over narrative illustrations in Anglo-Saxon religious manuscripts; these captions explain to the viewer what happened here in the picture. The equivalent Latin word 'hic' appears in the Latin titles of the Bayeux Tapestry, which was most probably made by Anglo-Saxon artists and embroiderers.

Reading

THE POEM *MAXIMS II*, LINES 48B–55A

In a further extract from *Maxims II*, the introductory poem in the C version of the *Chronicle*, the poet presents his reflections on the struggles of life in the world (lines 48b–55a). The compiler of the *Chronicle* perhaps considered it suitable wisdom to ponder as his readers read about the deeds of the kings in their own generation:

> [...]   **Tungol sceal on heofenum**
> **beorhte scinan, swa him bebead Meotud.**
> 50 **God sceal wið yfele; geogoð sceal wið yldo;**
> **lif sceal wið deaþe; leoht sceal wið þystrum;**
> **fyrd wið fyrde, feond wið oðrum,**
> **lað wið laðe ymb land sacan,**
> **synne stælan. A sceal snotor hycgean**
> 55 **ymb þysse worulde gewinn.**

> *A star belongs in the heavens, shining brightly as the Lord commanded. Good must fight with evil, youth with age, life with death, light with dark, army with army, enemy with another, foe against foe, dispute the land, accuse of wrong. Ever a wise man must meditate on the struggles of this world.*

The calendar

The dates in the *Chronicle* and other Old English writings follow the Roman calendar in using the system of *ides*, *nones*, and *kalends*, except that feast days are usually named individually, e.g. **midwintres dæg** *Christmas Day*. The *ides* (Latin 'idus') fall on the 15th day of March, May, July and October, and on the 13th day of the other months. The kalends are the first day of the month. The twelfth of the kalends – the day of the solstice and the equinox – is found by counting backwards.

The system can be illustrated by looking at the following table for the second half of December:

December

13	the ides of December (Latin 'idus Decembris')
14	nineteenth of the kalends of January
15	eighteenth of the kalends of January
16	seventeenth of the kalends of January
17	etc.
18	
19	
20	
21	twelfth of the kalends of January (the solstice, Old Eng. **sunstede)**
22	
23	tenth of the kalends of January
24	
25	Christmas (Old Eng. **midwintres dæg**)
26	St Stephen's Day
27	
28	fifth of the kalends of January
29	fourth of the kalends of January
30	third of the kalends of January
31	second of the kalends of January
January 1	the kalends of January (Latin 'kalendas Ianuarii')

Similarly, the *nones* (Latin 'nonas') can be defined as the ninth day by (inclusive) counting backwards from the *ides*.

In March, May, July and October the nones fall on the seventh of the month, and on the fifth of the other months.

Test yourself

1 Reread the study texts paying particular attention to the tenses of the verbs. Write the corresponding past tense for each infinitive in the list below.

Infinitive	Past tense
e.g. **wendan** *to turn*	**gewende** *turned, went*
a **gewunian** *to remain*	
b **niman** *to take*	
c **forðferan** *to depart*	
d **lætan** *to order*	
e **gehalgian** *to consecrate*	
f **betæcan** *to entrust*	

2 Choose the correct missing verb from the end of the sentence and write it in.

   a Her Cnut kyningc _____ út mid his scipon to Wiht [com/for].

   b Ic wiht _____ on wege feran [geseah/wiste].

   c Her on ðissum geare Cnut kyning _____ Þurkil eorl [geutlagode/geutlagodon].

   d Wulfstan arcebiscop and oðre biscopas … _____ þæt mynster æt Assandune [gehalgode/gehalgodon].

5 *Ymbe þa feower timan*
About the four seasons

In this unit you will learn about:
▶ *the writer Byrhtferth of Ramsey*
▶ *the 'th' ending of the present tense*
▶ *the subject of a sentence*
▶ *grammatical gender and the definite article*
▶ *connecting the definite article* **se**, **seo**, **þæt** *with the pronouns* **he**, **heo**, **hit**

You will read:
▶ *the description of the seasons from Byrhtferth of Ramsey's* Handboc (Enchiridion)
▶ *related passages from* Maxims II, The Seafarer *and* The Wife's Lament

 05.00

Ymbe þa feower timan
About the four seasons

Byrhtferth of Ramsey

Byrhtferth (c. 970–c.1020) was a monk and teacher at Ramsey Abbey, and an author of historical and scientific writings. In his position as **magister** (*teacher*), he compiled a bilingual Latin and English **handboc** or manual known otherwise by a Greek title *Enchiridion*. This was a textbook on the science of **gerim-cræft** *computus*, i.e. the mathematics of the calendar, which involved arithmetic, geography, astronomy, and rhetoric. Byrhtferth's readership was made up partly of the young monks and pupils of his own monastery, who knew Latin, but more widely also of the ordinary priests and clerics of the unreformed minsters and parishes, who used mainly English.

Byrhtferth's secondary aim therefore was to teach some basic Latin to those who did not know the language. But his main purpose was to teach computus and convey his enthusiasm for it: in his colourful prose Byrhtferth described the beauty of computus as **þære lilian blosman** *the blossom of the lily* and its profundity as **þære rosena swæc** *the fragrance of roses*. And he was full of respect for the institution that had fostered him**: þas þing we gemetton on Ramesige, þurh Godes miltsiendan gife** *these things we found at Ramsey, through God's merciful grace.*

Vocabulary builder

WEATHER

ceald	*cold*
drigge	*dry*
wæt	*wet*
wearm	*warm*

SEASONS

lengtentima	*spring*
sumor	*summer*
hærfest	*autumn*
winter	*winter*

TIME

hwil	*while*
tid	*hour*
dæg	*day*
monað	*month*
tima	*season*
gear	*year*

 05.01

Ymbe þa feower timan

About the four seasons

In each of the four descriptions, what two adjectives are used to classify the season?

Ymbe þa feower timan we wyllað cyðan iungum preostum ma þinga, þæt hig magon þe ranclicor þas þing heora clericum geswutelian.

About the four seasons we wish to proclaim to young priests more things, so that they can the more boldly declare these things to their clerics.

> **LANGUAGE INSIGHT**
>
> The verb **cyðan** *make known*, *proclaim* derives from **cuð** *known*; this still exists in modern English as the negative adjective *uncouth*, which initially meant *unknown*, *strange*, whence it later came to mean *unattractive in manners and language* and in some situations *uncultured*.

 05.02

1 LENGTENTIMA

Ver ys lengtentima, and he gæð to tune on .vii. idus Februarii, and he byð wæt and wearm, and þry monðas he byð betwux mannum, and he hæfð an and hundnigontig daga, and he hæfð emniht.

ys	*is*
gæð	*goes* from **gan** *to go* (pronounce vowels long)
tun	*estate, town* (see reading below)
.vii. seofon	*seven* 'séo-von'
on .vii. idus Februarii	*7th February*
monð-as	*months* 'mohn-thass' (plural)
be-twux	*among, betwixt*
mannum	*men, people* (dative plural)
an	*one* 'ahn' (long vowel)
hundnigontig	*ninety* 'hund-NEE-ghonti'
daga	*of days* (genitive plural)

LANGUAGE AND CULTURAL INSIGHT

Though early medieval Europeans knew nothing of a heliocentric universe, they inherited a sophisticated knowledge of the sun and the planets from Roman astronomy. The equinox (from Latin 'aequus' *equal* and 'nox' *night*) is the time when the sun appears to cross the equator, making the night and the day equal in length. The Old English **emniht** captures very well the sense of 'equi-nox', being a compound of **emn**, a phonetic assimilation from **efn** i.e. **efen** *even, equal* + **niht** *night*.

 05.03

2 SUMOR

Se oðer tima hatte æstas, þæt byð sumor. On lengtentima springað oððe greniað wæstmas, and on sumera hig weaxað and on hærfest hig ripiað. Sumor byð wearm and drigge, and þes tima byð þry monðas, and he hæfð hundnigontig daga, and he gæð to mannum on .vii. idus Mai, and he hæfð sunstede.

se	*the* (masculine singular definite article)
oðer	*second*
springað	from **springan** *to spring up*
oððe	*or* (conjunction)
greniað	*flourish* 'gré-niath' (from **grenian**, cf. **grene** *green*)
wæstm-as	*fruits* 'wæst-mas' (plural noun)
weaxað	from **weaxan** *wax, grow*
ripiað	from **ripian** *ripen*
drigge	*dry* 'drih-yeh'
þes	*this* (masc. nom. sg.)
.vii. idus Mai	*7th of the Ides of May* i.e. 9th May
sunstede	*solstice*

The sun was observed very closely as – so it seemed – it moved around the earth. The solstices are the two turning-points, one in summer and one in winter, when the sun, in the gradual shifting of its course through the sky, reaches its maximum distance from the equator. In summer the sun follows a more northerly course and 'stands' at the solstice on 21st June, thereafter following a daily more southerly course until it reaches its position at the winter solstice on 21st December. The Old English word **sun-stede** is again an elegant rendering of the Latin, a compound meaning literally *sun-place* or *sun-stead*, the second element occurring in modern English *homestead, farmstead* and *bedstead*, as well as in adjectives like *steady* and *steadfast*.

 05.04

3 HÆRFEST

Se þridda tima ys autumnus on Lyden gecweden and on Englisc hærfest. Boceras getrahtniað þæne naman for þære ripunge oððe for þære gaderunge. Hig cweðað 'autumnus, propter autumnationem uel propter maturitatem'. Se gæð on .vii. idus Augusti to tune, and he byð þry monðas, and he hæfð emniht, and he hæfð twa and hundnigontig daga, and he byð drigge and ceald.

se þridda tima	*the third season*
Lyden	*Latin*
gecweden	*called* (past participle of **cweðan**)
boceras	(plural of **bocere** *scholar*, cf. **boc** *book* 'bohk')
getrahtniað	*explain* (present tense)
þæne	*the* (masculine accusative case; see units 6 and 10)
nama	*name*
for	*because of*
þære	*the* (feminine dative; see units 8 and 10)
ripung	*ripening*
gaderung	*gathering*
cweðað	*say* (present tense of **cweðan** *say*)
.vii. idus Augusti	*7th August*

[The Latin etymology that Byrtferth gives, **autumnus propter autumationem uel propter maturitatem**, can be translated as *autumn, because of autumatio or maturity*.]

 05.05

4 WINTER

Se feorða tima ys genemned hiemps on Lyden and winter on Englisc. He hæfð sunstede and twa and hundnigontig daga, and he byð þry monðas, and he byð ceald and wæt.

 Language discovery

THE 'TH' OF THE PRESENT TENSE

It is hardly necessary to emphasize the importance of knowing whether a writer is talking about the present or the past, and like many European languages, English makes a basic formal distinction between present and past in its system of tenses. In Old English, the present tense can often be recognized in the third person, i.e. when the subject is *he, she, it, they*, by the ending in -**ð** or -**þ**. This is the same '-*th*' ending that we find in the King James Bible or Shakespeare's *the rain it raineth everyday* or in old proverbs such as *manners maketh the man*. And in Old English it is found in verbs such as **cymð** *comes*, **drincð** *drinks*, **selð** *gives*, or in the plural **wyllað** *want*:

We wyllað cyðan iungum preostum ma þinga

We want to tell young priests more things.

1 Find examples of the present-tense 'th' in the text about the four seasons and write them below.

    a *is* _____

    b *has* _____

    c *goes* _____

    d *spring up* _____

    e *flourish* _____

IDENTIFYING THE SUBJECT OF THE SENTENCE (THE NOMINATIVE)

The nominative is the normal form of the noun and the pronoun, the head-word which is listed in the dictionaries. In the following typical examples, a noun in the nominative case functions as the subject of the sentence, i.e. the person or agent, the 'doer' or 'experiencer' who carries out the action of the verb. In modern English the subject usually comes first and then the verb; this is not always true of Old English:

Her wæs Eadward gehalgod to cinge

Here Edward was consecrated as king

In the singular, a noun in the nominative case is unmarked by any ending, but when it refers to more than one entity the noun declines, i.e. takes an ending, to show that it is nominative plural. Again this nominative plural shows the subject of the verb, i.e. the doers of the action:

Boceras getrahtniað þæne naman for þære ripunge

Scholars explain the name as 'the ripening'.

2 In the following two sentences, underline the grammatical subject.
  a **Cyning sceal rice healdan**   *a king must rule a country* (unit 2).
  b **Her gewende Cnut cyng to Denemearcon**   *here king Cnut returned to Denmark* (unit 4).

GRAMMATICAL GENDER

Languages like Old English and German distinguish three fundamental categories of noun and use a different word for *the* with each category (the definite article). In Old English the three base forms for the definite article are **se**, **seo**, **þæt**:

the article **se** is used with masculine nouns such as **tima** *season*;

seo is used with feminine nouns such as **gaderung** *gathering*;

þæt goes with neuter nouns such as **mynster** *minster*.

In the same way, there are three words for *it*; these are the personal pronouns **he**, **heo**, and **hit**: the pronoun **he** means *he* as a personal pronoun or *it* when referring to a masculine noun; similarly, **heo** is either *she* or *it*; while **hit** means *it* in the neuter.

To give some quick examples of masculine nouns: **se nama** means *the name*, **se here** *the army*, **se mona** *the moon*, **se monað** *the month*, **se hafuc** *the hawk*, **se bera** *the bear* (note that the word **se** in these instances can also mean *that*). For feminine nouns, **seo tid** means *the hour* or *that hour*, **seo heall** means *the hall*, **seo glof** *the glove*, **seo eorþe** *the earth*, **seo sunne** *the sun*. Similarly, with neuter nouns: **þæt hus** means *the house*, **þæt scip** means *the ship*, **þæt ger** *'yér' the year*. All these examples show the base form, or the nominative.

It has been calculated that roughly forty-five per cent of the nouns you will meet are masculine, thirty-five per cent are feminine, and twenty-five per cent neuter (Quirk and Wrenn, p. 20). It is not usually possible to predict the gender of a noun from its form, although knowledge of the equivalent words in German will help.

In the late Old English period a new article **þe** developed and this eventually became Middle English and present-day English *the*. But until that process of gradual change had completed itself, speakers always made a distinction between the three grammatical genders of nouns. And the gender of a noun affected not only the article the but also other relevant words in the sentence.

So when Byrhtferth discusses the second season of the year he writes **se** because **tima** is masculine:

Se oðer tima hatte æstas, þæt byð sumor

The second season is called aestas, that is summer.

And when he refers to this season a little later, Byrhtferth uses the masculine **þes tima** and then the corresponding word for *it*, which has to be masculine **he**:

Sumor byð wearm and drigge, and þes tima byð þry monðas, and he hæfð hundnigontig daga, and he gæð to mannum on .vii. idus Mai, and he hæfð sunstede.

*Summer is warm and dry, and this season is three months, and it (O.E. **he**) has ninety days, and it (O.E. **he**) goes to men on 9th May, and it (O.E. **he**) has a solstice.*

If he were writing about *the sun*, **seo sunne**, a feminine noun, the corresponding pronoun would be **heo**, and if he were writing about a neuter noun **þæt ger** *the year*, the pronoun would be **hit**. So although it sounds like Byrhtferth is personifying the season, this is not necessarily so, since he is using **he** according to the rules of grammatical gender.

Here is Byrhtferth writing about the day, and its divisions and hours:

Se dæg hæfð þreo todælednyssa: seo forme hatte mane, þæt ys ærnemerigen, and seo oðer ys gecweden meridies, and seo þridde ys geciged suppremum, þæt ys on æfen oððe seo ytemeste tid (*Handboc*, II.3, ll. 127–30).

The day has three divisions: the first is called 'mane', that is early morning, and the second is called 'meridies', and the third is termed 'suppremum', that is in the evening or the last hour.

3 In the above sentence, note the variation in the definite article according to gender and fill in the table:

English	Old English	Gender
a the day		
b the hour		
c the division		

From now on, to help with the learning of gender along the lines of many modern language textbooks, the vocabulary explanations in each unit will list nouns together with their requisite definite article **se**, **þæt**, **seo** (meaning *the* or *that*). This is followed as before by the meaning in italics, where necessary the pronunciation in inverted commas, and any further information in brackets:

se tima   *season*   'tee-ma' (mod. Eng. *time*)

Reading

THE SEASONS

The reading section allows you to browse, to read some well-known texts discursively without worrying about the meaning of every single word.

1 From *Maxims II* (lines 3b–12)

In some lines from the beginning of the poem, the poet ponders **wyrd**, a term derived from the verb **weorðan** *to become*. A common word for *fate* in Old English poetry, **wyrd** means here *the becoming of events*, and the poet links it with the passing of the seasons. The passage can be seen as a set of associations and interconnections, in a modern punctuation best presented as a set of clauses joined by commas:

[...]   **Wind byð on lyfte swiftust,**

þunar byð þragum hludast, þrymmas syndan Cristes myccle,

5   **wyrd byð swiðost, winter byð cealdost,**

lencten hrimigost, he byð lengest ceald,

sumor sunwlitegost, swegel byð hatost,

hærfest hreðeadegost, hæleðum bringeð

geres wæstmas þa þe him God sendeð,

10   **soð bið swutolost, sinc byð deorost,**

gold gumena gehwam, and gomol snoterost

fyrngearum frod, se þe ær feala gebideð.

Wind in the air is swiftest,

thunder sometimes is loudest, the glories of Christ are great,

fate is strongest, winter is coldest,

spring the frostiest – it is cold the longest –

summer brightest with sun, sky is hottest,

autumn most glorious – brings to men

the fruits of the year which God sends them –

truth is clearest – treasure is dearest,

gold to everyman – and an old man most prudent,

wise with distant years, who has experienced much.

2 From the *Exeter Book*

The Seafarer, a poem about pilgrimage and exile, presents vivid images of winter and summer. Note the hyperbole of the following passage (lines 14–17):

hu ic earmcearig iscealdne sæ

15   **winter wunade wræccan lastum**

winemægum bidroren,

bihongen hrimgicelum. Hægl scurum fleag.

how I, wretched on the ice-cold sea,

remained the winter on the exile paths,

deprived of kinsmen,

hung round with icicles. Hail flew in showers.

A well-known passage presents the image of the *cuckoo* or **geac**, described as **sumeres weard** *summer's ward*, i.e. the guardian of summer. But for the exiled seafarer the cuckoo proclaims **sorge** *sorrow, trouble in mind* (lines 53–55a) :

> **Swylce geac monað   geomran reorde**
> **singeð sumeres weard   sorge beodeð**
> **bittre in breosthord.**

Also the cuckoo gives warning by its mournful speech; summer's guardian sings and proclaims sorrow, bitter at heart.

Another *Exeter Book* poem, *The Wife's Lament*, also an elegy on the theme of **wræc** *exile*, speaks ambivalently of the summer-long day (lines 37–8):

> **Þær ic sittan mot   sumorlangne dæg,**
> **þær ic wepan mæg   mine wræcsiþas …**

There I must sit the summer-long day.
There I may weep for the ways of my exile (trans. Bradley)

3 From the *Anglo-Saxon Chronicle*

As we saw in unit 3, annal C 1019 of the *Chronicle* tells us that king Cnut spent the winter of 1019–20 in Denmark. There were practical as well as political reasons for his stay. Because of adverse weather conditions, winter normally put a stop to travel until the sailing season could begin again at the end of the spring. Naturally enough, winter was a very conspicuous season. Perhaps because of this, people tended to count the winters rather than the number of years that a king lived or reigned. Thus the *Chronicle*, version F, writes about the founding of Normandy by the Viking Rollo:

F 876 Her Rodla ðurhferde Normandi mid his here, and he rixade fifti wintra.

Here Rollo took over Normandy with his army, and he ruled fifty winters.

4 From the Middle English *Harley Lyrics*

Byrhtferth writes that the *spring* **gæð to tune**, literally *goes to town* – in other words that it comes among the dwelling-places, or arrives in the world. A similar turn of phrase occurs in a famous Middle English poem, written long after the Old English period, in an anthology known (after its British Library shelf-mark) as the *Harley Lyrics*. Made about 1340, forty years or so before the time of the great Chaucer, the collection preserves a whole set of diverse early English poems. This stage of English sits roughly halfway in the development of the language between Old and Early Modern English. Although Middle English has lost the many case endings and gender distinctions of Old English, most of the words in this passage are Old English in origin. Pronunciation is very similar to Old English, but there are a different set of spelling conventions (**u** and **v** can be interchangeable, but **-ou-** in **toune** regularly represents the same 'oo' sound as **-u-** in Old English **tun**):

Lenten ys come wiþ loue to toune,

Wiþ blosmen ant wiþ briddes roune,

þat al þis blisse bringeþ.

Dayeseges in þis dales,

notes suete of nyhtegales,

vch foul song singeþ.

There are Old English equivalents for most of the words in this text: **lengten** *spring*, **ys (ge) cumen** *is come*, **wiþ** *with*, **lufe** (dat.) *love*, **to** *to*, **tun** *farmstead*, **blostm** *blossom*, **and** *and*, **bridd** *young bird*, **run** *mystery, counsel, runic letter*; **þæt** *that*, **eal** *all*, **þas blisse** (acc.) *this bliss*, **bringeþ** *bringeth*, **dæges-eage** *'the day's eye'* i.e. *daisy*, **in** *in*, **swet** *sweet*, **nihtegale** *nightingale*, **ælc** *'æltch' each*, **fugol** (later pronunciation 'foo-wol') *bird*, **sang** *song*, **singeþ** *singeth*. Only two or three words in the passage do not fit: the meaning of Middle English **roune** has changed to *'song'*; **dale** meaning *valley* comes from Old Norse **dalr** *valley* rather than Old English **dæl** *part*; and **note** is from Old French.

Byrhtferth at Evesham

In 1016 came the Battle of Assandun. Byrhtferth's noble patrons – Eadnoth bishop of Dorchester (formerly abbot of Ramsey from 992 to 1006) and Wulfsige (who had succeeded him as abbot) – both fell in the fighting. Ramsey came under the jurisdiction of Cnut, the new king, and it was probably he who appointed a new abbot. Wythmann was a foreigner from Germany, unused to the ways at Ramsey, and the monks reacted against his severe regime. In 1020 he was driven out. After going on pilgrimage to Jerusalem, he returned to Ramsey, resigned his position and became a hermit at Northeya. In the meantime, Cnut had decided to disperse the unruly monastery community, but was persuaded to change his mind by the abbot of Peterborough.

In these times of unrest there is a possibility that Byrhtferth also chose to leave his alma mater for voluntary exile elsewhere. In one of his later works, *The Life of St Ecgwine* (written in Latin), Byrhtferth tells the legendary story of the founder of Evesham Abbey in Worcestershire, and the book is respectfully dedicated to the monks of that abbey, almost as though he knew them. As Baker and Lapidge (1995) suggest, it is possible that during the troubles, the abbot of Evesham, who was a former monk of Ramsey, invited Byrhtferth to join him there.

Test yourself

1 Fill in the correct form of the present tense in the sentences below.

a We _____ cyðan iungum preostum ma þinga [wyllan].

b Lengtentima _____ to tune on .vii. idus Februarii [gan].

c He _____ an and hundnigontig daga [habban].

d On lengtentima _____ wæstmas [springan].

e On sumera _____ wæstmas [weaxan].

f On hærfest hig _____ [ripian].

g Winter _____ ceald and wæt [beon].

2 Translate the passage below.

Be ðære sunnan cweðe we þus. Ðonne heo uparist, þonne wyrcð heo dæg. Þonne heo nyðer byð astigen, þonne bringð heo þa niht (Byrhtferth, *Handboc*, II.3, lines 124–6).

3 The following passage comes from an anonymous eleventh-century school-text on gemstones and minerals. Read the extract and fill in the missing words in the translation.

a **Asbestus hatte sum stancynn on Claudea rice. Gif he wyrð onbyrnende, ne mæg hine wæter ne wind adwæscan.**

b **Sum stan is on Persa rice; gif þu hine mid handa ahrinest, he birneð sona. Se stan is haten piriten.**

c **Seleten hatte sum stan þæs gecyndu sind þæt he mid wexsendan monan wexseð and mid waniendan wanað. Se stan bið gemet on Persa rice.**

d **Sum stan hatte alexandrius. Se bið hwit and cristallum gelic.**

a A certain stone _____ asbestos in the kingdom of Claudea. If _____ starts (lit. becomes) burning, neither water nor wind _____ extinguish _____ .

b A certain stone is in the kingdom of the Persians; if you _____ it with the hand it immediately _____. The stone is called pyrites.

c Seletes is the name of a stone whose characteristics are that _____ waxes with the waxing moon and _____ with the waning one. The stone is found in Persia.

d A certain stone is called alexandrius; it _____ white and like to crystal.

SELF-CHECK	
I CAN …	
⃝	spot the 'th' ending of the present tense
⃝	identify the subject of a sentence
⃝	recognize the three different genders of the noun through the definite article *the*
⃝	distinguish **se**, **seo**, **þæt** and **he**, **heo**, **hit**
⃝	read the description of the seasons in Byrhtferth's *Handboc*

6 Ic geseah on swefne
I saw in a dream

In this unit you will learn about:
▶ *the context of* The Story of Joseph
▶ *the meanings of the past tense* **hēt**
▶ *the use of correlation:* **þa … þa** *when … then*
▶ *more past tenses*
▶ *the masculine accusative ending* -ne
▶ *the typical vocabulary of a dream vision*

You will read:
▶ **The Story of Joseph 1** *(from the Old English* **Hexateuch***)*
▶ *the opening lines of the poem* **The Dream of the Rood**

 06.00

Ic geseah on swefne
I saw in a dream

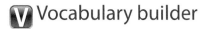 Vocabulary builder

DREAMS
swefn	*dream*
me mette	*I dreamed*
me þuhte	*it seemed to me*

EMOTIONS
lufode	*he loved*
hatedon	*they hated*
onscunodon	*they shunned*

The Story of Joseph 1

The story of Joseph and his brothers from the Book of Genesis is a compelling account of betrayal and reconciliation. It has had many retellings over the centuries, and it appears to have been popular in the Old English period. A translation of Genesis was made by a team of translators, and a group of artists made an illustrated version of the *Hexateuch* (the first six books of the Bible). *The Story of Joseph* also circulated as a separate text: in one manuscript now in the Parker Library at Cambridge. It occurs at the end of a collection of Archbishop Wulfstan's legal and political writings. Evidently there were political resonances to the story, for, as we will see in later units, a biblical story of fraternal rivalry had much to say to an age when brothers and half-brothers vied for the throne, suffered exile or worse, and at times seemed to struggle towards a hard-won reconciliation.

 06.01

Ða Iosep wæs syxtynewintre

When Joseph was sixteen

Ða Iosep wæs syxtynewintre, he heold hys fæder heorde mid hys broðrum. And he wæs mid Balan sunum and Zelphan hys fæder wifa; he gewregde hys broðru to heora fæder ðære mæstan wrohte.

Ða	*when* 'thah'
seo heord	*herd*
mid his broþrum	*with his brothers* (dative plural after **mid**)
þæt wif	*woman, wife* 'weef' (note the neuter gender)
wifa	*wives* 'wee-va' (plural)
gewregde	*accused* (past tense of **ge-wregan**)
heora	*their*
ðære mæstan wrohte	*of the greatest wrongdoing* (nominative **seo wroht**)

Check your comprehension against this translation.

When Joseph was sixteen, he kept his father's herd with his brothers. And he was with Bala's sons – and Zelpha's – his father's wives. He accused his brothers to their father of the greatest wrong.

 06.02

Soþlice Israel lufode Iosep ofer ealle his suna for þam ðe he hine gestrynde on his ylde, and het him wyrcean hringfage tunecan.

soþlice	*truly* 'sothe-li-cheh'
lufode	*loved* 'LU-vo-deh' (from **lufian** *to love*)
for þam ðe	*because*
strynan	*to gain, beget* (also spelt **strienan, streonan**)
yld	*old age* (also spelt **ield** *age*)
het	*ordered* 'hét' (i.e. **hēt** with long vowel) (from **hatan**)
wyrcean	*to make* 'wür-chan'

Truly Israel [i.e. Jacob] loved Joseph over all his sons because he had him in his old age, and he ordered a ring-coloured tunic to be made for him.

Language discovery

THE VERB HATAN AND ITS TWO PAST TENSES

The past tense **het** *ordered* comes from the unusual verb **hatan** 'hah-tan' *to call, order, promise*, which had several forms. One of these, **ic hatte** – meaning either *I am called* in the present, or alternatively *I was called* in the past tense – occurred in unit 3 in the riddle formula **saga hwæt ic hatte**. Another form will be seen in unit 24 in the king's coronation oath **ic þreo þing behate** *I promise three things*. With the prefix **be-** the verb means *to promise*. There is a related word **seo**

behæs *vow*, which became Middle English **behest** *promise, vow*. In the modern expression *at my behest*, meaning *on my instructions*, the sense of **hatan** as *call, order* is still present.

THE PAST TENSE HET

Linked to the meaning of modern English, *behest* is the other past tense form **het**, pronounced with a long vowel **hēt** ('hét' or 'hate'). It means *he/she ordered something to be done*. Like **sceal** (see unit 2), **het** is followed by the infinitive. A classic example of how it is used comes at the beginning of the poem *The Battle of Maldon*, where Byrhtnoth, the ealdorman of Essex, orders the deployment of his men:

Het þa hyssa hwæne hors forlætan, feor afysan.

Then he ordered each of the warriors to abandon (his) horse, drive (it) away.

The construction **het** can also occur without a direct object; conceivably the above sentence could have been:

Het þa hors forlætan.

He then ordered the horses to be abandoned.

(For a longer extract from *The Battle of Maldon* see unit 21.)

In older texts, or poems in an archaic style, **het** appears as **heht**; a celebrated instance is the inscription on the famous Alfred Jewel, now in the Ashmolean Museum in Oxford:

ÆLFRED MEC HEHT GEWYRCEAN

Alfred ordered me to be made.

Images of the Alfred Jewel are easily located online (see also Bibliography). The image on the front of the Jewel is an iconic figure; the large eyes and the emblems of authority in his hands symbolizing divine insight and royal wisdom. The boar's head was common on other Anglo-Saxon metalwork; but here its open jaws were evidently designed to grasp a wooden pointer that could be used by a reader to point to the line of text being read. Such a reading would take place on a formal occasion, from a book placed on a lectern.

The wording of the Alfred Jewel language mirrors a similar pattern in the Joseph text:

and het him wyrcean hringfage tunecan

and he ordered a ring-coloured tunic to be made for him.

Reading

 06.03

Þa hys gebroðru þæt gesawon

When his brothers saw this

Þa hys gebroðru þæt gesawon, þæt hys fæder hyne swiðor lufode þonne his oðre suna, ða onscunodon hi hine and ne mihton nane freondrædene wið hine habban.

When his brothers saw this, that his father loved him more than his other sons, then they shunned him and could not have any friendship with him.

Witodlice hyt gelamp þæt hym mætte, and he rehte þæt his gebroþrum; þurh þæt hi hyne hatodon þe swiþor.

So it happened that he had a dream, and he told that to his brothers; because of that [literally through that] they hated him the more.

Đa ... ða	*When ... then*
gesawon	*saw* 'yuh-SA-won' (plural of **geseah** *saw*)
hyne	*him* (accusative pronoun)
swiðor	*more* (comparative of **swiðe** *strongly, very much*)
onscunian	*shun* 'on-SHUN-yan'
mihton	*they could* (past tense of **magon** *they can*)
seo freondræden	*friendship*
habban	*have*
witodlice	*indeed, so* 'WI-tod-lee-cheh' (sentence adverb)
hyt gelamp	*it happened* 'hüt yuh-LAMP' (a set phrase)
rehte	*told, narrated* (irregular past tense of **reccan**)
hatodon	*they hated* (from **hatian** *to hate*)

Grammar

THE USES OF ÞA

The definite article **þā** (pronounced with long 'ah') and the adverb **þā** are technically homonyms, since they both have the same sound and spelling but a different meaning and origin. Directly before a noun phrase, as seen in unit 5, the word **þa** can be identified as the definite article, either the plural *the*, as in (1) **ymbe þa feower timan** *about the four seasons*, or the feminine accusative: (2) **þonne [seo sunne] nyðer byð astigen, þonne bringð heo þa niht** *when the sun is gone down then it brings the night*.

But at the beginning of a sentence, **þa** is usually either a time indicator *then*, or a connecting word *when*. The context usually helps us to decide. In examples (3) and (4) the word **þa** simply marks the adverb *then*:

(3) **Đa cwædon hys gebroðu, 'Byst ðu ure cyning?'**

Then his brothers said, 'Are you our king?'

(4) **þa geutlagode man Æþelweard ealdorman** (unit 4)

then they outlawed ealdorman Æþelweard.

Note the 'second-place' position of the verb. This is typical of clauses beginning with **her** and **þa**: the verb follows immediately after **þa** when it means *then*.

In example (5), however, the first **þa** means *when* while the second is *then*:

(5) **Þa hys gebroðru þæt gesawon, þæt hys fæder hyne swiðor lufode þonne his oðre suna, ða onscunodon hi hine.**

Again, note the word order in the second clause: **ða** is followed immediately by the verb **onscunodon**. But in the first part, where **ða** is a conjunction meaning *when*, the verb is sent to the end of the clause:

Þa hys gebroðru þæt gesawon, þæt hys fæder

[literally] *When his brothers that saw, that his father…*

This pairing up of the same word **ða** to connect two parts of a sentence is known in Old English grammar as correlation. Another instance is the correlation of **þonne … þonne** in sentence (2) above:

(2) þonne [seo sunne] nyðer byð astigen, þonne bringð heo þa niht.

Joseph's two dreams

1 JOSEPH'S FIRST DREAM

The story of Joseph continues in the following exercise. Fill in the missing past tenses from the following list: **abugon, bundon, cwædon, cwæð, hæfdon, hatedon, stodon, þuhte**. Solutions are in the key at the back of the book, and some of the sentences will be discussed in the Grammar section.

And he (a) _____ to him: 'Gehyrað min swefn, ðe me mætte. Me (b) _____ þæt we (c) _____ sceafas on æcere and þæt min sceaf arise and stode uprihte on middan eowrum sceafum, and eowre gylmas (d) _____ ymbutan and (e) _____ to minum sceafe.'
Ða (f) _____ hys gebroðu, 'Cwyst ðu la, byst ðu ure cyning oððe beoð we ðine hyrmen?' Witodlice þurh his swefn hig hyne (g) _____, and (h) _____ andan to him.

And he said to them: 'Hear my dream which I dreamed. It seemed to me that we were binding sheaves in the field and my sheaf seemed to arise and stand upright among your sheaves, and your sheaves stood about and bowed down to my sheaf.' Then his brothers said, 'Are you saying you are our king or we are your retainers?' So because of his dream they hated him and had enmity towards him.

þæt swefn	*dream* 'sweven' (cf. Middle Eng. **sweven**)
þe	*which*
me mette	*I dreamed*
se sceaf	*sheaf* 'SHÉaf' (cf. the mythical name **Scyld Scefing** *Shield Sheafson* in the poem *Beowulf*)
se æcer	*field* 'acker' (cf. mod. Eng. *acre*)
on middan	*in the midst*
ymbutan	*round about*
hyrmen	*retainers* 'hür-men' (**se hiereman** *retainer, subject*)
oððe	*or*
hyne	*him*

2 JOSEPH'S SECOND DREAM

Why would Joseph's family take exception to his telling of this dream?

Oðer swefen hyne mætte, and he rehte þæt hys broðrum, and cwæð, 'Ic geseah on swefne swylce sunne and mona and endleofun steorran, and ealle abugon me.' Þa he þæt hys fæder and hys broðrum rehte, ða aðreatode se fæder hyne, and cwæð: 'Hwæt sceal ðis swefen beon þe ðu gesawe? Sceolon we abugan ðe, ic and ðin modor and ðine gebroðru?'

Many of the words in the above text have appeared in this or preceding units, but make note of the following:

se steorra	*star* (plural **steorran** *stars*)
aðreatode	*rebuked* (past tense of **aðreatian**)
þe ðu gesawe	*which you saw*
seo modor	*mother*

Grammar

THE OBJECT OF A SENTENCE

In the typical structure of a sentence, the key elements are a subject (the doer or experiencer), the verb (the action) and the object (the thing or person acted upon by the verb), for example:

	Subject	Verb	Object	
1	**Israel**	**lufode**	**Iosep.**	*Israel loved Joseph.*
2	**He**	**gewregde**	**his broðru.**	*He accused his brothers.*

In these two sentences, the word order SVO (subject + verb + object) helps us to identify the doer of the action and distinguish him from the object of the sentence. The pattern here is the same in both Old English and modern English.

> **LANGUAGE INSIGHT**
>
> It is important to remember that the object of a sentence is a grammatical rather than a literal notion. We are not talking about objects in the real world, but simply about relationships between words in a sentence.

As an inflected language, Old English has a way of indicating the object other than by the order of the words. This is the main function of the accusative case (although it has other uses after a preposition or in time phrases). The accusative is marked by various endings which vary according to the gender and type of word.

THE -NE ENDING

Of all the accusative endings, the ending **-ne** is the easiest to distinguish, and marks various words that refer to a masculine noun in the accusative singular. It is found on the pronoun **hyne**, also spelt **hine**; the accusative form of the word **he**, as in the sentence:

Witodlice þurh his swefn hig hyne hatedon.

So because of his dream they hated him.

Note that the case ending allows the writer to be freer with the word order of the sentence – unlike the word order of modern English, the accusative pronoun tends to be placed before the verb:

adverbials	subject	object	verb
Witodlice þurh his swefn	**hig**	**hyne**	**hatedon.**

Note the word order also in the clause **for þam ðe he hine gestrynde on his ylde**, after the conjunction **for þam ðe** *because*:

conjunction	subject	object	verb	adverbial
for þam ðe	**he**	**hyne**	**gestrynde**	**on his ylde**
because	*he*	*him*	*gained*	*in his old age.*

The accusative ending **-ne** is also found on 'strong' adjectives qualifying a masculine noun; commonly found in poetry, it marks the noun phrase as the grammatical object of the sentence:

Ic... gefylle eal_ne_ middangeard   *I... fill all the world.* (unit 3)

The **-ne** ending is also found on the definite article:

Boceras getrahtniað þæ_ne_ naman for þære ripunge.

Scholars explain the name [autumn] as 'the ripening' (unit 5).

ME ÞUHTE *IT SEEMED TO ME*

The impersonal expression **me þuhte**, meaning *it seemed to me*, is often seen at the beginning of a dream narrative, informing the reader that what follows is only a seeming or apparition, and not an actual waking experience.

1 *The Dream of the Rood*

The Dream of the Rood is a poem contained in the religious anthology the *Vercelli Book*, so called because its owner apparently left the manuscript in Vercelli (where it is still kept in the cathedral library). Vercelli is in northern Italy, on the pilgrimage route to Rome: frequently travellers would stay there after crossing the Alps. The poem belongs to the medieval genre of the dream vision, and begins as follows (note the use of words and phrases that echo the vocabulary of the Joseph story):

> **Hwæt, ic swefna cyst   secgan wylle**
>
> **hwæt me gemætte   to middre nihte,**

syðþan reordberend   reste wunedon.

Þuhte me þæt ic gesawe   syllicre treow

5   **on lyft lædan   leohte bewunden**

beama beorhtost.

Listen, the best of dreams I will tell, what I dreamed in the middle of the night, after human beings remained in sleep. It seemed to me that I saw a wonderful tree being taken into the air, surrounded with light, the brightest of beams.

secgan	*to say, tell* 'sedge-an'
seo niht	*night*
syðþan	*after* (conjunction)
reord-berend	literally *speech-bearers*, i.e. a kenning or poetic expression for human beings, since animals do not use human language
lyft	*air*; **lædan** is the infinitive *to take*, but it means *being taken* after the verb *I saw*
leohte	*with light* (dative); **bewunden** literally *wound round*: i.e. surrounded with light
se beam	means either *tree* or *beam of light* (note the wordplay)

> **LANGUAGE INSIGHT**
>
> Impersonal verbs are verbs without a grammatical subject. These do not occur in present-day English because we supply a meaningless subject *it* (as in the phrase *it seemed to me that*…), which is not present in Old English **me þuhte þæt**…

2 COMPARISON WITH CHAUCER

In Chaucer's dream vision *The Book of the Duchess*, a Middle English poem written about 1370, the poet narrator begins his dream as follows. As you read the passage, look for words or expressions that it shares with the Old English dream visions:

Loo, thus hyt was; thys was my sweven.   [**hyt** *it*]

Me thoghte thus: that hyt was May,

And in the dawenynge I lay   [**dawnenynge** *dawning*]

(Me mette thus) in my bed al naked

And loked forth, for I was waked

With smale foules a gret hep   [**foules** *birds*; **hep** *multitude*]

That had affrayed me out of my slep,

Thorgh noyse and swetnesse of her song.   [**her song** *their singing*]

Chaucer's Middle English contains many words of Old English origin. It will be seen that his word for *dream* is **sweven**, spelt differently but pronounced the same as Old English

swefn. Chaucer also uses two impersonal verbs that occur in the Joseph passage and in *The Dream of the Rood*. In both instances the Old English construction consists of the dative **me** (pronounced 'may') followed by the verb:

Old English		Chaucer
me þuhte	*it seemed to me*	**me thoghte**
me mætte	*it dreamed to me*, i.e. *I dreamed*	**me mette**

By Shakespeare's time, the equivalent of Old English **me þuhte** and Middle English **me thoghte** was *methought*, which looks very close to *I thought*. But actually this is still an impersonal expression; it does not, strictly speaking, mean *I thought* but *it seemed to me*.

In classic Old English, by contrast, the language distinguished the two meanings by their form:

Infinitive	Present	Past
þyncan *seem* 'thün-chan'	**þyncð**	**þuhte**
þencan *think* 'then-chan'	**þencð**	**þohte**

In later English, both these verbs then coalesced as *thinketh* in the present and *thought* in the past tense.

3 COMPARISON WITH SHAKESPEARE

In Shakespeare's play *Richard III*, the Duke of Clarence, brother of Richard (Duke of Gloucester) – and his potential rival – is imprisoned in the Tower of London, where he has a dream (Act I, scene iv), an extract of which is given below. Note the occurrence of *methought* as an impersonal verb.

As an exercise in etymology, read through the passage and then, using the Index at the back of the book and a dictionary, identify words deriving from Old English. List any Old English words whose meaning has changed over time. For example: '*dream*', from Old English dream, originally meant *joy*.

Keeper: *What was your dream, my lord? I pray you tell me.*

Clarence: *Methoughts that I had broken from the Tower,*

And was embark'd to cross to Burgundy;

And in my company my brother Gloucester,

Who from my cabin tempted me to walk …

Methought that Gloucester stumbled, and in falling,

Struck me (that thought to stay him) overboard

Into the tumbling billows of the main …

Methoughts I saw a thousand fearful wrecks;

Ten thousand men that fishes gnaw'd upon;

Wedges of gold, great anchors, heaps of pearl,

Inestimable stones, unvalu'd jewels,

All scatter'd in the bottom of the sea.

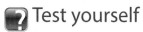 Test yourself

1 What is the difference between **me þuhte** and **ic þohte**?

_____

2 Translate the following.

a Witodlice þurh his swefn hig hyne hatedon. _____

_____

b Þa hys gebroðru þæt gesawon, þæt hys fæder hyne swiðor lufode þonne his oðre suna, ða onscunodon hi hine. _____

_____

7 Cnut cyning gret his arcebiscopas

King Cnut greets his archbishops

In this unit you will learn about:
- ▶ *the genre of the king's writ*
- ▶ *the declension of the strong noun*
- ▶ *the plurals of nouns*
- ▶ *the relative pronoun þe*
- ▶ *the salutation (greeting) in letters and proclamations*
- ▶ *the endings of the genitive case*
- ▶ *the concept of* frith

You will read:
- ▶ *an extract from king Cnut's Proclamation of 1020*
- ▶ *Cnut's writ to archbishop Lyfing*
- ▶ *the passage on* frith *in The Battle of Maldon (lines 36–9)*

 07.00

Cnut cyning gret his arcebiscopas

King Cnut greets his archbishops

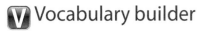 Vocabulary builder

LAW

lagu	*law*
riht	*justice*
unriht	*injustice*
miht	*power*
frið	*peace, protection*
mund	*protection*
spræc	*claim*

ADMINISTRATION

scirman	*shire governor*
scirgerefa	*shire reeve (sheriff)*
gewritu	*letters, documents*
freols	*legal privilege*
swutelung	*declaration*
gewitnys	*cognisance, witness*

The genre of the king's writ

While in Denmark in the winter of 1019–20, Cnut sent a remarkable proclamation to the English people in which he promised to be a **hold hlaford** *gracious lord* and to uphold the peace that had now been established in the kingdom.

The legal document known as a **writ** (from O.E. **ge-writ** *letter*) was a type of short administrative notice that probably came into use in the ninth century; there are many examples from the tenth and eleventh centuries. Very like a letter, the **writ** was composed on one side of a piece of vellum (parchment), which could then be folded and a wax seal attached. The issuing party, very often the king, sent the **writ** accompanied by his authenticating seal to the shire court, where its instructions could be put into force.

The manuscript context: The *York Gospels*

As we shall see in various units in this book, a suitable place to preserve copies of important documents was the blank page of a precious manuscript. A copy of the following document is written, along with some of Archbishop Wulfstan's impassioned Old English sermons, at the back of the famous *York Gospels* – the early eleventh-century de luxe illustrated gospel book (York Minster Library 1). Latin gospel books were often put on display on the altar (**weofod**) of an important church, and for permanent safe-keeping, other important documents such as charters and title-deeds were copied into them. The *York Gospels* were possibly presented as a special gift to archbishop Wulfstan by king Cnut and queen Emma.

 07.01

FROM *CNUT'S PROCLAMATION OF 1020*

Cnut cyning gret his arcebiscopas and his leodbiscopas and Þurcyl eorl and ealle his eorlas and ealne his þeodscipe, twelfhynde and twyhynde, gehadode and læwede, on Englalande freondlice.

And ic cyðe eow þæt ic wylle beon hold hlaford and unswicende to Godes gerihtum and to rihtre woroldlage.

Ic nam me to gemynde þa gewritu and þa word þe se arcebiscop Lyfing me fram Papan brohte of Rome, þæt ic scolde Godes lof upp aræran and unriht alecgan and full frið wyrcean be ðære mihte þe me God syllan wolde.

gret	*greets* 'grét' (irregular present tense)
leodbiscop	*bishop* (**leode** *people*)
se þeodscipe	*nation*
twelfhynde and twyhynde	*high- and low-ranking* (pronounce with short vowels)
gehadode	*ordained* 'yuh-HAH-do-de' (from **gehadod** past participle)
læwed-e	*lay* 'LÆ-weh-de'
freondlice	*in a friendly manner* (adverb)
ic cyðe eow	*I inform you, I proclaim to you*
unswicende	*faithful, undeceitful*
ðæt geriht	*right, justice, obligation*

riht	*just*
seo worold	*world*
seo lagu	*law*
seo ge-mynd	*mind, memory*
a-ræran	raise 'ah-RÆ-ran'
þæt unriht	*injustice* 'UN-riht' (**riht** rhymes with German 'nicht')
a-lecgan	*put down, lay down* 'ah-LEDGE-an' (became *allay* in mod. Eng.)
se frið	*peace*
seo miht	*power* (mod. Eng. *might*; pronounce to rhyme with **riht**)

Check your comprehension of the passage against the following translation.

King Cnut greets his archbishops and bishops and earl Thorkell and all his earls and all his nation, high-ranking and low-ranking, clergy and laity, in England with friendly greetings. And I proclaim to you that I will be a loyal lord and faithful to God's laws and to just secular law. I took to mind the writings and the words which archbishop Lyfing brought to me from Rome from the Pope, that I would raise up God's praise and bring down injustice and work full peace by the power which God wished to give me.

Language discovery

1 Plurals: Look again at the extract from Cnut's proclamation of 1020 and find examples of plural nouns.

2 Style: Identify any words or phrases that alliterate in the text.

3 Antonyms: In the text, find and translate as many words or phrases as you can that form antonyms, i.e. paired opposites on the pattern short / long, true / false, or amateur / professional, public / private etc.

Grammar 1

1 THE DECLENSION OF THE STRONG NOUN

The main type of noun in Old English is the so-called 'strong' noun; here the term 'strong' indicates the declension, i.e. the way the noun changes its endings to show case. The strong masculine noun, for example, has the following set of case endings:

	Singular	Plural
nominative	**se eorl** *the earl*	**þa eorlas** *the earls*
accusative	**þone eorl**	**þa eorlas**
genitive	**þæs eorles** *of the earl*	**þara eorla** *of the earls*
dative	**þam eorle** *to the earl*	**þam eorlum** *to the earls*

There are other patterns of noun declension: e.g. the strong feminine (which has a different set of endings), and the weak noun (weak nouns tend to end in **-n** in most cases except the nominative singular). The full details of noun declension can be learned in time; the important thing is to grasp some essentials first.

2 THE PLURALS OF NOUNS

The basic nominative plural ending for the main type of strong masculine nouns is formed by adding **-as**:

se biscop *the bishop*	**þa biscopas** *the bishops*
se eorl *the earl*	**þa eorlas** *the earls*
se freols *the privilege*	**þa freolsas** *the privileges*
se heofon *heaven*	**þa heofonas** *the heavens*
se flod *flood* 'flōd'	**þa flodas** *floods*
se wer *man*	**þa weras** *the men*

Strong neuter plurals end either in **-u** or like modern English *sheep* the plural remains unchanged as the 'zero' ending:

þæt gewrit *the letter*	**þa gewritu** *the letters*
þæt scip *the ship*	**þa scipu** *the ships*
þæt heafod *head*	**þa heafdu** *heads*
þæt scep *the sheep*	**þa scep** *the sheep* (plural)
þæt word *the word*	**þa word** *the words*
þæt þing *the thing*	**þreo þing** *three things*

Strong feminine nouns have a plural in **-a**:

seo glof *the glove*	**þa glofa** *the gloves*
seo benn *the wound*	**þa benna** *the wounds*
seo wynn *joy*	**þa wynna** *the joys*

and a small group of frequently met nouns have a plural in **-e**:

seo dæd *the deed*	**þa dæde** *the deeds*
seo wyrd *fate*	**þa wyrde** *the fates*

The plurals of 'weak' nouns have the usual weak ending **-an**:

þæt eage *the eye*	**þa eagan** *the eyes*
þæt eare *the ear*	**þa earan** *the ears*

An irregular noun is found as in modern English in **fōt** *foot* (pronounced 'foat') with plural **fēt** (pronounce long, rather like 'fate').

3 THE RELATIVE PRONOUN ÞE

The relative pronoun **þe** is a connector; it opens a clause beginning with *which* or *who*:

þa gewritu þe se arcebishop me fram papan brohte of Rome

the letters <u>which</u> the archbishop brought me from the Pope from Rome

on manegra goddra manna gewitnysse þe me mid wæron

with the witness of many good men <u>who</u> were with me.

After the relative pronoun, the verb tends to come later in the sentence than it does in modern English:

be ðære mihte þe me God syllan <u>wolde</u>

by the power which God wished to give me

Two additions to the Royal gospel book

On the adjoining pages of another gospel book (now in the British Library at shelfmark Royal I D.ix), in the characteristically 'handsome hand' of the Canterbury scribe Eadui Basan (for which see unit 10), there occur two texts relating to Cnut's dealings with Christ Church cathedral and monastery. The first of these is an agreement with the monks of Christ Church, the second a royal writ or message to Lyfing, who was archbishop of Canterbury when Cnut came to the throne. Both seem to date from 1018, when Cnut was in Kent granting the land at Hazelhurst to Christ Church (see unit 10), and before he departed for Denmark.

● **A NOTE ON SAWYER NUMBERS**

All writs and charters of the Anglo-Saxon period have been catalogued by P.H. Sawyer (available online as the Electronic Sawyer, see Bibliography). For convenience, in histories of the period, documents are identified by the Sawyer catalogue number. (In the case of Cnut's writ to archbishop Lyfing, the catalogue number is S 985).

1 A CONFRATERNITY NOTICE

A confraternity agreement for mutual support between, on the one side, Cnut and his brother Harald, who may have been with Cnut in England between 1016 and 1018, and on the other side the monks of Christ Church Canterbury. The first sentence 'In the name of our Lord Jesus Christ' is a rubric in Latin, the rest is Old English. Two of the other three names feature elsewhere in the charters.

+ In nomine domini nostri Iesus Cristi. Her is awriten CNUTES kynges nama, þe is ura leofa hlaford for worulde and ure gastlica broðor for Gode, and Harold þæs kinges broðor.

Ðorð ure broðor. Kartoca ure broðor. Thuri ure broðor.

2 FROM KING CNUT'S WRIT TO ARCHBISHOP LYFING

The following extract from Cnut's writ or letter to archbishop Lyfing and others begins, like his proclamation to the English nation, with a formula of greeting to the recipients **Cnut cing gret … freondlice**, *King Cnut greets … in a friendly manner*, followed by a solemn statement of purpose and **ic cyðe eow þæt** … *and I make known to you that* … But beyond the formalities, an actual dialogue is reported in this extract and the voices of king and archbishop can be heard in debate. The main topic under discussion is the freedom of Christ Church (**Cristes cyrice**), the cathedral in Canterbury.

Read the text and answer the questions in Practice.

Cnut cing gret Lyfing arcebiscop, and Godwine biscop, and Ælmær arcebiscop, and Æþelwine scirman, and Æþelric, and ealle mine þegnas, twelfhynde and twihynde, freondlice. And ic cyðe eow þæt se arcebiscop spæc to me ymbe Cristes cyrcean freols þæt heo hæfð nu læsse munde þonne hio hwilan ær hæfde. Þa lyfde ic him þæt he moste niwne freols settan on minan naman. Þa cwæð he to me þæt he freolsas genoge hæfde gyf hi aht forstodan. Þa nam ic me sylf þa freolsas and gelede hi uppan Cristes agen weofod on þæs arcebiscopes gewitnysse and on Þurkilles eorles and on manegra goddra manna þe me mid wæron

scirman	*shire governor* 'sheer-man' (**seo scir** *shire, province*)
þegn thegn	*official, minister* 'thane' (cf. **þegnian, þenian** *to minister*)
seo mund	*security, protection* (**mund-e** accusative)
hwilan, hwilum	*sometimes, once* 'hwee-lum' (dative plural of **seo hwil** *time*)
ær	*before, previously*
lyfde	*granted, conceded* (past tense of **lyfan**, also spelt **liefan**)
moste	*be allowed, might* (from **motan** *to be allowed*)
niw-ne	*new* (masc. acc. strong ending)
gyf	*if* (sends verb to end of clause)
aht	*anything*
forstodan	*were worth, stood for* (past of **forstandan**)
sylf	*self*
ge-lede	*laid* (also **gelegde**, past of **lecgan**)
hi	*them* 'hee' (the nom. and acc. of **hi** *they* is the same)
se weofod	*altar*
seo (ge)witnys, witnes	*knowledge, witness*

7 Cnut cyning gret his arcebiscopas King Cnut greets his archbishops   73

Practice

Reread the extract from Cnut's writ to archbishop Lyfing.

1 What was the archbishop's grievance? _____

2 What was Cnut's initial response? _____

3 How did he finally resolve the situation? _____

Grammar 2

1 THE SALUTATION (GREETING) IN LETTERS AND PROCLAMATIONS

In the opening greeting of a letter or writ, the adverb goes to the end of the sentence (for more detail on adverbs see unit 17). Here is an example:

Wulfstan arcebiscop gret Cnut cyning his hlaford

and Ælfgyfe þa hlæfdian eadmodlice.

Archbishop Wulfstan greets king Cnut his lord

and Ælfgyfu the lady humbly.

Often in the salutation of the king's writ, the verb **gret** *greets* is used with the adverb **freondlice**, as seen below:

Cnut cyngc gret Eadsige biscop and Ælfstan abbot and Ægelric and ealle mine þegnas on Cent freondlice.

The meaning should be clear enough when you are reading the Old English, but it presents problems for the translator, since although the adverb **freondlice** corresponds to *friendly*, this word in modern English is an adjective. Normally modern adverbs end in *-ly* (which of course derives from **-lice**), the exceptions being a few adjectives like *friendly* and *likely*; so we can send *friendly greetings* but we cannot say, for example, *she greeted him friendly*. To try and solve the problem some scholars translate **freondlice** as *amicably* while others use the phrase *in a friendly way*. Others translate the sentence as follows:

King Cnut sends friendly greetings to bishop Eadsige, and abbot Ælfstan, and Ægelric, and all my thegns in Kent.

> **LANGUAGE INSIGHT**
>
> Some present tenses in Old English have lost the standard **-th** ending in the 3rd person. The reasons are phonetic. If the stem or root of the verb ends in **-t** or **-d** it tends to assimilate the regular **-th** that would follow it. Examples are **stent** for the expected **standeð** and **gret** instead of **greteð**. The latter form, however, occurs in poetry e.g. **greteð gliwstafum** *he greets joyfully* in The Wanderer, line 52.

2 GENITIVE SINGULAR

For the genitive singular, meaning *of*, the endings can vary a lot, depending on the category of noun and its gender. The genitive ending of the common type of 'strong' masculine noun is usually **-s**, akin to the *apostrophe s* of present-day English:

uppan Cristes agen weofod

on Christ's own altar

on þæs arcebiscopes gewitnysse and on Þurkilles eorles

in the presence of the archbishop and of earl Thorkell

Note here the ending **-s** also affects the definite article **þæs** *of the*. Looking at the definite article is another way of recognizing a genitive, especially with nouns for which the genitive ending is not particularly distinctive. Where the masculine and neuter articles **se** and **þæt** change to **þæs** *of the* in the genitive, the feminine article **seo** goes to **þære** *of the*. So in the religious formula **on þære halgan þrinnesse naman** *in the name of the holy Trinity*, the base form **seo þrinnes** *the Trinity* would be in the nominative case. This becomes **þære þrinnesse** *of the Trinity* in the genitive.

3 GENITIVE PLURAL: OF DEEDS, OF MEN ETC.

As was pointed out in the presentation of numerals in unit 5, the genitive plural meaning *of deeds*, *of men* etc. ends regularly in **-a**, for example **tyn tida** *ten of hours*, i.e. *ten hours*. Other examples are:

twelf hund heafda *twelve hundred heads*

sida twa *two sides*

dæda demend *judge of deeds* (in *Maxims II*, see unit 2).

When an adjective describes and occurs with the genitive plural noun, it will usually take the strong ending **-ra**:

on manegra goddra manna gewitnysse

in the presence of many good men

eall cristen folc minra gewealda

all Christian people of my domains

For now, and to speed up the process of learning to recognize the form and meaning, we will follow a general rule of thumb: look out for the **-a** ending; in an appropriate context, it probably indicates the genitive plural.

THE CONCEPT OF **FRITH**

The word for *peace* in the Cnut's Proclamation is **frið**, cognate with German 'Frieden'. Elsewhere, in the compound **friðsocn**, it implies the *seeking out of a place of peace as sanctuary*. **Frith** meaning *sanctuary* is connected then with the strong medieval reverence for sacred spaces protected by the authority of Church and state. Describing the altar and reliquary of the saints at Hexham, a twelfth-century historian wrote in Latin of 'the stone chair which in English is called the *frith-stool*'. As Richard Fletcher points out in his book *Bloodfeud* (2002, 37): 'this sanctuary chair, simple, solid and dignified, can still be seen at Hexham, as can a similar one at Beverley. They are tangible reminders of one of the ways in which a violent society sought to limit and control aggression.' In the heroic narrative of *The Battle of Maldon* the question of **frith** as peace or protection becomes a dramatic and contentious issue.

Frith in *The Battle of Maldon* (lines 36–41)

The Battle of Maldon is a poem about lordship and loyalty, about making a choice between appeasement and war. In the following passage, during the negotiations before the battle, the Viking messenger lays down his ultimatum:

> **… Gyf þu þat gerædest   þe her ricost eart**
> **þæt þu þine leoda   lysan wille,**
> **syllan sæmannum   on hyra sylfra dom**
> **feoh wið freode,   and niman frið æt us,**
> **we willaþ mid þam sceattum   us to scype gangan,**
> **on flot feran   and eow friþes healdan.**

> *'… If you who are most powerful here advise*
> *that you will ransom your people*
> *and pay to the seamen at their own judgement*
> *money for peace, and take protection from us,*
> *we with the money will go to ship,*
> *travel on the sea, and keep peace with you.'*

line 36	**gyf þu þat gerædest** *if you advise this*; **þe … eart** *you who are…*; **ricost** *most powerful*
line 37	**lysan** *ransom*
line 38	**dom** *judgement*: **on hyra sylfra dom** *at their own judgement*
line 39	**feoh** *money*; **wið** *in exchange for*; **freode** *peace*; **niman** *take*; **frið** *protection*; **æt us**, *from us*
line 40	**mid þam sceattum** *with the coins*; **scyp** *ship*; **gangan** *go*
line 41	**flot** *sea*: **on flot** *to sea* (origin of the expression *afloat*) **eow friþes healdan** *keep the peace with you* (**healdan** takes a genitive object **friþes**)

In the context of a heroic poem, it is not hard to imagine how Byrhtnoth, the ealdorman of Essex, responds to this speech. For part of his reply, **yrre and anræd** *angry and resolute*, see the extract from the poem in unit 21.

Test yourself

Take the strong noun **se biscop** *the bishop* and write out its full declension in all four cases, and in singular and plural, with a translation. Use the declension of **eorl** in Grammar 1 as a model if necessary.

_____

_____

_____

_____

_____

_____

SELF-CHECK

	I CAN ...
⬤	decline the strong noun
⬤	recognize basic plurals
⬤	spot the relative pronoun **þe**
⬤	translate the salutation (greeting) in letters and proclamations
⬤	understand the endings of the genitive case
⬤	interpret the concept of **frith**

8 *He behet hyre þæt land æt Ealretune*
He promised her the land at Orleton

In this unit you will learn about:
▶ *marriage in Anglo-Saxon England*
▶ *the indirect object in a sentence*
▶ *the uses of the dative case*
▶ *the declension of the third person personal pronoun*
▶ *the forms of the feminine pronoun* **heo, hi, hire**

You will read:
▶ *the Worcestershire marriage agreement*
▶ *an extract from the* Life of Euphrosyne

 08.00

he behet hyre þæt land æt Ealretune
he promised her the land at Orleton

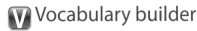 Vocabulary builder

MARRIAGE
wif	*woman, wife*
gesynscipe	*marriage*
wedd	*pledge*
morgengifu	*morning-gift*
land	*estate*

NEGOTIATION
ceap	*purchase*
to ðysum forwordan	*on these terms*
on dæge and æfter dæge	*in (her) lifetime and after (her) lifetime*

RELATED PAST-TENSE VERBS
behet	*promised*
sealde	*gave*
begeat	*acquired*
gyrnde	*yearned for*
onfeng	*received*

Marriage in Anglo-Saxon England

On the whole marriage in Anglo-Saxon England seems to have been designed to protect equally the property rights of both man and wife. Each was separately accountable under the law: if a man was found guilty of a crime, for instance, his wife could only be charged if she had been a willing accomplice. In order for a marriage actually to take place, the suitor had to meet with the woman's kinsmen, whose job it was to represent her best interests. The suitor was required to make *a pledge* (**wedd**) of money, the so-called *bride-price*, expressed in terms of a **ceap** or *purchase*, but the woman was free to accept or reject the man's offer. In addition, on the day after the marriage she received her **morgengifu** or *morning-gift*, which was her personal property, and according to the ancient law code of king Æthelberht of Kent, the morning-gift could pass eventually to the wife's kindred if she were childless. Primarily, then, the laws of marriage were concerned with pledges and gift-giving.

Grammar 1

THE DATIVE

1 Finding the indirect object

To illustrate this in present-day English, we could take the following two examples *he promised the land to her* or *he promised her the land at Knightwick*. Here the syntax or sentence structure consists of a subject, i.e. the doer, a verb i.e. the action, a direct object of the action, and an indirect object, representing the person who benefits from the action. This can be represented as follows:

subject	verb	object	indirect object
He	promised	the land	to her

subject	verb	indir. obj.	object	adverbial
he	promised	her	the land	at Knightwick

2 BASIC MEANING OF THE DATIVE

The basic meaning of the dative is *to* or *for*, marking the indirect object. In the Old English equivalent to the above example, **he behet hire þæt land æt Cnihtewican** the syntax is apparently similar, but because this is an inflected language with inflectional endings, it makes sense also to represent the structure in terms of the cases used, so that the subject is in the nominative case, the indirect object in the dative, and the direct object in the accusative:

subject	verb	indir. obj	object	adverbial
nominative		dative	accusative	
he	**behet**	**hire**	**þæt land**	**æt Cnihtewican**

It is possible to reorder the words of this sentence without changing its basic import, since the case endings do the work of bearing the meaning: **he hire þæt land æt Cnihtewican**

8 He behet hyre þæt land æt Ealretune He promised her the land at Orleton   **79**

behet or possibly **he hire þæt land behet æt Cnihtewican** or even **he hire behet þæt land æt Cnihtewican**.

3 DATIVE AFTER PREPOSITIONS

Many Old English prepositions such as **æt** (*at* or *from*), **mid** (*with*), **on** (*on*), **to** (*to* or *as*) are followed by a word or words in the dative case. It may help to picture the case endings as a useful way of knitting the words together to form a prepositional phrase, in various combinations such as:

preposition + noun:	*in town*
or preposition + *the* + noun:	*from the community*
or preposition + name:	*at Knightwick*

There are several examples in the study text below:

nominative	dative
se dæg *day, lifetime*	**on dæge and æfter dæge** *in (her) lifetime and after (her) lifetime*
se hired *the community*	**æt ðam hirede** *from the community*
Eanulfintun (place-name; masc.)	**æt Eanulfintune** *at Alton*
se arcebiscop *the archbishop*	**mid ðam arcebiscope** *with the archbishop*
ða forwerda *the terms* (fem. pl.)	**to ðysum forwordan** *for these terms*

4 THE DATIVE IN IDIOMATIC EXPRESSIONS

Various idiomatic uses of the dative can be derived from the basic meaning *to* or *for*:

<u>**ðam**</u> **ðe hire leofest wære**

to whoever was dearest to her i.e. to whoever she wished

he begeat ðæs arcebisceopes swuster him to wife

he acquired the archbishop's sister as his wife (literally <u>for himself</u> *as wife*).

The Worcestershire marriage agreement (S 1459)

In the eleventh century, *Worcester* (**Wigoreceaster**) was an important ecclesiastical and administrative centre. By a traditional arrangement, the man appointed to the archbishopric of York also held in plurality the bishopric of Worcester, probably for political and economic reasons. Worcester was a more prosperous diocese than York, and the double office promoted easier relations between the south and the politically more independent regions of the north. From 1002, the office was held by the capable figure of Wulfstan, sometimes known as Wulfstan the Homilist to distinguish him from others of the same name. Originally bishop of London, Wulfstan gained a reputation for rhetoric and eloquence. But as well as a composer of homilies and sermons and a church administrator, archbishop Wulfstan was also a politician and lawyer, who composed sets of laws implemented at great assemblies of king, nobility and clergy. A solid figure of continuity in a changing world, Wulfstan wrote these law-codes for both king Æthelred and his successor king Cnut. It is rare, however, that we glimpse anything at all of Wulfstan's family life or domestic arrangements as seen in this document, which is S 1459 in Sawyer's online catalogue (for mention of Wulfstan in the *Chronicle*, see unit 4, and for discussion of his rhythmical prose style, see unit 14).

For which family member is Wulfstan arranging this marriage?

 08.01

Her swutelað on ðysum gewrite ymbe ða forwerda ðe Wulfric and se arcebisceop geworhtan ða he begeat ðæs arcebisceopes swuster him to wife;

ða forwerda	*the terms, assurances* (from **seo foreweard** *agreement in advance*, cf. adjective **foreweard** *forward, future*)
begeat	*received* (past tense of **begytan** *acquire, receive*)
him to wife	*as his wife* (more literally *to him as wife*)

 08.02

þæt is ðæt he behet hyre þæt land æt Ealretune and æt Ribbedforda hire dæg, and he behet hire þæt land æt Cnihtewican – þæt he wolde hit hire begytan ðreora manna dæg æt ðam hirede on Wincelcumbe

hyre, **hire**	*her, to her, for her* (dative of **heo** *she*)
hyre dæge	*in her day* (i.e. in her lifetime)
wolde … begytan	*would acquire*
se hired	*community*

 08.03

and sealde hyre þæt land æt Eanulfintune to gyfene and to syllenne ðam ðe hire leofest wære, on dæge and æfter dæge, ðær hire leofest wære, and behet hire fiftig mances goldes and þritig manna and þritig horsa.

ðam ðe hire leofest wære	*to whoever was dearest to her* (i.e. to whoever she wished)
mances	*from* **mancus** *thirty silver pence, one eighth of a pound*

 08.04

Nu wæs ðyses to gewitnesse - Wulfstan arcebisceop, and Leofwine ealdorman and Aeþelstan bisceop and Aelfword abbod and Brihteh munuc, and manig god man toeacan heom, ægðer ge gehadode ge leawede - þæt ðas forewerda ðus geworhte wæran.

toeacan	*in addition to*
ægðer ge … ge	*both … and* pronounced 'either yay … yay'
ðas	*these* (the demonstrative – see unit 11)
ðus	*thus*
ge-worht	*made* (past participle of **wyrcean**)

08.05

Nu syndon to ðysum forwordan twa gewrita, oþer mid ðam arcebisceope on Wigereceastre and oþer mid Aeþelstane bisceope on Herforda.

oðer ... oðer   *the one ... the other*

Check your comprehension of the text against the following translation:

Here is declared in this document the agreement which Wulfric and the archbishop made when he received the archbishop's daughter as his wife. That is that he promised her the land at Orleton and Ribbesford for her lifetime, and he promised her the land at Knightwick, that he would obtain it for her for three people's lifetimes from the community at Winchcombe, and gave her the land at Alton to give and donate – to whoever she liked, in her lifetime or after her lifetime – wherever she liked, and he promised her fifty mancusses of gold and thirty men and thirty horses.

Now as witness to this were archbishop Wulfstan and ealdorman Leofwine and bishop Æthelstan and abbot Ælfweard and Brihtheah the monk, and many a good man in addition to them, both clergy and laity, that these terms were agreed thus. Now there are two copies of this, the one with the archbishop at Worcester and the other with bishop Æthelstan at Hereford.

Grammar 2

PERSONAL PRONOUNS, THIRD PERSON

1 Declension

Personal pronouns are classified according to first person (*I*, *we-two*, *we*), second person (forms of *you*), and third person (*she, he, it, they*). Third-person endings are as follows:

	masculine	neuter	feminine	plural
nominative	he	hit	heo	hi
accusative	hine	hit	hi	hi
genitive	his	his	hire	hira, heora
dative	him	him	hire	him, heom

Among the third person pronouns, the basic word for *he* is **he** (pronounced 'hay'). This is its form in the nominative case, when it functions as the subject of the sentence. But when the pronoun takes other functions, such as the object of the sentence, it changes its form. A comparison with modern English may be useful here, as the vestiges of the case system have survived in our modern pronouns. In the sentence *his father loved him*, the pronoun *he* has changed to *him* because it is the grammatical object i.e. the person or thing directly affected by the action. For native speakers it would be clearly wrong, i.e. grammatically unacceptable, to say or write *his father loved *he* (where **he* is the object of the action *loved*). Similarly in Old English, the nominative **he** changes to accusative **hine** in a similar context:

hys fæder <u>hyne</u> swiðor lufode þonne his oðre suna (see unit 6)

his father loved him more than his other sons.

Another example concerns the feminine pronoun. Basically, the word for *she* is **heo**. But when the context requires the idea of *benefit*, *giving to*, the pronoun switches to the dative **hire**, meaning *to her*, as a sentence from the Worcestershire marriage agreement shows:

he behet hyre þæt land æt Ealretune

he promised her the land at Orleton.

2 HISTORICAL CHANGES IN THE SYSTEM OF ENGLISH PRONOUNS

Many of the Old English pronouns have survived into modern English, sometimes with little change, as in *he*, *his*, *him*; or with some changes in spelling, as in the change from **hire** to modern English *her*. Though language is never strictly logical in all its forms, nevertheless, from the point of view of convenience, there were some flaws in the Old English pronoun system. A glance at the Pronoun table in Grammar 2 will elucidate.

Several of the forms have a multiple function and meaning: **his**, **him**, **hit**, **hi**, **hire**. Although the context usually made the message clear, when Old English began to lose its inflectional endings in the eleventh and twelfth centuries it became difficult to distinguish the meaning that was intended. The possibility of confusion was particularly acute for **hi**, which could mean *she* or *they*, for **him**, which could mean *to him*, *to it*, or *to them*; and for **hire**, which came to be pronounced and then spelt the same whether it meant *her* in the singular, or *their* in the plural. To solve the problem, speakers in the north, who were in daily contact with Danish settlers, began to imitate forms in the language of the Danes, Old Norse. As we shall see in unit 20, Old English and Old Norse were similar enough as cognate languages for people from the two speech communities to understand each other, and this facilitated borrowing between the two languages. The northern speakers of Old English borrowed **they**, **their** and **them** from Old Norse, and the new pronouns spread slowly southwards. Chaucer, in the fourteenth century, still used **her** to mean *their*, but the change had reached most forms of English by the time of Malory in the fifteenth century.

Practice

Write the correct form of the pronoun in the following sentences from unit 8.

Þa his gebroðru þæt gesawon, þæt hys fæder (a)_____ swiðor lufode þonne his oðre suna, ða onscunodon (b)_____ (c)_____.

When his brothers saw this, that his father loved him more than his other sons, then they shunned him.

Witodlice hyt gelamp þæt (d) _____ mætte, and he rehte þæt his gebroþrum; þurh þæt (e) _____ hyne hatodon þe swiþor.

So it happened that he had a dream, and he told that to his brothers; because of that [literally through that] they hated him the more.

From *The Life of Euphrosyne*

The following extract from the life of a female saint gives further insights into the process of wooing a young woman and securing a betrothal. The text was copied in a manuscript of the early eleventh century.

Read the passage, then answer the comprehension questions.

    a Why was Euphrosyne so well known in the town?

        _____

    b What did the father imply by the words he spoke to the young men seeking his daughter's hand in marriage?

        _____

    c Why did the father change his mind?

        _____

Þa asprang hire hlisa and wisdom and gelærednys geond ealle þa ceastre, forþam heo wæs on þeawum gefrætwod. And manige wurdon atihte þæt hi gyrndan hire to rihtan gesynscipe, and hit to hire fæder spræcon, ac he symle ongen cwæð, 'Gewurþe Godes willa.'

Þa æt nyxtan com him an þegen to, se wæs weligra and wurþra þonne ealle þa oþre and hire to him gyrnde. Þa onfeng se fæder his wedd, and hi him behet.

aspringan	_to spread, spring forth_
se hlisa	_sound, fame_ 'hleeza'
seo gelærednys	_learning, skill_
þeawas	_virtues_ (masc. nominative plural)
gefrætwod	_adorned_ (past participle of **gefrætwan**)
atiht	_drawn_ (past participle of **ateon**)
gyrnan	_to seek for, yearn for_ (takes the genitive case)
se gesynscipe	_marriage_
gewurþe Godes willa	_may God's will be done_
æt nyxstan, æt niehstan	_at last_
weligra	_wealthier_ (from **welig**)
wurþra	_richer, more worth_ (from **wurþ**, also spelt **weorþ**)
þæt wedd	_pledge_ (cf. modern English _wedding_)

💡 Language discovery

Reread the passage from _The Life of Euphrosyne_, paying attention to the precise use of the forms of the personal pronoun _she_, as used in various grammatical cases to describe the process of gift-giving and promising that accompanied the act of betrothal.

1 THE NOMINATIVE

<u>heo</u> wæs on þeawum gefrætwod   _she was adorned with virtues_

2 THE ACCUSATIVE

se fæder … <u>hi</u> him behet   _the father promised <u>her</u> to him_

3 GENITIVE AS POSSESSIVE

hire hlisa — *her fame*

manige … hit to hire fæder spræcon — *many spoke about it to her father*

4 GENITIVE USED AFTER THE VERB GYRNAN

Gyrnan belongs to a group of verbs which take an object in the genitive, where we would expect an accusative:

an þegen … — *a thegn*

hire to him gyrnde — *yearned for her for himself*

hi gyrndan hire to rihtan gesynscipe — *they yearned for her in lawful marriage*

5 THE DATIVE PRONOUN HIRE

For several uses of the feminine pronoun in the dative, see the above text of the Worcestershire marriage agreement; the examples include:

and he behet hire þæt land æt Cnihtewican

and he promised her the land at Knightwick

þæt he wolde hit hire begytan ðreora manna dæg æt ðam hirede on Wincelcumbe

that he would obtain it for her for three people's lifetimes from the community at Winchcombe

and sealde hyre þæt land æt Eanulfintune

and gave her the land at Alton

to gyfene and to syllenne ðam ðe hire leofest wære

to give and donate to whoever was most pleasing to her

● A NOTE ON SPELLING VARIANTS

Note alternative spellings with the letter **y** used for the vowel **i**: **hyne, hys, hym, hyre, hy**. This may be puzzling at first, but it is well to remember that absolute uniformity in spelling is a modern concept. It is generally true to say that almost all early English writers from king Alfred to William Shakespeare were liberal but not anarchic about their attitude to spelling. Shakespeare himself apparently spelt his name differently on different occasions, and even today a few words allow different vowels, such as *shown* and *shewn* or *grey* and *gray*, and they even allow different consonants in *realize* and *realise*. In the past, variant spellings of the same word were regarded as normal, or perhaps even useful as a way of adding interest and variety to a written text. You will have noticed already that the Old English consonants þ and ð alternate freely. Sometimes the scribe alternates the spelling purely for variety, but also for reasons of local dialect or house style (in a monastery scriptorium or writing hall).

LANGUAGE INSIGHT

On pronunciation matters, remember that **he** is pronounced with a long close vowel as (roughly) 'hay', **heo** is also pronounced long, and as one syllable, rather like 'Héo'. Note also that the pronoun **hi** for the fem. acc. singular and the nom. and acc. plural is pronounced 'hee', likewise with a long vowel. As we have seen already in the language of Byrhtferth (unit 5), the alternative spelling of plural **hi** was **hig**, pronounced 'hee', just as the **-ig** was pronounced 'ee' in adjectives such as **blodig** *bloody* 'bloh-dee'.

Reading

1 FROM THE *EXETER BOOK* POEM *MAXIMS I (LINES 81–3)*

In a very similar style to *Maxims II* from the C version of the *Chronicle*, this poem deals with the connections between the microcosm and the macrocosm, the human sphere and the natural world.

> **Cyning sceal mid ceape   cwene gebicgan**
> **bunum ond beagum: bu sceolon ærest**
> **geofum god wesan.**
>
> *A king must buy a queen with a transaction,*
> *with goblets and with rings: both must above all*
> *be generous with gifts.*

2 FROM *BEOWULF* (LINES 2016B–2019)

The following passage shows how a wife could become important as a pledge of peace between nations, a diplomatic presence at great feasts in the meadhall:

> **Hwilum mæru cwen,**
> **friðusibb folca   flet eall geondhwearf,**
> **bædde byre geonge,   oft hio beahwriðan**
> **secge sealde,   ær hie to setle geong.**

At times the great queen, peace-pledge of nations, processed all through the hall, encouraged the young men, often she gave a ring to a warrior, before she returned to her seat (Beowulf, lines 2016b–2019).

3 THE ROYAL WEDDING IN 1017 (FROM THE *CHRONICLE*)

As we saw in unit 4, the young king Cnut was able to bolster his position on the throne of England by marrying Æthelred's widow Emma, daughter of Richard duke of Normandy; she soon gave him a son. The annal D 1023 of the *Anglo-Saxon Chronicle* tells that **Imma seo hlæfdie mid hire cynelican bearne Hardacnute** *Emma the Lady with her royal heir Harthacnut* appeared at a great ceremony in honour of St Alphege. In the brief account of her marriage six years before, note the use of the verb **het** *ordered*:

from C 1017

… **þa toforan Kalendas Agusti het se cynigc fetian him þæs cyniges lafe Æþelrædes him to wife Ricardes dohtor.**

… then before the kalends of August, the king ordered king Æthelred's widow – Richard's daughter – to be brought to him as wife.

⟨?⟩ Test yourself

Translate the following personal pronouns into Old English.

a to her _____

b his _____

c to him _____

d to them _____

9 Ic sece mine gebroðru, hwar hig healdon heora heorda

I seek my brothers where they are keeping their herds

In this unit you will learn about:
▶ *the lexis of the pastoral economy*
▶ *possessives*
▶ *the conjugation of verbs in tense, person, and number*
▶ *the variety and origin of place-names in* -ford *and* -ley

You will read:
▶ **The Story of Joseph 2** *(from the Old English* Hexateuch*)*

 09.00

Ic sece mine gebroðru, hwar hig healdon heora heorda.
I seek my brothers where they are keeping their herds.

Vocabulary builder

FARM ANIMALS

heorde	*herds*
feoh	*cattle, money*
neat	*cattle*
oxan	*oxen*
swin	*pigs*
scep	*sheep*

LAND

stow	*place*
dene	*valley*
leah	*clearing*
læs	*pasture*
hæþ	*heath*

CROPS

hiege	*hay*
æte	*oats*
hwæte	*wheat*
bære	*barley*
lin	*flax, linseed*

The pastoral economy

The Old English *Story of Joseph* takes place against a background of a pastoral economy that must have been immediately recognisable to eleventh-century English people from their own experience. Throughout the period the principal farm animals were cattle, pigs and above all sheep.

CATTLE

Cattle (**feoh** or **neat**) in Anglo-Saxon times were important for labour, especially for ploughing, and cultivated land was measured by the number of plough teams. Interestingly, the word **feoh** originally meant *cattle*, but its meaning gradually evolved through *moveable goods* and *property* to *money*; from this latter use is derived the modern word *fee*, perhaps influenced also by the French 'fee' meaning a *fief*.

PIGS

Pigs or swine were **swin** (pronounced 'sween'). As manuscript illustrations and archaeology reveal, Anglo-Saxon pigs were dark and hairy and looked rather like small wild boar. They were often pastured in areas of open woodland, especially in the autumn when the ground was covered with acorns and beech mast.

SHEEP

Sheep (**scēp**) had multiple uses, for milk and meat (**meolc**, **flæsc-mete**), but above all for wool (**wull**). The increasing quantities of sheep bones, sheep shears and spindles in archaeological sites of late Anglo-Saxon England point to the great importance of sheep in the economy of the time, when England began to develop its highly lucrative trade in wool and textiles. Several common types of place-name contain the element *Shep-* or *Ship-*, usually deriving from Old English variants **sceap**, **scep** or **scip**; examples include:

Sheppey: **sceap** or **scep + iege** *island*

Shipley: **sceap + leah** *clearing* or *pasture*; for the name **leah**, see below.

Shipton: **sceap + tun** *estate, farm*

Shifford: **sceap + ford** *ford*

> **CULTURAL INSIGHT**
>
> The crossing-place or ford was crucial on large rivers like the Thames and Severn. The name Oxford illustrates this well: *the ford of the oxen*, first recorded in a document of 900 in the oblique case form of **Oxnaforda**; further upstream to the west of Oxford is *Swinford*, near Eynsham, and several miles further up the Thames is *Shifford*, near Kingston Bagpuize.

Grammar 1

THE POSSESSIVE (*HIS, HER, THEIR* ETC.)

The Old English personal pronoun had a genitive form, e.g. **ān heora** *one of them*. This form also served as the possessive pronoun (i.e. *their*). The possessives resemble their modern English equivalents, although the pronunciation of the vowels has changed over time:

Singular				
1	**ic** *I*	'itch'	**min** *my*	'meen'
2	**þu** *thou*	'thoo'	**þin** *thy, your*	'theen'
3	**he** *he*	'hay'	**his** *his*	'hiss'
	heo *she*	'HÉo'	**hire** *her*	'HIRReh'
	hit *it*	'hit'	**his** *its*	'hiss'

Dual				
1	**wit** *we-two*	'wit'	**uncer** *both of our*	'un-ker'
2	**git** *you-two*	'yit'	**incer** *both of your*	'incher'

Plural				
1	**we** *we*	'way'	**ure** *our*	'OO-reh'
2	**ge** *you*	'yay'	**eower** *your*	'Éo-wer'
3	**hig** *they*	'hee'	**heora** *their*	'HÉora'
			hira *their*	'HIRRa'

Examples of the possessive have occurred in the study texts: **to heora clericum** *to their clerics* (unit 5), **he gewregde his broðru to hira fæder** *he accused his brothers to their father* (unit 6).

In similar contexts, the possessives **min**, **þin**, **ure**, **eower** take endings when used with a noun; these strong adjective endings will be covered in unit 14. They usually do not hinder recognition of the possessive and its meanings, e.g. **þine gebroðru healdað scep on Sichima** *your brothers are keeping the sheep at Sichim* and **ic sece mine gebroðru** *I seek my brothers* (see text of *Story of Joseph 2* below).

> **LANGUAGE INSIGHT**
>
> The plural of **broðor** *brother* in Old English was either **broðru** *brothers,* or **gebroðru** with its suggestion of *brothers together* or *group of brothers* expressed by the prefix **ge-**, hence **gebroðru** could also mean *a group of monastic brethren,* i.e. *monks.*

The Story of Joseph 2

We left the Joseph story in unit 6 with the brothers' emotions turning to hatred as their young upstart brother recounts his dreams. Joseph has now remained at home for some time. Meanwhile his brothers have been away too long with the herds on the pastures at Shechem. What does his father decide to do?

 09.01 Read and listen to the story, then answer the questions in Practice below.

Þa hys gebroðru wæron to lange on Sichem *When his brothers were too long in Shechem*

Þa hys gebroðru wæron to lange on Sichem mid heora fæder heordum on læswum, ða cwæð Israel to him, 'Þine gebroðru healdað scep on Sichima. Far to him and loca hwæðer hyt wel sy mid him and mid heora heordum, and cum to me and cyð me hu hyt sy.

on læswum	*on the pastures* (dative plural of **seo læs** *pasture*)
far	*go* (imperative of **faran**)
loca	*look* (imperative of **locian**)
sy	*is* (subjunctive mood of **is** and **bið**; for explanation, see unit 13)

 09.02

He com ða to Sichem *He came then to Shechem*

He com ða to Sichem fram Ebron dene. And hyne gemitte ðær an man, þa he eode on gedwolan, and axode hyne hwæt he sohte.

He andswarode and cwæð, 'Ic sece mine gebroðru, hwar hig healdon heora heorda.'

Ða cwæð se man to him, 'Hi ferdon of ðisse stowe. Ic gehyrde ðæt hi cwædon þæt hig woldon to Dothaim.'

Iosep ferde to Dothaim æfter his gebroðrum.

gemitte	*met* (**gemittan** *to meet, find*)
se gedwola	*error, wandering*
sohte	*sought* (**secan** *to seek* 'sé-chan')

Practice

 09.03 Read and listen to the text then answer the following questions.

1 What was Joseph supposed to do when he found his brothers?

_____

2 What was Joseph doing when the man spoke to him?

_____

3 How did the man know where Joseph's brothers had gone?

_____

Grammar 2

PRINCIPLES OF VERB CONJUGATION

As we saw in unit 4, the two basic types of verb in Old English are weak and strong. In the grammars of languages like Latin and Old English, verbs conjugate, or in other words, they take a set of inflections or endings to indicate the tense or time of the action, the person doing or experiencing the action (e.g. **I, thou, she**), and the number, i.e. to distinguish singular and plural (**thou** or **you**, **she** or **they** etc.). Modern English only uses endings to show such distinctions in the third person of the present tense:

she plays (-*s* ending)   but   *they play* (no ending)

The past tense, however, does not distinguish singular and plural:

she played   and   *they played*

But Old English is different. In units 4 and 6 it was seen that the past tense of the verb marks the plural ending with the ending **-on**:

wunode (*he* or *she*) *remained*   **wunodon** (*they*) *remained*

fōr (*he* or *she*) *travelled*   **fōron** (*they*) *travelled*

The two types of verb form their past tenses differently: weak verbs have a consonant **-d-** as part of the ending (e.g. **wunode** *remained*) while strong verbs change the internal vowel (e.g. **faran** *to travel* – **fōr** *travelled*).

For verbs it is best to learn some basic patterns first and then slowly but surely assimilate the others as they arise. This unit will focus on the conjugation of two common verbs: the class II weak verb **lufian** *to love* and the class III strong verb **singan** *to sing*.

The conjugation of the weak verb lufian

In unit 5 we saw that the present tense of most verbs has some form of '*th*' ending in the third person. Though the exact forms may differ, the present singular usually has **-ð** contracted from **-eð**, while the plural has **-að**:

singeð sumeres weard

summer's guardian sings   (*The Seafarer*, line 54a)

We wyllað cyðan iungum preostum ma þinga

we want to tell young priests more things   (Byrhtferth of Ramsey)

The verb **lufian** 'LU-vian' is related to the noun **seo lufu** 'LU-vu'. For the present tense singular, it changes its inflection according to person, but in the plural there is simply one inflectional ending:

Present tense			
singular		**ic lufige**	*I love*
		þu lufast	*you (sg.) love (thou lovest)*
		heo lufað	*she loves*
plural		**we lufiað**	*we love*
participle		**lufiende, lufigende**	*loving*

In the past tense, the ending is the same for **ic** and **heo** (first and third person singular) and there is, again, a common inflection for the plural:

singular		**ic lufode**	*I loved*
		þu lufodest	*you loved*
		he/heo lufode	*he/she loved*
plural		**we lufodon**	*we loved etc.*
past participle		**gelufod**	*loved*

Other weak verbs which follow the pattern of **lufian** are: **andswarian** *answer*, **āscian** *ask*, **blissian** *rejoice*, **geearnian** *earn*, **ferian** *carry*, **folgian** *follow*, **fremian** *benefit*, **gaderian** *gather*, **leornian** *learn*, **locian** *look*, **ge-nerian** *save*, **swutelian** *declare*, **ge-þāfian** *allow*, **ge-utlagian** *outlaw*, **wacian** *wake, keep watch*, **wunian** *dwell, remain*.

Conjugation of the strong verb singan

The verb **singan** has a corresponding noun **se sang** *song, singing, poem* with related compounds **blisse-sang** *song of joy* and **lof-sang** *song of praise*. Its present and past tenses are given in the table below:

present	singular	**ic singe**	*I sing*
		þu singst	*you (sg.) sing*
		heo singð	*she sings*
plural		**we singað**	*we sing*
participle		**singende**	*singing*

past	singular	**ic sang**	*I sang*
		þu sunge	*you sang*
		he, heo sang	*he/she sang*
plural		**we sungon**	*we sang etc.*
participle		**gesungen**	*sung*

In the past tense of strong verbs, there is a change of vowel to mark off the past from the present, and another vowel change within the past tense itself, so that:

ic sang *I sang*	differs from	**þu sunge** *you (sg.) sang*
he, heo sang *he, she sang*	differs from	**we, ge, hi sungon** *we, you, they sang*

Verbs with the same pattern as **singan** include:

byrnan *burn,* **climban** *climb,* **drincan** *drink,* **hlimman** *resound,* **gelimpan** *happen,* **springan** *sprout,* **swimman** *swim,* **swincan** *toil,* **winnan** *strive,* **yrnan** *run*

Sometimes in strong verbs the present tense drops or alters its final '*th*' ending for phonetic reasons, so that **bindan** *bind* or **findan** *find* have present tenses **bint** and **fint**. Other patterns are:

infinitive	present tense
helpan *help*	**hilpð** *helps*
delfan *dig*	**dilfð** *digs*
meltan *melt*	**milt** *melts*
gyldan *pay*	**gylt** *pays*

Therefore, when learning a new verb as a vocabulary item, it is best to note down the four principal parts with changeable vowels, i.e. its present tense (3rd person singular i.e. **he** or **heo**), its two past tense forms in the singular and plural, and finally the past participle:

infinitive	3rd sg. pres. tense	1st/3rd sg. past	pl. past	past participle
singan	singð	sang	sungon	sungen
byrnan	byrnð	barn	burnon	geburnen

LANGUAGE INSIGHT

Participles

The so-called 'present' participle marks an incomplete action such as *singing*, whereas the 'past' participle is not a past tense as such but a word that expresses completion – at any time, whether past, present or future. In this sense it functions like an adjective, in that it premodifies a noun, e.g. *the well sung hymn*, *the well tempered clavier*. It can be combined with *to have* to give a perfect tense *I have sung*, or it can combine with *to be* in passives: *the hymn is sung, the hymn was sung, the hymn will be sung*. In these three examples, the auxiliary verb *to be* changes to mark the tense, but the past participle remains unchanged.

THE PLACE-NAME ELEMENT -LEY

The name **leah** ('léah') is one of the most common topographical names in Old English, and comes into modern English as *lea* or as the place-name element *-ley*. It had a range of meanings, discussed by the place-name specialists Gelling and Cole (2014: 237–42; see Bibliography). Mostly associated with woodland, it originally signified a *glade* or *clearing* and so *wood-pasture*. Sometimes it occurs with the name of a man such as Beorn in Barnsley, Becca in Beckley, Blecca in Bletchley, Ceolmund in Cholmondeley and Chumleigh, Cyneheard in Kinnerley, Eardulf in Ardley; or with the name of a woman Ælfgyð in Alveley or Aldgyð in Audley. These are probably the names of the original holders of the land. As in the case of Farnley in Yorkshire (from **fearn** *fern*), the **leah** element could be combined with many other kinds of natural and agricultural elements:

Trees:

seo ac *oak* (Oakley), **se æsc** *ash* (Ashley), **seo beorc** *birch* (Berkeley), **seo lind** *lime* (Lindley), **seo plume** *plum* (Plumley), **se þorn** *thorn* (Thornley), **se wiðig** *withy, willow* (Weethley, Widley)

Crops and plants:

seo æte, seo ate *oats* (Oatley), **se hæþ** *heath* (Hadley), **þæt hiege** *hay* (Hailey), **se hwæte** *wheat* (Wheatley), **þæt lin** *flax, linseed* (Linley); another kind of crop is the sticks or staves that were cut and gathered at Staveley, from Old English **stæf** *staff*, plural **stafas** ('sta-vas').

Physical features:

brad *broad* (Bradley), **efen** *even, smooth* (Evenley), **lang** *long* (Langley), **þæt (ge)mære** *boundary* (Marley), **se mor** *marsh* (Morley), **roh** *rough* (Rowley), **se stan** *stone* (Stanley).

Farm animals (here -ley means *meadow, pasture*):

se bula *bull* (Bulley), **seo cu** *cow* (Cowley), **seo gat** *goat* (Gateley); **se oxa** *ox* (Oxley), **þæt scip** *sheep* (Shipley).

💡 Language discovery

Using an Ordnance Survey map of an English town and countryside that you know well, see if you can identify any names in the region which use place-name elements beginning with *Ox-*, *Swin-*, *Shep-*, *Ship-*, or *Shiff-*. Check their etymology in a book on the place-names of the area (e.g. the publications of the Place-Name Society). Try a similar task tracing the *-ford* or *-ley* place-names in your chosen area. What other place-name elements predominate in the topography of your region?

🛈 Test yourself

1 Using the model of the verb table for **lufian** *to love*, write out a paradigm for the weak verb **blissian** *to rejoice*. Include the personal pronouns, and show all the forms of the present tense, present participle, past tense and past participle.

2 Translate these phrases into Old English using the correct form of the strong verb.
   a It happened _____
   b I swam _____
   c we drank _____
   d you found it _____

10 Ðis syndan ðæs dennes landgemæru to Hæselersc

These are the bounds of the pasture at Hazelhurst

In this unit you will learn about:
- ▸ *charter bounds and descriptions of the landscape*
- ▸ *declension of the definite article* the
- ▸ *further uses of the accusative and dative*
- ▸ *the* -an *endings of the weak declension*

You will read:
- ▸ *the* Hazelhurst Charter *written by the Canterbury scribe Eadui Basan*
- ▸ *descriptions of 'Roman' landscape features in the poems* Beowulf *and* The Ruin

10.00

Ðis syndan ðæs dennes landgemæru to Hæselersc

These are the bounds of the pasture at Hazelhurst

Vocabulary builder

FIELDS

se æcer	*field, acre*
se croft	*croft, small field*
seo denu	*valley* (not to be confused with **dun** *hill* or **denn** *swine pasture*)
se feld	*open land*
se leah	*clearing, wood-pasture*

WATERWAY

seo dic	*ditch, dike* 'deetch'
se burna	*stream*
se broc	*brook,* 'broak'
þæt fenn	*fen, marsh*
seo hyð	*landing-place on a river* (cf. the place-name *Hythe*)
se mere	*pool, lake*
se wylle, wiell, wælle	*spring, stream*

LANDHOLDING

seo hid	*hide* 'heed' (land supporting one household; a unit of tax assessment)
se port	*town* (esp. with market or harbour; from Latin 'porta')

seo stow	*place, site* (e.g. *Stow-on-the-Wold*; cf. *Chepstow = market town*)
se tun	*estate*
se wic	*place, settlement, trading centre* 'weetch' (e.g. *Sandwich*)

LAND MANAGEMENT

se geard	*enclosure* 'YÉard' (cf. the O.E. name for the *world* **middangeard**)
se graf	*grove* 'graaf'
se hege	*hedge, fence* 'hay-a'
seo hegeræw	*hedgerow*
þa landgemæru	*estate boundaries*
þæt gemære	*boundary*

THE OLD WAYS

seo eorðbyrig, eorðburh	*earthwork*
se beorg	*barrow* (often pre-historic); also means *hill*
se hlæw	*mound, burial-mound* (-low in names, e.g. *Wenslow – Woden's Low*)
se stan	*stone, standing stone*
se stapol	*pillar, post*
seo stræt	*paved road, high road* (from Latin 'strata via')
se weg	*path*

Charter bounds and descriptions of the landscape

To a considerable extent, the present-day English landscape was named or, in the case of ancient settlements, re-named by speakers of Old English. The fields, the boundary ditches and borders of estates and woodland – the names of many of these landmarks were established in the Old English period. We know this from the evidence of place-names still in use, and from the descriptions in documents.

Land ownership in Anglo-Saxon England was recorded for posterity in numerous bilingual land charters. A charter, called a **boc** (literally a *book*) in Old English, was a title-deed. Typically it consisted of a religious preamble and record of the transaction in Latin, a description of the **landgemæru**, or the *boundary markers* of the property in Old English, and a list of witnesses. When a land transaction took place and a property changed hands, there was no survey or detailed plan of the property; instead, all the participants and their witnesses walked or rode on horseback around the bounds of the estate, fixing its features in their memories.

> ● **OLD–MODERN CONNECTIONS**
>
> The Old English description of the bounds often tallies remarkably with the present-day shape of a piece of land. As John Blair writes on the Old English namers of the landscape: 'Their topographical vocabulary was astonishingly rich and sensitive: the modern usages of "hill", "valley", "stream", or "wood" are blunt instruments compared with the range of lost terms which are preserved in place-names, enabling us to decode the landscape as the Anglo-Saxons saw it.' Blair's comment is supported by detailed study: Margaret Gelling and Ann Cole in *The Landscape of Place Names* (Donington, 2014) demonstrate on the basis of maps, sketches, and diagrams how many place-names relate to the lie of the land and/or the long-term and human-influenced features of the landscape.

The *Hazelhurst Charter*

In the year 1018, king Cnut granted some land, a copse called **Hæselersc**, now *Lower Hazelhurst* near Ticehurst in Sussex, to archbishop Ælfstan Lyfing. The event was recorded in a Latin charter (S 950 in the Electronic Sawyer online catalogue). The important scribe Eadwig Basan, who around the same time also penned Cnut's writ to archbishop Lyfing in the Royal gospel book (see unit 7 above), produced the principal copy of this Latin charter, adding Old English bounds and a list of witnesses.

The text below gives a transcription of the Old English charter bounds in the manuscript, with the original punctuation and mostly with the original word division. The only capital letter is on the first word, marking the new section; for the modern reader, the question of capitalization becomes an issue when identifying the names of places or landmarks that occur in the charter, for most names in Old English are descriptive and informative rather than mere labels. The name Thornhill, for instance, would mean literally *thorn hill*, a hill with a thorn tree.

The charter bounds here encompass a piece of land at Hazelhurst known as a **denn**. This place-name element developed only in the Weald region (Kent and Sussex) to designate a *woodland pasture*, usually a swine pasture, at some distance from the parent estate. An example is the modern place Tenterden, meaning originally the **denn** of the people of Thanet, which is in fact 45 miles away on the coast to the east. Over time the **denn** developed into an independent settlement in its own right, sometimes with the name of an original owner or inhabitant attached to it: Beaduric in Bethersden, Bidda in Biddenden, Ciolla in Chillenden (note the newer *ch* spelling that preserves the old pronunciation of **ci**).

 10.01

Ðis syndan ðæs dennes landgemæru to Hæselersc

These are the bounds of the pasture at Hazelhurst

Ðis syndan ðæs dennes landgemæru to hæsel ersc. ærest andlang fearnleges burnan. oð runan leages mearce. of runan leages mearce be holan beames mearce. of holan beames mearce swa on geriht to wiglege bufan ðære smiðan to þam geate. of þam geate innan þæne sihter. andland sihtres innan þæne bradan burnan. niðer andland bradan burnan. be þæs arcebiscopes mearce eft innan fearnleages burnan.

These are the estate boundaries of the denn at Hazelhurst. First along Fernglade Brook to the border of Roughglade, by Hollow Tree Border; from Hollow Tree Border thus straight ahead to Sacred Glade, above the smithy to the gate; from the gate into the ditch, along the ditch into the broad brook, down along Broad Brook, by the archbishop's boundary back into Fernglade Brook.

The many descriptive elements in the text include:

se ersc	*stubble-field*
ðæt wig	*sacred place, shrine* (also spelt **weoh**)
seo smiþðe	*forge, smithy*
þæt geat	*gate*

se sihter, seohter	*drain, ditch*
se fearn	*fern* + **se leah** *glade, clearing* (cf. the modern name *Farnley* in Yorkshire)
se burna	*burn, brook, stream*
runanleages	*of ?rough glade*, i.e. *Rowley*

The cultural context of the *Hazelhurst Charter*

1 THE WITNESS LIST

The witness list of the charter contains some familiar names: Cnut, Wulfstan, Ælfgyfu, earl Thorkell, and earl Godwine. Thorkell is the earl of East Anglia, exiled by Cnut in 1021 but restored to power in 1022. The other earl is to be identified as the father of the famous Harold II, who ruled England in 1066. This is one of the first appearances in the historical record of earl Godwine, a nobleman who was to become head of the most powerful family in the England of Cnut and Edward the Confessor.

In the Latin text, Ælfgyfu is entitled 'regina', Latin for *queen*, although the consort of the king was normally termed **ðæs cyninges wif** *the king's wife*. But Cnut's new wife – Emma of Normandy, whom Cnut had married in 1017 – was the most politically active of royal women since Eadgifu in the mid-tenth century, and she came to be called by the honorific title of **seo hlæfdige** ('HLÆF-di-yuh'), *the Lady*. The strength of her influence is indeed discernible even here in this document. As the Latin of the main text reveals, Cnut had given the grant at his queen's instigation. Emma was not of course new to England, having been the wife of the previous king Æthelred Unræd from 1002. On that first marriage, when she was a very young woman, her foreign name had been changed to Ælfgyfu (also spelt Ælfgifu; pronounced 'Ælf-yivu'). But like Godwine, Emma rose to much greater power and prominence during the reign of king Cnut.

2 THE SCRIBE EADWIG BASAN

The stately handwriting of the *Hazelhurst Charter* has been recognized as that of a Christ Church monk called Eadwig Basan. During his career, Eadwig (pronounced 'Éa-dwi', and also spelt Eadui) produced a number of fine illustrated manuscripts, including Latin gospel books and a book of psalms. In this period, the style of Latin script was known as Anglo-Caroline minuscule, but Eadwig developed a new variant on the style, which was widely imitated and became the dominant form of Anglo-Latin handwriting before the Norman Conquest. Notice how he changed his script or font when he switched from Latin to English:

Grammar 1

THE DEFINITE ARTICLE

You will see that the text illustrates various cases of the masculine definite article **se**; in the accusative, genitive and dative cases the forms are **þæne**, **þæs**, and **þam**. There is also an example of the feminine form **þære**. This kind of information can be presented usefully in a table (to aid pronunciation, length is marked by a macron over the vowel, e.g. **þǣm**, pronounced with a long drawn-out 'æ' sound):

	Masc.	Neut.	Fem.
Nom.	se	þæt	seo
Acc.	þæne	þæt	þā
Gen.	þæs	þæs	þǣre
Dat.	þām	þām	þǣre

The plural does not distinguish gender; in the four cases (nom., acc., gen., dat.) the forms are: **þā**, **þā**, **þāra** and **þǣm**. (Other spellings of the above forms do occur in the manuscripts, notably **þone** for **þæne** and **þan** for **þam**.)

THE STRONG NOUN

The basic kind of noun in Old English, the strong declension, varies its case endings depending on its gender. Here is a table illustrating three strong nouns in the singular:

Singular			
Nom.	**se bēam** *the tree*	**þæt land** *the land*	**sēo mearc** *the border*
Acc.	**þæne bēam**	**þæt land**	**þā mearce**
Gen.	**þæs bēames** *of the tree*	**þæs landes**	**þǣre mearce**
Dat.	**þǣm bēame** *to the tree*	**þǣm lande**	**þǣre mearce**
NB The dative is also used after a preposition, e.g. **to þam geate** *to the gate*.			

Practice 1

In the following extract from the bounds of a Worcester charter (S 1393), fill in the correct forms of the definite article.

Ofer (a) _____ weg west riht to (b) _____ ealdan dic;

æfter (c) _____ dic to (d) _____ bradan stræt.

Of (e) _____ bradan stræt be (f) _____ grafe innan

(g) _____ port stræt; æfter stræte innan Dillameres dic.

Over the way westwards to the old ditch;

along the ditch to the broad road.

From the broad road by the grove into the town road;

along the road into Dillamere ditch.

Grammar 2

INTRODUCTION TO THE WEAK (-AN) DECLENSION

The so-called 'weak declension' is a term used for a characteristic set of endings on noun or adjective. The typical weak ending is **-an**, and it appears in the oblique cases, i.e. all the cases except the nominative case. An example of a weak noun is **seo smiþðe** *the smithy, forge*. In the dative case we have **bufan ðære smiþðan** *above the smithy*. Similarly, the 'dictionary entry' or nominative form of *the broad stream* would be **se brada burna** but, as we can see in the above text, the preposition **innan** *into* takes the accusative, which gives the **-an** endings **innan þæne bradan burnan** *into the broad stream*.

THE WEAK ENDING ON ADJECTIVES

Usually after the definite article (*the*), adjectives take the weak (**-an**) endings, for example the common phrase in the *Chronicle*, **on þam ilcan geare**. In the nominative the phrase would be **þæt ilce gear**, but – as stated above – in the oblique cases (acc., gen., dat.) the adjective takes **-an**. So the basic rule is that the weak ending is **-an** except in the nominative. The masculine nominative takes **-a** while the neuter and feminine ending is **-e**.

Other examples of the nominative include **se grena weg**, **seo greate dic**, **seo mæste wroht**; in the oblique cases these adjective endings appear as:

Acc.	**on þæne grenan weg** *onto the green way* (accusative after **on**)
Gen.	**ðære mæstan wrohte** (unit 6) *(accused) of the greatest wrong*
Dat.	**æfter þan grenan wege** *along the green way* (dative after **æfter**)
	to þære greatan dic *to the great ditch* (dative after **to**)

The preposition **on** takes an accusative when it means *onto* (i.e. movement) and takes a dative when it means *on* (i.e. static location). Note the different cases used in the following two phrases:

1 accusative after **on** expressing movement onto something:

on þæne grenan weg

onto the green way

2 dative after **on** expressing location in time:

on ðam ilcan lenctene (ASC C 1002)

in the same spring

OTHER USES OF THE WEAK ENDING

The weak ending is met in other 'definite' contexts, i.e. phrases where the meaning is definite and specific, even if the definite article is not present:

Accusative

þurh Godes miltsiendan gife (unit 5)

through God's merciful grace

Dative

æt Niwantune i.e. **æt niwan tune**

at Newton

be holan beames mearce

by Holbeam's boundary, by the boundary of Hollow Tree (In this instance, the original name persisted long after its meaning became obscure, so that a modern place-name near Hazelhurst is *Holbeanwood*.)

Practice 2

Translate this extract from the charter S 1393.

Of þære dice ende innan þa wællan. Of þære wællan in þa sandihte stræt; æfter stræte norð on bisceopes scirlett, ofer bisceopes scirlett in lin aceran wege þam innmæstan. Of lin aceran innan ðone hege, æfter þam hege on brocc holes weg. Of brocc holes wege innan þone croft. Of þam crofte be þam gearde innan leofesunes croft.

_____

_____

_____

_____

_____

_____

_____

'Roman' remains in the Old English landscape

It is clear that the many old Roman and pre-Roman routes and ridgeways and the many ritual mounds and monuments that occur across the countryside were used and re-used by the Anglo-Saxons, who named them accordingly. In _The Old Ways: A Journey on Foot_ (London, 2013), Robert Macfarlane offers the perspective of a literary critic and cultural historian (p. 13):

It's true that, once you begin to notice them, you see that the landscape is still webbed with paths and footways – shadowing the modern-day road network, or meeting it at a slant or perpendicular. Pilgrim paths, green roads, drove roads, corpse roads, trods, leys, dykes, drongs, sarns, snickets – say the names of paths out loud and at speed and they become a poem or rite – holloways, bostles, shuts, driftways, lichways, ridings, halterpaths, cartways, carneys, causeways, herepaths.

The archaeologist Sarah Semple has studied in detail the Anglo-Saxon re-use of the older monuments of the landscape; her work appears to confirm the insights of writers like Macfarlane, and before him Edward Thomas or Hilaire Belloc.

1 STRÆT

The word **stræt** was derived in the very early period from Latin 'via strata', and while in major settlement-names it clearly means _Roman road_, it can also mean _paved road_, as below in _Beowulf_ 320a. As Gelling and Cole show (pp. 92–4), **Stræt** can occur as a simplex name: there is a place called Street in Herefordshire and Kent, and two towns of that name in Somerset, and there are two places named Strete in Devon. **Stræt** can form compounds with **ham**, **feld**, **leah** and **ford** yielding place-names such as _Stretham_, _Stratfield_, _Streatley_ and the common _Stratford_. The popular name _Stratton_ (also spelt _Stretton_) suggests a functional settlement for the _estate_ (**tun**) in relation to the **stræt** or main road that ran through it and allowed agricultural products to be moved easily to market. Roman roads are landmarks: convenient, well built, and they move straight across the countryside (unlike the winding roads of later centuries).

In this passage from *Beowulf* (lines 320–4), Beowulf and the Geats have arrived in Denmark by ship. They now travel across the countryside on the **stræt**, *the paved road*, and ascend the **stig** *path* (cf. **stigan** *to climb*; see unit 2) on the way to Hrothgar's hall, described here as **sele** (line 323):

320 Stræt wæs stanfah,   stig wisode

gumum ætgædere.   Guðbyrne scan

heard hondlocen,   hringiren scir

song in searwum,   þa hie to sele furðum

in hyra gryregeatwum   gangan cwomon.

320   *The street was paved with stone, the path guided*

the men together. The battle-corslet shone:

hard, hand-linked, the ring-iron bright

sang in the armour, when they to the hall first

came walking in their fear-inspiring wargear.

320a	**stanfah** *stone-paved* (**fāh / fāg** often implies *stained* or *coloured* and sometimes simply *adorned*: the hall in *Beowulf* is **bān-fāg**, meaning *adorned with bone antlers*)
320b	**stig** *path*; **wisode** *guided* (from **wisian** *to guide*) followed in 321a by an object **gumum** *the men*, in the dative case
321b	**guð-byrne** as compound consists of **guð** *war* + **byrne** *mail-coat*; **scan** *shone*
322	**hring-iren** describes the *interlinking rings* that make up the coat of chainmail
322b	**scir** *bright* pronounced 'sheer'
323a	**song** alternative form of the past tense **sang** *sang* (from **singan** *to sing*)
323b	**se sele** *the hall* is a frequent synonym for **seo heall**
324	**gryre**- means *fear-inspiring*, while **geatwe** is a feminine plural meaning *wargear*

2 FAWLER

In Anglo-Saxon England, particularly in the early period, the ruins of old Roman villas still dotted the countryside, and sometimes their presence was remembered in the place-names. The mosaic floors were known as **fag flor** *the coloured floor*, **fag** (or **fah**) being an adjective with various connotations from *variegated* and *dappled* to the more negative *stained*. *Fawler* in Oxfordshire is a modern place-name derived from **fag flor**, the fricative '**g**' becoming '*w*' (as in the change from Old English **boga** to modern *bow*). Archaeology has confirmed the origin of the name: a Roman villa has been found on the site. It seems that sometimes the local hall or even church was built on or near these older sites.

Strikingly, given that the poem is set in Denmark, *Beowulf* has a variegated floor, in the hall of king Hrothgar. The detail is mentioned in the description of the monster Grendel breaking down the door and advancing onto the floor to attack the sleeping Geats (724b–727):

Raþe æfter þon	*Quickly after that*
on fagne flor feond treddode,	*onto the decorated floor the enemy stepped,*
eode yrremod; him of eagum stod	*advanced angrily; from his eyes stood*
ligge gelicost leoht unfæger.	*most like a flame an ugly light.*

For what happens next in the narrative, and for the text of the fight between Beowulf and Grendel, see unit 22.

3 CEASTER

Roman walls and other remains still existed, remembered in the Chester place-names (see unit 1) and evoked splendidly in the *Exeter Book* poem *The Ruin* (lines 31b–41a), probably about **Baþanceaster**, i.e. *Bath*, where king Edgar staged his second, imperial coronation:

35   **Hryre wong gecrong**

       gebrocen to beorgum   þær iu beorn monig

       glædmod and gold beorht   gleoma gefrætwed

       wlonc and wingal   wighyrstum scan,

40   **seah on sinc, on sylfor,   on searogimmas,**

       on ead, on æht,   on eorcanstan,

       on þas beorhtan burg   bradan rices.

       Stanhofu stodan,   stream hate wearp

       widan wylme;   weal eall befeng

       beorhtan bosme   þær þa baþu wæron,

       hat on hreðre.

The site is fallen into ruin, reduced to heaps, where once many a man blithe of mood and bright with gold, clothed in splendours, proud and flown with wine, gleamed in his war-trappings, and gazed upon treasure, on silver, on chased gems, on wealth, on property, on the precious stone and on this bright citadel of the broad kingdom; and the stone courts were standing and the stream warmly spouted its ample surge and a wall embraced all in its bright bosom where the baths were, hot at its heart.

(*The Ruin*, lines 31B– 41A; translated by S.A.J. Bradley)

31b	**se hryre** *fall*; **wong = wang** *site, field*; **gecrong** *fell* (from the poetic **cringan**)
32	**gebrocen** *broken* (from **brecan** *to break*); **beorgum** *to heaps, mounds*; **iu** *once*
33	**glæd-mod** *glad of mind*; **gefrætwed** *clothed, adorned*
34	**wlonc** *proud*; **wīn-gāl** *inebriated with wine*; **wig-hyrstum** *in war-trappings* (dat.)
35	**seah on** *looked upon*; **sinc** *treasure*; **sylfor** *silver*; **searo** *intricately crafted*; **gimmas** *jewels*
36	**ead** *prosperity*; **æht** *possessions*; **eorcan-stan** *precious stone*
38	**stan-hofu** *stone courts*; **hate** *hotly, fervidly*; **wearp** *threw out*
39	**widan wylme** *in a broad surge* from **wylm** (or **wielm**) *surge*; **weal** *wall*; **befeng** *embraced*
40	**þa baþu** *the baths*, cf. the names for the city of Bath: **æt Hataþaþum** *At the Hot Baths* or **Baþanceaster** *Bath City*
41a	**hāt** *hot*; **hreðer** *heart*

? Test yourself

Without looking back to the original text, see if you can fill in the missing words or phrases of the *Hazelhurst Charter* bounds. You may recall that one of the features of this estate was a stream and the other a hollow tree:

Ðis syndan (a)_____ dennes landgemæru to Hæselersc. Ærest andlang

(b) fearnleges _____ oð runan leages mearce. Of runan leages mearce be

(c) _____ _____ mearce. Of (d) _____

_____ mearce swa on geriht to Wiglege, (e) _____

smiþðan to (f) _____ geate. Of (g) _____ geate innan

(h) _____ sihter, andland sihtres, innan (i) _____

bradan burnan. Niðer andland bradan burnan, be (j) _____

arcebiscopes mearce, eft innan fearnleages burnan.

SELF-CHECK	
	I CAN ...
⚪	understand the endings of the definite article
⚪	recognize further uses of the accusative and dative
⚪	identify the **-an** endings of the weak declension
⚪	read charter bounds and other descriptions of the landscape

11 *Her swutelað on ðysum gewrite*
Here it declares in this document

In this unit you will learn about:
- ▶ *the declaration*
- ▶ *fixed phrases and formulas*
- ▶ *the two-stress phrases of rhythmical prose*
- ▶ *the inflected infinitive* to habbanne
- ▶ *the declension of the demonstrative* þes this

You will read:
- ▶ *the declaration of Godwine to Leofwine the Red (S 1220)*

 11.00

Her swutelað on ðysum gewrite

Here is declared in this document

Vocabulary builder

VERBS FROM CHARTERS AND DECLARATIONS

gretan	*to greet*
swutelian	*to declare*
geunnan	*to grant*
giefan / gyfan	*to give, bestow*
sellan	*to give, sell*
geldan	*to pay*
gebyrian	*to belong*
habban	*to have*
wealdan	*to rule, administer*

Canterbury in the early middle ages

Canterbury, in the year 1000, centred on the cathedral of Christ Church in the city itself, and the monastery of St Augustine's just outside the city walls; both were established around the year 600 after Pope Gregory the Great sent a mission to Æthelberht, king of Kent. The leader of this mission was an Italian with the same name as the early-fifth-century patristic writer, Augustine of Hippo. This other Augustine became the first archbishop of Canterbury and eventually gave his name to the monastery. As the seat of the archbishopric, urban Canterbury flourished in the early middle ages. By the reign of Cnut (1016–35), Christ Church had followed in the wake of tenth-century reforms and installed monks to run the cathedral rather than the normal secular clergy, so that there were now two monastic communities at the city. Usually they acted as partners, as in the present document here, although on occasions rivalry did break out between the two institutions.

THE DECLARATION

The following type of document is known as a *declaration*, or **swutelung**, typically opening with the formula **her swutelað** *here it declares, here is declared*. The text records the grant by a certain Godwine of a Kentish **dænn** *swine-pasture* (cf. the *Hazelhurst Charter* in unit 10) to a man called Leofwine the Red – presumably this Leofwine had red hair and was so called to distinguish him from others of the same name. (The document may be found on the Electronic Sawyer online as S 1220.) In the course of the transaction, which took place some time between the years 1013 and 1020, Leofwine receives the pasture as an **ece yrfe** *eternal* i.e. *permanent inheritance*, then attaches it to his land at Boughton Malherbe ('BAW-ton MAL-er-bee'), about half way between Maidstone and Ashford in Kent.

> **LANGUAGE INSIGHT**
>
> Note the text's insistence that Godwine grants the land to Leofwine, the completion of the action being emphasized with the (optional) perfective prefix **ge-** on the verb **ge-ann** (pronounced 'yuh-AHN'). In the second sentence, however, where the later recipient of the grant is still unknown and this future grant is not yet completed, the form of the verb used is **ann**, without the prefix. For more on the **ge-** prefix, look back to unit 4.

 11.01 Listen and read the text then answer the questions below.

1 How much does Leofwine pay to receive the swine-pasture?

_____

2 What members of Canterbury society are called upon to witness the transaction?

_____

Leofwine reada *Leofwine the Red*

Her swutelað on ðysan gewrite þæt Godwine geánn Leofwine readan ðæs dænnes æt Swiðrædingdænne on ece yrfe, to habbanne and to sellanne, on dæge and æfter dæge, ðam ðe him leofost sy, æt þon sceatte ðe Leofsunu him geldan scolde: þæt is feowertig penega and twa pund and eahta ambra cornes. Nu ann Leofwine þæs dænnes ðon ðe Boctun to handa gega æfter his dæge.

Here it declares in this document that Godwine grants to Leofwine the Red the swine pasture at Southernden as a permanent inheritance, to keep and to give, in his day and after his day, to whoever is dearest to him, for the price which Leofsunu had to pay him, that is: forty pence and two pounds and eight ambers of corn. Now Leofwine [may] grant the pasture into the hands of whoever Boughton may pass after his day.

11.02

Nu is þyses to gewittnesse: Lyfingc bisceop and Ælfmær abbud, and se hired æt Cristescyrcean and se híred æt sancte Augustine, and Síred, and Ælfsige cild, and Æþelric, and manig oþer god man binnan byrig and butan.

Now as witness of this are (arch)bishop Lyfing and abbot Ælfmær, and the community at Christ Church, and the community at Saint Augustine's, and Sired, and Ælfsige Child, and Æthelric, and many another good man within the city and without.

Listening

 11.03 Listen again to the passage on the audio recording and use the vocabulary below to help you follow the text. As you listen, be aware of the sounds of Old English, especially the long vowels in the passage and the rhythmical phrasing of the prose style.

swutelian	*to declare* (**swutelað, swutelode, swutelodon, geswutelod**)
geunnan	*grant* (pres: **ānn, unnon**, past: **uðe, uðon**, past part. **geunnen**)
Godwine geánn … ðæs dænnes	*G. grants the swine-pasture* (**geunnan** takes a genitive object rather than accusative – see Grammar in unit 13)
Leofwine readan	*to Leofwine the Red* (dative; weak adjective; see unit 10)
ece	*eternal* (see Language discovery below)
seo yrfe	*inheritance, bequest* (also spelt **ierfe**)
sellan	*to give, sell* (also spelt **syllan**)
ðam ðe	literally *to-that-one who*
leof	*dear*
se sceatt	*coin, price*
æt þon sceatte	*at the price* (dative; spelling **þon** for **þam**)
geldan	*pay*
feowertig	*forty*
se peneg	*penny* (also **peaneg, pening**)
þæt pund	*pound*
amber	*pitcher, measure, amber*
ðon ðe = ðam ðe	*to the one who*
gega	*should go* 'yuh-GAH' (subjunctive)

 11.04

nu	*now*
Lyfingc bisceop Lyfing	*archbishop of Canterbury from 1013 to 1020*
Ælfmær abbud Ælfmær	*abbot of St Augustine's Abbey, Canterbury*
cild	*child, youth of aristocratic birth* (hence the title **Childe** in later ballads)
manig oþer	*many another*
god man	*good man*; the vowel is long in **gōd** (sounds like 'goad')
binnan	*within*
byrig	*city, stronghold* (dative form of **seo burh** / **seo burg**)
butan	*without*

GEWITNES

The feminine noun **gewitnes** means *knowledge, cognisance, testimony, witness*, and derives from the verb **witan** *to know*. **Nu is þyses to gewittnesse** literally *now is of-this (genitive) as witness* or in more natural word order *now as witness of this is*…serves as a formula to introduce the list of witnesses to the transaction. As with many such formulas, the wording or tense can vary slightly, so that we also find: **nu wæs ðyses to gewitnesse** in the past tense.

Another grammatically more complex formulation is to say *this was spoken …with the witness (cognisance) of X, and of Y and of Z…* Here each of the male names of witnesses that follow in the list is given an **-es** ending for the genitive case:

Ðis wæs gespecen …on Lyfinges arcebiscopes gewitnesse, and Ælfmeres abbodes, and Æþelwines sciregerefan, and Siredes ealdan, and Godwines Wulfeages sunu …

This was said … with the cognisance of archbishop Lyfing … and abbot Ælfmer … and Æþelwine the sheriff, and Sired the Old, and Godwin Wulfeah's son …

Not all of those present at a meeting were necessarily named, and sometimes the list of witnesses ends conventionally with a disclaimer such as **and manig oþer god men** *and many other good people*, or **mænig god cniht toeacan ðysan** *many a good retainer as well as these*. In the latter phrase it is worth noticing incidentally the process of semantic change. The word **cniht**, which originally meant *young man*, was, by the eleventh century, beginning to develop its later meaning of *knight*.

 Language discovery

Look through the declaration again noting any words or phrases that seem to follow a fixed structure or formula.

FIXED PHRASES AND FORMULAS

The vocabulary of the text typifies many of the formulaic phrases commonly found in declarations, writs, and other documents.

Her swutelað on ðysan/ðyssum gewrite (literally *here declareth in this writing*) is the standard formula for opening this type of **swutulung**, *declaration, notification*; the verb **swutelian** *to declare*, which occurred in unit 5, derives from an adjective **swutol** or **sweotol** meaning *clear*. As with the definite article **þam** and **þan**, there are different ways of spelling **ðysan** and **ðyssum** (see Grammar).

on ece yrfe *as a perpetual inheritance*. The common adverb and adjective **ece** usually means *eternal*.

to habbanne and to sellanne *to have and to give*: the recipient is free to dispose of the land as he or she sees fit. This formula is reminiscent of the time-honoured phrase *to have and to hold*, a variant of which appears in the poem *Beowulf* (line 658a). For the inflected infinitive, see Grammar.

on dæge and æfter dæge *in his day and after his day*. Here the word **dæg** is used metaphorically to signify *lifetime*. Another common expression is **þreora manna dæg** to signify *for three people's lifetimes*, after which the leased property would revert to the original owner, such as a cathedral. Also connected with this usage is a phrase such as **on Æþelrædes dæge cyninges** *during the reign of king Æthelred*.

The relative clause **ðam ðe him leofost sy** depends on the preceding formula **to sellanne** and implies that the recipient is free to give the land to whoever he please, to whom it may be dearest to him. The final word **sy** (here translated *may be*) is the subjunctive form of the verb **is**. Another form of the subjunctive **wære** *would be* occurs in the formula **ðam ðe hire leofost wære** *to whom it would be dearest to her*, in other words, *to whoever she please* (see unit 8).

A similar linguistic pattern recurs in the next sentence of our passage in the relative clause **ðon ðe Boctun to handa gega** literally *to whom Boughton may pass into the hands*, with **ge-ga** here being the subjunctive of the verb **gan** or **ge-gan**. For the forms of the subjunctive, see the text and grammar in unit 13.

THE TWO-STRESS PHRASES OF RHYTHMICAL PROSE

The language of the administrative documents draws on the traditional forms of oral parley and debate for some of its stylistic effects. One popular feature of style in all genres of Old English discourse is the two-stress phrase, an example in modern English being *hands and feet*. The latter phrase has one weak syllable between two strong, or stressed syllables, and its pronunciation could be represented 'HANDS and FEET' or by a notation that marks the pattern:

hands and feet / x / (strong-weak-strong)

where / is a stressed or emphatic syllable and x is a weak or unstressed syllable.

A two-stress phrase can vary in length, because the number of weak syllables can range from one to four or more:

LONdon TOWN	/ x /
CIty of OX-ford	/ x x / x
saint DAvid's caTHEdral	x / x x / x
saint AuGUStine's ABBey	x x / x / x

The two-stress phrase can also combine with other effects like rhyme, half-rhyme, assonance (similar vowel sounds) or alliteration (similar initial consonants); examples are *kith and kin* (alliteration and assonance), *hearth and home* (alliteration), *sticks and stones* (alliteration).

A series of two-stress phrases can form a memorable saying:

sticks and stones may | break my bones but | words will never hurt me

This proverb could be analysed as three two-stress phrases each highlighted by memorable alliteration, rhyme and half-rhyme.

In terms of phonetics, the stressed syllable of a modern English word does not normally depend on the regional accent or dialect of a particular native speaker. There are exceptions, such as 'GArage' and 'gaRAGE', but normally we all follow the pattern 'MInister', 'PRINcess' or 'SHEPherd'. And whether you are from Pembrokeshire, Belfast or Ohio, you will nevertheless still place the stress on the second syllable of the word caTHEdral. Word stress may be different in other languages, however, even for related words; so, for example, the French say 'cathéDRALE'. Although the stressed syllable in a particular modern English word is usually fixed, it can occasionally shift when two similar words are contrasted, such as *inhale* and *exhale*. Normally we say 'inHALE', but when the two words come together we may well say 'INhale and EXhale'.

With these principles in mind, try reading the Old English swutulung documents out loud, since the style of their language seems to draw heavily on the patterns and rhythms of speech. These are formal declarations made before witnesses in which the words must be weighed, and form must balance content.

Prominent in their language is the two-stress phrase made up of two nouns, adjectives, verbs or adverbs each with a stress on its most prominent syllable. In the above document for instance, listen to the chiming effects of the ending on the two-stress phrase made up of two inflected infinitives:

to HABBanne and to SELLanne,

or the similar rhetorical contrast of the formula

on dæge and æfter dæge,

perhaps pronounced contrastively as '**ON dæge and ÆFter dæge**', or the alliterative rhythm of the final phrase:

BINnan byrig and BUtan.

Other examples include the alliteration of **swa full and swa forð** as *fully and completely*, rhyme in **unforboden and unbesacan** *unforbidden and uncontested* **and ægðer ge gehadode ge leawede** *both clergy and laity*. Parallelism (where the two elements of the phrase have the same structure or parallel pattern) highlights the antithesis in the formula **on wuda and on felde** *in wood and in field*.

Some formulas are a kind of shorthand, and require further explanation. A grant of land **mid mete and mid mannum** means literally *with food and with men* and relates to the food-provision and labour that went with the estate. The term **mid sake and mid socne**, sometimes called *sake and soke*, means jurisdiction and probably refers to the right to hold a court in the area and/or to profit from any fines exacted.

One final point to note is that many of the terms and formulas used in declarations are also used in other legal documents (for examples, look back to the king's writ in unit 7 and the marriage agreement in unit 8).

Practice

Cnut gives the archbishop more land (S 988; Harmer no. 30)

1   In the following royal writ, fill in the gaps with the most likely word as suggested by the context.

Cnut cyngc (a) _____Eadsige bisceop and Ælfstan abbod and Ægelric and ealle (b) _____ þegenas on Cent (c) _____. And ic (d) _____eow þæt ic hæbbe geunnan Æþelnoðe arcebisceope ealre þare landare þe Ælfmær hæfde and mid rihte into Cristes cyricean gebyrað, binnan (e) _____ and butan, on (f) _____ and on felda, swa full and swa (g) _____ swa Ælfric arcebiscop hyre weold oþþe ænig his forgengena.

2   Translate the following the document (S 1222).

Ic Þored geann þæt land æt Horslege þam hirede æt Cristes cyrcean for mine sawle swa full and swa forð swa ic sylf hit ahte.

_____

_____

3   Translate (S 1225).

Þis sendan þa land þe Þurkytel gean Gode and sancte Marian and sancte Eadmunde: þæt is þæt land æt Culeforde þæt his agen wæs, swa hit stænt, mid mete and mid mannum, and mid sake and mid socne, and eal þæt land æt Wridewellan; and þæt land æt Gyxeweorðe swa hit stent mid mete and mid mannum.

_____

_____

_____

_____

_____

_____

Grammar

THE INFLECTED INFINITIVE

The phrase **to habbanne and to sellanne** *to keep or to give, to have or to sell* is expressed in the form of **to** + the inflected infinitive, which had a regular ending normally spelt **-anne** or **-enne**.

A similar formula in the marriage agreement in unit 8 is **to gyfene and to syllenne** (note the spelling variant **syllenne** for **sellanne**).

The preposition **to** + inflected infinitive was often used to express cause or purpose (for examples, see *The Story of Joseph 2*, in unit 13 below)

THE DECLENSION OF THE DEMONSTRATIVE ÞES (*THIS*)

	Masculine	Neuter	Feminine	
nom.	**þes**	**þys**	**þēos**	*this*
acc.	**þysne**	**þys**	**þās**	*this*
gen.	**þyses**	**þysses**	**þysse**	*of this*
dat.	**þyssum**	**þyssum**	**þysse**	*to this*

Note that the vowel **-y-** in **þys** is sometimes spelt with **-i-** as **þis**, and that **þis** can also occur as **ðis**. The plural forms are **þās, þās, þyssa, þyssum** *these, these, of these, to these*, the first two being pronounced with a long 'ah' vowel (marked **ā** with a macron over the vowel to show length, a convention used in modern grammars of Old English).

NOTES ON THE USE OF ÞES (*THIS*)

Many of the forms of the demonstrative **þes** have been seen already in previous units. In Riddle 66 (unit 3), the speaker begins:

ic eom mare þonne þes middangeard

I am greater than this middle world

where **middangeard** is a masculine noun, while a neuter nominative **ðis swefn** *this dream* occurred in Jacob's question to his son Joseph (see unit 6):

Hwæt sceal ðis swefn beon?

What is this dream supposed to be?

An example of the genitive is:

nu is þyses to gewittnesse

now as witness of this is

Various uses of the dative include:

her swutelað on ðysum gewrite

here declareth in this document

her on þyssum geare

here in this year

hi ferdon of ðisse stowe

they went from this place (unit 9).

LANGUAGE INSIGHT

A common variant of **þyssum** is **þysan** or (with the letter **eth**) **ðysan**, so that we find **her swutelað on ðysan gewrite** *here declareth in this document* instead of **on ðysum gewrite**. The explanation demonstrates phonetic change in the late Old English period; speakers pronounced the ending **-um** weakly, with a reduced vowel (known as schwa in phonetics) that was difficult to distinguish from **-an**. Spoken language is in a process of constant change and here is an example of a sound change caught on record in a written document.

SINGULAR *THIS* AS PLURAL

In a document describing a gift to Bury St Edmunds, the neuter singular functions as a general *this*, but the singular **þis** is followed by the plural **sendan**, i.e. **syndon**:

Þis sendan þa land þe Þurkytel gean Gode and sancte Marian and sancte Eadmunde
These are the lands that Thorketel grants to God and saint Mary and saint Edmund.

A similar phrase with a different spelling occurs in the *Hazelhurst Charter*, in the phrase introducing the Old English description of the estate (see unit 10):

Ðis syndan ðæs dennes landgemæru to Hæselersc
These are the bounds of the estate at Hazelhurst.

In modern English grammar, of course, the demonstrative form *this* is resolutely singular, and only *these* could combine with the plural verb *are*.

Examples of *this* in the plural

As far as plural forms of the demonstrative are concerned, we saw Byrhtferth's reason for writing about the calendar in unit 5:

þæt hig magon þe ranclicor þas þing heora clericum geswutelian

so that they [the priests] may declare these things the more boldly to their clerics.

And in the dative plural we have the following use:

nu syndon to ðysum forwordan twa gewrita

now for these terms of agreement there are two documents.

❓ Test yourself

Replace the definite article with the appropriate form of the demonstrative *this*; for example:

se wer: þes wer; heo lufað þone wer: heo lufað þisne wer

a se ceorl _____

b he hatað þone cyning _____

c he lufað þa cwen _____

d þæs cynges land _____

e he hit geaf þam ceorle _____

f þa eorlas _____

g he hit geaf þam eorlum _____

SELF-CHECK

I CAN ...
understand fixed phrases and formulas in declarations
pronounce rhythmical two-stress phrases
form the inflected infinitive **to habbanne**
decline in all cases, in singular and plural, the demonstrative **þes** *this*

12 *wordhord*
word-hoard

This unit will focus on vocabulary building, revising select topics from units 1–11 and adding more items to the **wordhord**, the compound noun used by Anglo-Saxon poets for their treasure hoard, their thesaurus or repertoire of poetic words, phrases, themes.

In this unit you will learn how to:
▶ *decline the basic nouns for parts of the body*
▶ *count in Old English*
▶ *read Roman numerals*
▶ *employ different techniques for storing and learning vocabulary*

You will read:
▶ *short extracts from Byrhtferth's* **Handboc** *or* **Enchiridion**
▶ *a passage from the* **Exeter Book** *poem* **The Seafarer**
▶ *Riddles 36 and 86*

The Fuller brooch

The famous ninth-century Fuller brooch, a disc brooch used for fastening the cloak at the shoulder, is an ornate piece of silver metalwork with an elaborate allegorical decoration (for an image, see references in the Bibliography). In the main frame, four figures are grouped around the image of a man who holds plant stems in his hands and stares straight out from the centre of the brooch. Each figure mimes a clear and unmistakable action: one puts hand to open mouth in a gesture of taste, another – with hands behind his back – smells a piece of vegetation, a third touches hand to hand and foot to foot, a fourth puts right hand to ear in a gesture of hearing. Like the central figure of the Alfred Jewel, which represents Wisdom, the central figure here is Sight, or Spiritual Vision, with large round eyes that gaze out at the viewer like a Greek icon.

In the next section, we will consider the Old English words that such images of the five senses represent:

eye	**ēage** pronounce 'Éa-yuh' (*eyes* **ēagan**)
ear	**ēare** (*ears* **ēaran**)
nose	**nosu** pronounce 'nozzu' (medial '-**s**-' is pronounced as '**z**')
mouth	**mūð** 'mooth'
tongue	**tunge**
hand	**hand** (*hands* **handa**)
foot	**fōt** 'foat' (*feet* **fēt**, pronounced 'fate')

V Vocabulary builder 1

THE HUMAN BODY

The difference between the old and new forms of the words often lies in the vowel sounds. To help to remember the following list, and to make the right old–modern connections, say or chant the words out loud. The occasional long vowels are worth highlighting; they are marked here with an editorial macron (e.g. the **ē** in **fēt** *feet*) to emphasize their length, so that **fēt** is pronounced rather like modern Scots 'fate'.

body	**bodig** pronounce as in modern English *body*
head	**heafod** cf. German cognate 'Haupt' and Latin 'caput'
(pronounce -f- as 'v': in Middle English the 'v' sound eventually dropped, leaving 'head')	
eye	**ēage** pronounce 'Éa-yuh' (*eyes* **ēagan**)
nose	**nosu** pronounce 'nozzu' (medial -s- is pronounced as 'z')
mouth	**mūð** 'mooth'
ear	**ēare** pronounce as two syllables 'Éa-ruh' (*ears* **ēaran**)
neck	**swēora** or **hnecca**
back	**hrycg** pronounce 'hrüdge' (modern English *ridge*)
	bæc (modern English *back*)
shoulder	**eaxl** (cf. modern English *axle*) or **sculdor**
arm	**earm**
elbow	**elnboga**
hand	**hand**
finger	**finger**
thumb	**þūma**
index finger	**scytefinger** (from **scyte** *shooting*, e.g. a bow and arrow)
side	**sīde**
stomach	**wamb** or **womb**
leg	**scanca** (cf. Edward Longshanks or *shank's pony*)
knee	**cneow** (**on cneowum** *on their knees*)
foot	**fōt** 'foat' (*feet* **fēt** 'fate')

POETIC WORDS FOR THE LIVING BODY

As well as the everyday words for the body such as **bodig** and **lic**, there are many poetic expressions for the living body. These include **feorhhus** *life-house*, **feorhbold** *life-mansion*, **feorhhord** *life-treasury*. There is **bānhūs** *bone-house*, the poet Seamus Heaney's favourite: it occurs in *Beowulf* and is echoed in Heaney's poem *Bone Dreams*. For more examples, see *Stephen Pollington's Wordcraft* (1993).

DECLENSION OF NOUNS OF SENSORY PERCEPTION

As Old English nouns, our six primary words for sense perception – eyes, ears, nose, mouth, hands and feet – are classified grammatically according to their declension, the type of endings which accrue to them in sentences. Where **muð** belongs to the strong masculine declension, **eage** and **eare** are weak neuter nouns, while the other three are irregular, **fot** being irregular masculine and **hand** and **nosu** irregular feminine nouns:

	Strong	Weak	Irregular			
Sing.	masc.	neuter	masculine		feminine	
Nom.	**mūð**	**ēage**	**ēare**	**fōt**	**hand**	**nosu**
Acc.	**mūð**	**ēage**	**ēare**	**fōt**	**hand**	**nosu**
Gen.	**mūðes**	**ēagan**	**ēaran**	**fōtes**	**handa**	**nosa**
Dat.	**mūðe**	**ēagan**	**ēaran**	**fēt**	**handa**	**nosa**
Plural						
Nom.	**mūðas**	**ēagan**	**ēaran**	**fēt**	**handa**	
Acc.	**mūðas**	**ēagan**	**ēaran**	**fēt**	**handa**	
Gen.	**mūða**	**ēagena**	**ēarena**	**fōta**	**handa**	
Dat.	**mūðum**	**ēagum**	**ēarum**	**fōtum**	**handum**	

NUMBERS ONE TO TWELVE

It is worth learning Old English numbers alongside Latin numerals in the form in which they were written in Old English manuscripts and as they appear in many printed editions. The Latin notation was the only one used until the arrival of Arabic numerals in the twelfth century. Long vowels are marked for convenience (e.g. **ān**, pronounce 'ahn').

.i.	**ān** 'ahn'
.ii.	**twegen** 'twayen' also **twā** 'twah' (fem.) and **tu** 'two' (neuter)
.iii.	**þrý** also **þrīe** (masculine), **þrēo** (feminine and neuter)
.iv.	**fēower**
.v.	**fíf**
.vi.	**syx** (also spelt **siex**)
.vii.	**seofon** (two syllables 'SEHuh' + 'vun')
.viii.	**eahta** (pronounce 'h' as the 'ch' in Loch Ness); rarely also **ehtuwe**
.viiii. or ix.	**nigon** 'ni' + 'gon'
.x.	**týn**
.xi.	**endlufon** or **endleofon** (pronounce -f- between vowels as 'v')
.xii.	**twelf**

Practice 1

NUMERALS AND PARTS OF THE BODY IN RIDDLES

 12.00

Ic wiht geseah on wege feran

I saw a creature travel on the wave.

In the two riddles below, the main figure is a strange **wiht** (*wight*, *being*, *creature*) with an unusual physical appearance. In Riddle 36, for instance, the wight is described as having **siex heafdu** *six heads*.

Read or listen to each text and note the numerals used, then suggest a solution to the riddle. [Essential new words and phrases are **on wege** *on the wave*, **wrætlice** *marvellously*, **wundrum gegierwed** *girded with wonders*, **cwom** *came*, **on mæðle** *at their talk*, **mode snottre** *with a prudent mind*.]

 12.01

(a) from Riddle 36

    Ic wiht geseah   on wege feran,

    seo wæs wrætlice   wundrum gegierwed.

    Hæfde feowere   fet under wombe

    ond ehtuwe   ufon on hrycge;

5   **hæfde tu fiþru   ond twelf eagan**

    ond siex heafdu.   Saga hwæt hio wære.

 12.02

(b) Riddle 86

    Wiht cwom gongan   þær weras sæton

    monige on mæðle,   mode snottre;

    hæfde an eage   ond earan twa,

    ond twegen fet,   twelf hund heafda,

5   **hrycg ond eaxle,   anne sweoran**

    ond sida twa.   Saga hwæt ic hatte.

Vocabulary builder 2

MORE NUMERALS

The -teen numerals end in **-tȳne**:

13 **þrēotȳne**   14 **fēowertȳne**   15 **fīftȳne**   16 **syxtȳne**   17 **seofontȳne**

18 **eahtatȳne**   19 **nigontȳne**.

The number **twentig** sounds almost exactly the same as modern English *twenty*, since the combination of letters **-ig** was regularly pronounced as a short 'ee' sound. The same is true of 30 **þrītig**, 40 **fēowertig**, 50 **fīftig**, and 60 **sȳxtig**. Thereafter up to 120 an ancient and original system of counting takes over in which the names for 7, 8, 9, 10, 11, 12 end with the suffix **-tig**, and each is preceded by **hund**, even though **hund** normally means *hundred*:

70	**hundseofontig**	100	**hundteontig**
80	**hundeahtatig**	110	**hundendleofantig**
90	**hundnigontig**	120	**hundtwelftig**

THE SYNTAX OF NUMBERS

To express the figure XXIV, Old English said **feower and twentig** in the style of the nursery rhyme 'four and twenty blackbirds'. Often the following noun was put into the genitive plural (ending in **-a**) so that the idea is expressed as 'four and twenty of blackbirds': examples are, **dæg** *day*, **tyn daga** *ten of days*, **þrittig daga and tyn tida**, *thirty days and ten hours*. With large numbers, the noun may be repeated: **þreo hund daga and feower and fiftig daga**, i.e. *three hundred and fifty-four days*.

ROMAN NUMERALS

It is worth recalling the basic principles of the Roman system of numerals that is often used in Old English manuscripts and printed editions. Based on the letters M, D, C, L, X, V, and I representing the hierarchy thousand, five hundred, hundred, fifty, ten, five, and one, the main principle is cumulative: the most senior letter comes first and any junior letters that appear to its right are simply added to it.

So we have:

VI	six	VII	seven	VIII	eight
XI	eleven	XII	twelve	XIII	thirteen
XV	fifteen	XVI	sixteen	XVII	seventeen
XX	twenty	XXI	twenty-one		
LI	fifty-one	LVI	fifty-six		
LXXII	seventy-two				
CLXXXVII	one hundred and eighty-seven (C is Latin 'centum' = 100)				

If, however, a junior letter precedes a senior, then its value is subtracted. This gives the following numbers:

IV	four (sometimes written by scribes as IIII)
IX	nine
XL	forty
XC	ninety (etc.)

BYRHTFERTH OF RAMSEY ON NUMBERS

The following is Byrhtferth's passage on **getæle** *counting*, i.e. his explanation of Roman numerals. There is perhaps one error or confusion in his list, namely the symbol for six: probably he meant to write **V and I getacnað syx** *V and I signify six*.

Þas stafas synt on Ledenum getæle: I getacnað an, V getacnað fif, X getacnað tyn, L fiftig, C centum hundred, M þusend, I and V syx, X and I endlufon, X and L feowertig, L and X, syxtig, X and C hundnigontig, D and C syx hundred, duo CC twa hundred, CCC þreo hundred, CCCC feower hundred, D and CCCC nigon hundred, M þusend.

For multiplication, Byrhtferth uses **siðon** *times*:

Nim twelf siðon þrittig; do togædere; þonne hæfast ðu þreo hund daga and syxtig.

Take twelve times thirty; add together; then you have three hundred and sixty days.

Like many medieval writers Byrhtferth is fascinated by the symmetry and interconnections of numbers. In his *Handboc* he writes about:

þa feower timan *the four seasons*: **lengtentima, sumor, hærfest, winter,**

þa feower gesceaft *the four elements*: **lyft, fyr, wæter, eorðe,** and their related adjectives: **ceald** *cold*, **wearm** *warm*, **wæt** *wet*, **drigge** *dry*,

þa feower mægna *the four virtues* (literally *the four powers*): **rihtwisnys** *righteousness*, **snoternys** *wisdom*, **ge-metgung** *moderation* and **strengð** *strength*.

For more on Byrhtferth, look back to unit 5.

Practice 2

1 Translate the following text on the Annus solaris (*the solar year*).

Annus solaris hæfð þreo hund daga and fif and syxtig, and twa and fiftig wucena, and twelf monðas. And soðlice ðæt ger hæfð eahta þusend tida and syx and syxtig.

(Byrhtferth, *Enchiridion*, ed. Baker and Lapidge, II.3, 178-80)

2 Fill in the missing numbers of hours:

On anum dæge and þære nihte beoð (a) _____ tida, and on twam dagum beoð (b) _____ tida, and on þrim dagum beoð (c) _____ . On feower dagum syx and hundnigontig. On fif dagum beoð (d) _____ tida and (e) _____ tida.

Language discovery

HOW TO LEARN VOCABULARY

The study of vocabulary serves two purposes. Practically speaking, a wide knowledge of the lexical patterns of the language accelerates the process of learning to read the texts. More theoretically, the systematic study of the Old English lexicon throws light on the way the speakers viewed the world, on the things and phenomena they thought necessary to name and label. It is part of the study of Old English culture, equally relevant to both literature and history.

The lexical fields studied so far in units 1–11 include the language of riddles, kingship, family and marriage, education, time and the seasons, lordship and land use. For the rest of this unit, several ways of studying, recording and learning vocabulary will be explored. The area of lexis chosen is the animal world, but the methods and exercises presented here can easily be adapted and applied to other areas of vocabulary, depending on your interests.

1 Basic word lists

To activate connections in your mind, list words in different ways:

1a English, Old English

adder **seo næddre**, *bear* **se bera**, *beaver* **se befor**, *badger* **se brocc**, *boar* **se bar** or **se eofor**, *deer or stag* **se heorot** or **heort**, *horse* **þæt hors**

1b Old English, English

se cran *crane*, **se crawe** *crow*, **se earn** *eagle*, **seo gos** *goose*, **se hafoc** *hawk*, **se higera** *jay*, **se hræfn** *raven*, **se hremn** *raven*, **se swan** *swan*

1c Old English synonyms:

[HORS] **eoh**, **hors**, **mearh**, **wicg**

2 Learning words in context: *The Seafarer*

Relate the words you learn to the text in which you first read them. For example, some well-known lines in the *Exeter Book* poem *The Seafarer* enumerate the many seabirds that the protagonist encounters on his long winter pilgrimage. The birds are solitary creatures, tokens of his isolation, but at the same time emblems of his determination and resolve. Because he is resolved to travel, he prefers the gannet's cry and the curlew's song to the laughter of men, and he prefers the singing of the gull to the drinking of mead in the hall. The following are the birds named in the passage:

seo ilfetu	*swan*
se hwilpe	*curlew*
se ganet	*gannet*
se mæw	*seagull*
se stearn	*tern*
þæt earn	*eagle*

In this context it makes sense to learn the words in the order in which they appear in the poem (lines 18–26):

> Þær ic ne gehyrde   butan hlimman sæ,
>
> iscaldne wæg.   Hwilum ylfete song
>
> 20   dyde ic me to gomene,   ganetes hleoþor
>
> and huilpan sweg   fore hleahtor wera,
>
> mæw singende   fore medo drince.
>
> Stormas þær stanclifu beotan,   þær him stearn oncwæð
>
> isigfeþera;   ful oft þæt earn bigeal
>
> 25   urigfeþra.   Nænig hleomæga
>
> feasceaftig ferð   frefran meahte.

> *There I heard nothing but the sea resounding,*
>
> *the ice-cold wave. At times the song of the swan*
>
> *I made my joy, the gannet's cry*
>
> *and the curlew's melody for the laughter of men,*
>
> *the gull singing rather than the drinking of mead.*
>
> *Storms beat stone cliffs there, where the tern replied*
>
> *icy-feathered; very often the eagle called back*
>
> *dewy-feathered. No protecting kinsmen*
>
> *could comfort the desolate spirit.*

3 Making more informative word-lists

When listing vocabulary for the purpose of memorisation, it is useful to record any relevant information on grammar, usage or pronunciation. For verbs, especially strong verbs, you could list the forms of the past tense. For the names of people, things and concepts, it is suggested that you record each noun with its gender and (if you wish) its plural. Learn the gender of the noun by marking it with the definite article:

se gat *the goat*   **þæt hors** *the horse*   **seo culfre** *the dove*

Alternatively, follow the policy of Old English dictionaries and mark the gender by an abbreviation for masculine, neuter, and feminine:

gāt (m.) *goat*   **hors** (n.) *horse*   **culfre** (f.) *dove*

Note also any particularities of pronunciation, such as the medial '-f-' of **culfre**, pronounced 'v', which may help to connect the word with its modern equivalent *culver dove*. Although the original texts do not usually indicate long vowels, you may wish to mark (with a macron) the long vowel of **gāt** to show that it is pronounced 'gaht'. Often this long 'ah' vowel appears in words which in modern English have a long 'o' sound; examples are **drāf** *drove*, **stān** *stone*, **tāde** *toad*. Similarly, the long **ū** of **mūs** points to the later *ou* of *mouse*, and the long **ō** of **gōs** looks ahead to the *oo* of the modern word *goose*. The sounds of the words are thus set to work usefully; the pronunciation establishes connections by which the lexical items can be remembered. If the word can be associated with an image or illustration (e.g. from Anglo-Saxon manuscript art) this will also help to reinforce the learning of the word visually.

4 Old–modern connections

Attention to changes in meaning brings life to the history of vocabulary. The process of semantic change sometimes preserves old words in the language with new, specialized meanings. Generally **fugol** meant *bird*, rather than the specific meaning that *fowl* has assumed in more recent times. Similarly, the general word for *animal* is **se dēor** (cognate with modern German 'Tier'); again, in later times, this word has taken on the more particular meaning of *deer*. Occasionally also the reverse process takes place and a word with a specific meaning has become more general: thus the modern word *bird* was originally **bridd**, which designated *a young bird* or *fledgeling*.

5 Word-hoard

A potentially useful way of acquiring a set of vocabulary items, such as names of animals, is to organise the items into a semantic field, a set of words associated by meaning. Words can be written on cards and sorted into categories in different piles. One such group could be placed under the heading *herd*, Old English **heord**. In making such an arrangement, you will immediately see that Old English had more synonyms for the concept *cattle* than does modern English, and that wealth, money and livestock were more closely associated than they are in the present-day language.

HERD	HEORD
oxherd	**se oxanhyrde**
shepherd	**se sceaphyrde**
cattle	**se ceap** (also means *purchase*, *trade*)
	þæt feoh (also means *money*, cf. *fee*)
	þæt neat, **þæt nyten**, **þæt orf**
cow	**seo cu** or **þæt hriðer**
ox	**se oxa** or **þæt hriðer**
cattleshed	**seo scipen** (cf. German 'Schuppen'; modern English *shippen*)
sheep	**se scēap**, or **se scēp**, or **se scīp**
sheepfold	**þæt scēapwīc** 'SHÉap-weech'

6 Connections with place-names

Many Old English words are preserved in the names of places. Focussing on the natural world, you can learn new vocabulary and also study evidence about which animals were considered important in Old English land-use and agriculture. So **se oxa** *the ox* is associated with a dairy farm (**wic**) at *Oxwich* (Nf), with an enclosure **hæg** at *Oxhey* (Hrt), with a *ford* or *river-crossing* for the *oxen* at *Oxford* – originally **Oxenaford** *ford of the oxen* (genitive plural), and with an *island* (**ēg**) of the oxen at *Oxney* (K).

7 The **mere**: a case-study

A variety of creatures are associated with **mere**, the word for *pond* or *lake*: **se bridd** *young bird*, **se bula** *bull*, **se catt** *wild cat*, **se cran** *crane* or *heron*, **se crawa** *crow*, **se frosc** *frog*, and **se wulf** *wolf*. The equivalent modern place-names are *Bridgemere* (Ch), *Boulmer* (Nb), *Catmore* (Brk), *Cranmere* (Ha), *Cromer* (Hrt), *Frogmore* (D, Do, Hrt), and *Woolmer* (Ha) – the missing 'f' in the latter name is reflected also in later spellings of the personal name *Wulfstan* as *Wulstan*. From a literary point of view, the most famous creature associated with a **mere** is Grendel, the monster in *Beowulf*. A special case is the name of the type *Merton, Marten, Marton*, deriving from Old English **mere** *pond* combined with **tun** *estate*. The ponds indicated by these names were functional: situated on common land routes to provide water and refreshment for travellers (who presumably travelled on horseback if they could afford it). In addition, they supplied water, fish, water-fowl and reeds for the local economy.

8 More names in -**tun**

As an element in place-names, the Old English **tun** (pronounced **tūn** 'toon'), the word for *estate*, often combines with a word denoting agricultural or economic use. This can include crops in *Flaxton, Linton, Ryton* and trees such as *Pirton* or *Appleton* (see unit 2). Other **tun** names reflect the animal husbandry or farming practised at the location, or associate the estate with a particular species of bird or animal, such as *Everton*, associated with the *boar*, **se eofor** (pronounced as two syllables 'Éo-vor'):

Shepton (So), *Shipton* (O)	**se scēp** or **se scīp** *sheep*
Rampton (C)	**se ramm** *ram*
Natton (Gl), *Netton* (W)	**þæt neat** *cattle*
Calton (WRY), *Kelton* (Cu)	**þæt cealf** *calf*
Calverton (Bk, Nt)	**cealfa** *of the calves* (gen. plural)
Butterton (St)	**seo butere** *butter*
Honiton (D)	**þæt hunig** *honey*
Everton (Bd, La, Nt)	**se eofor** *boar, wild boar*

NOTE: the abbreviations in this section refer to the traditional pre-1974 counties in which the places occur, thus Bd is Bedfordshire, Bk Berkshire, C Cambridgeshire, Ch Cheshire, Cu Cumberland, D Devon, Do Dorset, Du Durham, Gl Gloucestershire, Ha Hampshire, Hrt Hertfordshire, K Kent, La Lancashire, Nb Northumberland, Nf Norfolk, Nt Nottinghamshire, Nth Northamptonshire, O Oxfordshire, So Somerset, St Staffordshire, W Wiltshire, and WRY is the West Riding of Yorkshire.

> **CULTURAL INSIGHT**
>
> Most of the shires and counties of England were administrative units based on the West Saxon system of administration and founded at various times in the Old English period. For the **scirgemot** or *shire-court* in action, see units 19 and 20.

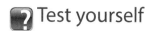 ## Test yourself

Give the etymology of the following place-names and identify the Old English birds or animals referred to.

Example: Crawley 'Crow Glade' from **se crawa** *crow*

1 Cowden (K) _____

2 Shapwick (Do) _____

3 Gateford (Nt) _____

4 Earnley (Sx) _____

5 Carnforth (La) _____

6 Horsforth (Nf) _____

7 Shipley (frequent) _____

8 Hartburn (Du) _____

9 Woolley (Brk) _____

10 Hardwick (frequent) _____

11 Chalvey (Bk) _____

12 Hunton (Ha) _____

13 Eversholt (Bd) _____

14 Shiplake (O) _____

SELF-CHECK	
I CAN ...	
●	decline the basic nouns for parts of the body
●	count in Old English
●	read Roman numerals
●	employ different techniques for learning and storing vocabulary

13 *And dydon hyne on þone wæterleasan pytt*

And they put him into the waterless well

In this unit you will learn about:
▶ *rivalry for the throne around the year 1000*
▶ *language and style: expressing intentions*
▶ *basic uses of the subjunctive*
▶ *the prefixes ā-, of-, and be-*
▶ *metaphorical uses of* handa *hands*
▶ *the meanings of* ceap

You will read:
▶ *the accounts of Edward the Martyr from the* Anglo-Saxon Chronicle
▶ The Story of Joseph 3, *from the Old English* Hexateuch

 13.00

And dydon hyne on þone wæterleasan pytt
And they put him into the waterless well

Ⓥ Vocabulary builder 1

SPEECH ACTS

cwædon him betwynan	*they said among themselves*
uton secgan þæt...	*let's say that …*

DEBATE

Hwæt fremað us?	*What will it benefit us?*
selre ys þæt...	*it's better that …*
hyt swa mihte beon	*it may be so*

ⓠ Language discovery

Consider the verbs in the following modern English expressions:

1 So be it.
2 As it were.

3 Peace be with you.

4 God save the Queen.

5 Long live the Prince.

Normally the verbs used would be *is*, *was*, *is*, *saves*, **and** *lives*, **respectively. Why are the verbs in a different form to what is expected? What extra meanings are conveyed by the forms of the verb given here? For more discussion see Grammar 1.**

Rivalry for the throne around the year 1000

Rivalry between half-brothers was a perennial problem of tenth- and eleventh-century royal politics. The problem became acute on two occasions after the unexpected departure of a strong and forceful ruler; the first such occasion being the death of Edgar the Peaceable in 975, the second that of Cnut in 1035. In 975 opinion was sharply divided over which of Edgar's two sons should succeed him; even the great monastic reformers St Dunstan and St Æthelwold could not agree. In the end, the older half-brother Edward succeeded, but three years later, on a journey to visit his stepmother in Dorset, he was ambushed and killed near Corfe Castle by unknown assailants. Immediately his half-brother Æthelred (later called **Unræd** *the ill-advised*) succeeded him; he was young enough to be innocent of blame, but it was an unhappy start to his reign.

Looking back a generation later, the writer Wulfstan referred to the murder of Edward as **hlafordswice** *betrayal of a lord*, from the verb **beswican** *to betray*, connected with the noun **swicolnes** *deceit* and the participle **unswicende** *faithful* (literally *undeceitful*) used in Cnut's Proclamation of 1020 (see unit 7). In the successive versions of the *Anglo-Saxon Chronicle*, the level of shock and indignation at the treachery – possibly by members of Edward's own kindred – increased with each retelling of the events (see study text below).

It is a measure of the awe with which the sacred office of kingship was regarded that, like his nephew Edward the Confessor after 1066, this king too was popularly considered a saint and came to be known as Edward the Martyr.

Edward the Martyr: three versions of the *Chronicle*

With each successive version of the *Anglo-Saxon Chronicle*, the story of Edward the Martyr's murder (by supporters of his half-brother Æthelred) is given further significance. The earliest version, manuscript A, gives bare facts, C mentions the martyrdom, while D publishes a prose poem – a kind of homily in balanced, rhythmical phrases – on the saintliness of the king and the futility of earthly endeavour. Here the writer employs contrasting words and phrases to emphasize his points about the situation **ær** *previously* and **nu** *now*: **ofmyrþredon** *murdered* and **mærsode** *glorified*, **eorðlic cyning** *earthly king* and **heofonlic sanct** *heavenly saint*, **his gemynd adilgian** *to blot away his memory* and **on heofonum and on eorþan tobrædan** *to spread it widely over heaven and earth*.

A 978 Her wearð Eadweard cyning ofslegen. On þis ylcan feng Æðelred æðeling his broðor to rice.

Here king Edward was slain. In the same year prince Æthelred his brother succeeded to the kingdom.

C 978 Her on þysum geare wearð Eadweard cyning gemartyrad, and Æþelred æþeling his broðor feng to þam rice, and he wæs on þam ylcan geare to cinge gehalgod. On þam geare forðferde Alfwold, se wæs bisceop on Dorsætum, and his lic lið on þam mynstre æt Scireburnan.

Here in this year king Edward was martyred and prince Æthelred his brother succeeded to the kingdom, and he was in the same year consecrated as king. In that year Alfwold passed away, who was bishop in Dorset, and his body lies in the minster at Sherbourne.

D 979 Her wæs Eadweard cyning ofslægen on æfentide æt Corfes geate on .xv. Kalentas Aprilis, and hine mon þa gebyrigde on Werhamme, butan ælcum cynelicum wurðscipe. Ne wearð Angelcynne nan wyrse dæd gedon, þonne þeos wæs, syþþan hi ærest Britenland gesohton. Menn hine ofmyrþredon, ac God hine mærsode. He wæs on life eorðlic cyning, he is nu æfter deaðe heofonlic sanct. Hyne noldon his eorðlican magas wrecan, ac hine hafað his heofonlic fæder swyðe gewrecan. Þa eorðlican banan woldon his gemynd on eorðan adilgian, ac se uplica wrecend hafað his gemynd on heofonum and on eorþan tobræd. Þa ðe noldon ær to his libbendan lichaman onbugan, þa nu eadmodlice on cneowum gebugað to his deada banum. Nu we magan ongytan þæt manna wisdom, and heora smeagunga, and heora rædas syndon nahtlice ongean Godes geðeaht. Her feng Æðelred to rice, and he wæs æfter þæm swyðe hrædlice mid micclum gefean Angelcynnes witan gehalgod to cyninge æt Cyngestune.

Here in this year king Edward was slain in the evening at Corfe Castle on the fifteenth of the kalends of April, and they buried him then at Wareham without any royal honour. No worse deed had been done in the English nation than this was, since they first settled the land of Britain. Men murdered him but God glorified him; in life he was an earthly king: now after death he is a heavenly saint. His earthly kinsmen would not avenge him, but his heavenly Father has very much avenged him. The earthly killers wished to purge his memory on earth, but the heavenly Avenger has spread his memory in heaven and earth. The men who would not bow to his earthly body now humbly bend their knees to his mortal remains. Now we can see that the wisdom of men and their thoughts and plans are as nothing to God's providence. Here Æthelred succeeded to the kingdom, and thereafter very quickly, to the great joy of England's Assembly, he was consecrated king at Kingston.

geat	*gate* (the word implies a **burhgeat**, or *fortification with enclosure and walled gatehouse*, see the extract from Wulfstan's *Promotion Law* in unit 20)
gebyrigde	*buried* (from the verb **gebyrgan** *to raise a mound*, connected with **beorg** *mound*)
seo dæd	*deed*
wyrs	*worse*
wearð… gedon	*was done*

gesohton	*sought out* (from **secan** *to seek*; often used with the meaning *to come to, travel to a country*)
Britenland	*Britain*
of-myrþredon	*murdered* (stress the **m**-syllable to alliterate with the next verb)
mærsode	*glorified, made famous* (cf. **mære** *famous*)
sanct	*saint*
magas	*kinsmen*
wrecan	*to avenge*
se bana	*killer*
gemynd	*memory*
wrecend	*avenger*
tobræd	*spread widely*
þa ðe noldon ær	*those who previously had not wanted*
eadmodlice	*humbly*
smeagunga	*thoughts, meditations*
rædas	*plans, advice*
geðeaht	*counsel, design, providence*
hrædlice	*quickly*
gefea	*joy*
witan	*councillors* (i.e. *the Assembly*)

The Story of Joseph 3

EXPRESSING INTENTIONS

Almost any narrative thrives on exploring the purposes and intentions of its characters. Readers of stories are fascinated by the uncertainty and are impelled to read further to find out what happens next. In the following extracts from the Joseph Story, the verb **þencan** (*to think, intend*) describes the conflicting intentions of Joseph's brothers and Ruben: on the one hand, we have **hi ðohton hyne to ofsleane** *they thought to slay him* and, on the other hand, there is Ruben's intention **he ðohte hyne to generienne of heora handum** *he thought to rescue him from their hands*. Here, as we saw in unit 11, the inflected infinitive (**to** + infinitive + ending) is used to express purpose and adds interest and tension to the narrative.

13.01

Þa hi hyne feorran gesawon

When they saw him from afar

What will the brothers do with their half-brother Joseph when he falls into their hands?

The words underlined are examples of the subjunctive mood of the verb, which expresses conjecture and anticipation (further explanations follow).

Þa hi hyne feorran gesawon, ær ðam þe he him to <u>come</u>, hi ðohton hyne to ofsleane, and cwædon him betwynan, 'Her gæð se swefniend. Uton hyne ofslean and don on þone ealdan pytt and secgan þæt wildeor hyne fræton. Ðonne byð gesyne hwæt him hys swefen <u>fremion</u>!'

13 *And dydon hyne on þone wæterleasan pytt* And they put him into the waterless well   135

gesawon	*they saw* 'yuh-SAH-won' (Note long vowel in **sāwon**) (cf. **seah** *he saw*, **sēon** *to see*)
feorran	*from afar*
ær ðam þe	*before* (conjunction)
hi ðohton	*they thought* (Note long vowel **ðōhton**)
to ofsleane	*to kill* (inflected infinitive)
cwædon	*they said* (Note long **-æ-** vowel) (but **he cwæð** *he said*, with short vowel)
se swefniend	*dreamer* (cf. **swefn**, **swefen** *dream*; see unit 6)
ofslean	*to kill* (normal infinitive)
don	*to put* (the long vowel **dōn** rhymes with 'Doane') (NB **dōn** literally means *to do*)
se pytt	*pit* (from Latin 'puteus'; Old English **wælle** means *spring*)
wildeor	*wild animals* (**wild** + **deor**)
fræton	*they ate* (used to describe animals)
gesyne	*seen* 'yuh-SEE-nuh' (past participle)
fremion	subjunctive of **fremian** *to benefit*

Grammar 1

1 INTRODUCTION TO THE SUBJUNCTIVE

The subjunctive expresses the idea of conjecture. It can appear after a conjunction of time. Here is an example from the Joseph story from the study text in this unit:

ær ðam þe he him to <u>come</u>   *before he reached them*

Here the conjectural subjunctive **com-e** (instead of indicative **com**) is used to talk about an event that was being anticipated in the future. A further example of anticipation from the same text is the brothers' speech as they plot to kill Joseph:

'Ðonne byð gesyne hwæt him hys swefen <u>fremion</u>!'

'Then it will be seen how his dreams may benefit him!'

A protracted sense of anticipation runs through the whole passage from the moment when the possibility of Joseph's arrival was first aired (and marked by the subjunctive) to the moment when he actually did arrive (marked by the indicative), whereupon he was seized by the brothers and thrown into the pit:

Sona swa he to hys broðrum com, swa bereafodon hi hyne hys tunecan and dydon hyne on ðone wæterleasan pytt.

As soon as he came to his brothers, they deprived him of his tunic and put him into the waterless well.

Between these two moments marked by **come** (subjunctive) and **com** (indicative) is the debate between the brothers, during which Joseph's fate hangs in the balance. A similar period of anticipation then follows as Joseph's brothers, Ruben and Judah, discuss with the other brothers what is to be done with Joseph now that he has been taken prisoner.

2 FORMS OF THE SUBJUNCTIVE

In present-day English, the subjunctive still exists to a limited extent; it is a mood of the verb that expresses an idea of wish or conjecture or concession (e.g. *so be it*) and so contrasts with the regular mood of the verb, the indicative, used for assertions (e.g. *so it is*). Sometimes the same idea or mood can be expressed by the auxiliary *may*, *might*, as in *long may it prosper*, or perhaps in a prayer or petition *may the situation remain stable*. Generally, the subjunctive in modern English exists in a few fixed and formal expressions like *long live the king* (cf. the indicative *the king lives long*) or in certain formal contexts such as *the king required that each town render tribute*.

In Old English, the subjunctive mood was found more widely. In form the present subjunctive can often be recognized by its lack of the **-th** ending associated with the present indicative as in *he maketh*. So in this unit we have **syllon** (subjunctive) instead of regular indicative **syllað**. And in the declaration of Godwine to Leofwine the Red (unit 11), the normal present tense **gæð** (*goes*) becomes subjunctive **gā** or **ge-gā**, and in the plural, the present subjunctive would be **gān**. The past subjunctive is harder to spot, particularly in late Old English spellings. Indicative **cōm**, **cōmon** *came*, becomes subjunctive **cōme**, **cōmen**. For irregular verbs, there are anomalous forms. The indicative **bið** (*is*) becomes **bēo** in the subjunctive, e.g. the closing remark in one of Cnut's writs (*Harmer, no. 29)* **beo gerefa se þe beo** *be the reeve whoever he may be*. The plural subjunctive is **bēon**. A second alternative form of the present subjunctive of *to be* is **sy**, while yet another form is the past subjunctive **wære**; they occur in the formula **ðam ðe him leofost sy** in the Leofwine document and **ðam ðe hire leofest wære** and **ðær him leofost wære** in the Worcestershire marriage agreement (unit 8 above).

 13.02

Soðlice þa Ruben ðis gehyrde, he ðohte hyne to generienne

Truly when Ruben heard this he thought to save him

Soðlice þa Ruben ðis gehyrde, he ðohte hyne to generienne of heora handum, and cwæð, 'Ne ofslea we hyne, ne we hys blod ne ageotan, ac wurpað hyne on ðone pytt, and healdað eowre handa unbesmitene.' Þæt he sæde, for þam ðe he wolde hyne generian of heora handum and hys fæder agyfan.

ge-nerian	*to save*
ageotan	*to spill*
unbesmiten	*untarnished*
agyfan	*to deliver, give over to*

Sona swa he to hys broðrum com

As soon as he came to his brothers

Sona swa he to hys broðrum com, swa bereafodon hi hyne hys tunecan, and dydon hyne on ðone wæterleasan pytt. And þa hi woldon etan, hi gesawon twegen Ismahelitisce wegfarende men cuman of Galaad, and læddon wyrtgemang on heora olfendon, and tyrwan and stacten, on Egypta land.

sona swa	*as soon as*
berēafian	*to deprive* (cf. **se rēaf** *garment, booty*)
dydon	*they did* (here it means *they put*)
twegen	*two*
Ismahelitisc	*Ismaelite*
wegfarend	*wayfaring*
seo wyrtgemang	*mixture of spices*
olfendon	*camels* (**se olfenda** false etymology from Latin 'elephantem')
se tyrwa	*resin*
stacten	*myrrh*

Grammar 2

PREFIXES ON VERBS

As well as the perfective **ge-** prefix with its emphasis on the idea of completed action, there are other prefixes before verbs. The study text in this unit has **ā-**, **of-**, and **be-**. Like **ge-**, these prefixes are weakly stressed. It is important to note that the main stress comes on the stem or root syllable of the verb:

ageotan	*to spill, shed*	'ah-YÉotan'
bereafodon	*they deprived*	'be-RÉa-vo-don'

THE Ā- PREFIX

The **ā-** prefix (pronounced long as 'ah') can intensify the meaning, as in the case of **geofan** *give* becoming **āgeofan** *deliver*, but often **ā-** behaves rather like **ge-** in that it adds perfective force, a sense of completion:

fysan *to drive*	**afysan** *to drive away*
geotan *to pour*	**ageotan** *to spill*

THE OF- PREFIX

Similarly, **of-** (pronounced 'off-') has perfective force:

ofgyfan	*to give up*	**ofslean**	*to strike down*, i.e. *slay, kill*
ofmyrþrian	*to murder*	**ofsniðan**	*to cut down, kill*
ofsendan	*to send for*		

THE PRODUCTIVE BE- PREFIX

Prefixes are described in linguistic terms as productive if they can be readily used to form new words, as in the case of **be-**, which is still used in modern English. The Old English prefix **be-** was likewise productive and had several meanings. A basic meaning is *round about* as in the following:

lucan *to lock*	**belucan** *to enclose, lock up*
settan *to put*	**besettan** *to beset, surround*
sittan *to sit*	**besittan** *to besiege*
standan *to stand*	**bestandan** *to stand round* cf. unit 21, *Maldon*, line 68
windan *to wind*	**bewindan** *to wind round, encircle*

> **LANGUAGE INSIGHT**
>
> The verb **bewindan** features in the poem *The Dream of the Rood* (line 5), in a well-known phrase **leohte bewunden** *surrounded with light*, describing the cross itself in the vision at the start of the poem (see Reading in unit 6).

A similar meaning for **be-** is found in modern English words such as **benight**, **besiege**, **bestraddle**, **betake**, all of which seem to have come into existence after the Old English period – sometimes, as in the case of **besiege**, the older English prefix combining with a newer word imported from French.

Another use of **be-**, corresponding to the modern **be-** in **bewail**, is to convert an intransitive verb into a transitive one, i.e. the **be-** converts a verb which normally stands on its own into one which requires an object: *the monk was wailing* as opposed to *the monk was bewailing his wicked deeds*. Some Old English examples show how this works:

wēpan	*to weep*	**bewēpan**	*to bewail*
delfan	*to dig*	**bedelfan**	*to dig round, bury*
scīnan	*to shine*	**bescīnan**	*to illuminate*
þencan	*to think*	**beþencan**	*to think about something, ponder*

A third meaning of **be-** (sometime spelt **bi-**) is privative: it adds a sense of depriving to the verb, as in the modern English *bereft*. For example, recall the proverb **cyning sceal beagas dǣlan** in unit 2. If the prefix is added, it alters the meaning pejoratively:

dǣlan *to distribute*	**bedǣlan** *to deprive*
niman *take*	**beniman** *take away*

In poetic elegies, **eðle bidǣled** means *deprived of homeland* (as in the *Exeter Book* poem, *The Wanderer*, line 20). The example **bereafodon** *they deprived* in *The Story of Joseph* is particularly apt, as **rēaf** also means *garment*, and it is this which the brothers remove, literally *be-reave*, from their brother, leaving him bereft:

Sona swa he to hys broðrum com, swa bereafodon hi hyne hys tunecan.

As soon as he reached his brothers, they deprived him of his coat.

13 *And dydon hyne on þone wæterleasan pytt* And they put him into the waterless well   **139**

V Vocabulary builder 2

METAPHORICAL USE OF **HANDA** *HANDS*

As books like *Metaphors we Live by* (Lakoff and Johnson, 2003) show, languages employ many metaphors which are so completely assimilated into the structure of our vocabulary that we barely notice them. It is interesting to consider how Old English metaphors construe the world when compared and contrasted with the language of the present. As already suggested in unit 11, **on dæge** *in his lifetime* is an obvious metaphorical use of the word *day*, as is the phrase **to handa gan** *to come into the hands of* or the description of the act of giving **unnendre handa** *with a giving hand* or **unnendre heortan** *with a giving heart*. In these phrases, the act of giving, taking and receiving derives from a metaphor of the body. They may be compared with similar expressions in the biblical passage, where the *hands* metaphor is used to denote ideas firstly of captivity and then of innocence and guilt:

he wolde hyne generian of heora handum and hys fæder agyfan

he wanted to rescue him from their hands and deliver him to his father

selre ys þæt we hyne syllon to ceape Ismaelitum þæt ure handa beon unbesmitene

it is better that we sell him to the Ismaelites so that our hands may be untarnished

CEAP *TRADE*

The verb *to buy* comes from the Old English **bycgan** *to pay for*. In the same semantic field belongs the noun **se cēap** ('chéap'), which like **feoh** *fee, money* could also mean *cattle* but usually denoted *trade* and related ideas, with a verb **cēapian** *to bargain*, *trade*, *buy* (derived like German 'kaufen' *to buy* from Latin 'caupo'). A series of related concepts are found as compounds. A word-list in a manuscript records **cēap-dæg** *market-day*; elsewhere we find **cēapland** *purchased land*, **cēapman** *trader*, **cēapscip** *trading vessel*, **cēapsetl** *toll-booth* and **cēapstræt** *market*. Another word for a *market* is **seo cēapstow** which combines **cēap** with the general word for a place **seo stow**, as in the town *Stow-on-the-Wold* and, of course, *Chepstow*. Similarly **seo cēapung** *trade* is the origin of place-names of market towns like *Chipping Norton* and *Chipping Camden*.

> **LANGUAGE INSIGHT**
>
> The phrase **butan cēape** *without price*, i.e. gratis, has given rise to the adjective *cheap* in modern English.

13.04

Hwæt fremað us?

What will it benefit us?

The words underlined are further examples of the subjunctive mood of the verb, here expressing conjecture and anticipation.

Þa cwæð Iudas to hys gebroðrum, 'Hwæt fremað us ðeah we urne broðor <u>ofslean</u>?
Selre ys þæt we hyne <u>syllon</u> to ceape Ismaelitum þæt ure handa <u>beon</u> unbesmitene;

he ys ure broðor and ure flæsc.' Þa cwædon hys gebroðru þæt hyt swa mihte beon. And þa þær forun Madianisce cypan, hi tugon hyne up of þam pytte and sealdon hyne Ismaelitum wið ðrittigum penegum. And hi hyne læddon on Egypta land.

selre	*better*
se cēap	*price, transaction*
mihte	*it could* (past tense of *magan*)
þæt flæsc	*flesh* (pronounce with long vowel)
cypan	*merchants* (**se cypa**; cf. surnames *Chapman, Cooper*)
tēon	*to pull, drag* (**tyhð, tēah, tugon, getogen**)
lædan	*to lead, carry*

 Test yourself

Reread the study texts from *The Story of Joseph* in this unit and answer the following questions.

1 What did the brothers do before they put Joseph in the waterless well?

_____

2 What were they about to do when they saw the two Ismaelite wayfarers?

_____

3 Compare Ruben's and Judah's actions and motivations.

_____

4 For a medieval Christian audience, what might be the significance of the price for which the brothers sell Joseph?

_____

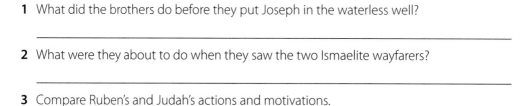

SELF-CHECK

	I CAN ...
○	recognize ways of expressing intention in Old English
○	understand and interpret the uses of the subjunctive
○	distinguish the meanings of the prefixes **ā-**, **of-**, and **be-**
○	analyse metaphorical uses of **handa** *hands*
○	understand the meanings of **ceap**

14

Nys se cnapa her
The boy is not here

In this unit you will learn about:
▶ *forms of the negative*
▶ *the manuscripts of* The Story of Joseph
▶ *text and illustration*
▶ *'fronting' the object*
▶ *the endings of the strong adjective*
▶ *strong adjectives in Old English poetry*
▶ *stressed syllables and rhythmic patterns in Old English prose*

You will read:
▶ The Story of Joseph 4
▶ *extracts from* The Seafarer *and* Beowulf
▶ *a passage from Wulfstan's* Sermo Lupi

 14.00

Nys se cnapa her
The boy is not here

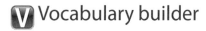 Vocabulary builder

NARRATIVE VERBS

tær	*tore*
namon	*took*
ofsniðon	*killed*
bedypton	*dipped*
brohton	*brought*
cwædon	*said*
fræton	*devoured*
scrydde hyne	*clothed himself*
weop	*wept*
gesamnodon	*assembled*
gefrefrodon	*consoled*
sealdon	*sold*

NEGATIVES

ne	*not*
næfre	*never*
nænig	*not any, none*

naht	*not*
nalas	*not at all*
nan	*none*
nealles	*not at all*

Grammar 1

EXPRESSING A NEGATIVE WITH THE WORD **NE**

The basic way of forming a negative in many European languages is to place a negative particle before the verb. In Latin the negative is 'non', in French 'ne… pas', in Russian 'nye'. Old English also places a particle **ne** before the verb, so that **hi ne mihton** means *they could not* or *they were not able to*.

CONTRACTED **NE** WITH VERBS *TO BE* AND *TO HAVE*

Before the verb *to be* when it begins with a vowel or 'w' and before the verbs **habban** or **willan**, the negative **ne** is contracted. It drops its vowel **-e** and blends with the following word:

ic eom *I am*	**ic neom** *I am not*
heo ys *she is*	**heo nys** *she is not*
hit wæs *it was*	**hit næs** *it was not*
we wæron *we were*	**we næron** *we were not*
ic hæbbe *I have*	**ic næbbe** *I do not have*
heo hæfð *she has*	**heo næfð** *she does not have*
ic hæfde *I had*	**ic næfde** *I did not have*
ic wylle *I want*	**ic nylle** *I do not want*
ic wolde *I wanted*	**ic nolde** *I did not want to*

The contrastive pairs **wylle, nylle** and **hæbbe, næbbe** have survived into modern English in disguised spellings. *Will I, nill I* or *will he, nill he* became *willy nilly*, in other words, something like 'whether one likes it or not'. And in the expression *hob nob* from **hab nab**, the pair **hæbbe næbbe** has changed its meaning more drastically: from *have it or don't have it* to the reciprocal notion of *give and take*; eventually this meant two friends giving and taking drinks and proposing toasts to each other, i.e. *hob-nobbing* or being on familiar terms with each other.

Other words such as **æfre** *ever* and **an** *one* can also be preceded by the particle **ne** to make them negative. Again the two words are written together as one word **næfre** and **nan** and these survive as *never* and *none*. For an example in context see Joseph in unit 6, on the brothers' animosity:

ða onscunodon hi hine and ne mihton nane freondrædene wið hine habban

then they shunned him and were not able to have any friendship with him

Notice here that the negative particle **ne** is repeated twice, once before **mihton** and once in the determiner **nan** (= **ne + an**).

Two further examples of negative contractions are found in the next section of Joseph. In the absence of Ruben, who had hoped to rescue his brother from the dry well and return him to his father, the brothers have sold Joseph to the Midianite traders. Ruben returns only to find the well empty:

Þa Ruben eft com to þam pytte and þone cnapan þær ne funde, ða tær he hys claðas and cwæð to hys broðrum, 'Nys se cnapa her! hwyder ga ic?'

When Ruben came back to the well and could not find the boy there, he tore his clothes and said to his brothers, 'The boy is not here! Where will I go?'

Later the brothers hypocritically try to console their father, but to no avail:

he nolde nane frefrunge underfon

he would not receive any consolation

THE MANUSCRIPTS OF *THE STORY OF JOSEPH*

The Old English *Story of Joseph* appears in four manuscripts with the following locations and library shelf marks:

▶ Oxford Bodleian Library, Laud Misc. 509 (*Hexateuch, Judges*); the manuscript once concluded with the *The Life of St Guthlac,* now in London, British Library, Cotton Vespasian D. xxi (for Guthlac, see unit 16)
▶ London, British Library, Cotton Otho B. x (an anthology of saints' lives); the manuscript was destroyed in the disastrous fire at the Cotton library in the eighteenth century.
▶ London, British Library, Cotton Claudius B iv (the *Illustrated Hexateuch*), a Bible translation from Genesis to Joshua; contains about four hundred illustrations in which text and image often work together to convey the message of the story.
▶ Cambridge, Corpus Christi College 201 (the Corpus Wulfstan anthology), a collection of laws, sermons and legal treatises by the famous archbishop of York, with other texts in prose and verse added mostly at the end of the anthology. For the story of Apollonius of Tyre see unit 23 below.

Each of these four manuscripts has its particular context and purpose. What they have in common is an insistence on the exemplary and hagiographic nature of the Joseph story – in two of the above manuscripts the story is juxtaposed with legends of the saints as though it is regarded as another story from the same genre.

THE STORY OF JOSEPH 4, FROM THE OLD ENGLISH *HEXATEUCH*

Text and illustration

The Old English *Hexateuch* narrates the story of Jacob's loss of his son Joseph in a series of four illustrations interspersed with short lines of text. The effect is to highlight the person in grief, who always stands or sits on the right of the picture, in broadly the same position. In three of the pictures (which can be seen in images online), the grieving figure points to his eyes, a medieval iconographic convention used to indicate tears, for instance in the figure of Edith weeping for Edward in the slightly later Bayeux Tapestry.

The text, which is given below, recounts the deception the brothers practise on their father; it centres on the image of *the coat of many colours*, **seo tunece**, a feminine noun referred to later by the accusative pronoun **hi** (*it, her*) in the crucial phrase **ða ða he hi gecneow** *when he recognized it.*

> ● **BIBLIOGRAPHICAL NOTE**
>
> A published facsimile of the *Hexateuch* exists, and reproductions may be found online, and in books on Anglo-Saxon England; for full references see Bibliography at the end of the book. It is worth noting that references to manuscripts are usually given by folio number rather than page number; a folio number refers to the full page, both front (recto) and back (verso). For example, the pictures of Jacob and Joseph weeping are found on facing pages: folios 54v and 55r of the *Hexateuch* manuscript (where r means recto and v means verso).

14.01

Þa Ruben eft com to þam pytte

When Ruben came back to the well

Þa Ruben eft com to þam pytte and þone cnapan ðær ne funde, ða tær he hys claðas and cwæð to hys broðrum, 'Nys se cnapa her! hwyder ga ic?'

se cnapa	*boy, lad* (also occurs as **cnafa 'kna-va'**, cf. *knave*)
claðas	*clothes* (**se cla\u0111** *garment* 'klahth')
hwyder	means *whither* in the directional sense of *where to*; the corresponding word for *where* expressing stationary location is **hwær** (also spelt **hwar**).

14.02

Þas tunecan we fundon

We have found this tunic

Þa namon hi an ticcen and ofsniðon hyt and bedypton hys tunecan on þam blode, and brohton to heora fæder, and cwædon, 'Þas tunecan we fundon; sceawa hwæðer hyt sy ðines suna þe ne sy.'

Ða cwæð se fæder ða ða he hi gecneow, 'Hyt ys mines suna tunece.'

Þa cwædon hi, 'Wildeor fræton Iosep.'

He totær hys reaf and scrydde hyne mid hæran and weop hys sunu lange tide.

þæt ticcen	*goat kid*
þæt blod	*blood*
þæt reaf	*garment*
seo hære	*sackcloth* (the garment is thought of as a *hairshirt*)

THE FRONTING OF THE DIRECT OBJECT

As in modern English, but more frequently and consistently, it is possible to emphasize the object of a sentence by placing it first, at the front of the sentence. So **þas tunecen we fundon** (where **þas** marks the accusative, see unit 11) means literally *this tunic we found*, in other words *we have found this tunic*. In a translation, in order to capture the particular emphasis of the fronting, one could use a paraphrase: *look at this tunic that we have found*. In this respect, the artist-illustrator of the Old English *Hexateuch* read the text closely. The emphasis on the 'pointing word' **þas** *this* is brought out very strongly in the gestures of the brothers and in the prominent position of **seo tunece** in the middle of the picture. Note also the use of **sy**, the subjunctive of **beon** *to be*, in the next part of the brothers' speech: **sceawa hwæðer hyt sy ðines suna þe ne sy** *see whether it may-be your son's or not*.

 14.03

he nolde nane frefrunge underfon

he would not take any comfort

Soðlice hys bearn hi gesamnodon to þam þæt hi heora fæder gefrefrodon: he nolde nane frefrunge underfon, ac cwæð wepende, 'Ic fare to minum suna to helle.'

gesamnodon	*gathered*
to þam þæt	*so that*
hi … gefrefrodon	*they … consoled*
seo frefrung	*consolation*
hell	*Gehenna, Hades, hell*

 14.04

Ða Madaniscean sealdon Iosep on Egypta land

The Midianites sold Joseph in Egypt

Ða Madaniscean sealdon Iosep on Egypta land Putifare, þam afyredan, Faraones cempena ealdre.

se afyreda	*eunuch*
se cempa	*warrior* (**cempena** *of warriors*)
ealdor	*chief, captain, prince*

Reading

Reread the passages from the Joseph story and answer the following questions.

1 What did the brothers do with Joseph's tunic?

_____

2 How do both Ruben and Jacob react to Joseph's disappearance? Consult the images online. What parallels can be drawn between the two passages and their illustrations?

_____

3 What happened to Joseph when he arrived in Egypt?

_____

Grammar 2

IDENTIFYING THE STRONG ADJECTIVE

When an adjective appears without a definite determiner such as **se** (*the* or *that*) or **þes** (*this*), then it takes a set of prominent endings to indicate case, gender and number:

masculine accusative

ic… gefylle ealne middangeard	*I… fill all middle earth* (unit 2)

neuter genitive

mid ten pundan reodes goldes	*with ten pounds of red gold* (unit 11)

feminine dative

unnendre heortan	*with a generous heart* (unit 8)

nominative plural

ealle his eorlas	*all his earls* (unit 7)

genitive plural

ðreora manna dæg	*for the lifetime of three people* (unit 8)

dative plural

sibban oððe fremdan (**-an** for **-um**)	*to relatives or strangers* (unit 8)

From your reading so far, many of these inflectional endings will already be familiar, especially the masculine accusative ending **-ne** (for example in the pronoun **hyne**) and the nominative plural **-e**. There are also parallels with the strong ending in the demonstrative genitive '**-s**' of the demonstrative **ðysses** meaning *of this* and in strong nouns, e.g. the genitive **eorles** or **goldes**.

These so-called strong endings also occur in the predicative use, i.e. when an adjective comes after the verb *be, is, are, was, were, remained* etc. Here are two examples of the strong plural **-e** ending:

þrymmas syndan Cristes myccl<u>e</u>

Christ's glories are great (unit 4)

þæt ðas forewerda ðus geworht<u>e</u> wæran

that these terms were made thus (unit 11)

(For the full declension of the strong adjective, see unit 18.)

STRONG ADJECTIVES IN OLD ENGLISH POETRY

When reading Old English poetry, watch out for the masculine **-ne** ending of the direct object, which can be crucial for making clear who did what to whom. Here, to cite again the same passage from the poem *The Seafarer*, is an example in which the speaker states that all he could hear was the sea and ice-cold wave, where the adjective *ice-cold* takes the adjective ending:

> **Þær ic ne gehyrde   butan hlimman sæ,**
>
> **iscald<u>ne</u> wæg**.
>
> *There I heard nothing but the sea resounding,*
>
> *the ice-cold wave* (*The Seafarer*, lines 18–19a)

In unit 10, we considered an extract from the episode in *Beowulf* where the monster steps onto the decorated (colourfully patterned) floor of the Danish hall (lines 724b–727); here again is the same strong ending on the adjective:

>   **Raþe æfter þon**
>
> **on fag<u>ne</u> flor   feond treddode,**
>
> **eode yrremod;   him of eagum stod**
>
> **ligge gelicost   leoht unfæger**.
>
> *Quickly after that*
>
> *onto the decorated floor the enemy stepped,*
>
> *advanced angrily; from his eyes stood*
>
> *most like a flame an ugly light.*

Here is an example from the same episode in *Beowulf*, lines 740–742a:

> **Ne þæt se aglæca   yldan þohte,**
>
> **ac he gefeng hraðe   forman siðe**
>
> **slæpend<u>ne</u> rinc,**
>
> *The assailant did not think to delay,*
>
> *but he quickly seized at the first opportunity*
>
> *a sleeping warrior.*

As the story of Grendel's monstrous visit unfolds, we see that he even tries to seize Beowulf himself, who appears to be asleep; Beowulf is described as **hige-þihtig**, a compound adjective meaning *resolute-courageous*, here marked by the strong accusative ending **-ne**:

Forð near ætstop,

nam þa mid handa   higeþihtigne

rinc on ræste,

He stepped forward closer,

seized with his hands the <u>courageous</u>

warrior asleep.

For Grendel's surprise at what happens next, and for the rest of this episode from the poem *Beowulf*, turn to unit 22.

The rhythms of Old English

As we saw when examining the style of the writs and declarations in unit 11, in order to appreciate the rhythm of a language, you need to learn how to divide words into their constituent syllables. The pattern of stressed syllables in a sentence gives the rhythm.

A syllable is made up of a vowel with its preceding and following consonants; in linguistic terminology, the syllable can be described as having an onset, vowel and coda. So a one-syllable word such as the past tense **com** (here given with its long vowel marked as **cōm** 'kohm') consists of:

onset	+	vowel	+	coda
c	**+**	**ō**	**+**	**m**

But in the past subjunctive, the verb becomes **cōme**, which has two syllables:

onset + vowel + coda	and	onset + vowel + coda
c + ō –		**m + e –**

The two syllables of **cōme** both lack a consonant in the coda, but they are not equally stressed, since the emphasis falls on the longer and heavier first syllable, as it does in the words **roamer** or **comber** (cf. *beachcomber*). To represent the rhythm of **cō-me** we can use capital letters **CO-me** or the symbols / x. Returning to some of the rhythmical formulas from unit 11, we can represent their rhythm as follows:

to habbanne and to sellanne	**to HAB-ban-ne and to SEL-lan-ne,**
binnan byrig and butan	**BIN-nan byrig and BU-tan**
swa full and swa forð	**swa FULL and swa FORÐ**
unforboden and unbesacan	**un-for-BO-den and un-be-SA-can**

The point of the latter example is that the main stress tends to be on the root or stem of the word rather than on any weaker prefixes.

From Wulfstan's *Sermo Lupi*

Archbishop Wulfstan's most famous sermon was delivered originally in 1012 as a call to the nation to repent of its sins, which he believed had led to the military disasters that had befallen them. Note the rhythmical two-stress phrases (marked here by the punctuation):

And eac we witan ful georne hwar seo yrmð gewearð, þæt fæder gesealde: his bearn wið wurðe, and bearn his modor, and broðor sealde oþerne, fremdum to gewealde; and eal þæt sindon micele – and egeslice dæda, understande se ðe wille. And git hit is mare and mænigfealdre, þæt derað þisse þeode: manige sind forsworene, and swiðe forlogone, and wed synd tobrocene, oft and gelome.

And also, we know very well where that crime occurred: that a father sold his son for profit, and a son his mother, and one brother sold another, into the power of strangers, and all these are great – and terrible deeds, may he understand who will. And yet there is a greater and more numerous one that harms this nation: many are perjured, and greatly forsworn, and pledges are broken, again and again.

seo yrmð	*misery, crime* (also spelt **iermð**, cf. **earm** *poor, miserable*)
þæt wurð	*price*
geweald	*power:* **fremdum to gewealde** *into the power of strangers*
mænigfeald	*manifold, numerous*
derian	*damage, harm* (verb with dative object)
oft	*often*
gelome	*frequently*

Practice

OLD ENGLISH PROSE STYLE

Exploring Wulfstan's literary style. Reviewing the section on the oral-formulaic style of the declaration, find the following stylistic devices and linguistic features in the passage from *Sermo Lupi*.

1 In the first sentence, find:
   a words that alliterate on initial **w-** (ignore the unstressed **ge-** prefix)
   b an example of full rhyme
   c a two-stress phrase with the verb in the subjunctive.

2 In the second sentence, find
   a alliteration on the consonants **m-** and **sw-**
   b three words that rhyme
   c two adverbs forming a two-stress phrase.

3 **Marking stress and rhythm.** The first part of the second sentence could be written using capitals to mark the heavily stressed syllables:

   And git hit is MAre and MÆnigfealdre, þæt DErað þisse ÞEOde

Write out the second half of this sentence, marking stressed syllables in the same way.

Test yourself

Strong adjectives. Reread the Wulfstan passage and list any adjectives with strong inflectional endings.

_____

_____

_____

_____

SELF-CHECK

I CAN ...

○	recognize forms of the negative
○	identify strong adjective endings
○	identify and pronounce stressed syllables
○	analyse rhythmic patterns in Old English prose

15 Ic symle wilnode to munuclicum life gecyrran

I always wanted to convert to the monastic life

In this unit you will learn about:
▶ *Anglo-Saxon monastic life*
▶ *more uses of the subjunctive mood*
▶ *the pronoun* mon / man
▶ *verbs that take an object in the genitive case*
▶ *the irregular verbs* dōn, willan, gān

You will read:
▶ *extracts from* The Monastic Signs
▶ *a passage from* The Life of St Euphrosyne
▶ *Riddles 47 and 48 from the* Exeter Book

 15.00

Ic symle wilnode to munuclicum life gecyrran
I always wanted to convert to the monastic life

Vocabulary builder

MONASTIC PEOPLE

se abbud	the abbot (head of the **hired** community)
se profost	the provost; second-in-rank after the abbot (pronounce medial '**-f-**' as 'v')
se diacan	deacon, dean (see D. Banham 1991, p. 57)
se hordere	cellarer (in charge of food, drink and provisions)
se cyricweard	sacrist (looks after sacred vessels and shrines in the church)
se magister	master, teacher
se mete-rædere	mealtime reader (reads out loud to the monks at meals)

TABLE		FOOD	
fyldstol	*folding chair*	**mete**	*food*
sceat	*sheet, cloth*	**briw**	*soup*
wapan	*towel, napkin*	**hunig**	*honey*
syx	*knife*	**laf, hlaf**	*loaf*
disc	*dish*	**sealt**	*salt* (**seltan** *to salt*)
sticca	*skewer*	**pipor**	*pepper*

DAIRY	VEGETABLES
meolc *milk*	**beana** *beans*
cyse *cheese*	**grene wyrta** *green vegetables*
butere *butter*	**læc, leac** *leek*

(For more monastic vocabulary, see Bibliography, especially D. Banham, *Monasteriales Indicia*, 1991.)

Anglo-Saxon monastic life

The monasteries were an important bulwark of education and literary activity in the Old English period. Monks led an extremely regulated life, summoned by the ringing of a bell to the frequent monastic hours, i.e. church services and communal prayer, and to intervening periods of manual labour and reading. For those brothers who possessed particular skills, the work periods involved teaching in the monastic school, perhaps composing literary works of various kinds or, more likely, copying other people's compositions in the monastery scriptorium. Periods of silence were built into the working pattern at certain times of the day, including special mealtimes when a reader was employed to read a devotional work while the monks ate in the dining hall.

The great age of the Old English monastery began in the middle of the tenth century, particularly during the reign of Edgar the Peaceable, father of Æthelred the Unready. This king was able to encourage the Continental monastic reform movement promoted by his reforming bishops Æthelwold, Dunstan and Oswald, who were later honoured as saints.

At the beginning of the century, there were many secular minsters but only a few regular monasteries, an example being Glastonbury in the Somerset Levels, but by the year 1000 substantial numbers had been founded or re-founded. From 964, when Æthelwold replaced the secular clergy at the Old Minster in Winchester with his Abingdon monks, it became common for abbots to be appointed as bishops. By the eleventh century, England was unusual for having monastic cathedrals in three of its important cities: at Winchester, Worcester and Canterbury.

Language discovery

Explore the study text on the basis of the following two questions. For further commentary see Grammar 1.

1 *IF, AS IF* AND *WHEN*

Look for the verbs which are used with **gif** *if* and **ðonne** *when*, and **swilce** *as if*. Do you notice anything unusual about the form of these verbs?

2 THE PRONOUN **MAN**

To gain an insight into the Old English pronoun **man / mon**, it is useful to take a very modern situation in a sister language like German. On the doors of restaurants in Mediterranean tourist resorts you sometimes see two notices, one in English and one in German:

ENGLISH SPOKEN   MAN SPRICHT DEUTSCH

Can you analyse the difference in the language of these notices? Both serve to inform English and German speakers that the waiter will understand their language, but what is this little pronoun 'man'?

THE MONASTIC SIGNS

The following extracts from the monastic sign language (ed. Debby Banham, *Monasteriales Indicia*, 1991, see Bibliography) describe hand signals for use during periods of silence in the life of the monastery. As each hand gesture is a sign (**tacen**), an unreal representation, the verb is chosen accordingly.

 15.01

Huniges tacen is þæt þu sette
þinne finger on þine tungan.

The sign of honey is that you should set
your finger on your tongue.

þæt tacen	*sign* 'tahkun' (cf. *token*)
þu sette	subjunctive of **þu settest**
seo tunge	*tongue*

 15.02

Ðonne þu fisc habban wylle
þonne wege þu þyne hand
þam gemete þe he deþ his tægl
þonne he swymð.

When you may want to have fish,
then wave your hand
in the way which it does its tail
when it swims.

wylle	subjunctive of **þu wyllt** (see **willan** in Grammar below)
wegan	*to wave* (cf. **se wæg** also spelt **weg**, *wave, motion*)

15.03

Ðæs diacanes tacen is

þæt mon mid hangiendre hande do

swilce he gehwæde bellan cnyllan wille.

The sign of the deacon is

that one should do with hanging hand

as if one would ring a little bell.

se diacen	*deacon* (or *dean*, see Banham, p. 57)
do	subjunctive of **deþ** *does* (see Grammar)
gehwæde	*little* ('yuh- HWÆ- de')
swilce	*as if* (conjectural **swilce** is followed by the subjunctive)

Grammar 1

1 SUBJUNCTIVE AFTER *IF, AS IF* AND *WHEN*

In Old English the verb dependent on **gif**, **swilce** or **þonne** goes to the end of the clause:

ðonne þu fisc habban wylle…

When you want to have fish…

Because it expresses a hypothesis, the verb is put in the subjunctive as **wylle** or **wille** rather than indicative **wilt**. In this case, you could also translate *whenever you may want to have fish* or, possibly, *if you wanted to have fish, then*… But often a simple translation such as *when you want to have fish* is the most elegant modern equivalent, even if it does not retain all the connotations of the original Old English.

In the opening lines of the *Exeter Book* poem *Wulf and Eadwacer*, there is a clear example of a contrast between the subjunctive after **swylce** *as if* and the indicative after **gif** *if*:

Leodum is minum swylce him mon lac gife.

Willað hy hine aþecgan, gif he on þreat cymeð

To my people it is as if they were given a present

They want to consume him if he comes in a troop

Although the speaker and situation are not stated, the choice of verbs here is nevertheless precise, employing subjunctive and indicative to make distinctions of mood between the **swylce** and the **gif** clauses. There is conjecture in the subjunctive clause **swylce him mon lac gife** where the subjunctive is dependent on **swylce** *as if*. This is followed by the declarative meaning of the indicative **gif he on þreat cymeð** *if he comes in a troop*, which implies that this is the expected course of events. Nevertheless, the subjunctive mood sets the tone for the whole lyric, which is strong on feeling but enigmatic and riddle-like in meaning. (For this poem, see the anthologies by Richard Hamer or Elaine Treharne in the Bibliography.)

2 TRANSLATING THE PRONOUN **MAN / MON**

The much used impersonal pronoun **man**, or in its alternative spelling and pronunciation **mon**, has appeared in various texts so far, usually translated as *they*. Recall the passage from the *Anglo-Saxon Chronicle* in unit 4:

And Cnut cyning com eft to Englalande, and þa on Eastron wæs mycel gemot æt Cyringceastre, þa geutlagode man Æþelweard ealdorman and Eadwig 'ceorla cyngc' (*Anglo-Saxon Chronicle*, version C, the year 1020).

Although the nearest modern equivalent might be the pronoun *one*, used in such expressions *as one should not do that*, this does not cover all the contexts in which **man** is used. Just as the German sentence 'man spricht Deutsch' cannot be translated as *one speaks German*, so **geutlagode man** does not mean *one outlawed…*

As a general rule, Old English **man** can be translated either with *they* or with a passive construction:

þa geutlagode man Æþelweard ealdorman

either   *then they outlawed ealdorman Æthelweard* (where *they* is general)

or   *then ealdorman Æthelweard was outlawed* (passive)

3 VERBS WHICH TAKE A GENITIVE OBJECT

Some verbs take an object in the genitive case. In other words, where you would expect the accusative case, the object of the sentence has genitive endings, for example in the grant of land to Leofwine the Red in unit 11:

Godwine geānn Leofwine readan ðæs dænnes æt Swiðrædingdænne.

Godwine grants to Leofwine the Red the pasture at Southernden.

This example, from unit 11, shows the object in the genitive object after the verb **geunnan** *to grant*. Although it seems to mean literally *Godwine grants of the pasture*, the intended meaning is *Godwine grants the pasture*. It may be useful in understanding this idiomatic usage to consider some phrasal verbs in modern English such as *look for a monastery*, *he will petition for an audience* or expressions such as *to have need of* or *he is desirous of a hearing*. These phrases, which combine verb, adjective or noun with a preposition, are the nearest modern equivalents. In each case the verb does not take a direct object; it needs the preposition to make a well-formed verb phrase.

The genitive follows verbs such as

beþurfan *need*, **brūcan** *enjoy*, **gyrnan** *desire*, **neodian** *require*, **þyrstan** *thirst for*, **wēnan** *expect*, **gewilnian** *desire*

An example from the *Monastic Signs* is the word **disc** *dish*, put into the genitive as object of the verb **beþurfan** *to need*:

Gif þe disces beþurfe, þonne hefe þu up þine oþre hand and tospræd þine fingras.

If you have need of a dish, then raise up your other hand and spread your fingers.

The verb **wilnian** *to desire, seek* is used in a similar way; in the *Life of Euphrosyne*, for instance, the gate-keeper of the monastery reports to the abbot the arrival of a mysterious young stranger:

Þa eode se geatweard to þam abbode, and cwæð him to, 'Fæder, her is cumen an eunuchus of cinges hirede, wilnað þinre spræce.'

Then the gate-keeper went to the abbot and said to him, 'Father, a eunuch has come here from the king's court and seeks an audience with you' [literally desires of your speech*].*

The Life of Euphrosyne

A key to the following passage from *The Life of Euphrosyne* is a set of antonyms or opposites: **wiflic–werlic**, **fæmne–wer**, **bryd–brydguma**, **æfentid–mergen** (see word index at the back of the book).

Where does Euphrosyne decide to go, and how can she put this plan into action?

15.04

Eufrosina þa þohte þus

Euphrosyne then thought thus

Eufrosina þa þohte þus cweðende, 'Gif ic nu fare to fæmnena mynstre, þonne secð min fæder me þær, and me þær findað, þonne nimð he me neadunga ðanon for mines brydguman þingan. Ac ic wille faran to wera mynstre þær nan man min ne wene.' Heo þa þone wiflican gegyrlan ofdyde, and hi gescrydde mid werlicum. And on æfentid gewat of hire healle, and nam mid hire fiftig mancsas, and þa niht hi gehydde on digelre stowe.

seo fæmne	*virgin, woman* (genitive plural **fæmn-ena**)
nimð	*takes*
neadunga	*by force*
ðanon	*thence, from there*
for mines … **þingan**	*for the sake of my* …
wene	*expect* (present subjunctive of **wēnan** *suppose, expect*)
se gegyrela, gegierela	*clothing* (cf. **gearwian** and **ge-gierwan** *to prepare, clothe*)
scrydan	*to clothe* (from **þæt scrud** *clothing, garment*, cf. *shroud*)
hydan	*hide* (**hi gehydde** *hid herself*, cf. **hi gescrydde** *clothed herself*)
digel	*secret*

In a study on the etymology of the word *girl*, Fred C. Robinson has argued that Middle English **gerle** does not, as is sometimes stated, come into English in the medieval period as a Low German loanword *'gör'* *child*. Instead, he argues by analogy. The Old English word **bratt** originally meant *over-garment*, *apron*, and then later denoted *a pinafore* as worn by a child. Eventually the child was referred to by the garment they wore, *the brat*. Similarly with **gegierla**. With its optional **ge-** prefix omitted, this is **gierla**, *a garment worn by a young woman*, which came to be associated with the *girl* herself.

 15.05

Þa eode se geatweard to þam abbode

Then the gate-keeper went to the abbot

Þa þæs on mergen com Pafnutius to þære ceastre, and þa æfter Godes willan eode he into cyrcan. Eufrosina betwux þysum com to þam mynstre, þe hire fæder tó sohte. Þa eode se geatweard to þam abbode, and cwæð him to, 'Fæder, her is cumen an eunuchus of cinges hirede, wilnað þinre spræce.'

Se abbod þa ut eode, and heo sona feoll to his fotum, and onfangenre bletsunge hí togædere gesæton.

se mergen	morning (also **morgen** *morn*)
se geatweard	gate-keeper
seo spræc	speech 'spræch'
tó	towards
feoll	fell (from **feallan** *to fall*)
onfangenre bletsunge	having received a blessing (imitates a Latin construction)
gesæton	they sat (**sittan**)

 15.06

For hwilcum þingum come þu hider?

For what reasons did you come here?

Þa cwæð se abbod, 'Bearn, for hwilcum þingum come þu hider?'

Ða cwæð heo, 'Ic wæs on cinges hirede, and ic eom eunuchus, and ic symle wilnode to munuclicum life gecyrran. Ac þyllic lif nis nu gewunelic on ure ceastre. Nu geaxode ic eowre mæran drohtnunge, and min willa is ðæt ic mid eow eardian mote, gif eower willa þæt bið.'

for hwilcum þingum	for what reasons
gecyrran	to convert, turn
þyllic	such
gewunelic	usual
geaxian, geacsian	to hear of (perfective **ge-** + **āscian** *to ask*; see unit 4)
mære	great, famous
seo drohtnung	way of life
eardian	to live, dwell

Reread the passages from *The Life of Euphrosyne* and answer the questions below.

1 Why does Euphrosyne avoid the women's convent?

_____

2 What does Euphrosyne do before departing from the hall?

_____

3 What happens when the abbot comes out to see the visitor?

_____

4 Why does the stranger want to join the monastery?

_____

Grammar 2

COMPARING REGULAR AND IRREGULAR VERBS

Review the forms of the regular verbs **deman** *judge* (weak verb) and **cuman** *come* (strong verb) and compare them with the paradigm for three frequent but irregular verbs **dōn** *do*, **willan** *want* and **gān** *go* (note long vowels marked **ā, ē, ō, æ**):

	Regular		Irregular		
Weak	Strong		dōn	willan	gān
infinitive	dēman	cuman	dōn	willan	gān
present indicative					
1 singular	dēme	cume	dō	wille	gā
2	dēmst	cymst	dēst	wilt	gǣst
3	dēmð	cymð	dēð	wile	gǣð
1, 2, 3 plural	dēmað	cumað	dōð	willað	gāð
present subjunctive					
1, 2, 3	dēme	cume	dō	wille	gā
1, 2, 3	dēmen	cumen	dōn	willen	gān
past indicative					
1, 3 singular	dēmde	cōm	dyde	wolde	ēode
2	dēmdest	cōme	dydest	woldest	ēodest
1, 2, 3 plural	dēmdon	cōmon	dydon	woldon	ēodon
past subjunctive					
1, 2, 3	dēmde	cōme	dyde	wolde	ēode
1, 2, 3	dēmden	cōmen	dyden	wolden	ēoden

Reading

MORE EXTRACTS FROM THE OLD ENGLISH *THE MONASTIC SIGNS*

The Old English treatise *The Monastic Signs* occurs in an eleventh-century compendium of Benedictine monastic texts in London, British Library, Cotton Tiberius A. iii.

Ærest þæs abbudes tacen is þæt mon his twegen fingras to heafde asette, and his feax mid genime.

First the abbot's sign is that you put your two fingers to your head and take hold of your hair.

Ðonne is þæs horderes tacen þæt mon wrænce mid is hand swilce he wille loc hunlucan.

Then the cellarer's sign is that one turns with one's hand as if one wanted to open a lock.

Gyf þu mete-rædere fyldstol habban wille, oþþe oþrum men, þonne clæm þu þine handa togædere and wege hi, þam gemete þe þu dest þonne þu hine fyldan wylt.

If you want to have a folding stool for the mealtime-reader for another person, then put your hands together and move them in the way that you do when you want to fold it.

Gyf þu sceat habban wille oððe wapan, þonne sete þu þine twa handa ofer þinum bearme and tobræd hi swillce sceat astrecce.

If you want to have a sheet or a napkin, then place your two hands over your lap and spread them as if you were stretching out a sheet.

More riddles from the *Exeter Book*

The *Exeter Book* was certainly owned by bishop Leofric in Exeter from the mid-eleventh century, but by then the book had already been in use for several generations. Scholars agree that the handwriting indicates a date of origin of about 975, although opinions differ as to who wrote the book and who owned it before Leofric. While some have made a case for Exeter as the actual origin of the manuscript, others argue for a large writing workshop in southwest England that had connections with Canterbury. One possibility is the great abbey at Glastonbury.

A striking feature of the *Exeter Book* is the variety of poems it contains, and the following two poems illustrate this range. Both suggest a monastic context, of work and worship, but in different moods, one making fun of a colleague, the other celebrating the mysteries of the faith.

What are the solutions?

RIDDLE 47

> **Moððe word fræt: me þæt þuhte**
> **wrætlicu wyrd,   þa ic þæt wundor gefrægn,**
> **þæt se wyrm forswealg   wera gide sumes,**
> **þeof in þystro,   þrymfæstne cwide**

5   ond þæs strangan staþol.   Stælgiest ne wæs

wihte þy gleawra,   þe he þam wordum swealg.

A moth ate words: that seemed to me

a wondrous fate, when I heard of that wonder,

that the worm swallowed a man's song,

a thief in the dark (swallowed) a glorious saying

and its strong foundation. The stealing guest was

was not one bit the wiser when he swallowed the words.

LANGUAGE INSIGHT

The word **þrymfæst** is a compound, made up of **þrymm** *glory* and **fæst** *firm*, forming a poetic adjective *glorious*. Similar compound adjectives include: **tirfæst** *glorious*, **arfæst** *gracious*, **stedefæst** *steadfast*, **gemetfæst** *moderate*. When the adjective **fæst** is used as an adverb it becomes **fæstlice** (e.g. unit 21, *The Battle of Maldon*, line 81).

RIDDLE 48

Ic gefrægn for hæleþum   hring endean,

torhtne butan tungan,   tila (þeah he hlude

stefne ne cirmde)   strongum wordum.

Sinc for secgum   swigende cwæð:

5   'Gehæle mec,   helpend gæstra.'

Ryne ongietan   readan goldes

guman galdorcwide,   gleawe beþencan

hyra hælo to Gode,   swa se hring gecwæð.

I heard a ring speaking before men,

bright, tongueless, prosperously (though with a loud

voice it did not speak) with strong words.

The treasure before men silently spoke:

'Save me, helper of souls.'

May men understand the mysteries of the red gold,

the magical speech, may they wisely ponder

their salvation in God, as the ring said.

Test yourself

Look through the list of words in the vocabulary builder in this unit and identify the missing Old English word and its translation in the following descriptions from *The Monastic Signs*:

Ðæs (1a) _____ taccen is þe þa cild bewat þæt man set his twegen fingras on his twa eagan and hebbe up his litlan finger.

*The **(1b)** _____'s sign who guides the children is that one places his fingers on his two eyes and raises up his little finger.*

Gyf þe (2a) _____ genyodige þonne snid þu mid þinum fingre ofer þonne oþerne swylce þu cyrfan wille.

*If you have need of a **(2b)** _____ you cut with your finger over the other as if you wanted to carve.*

(3a) _____ tacan is þæt þu wecge þine fyst swilce þu
(3b) _____ hrere.

*The sign of **(3c)** _____ is that you move your fist as if you were stirring*
(3d) _____.

Ðonne þu (4a) _____ habban wylle, þonne geþeoddum þinum þrim fingerum hryse þine hand swylce þu hwæt (4b) _____ wylle.

*When you want to have **(4c)** _____then, with your three fingers joined, drop your hand as if you want **(4d)** _____ something.*

SELF-CHECK

I CAN ...
identify the subjunctive mood in clauses starting with *if*, *as if* and *when*
translate the pronoun **mon / man**
recognize verbs that take an object in the genitive case
conjugate the irregular verbs **dōn, willan, gān**

16 *Đæt gelamp on sumere nihte*
It happened one night

In this unit you will learn about:
- ▶ *hermits in Anglo-Saxon England*
- ▶ *connections between the definite article* the *and the personal pronoun* he, she, it
- ▶ *the determiner* **sum**
- ▶ *conjunctions and adverbs of time*
- ▶ *word order and correlation with* **sona swa** *as soon as*

You will read:
- ▶ *the two 'raven episodes' from the Old English prose* Life of St Guthlac
- ▶ *extracts from the Old English* Bede *and the* Anglo-Saxon Chronicle

 16.00

Đæt gelamp on sumere nihte
It happened one night

Vocabulary builder

ADVERBS OF TIME

þa	*then*
ongean	*again*
sona	*immediately*
þonne	*then*
gyta	*still*
iu geara	*years before*
iu	*formerly*
ær	*previously*
eft	*back*
þanon	*whence, from where*

CONJUNCTIONS

þa	*when*
mid þy	*while*
sona swa	*as soon as*
efne swa	*as if*
þæs	*when*
þætte	*that*
swa hwær swa	*wherever*

| for þon ðe | because |
| hwær | where |

ADVERBIALS OF TIME

on sumere nihte	one night
on þam ylcan timan	at the same time
nænig hwil to þan	not long afterwards
ymbe twa winter	after two winters

Hermits in Anglo-Saxon England

The hermit or anchorite, the spiritual warrior who spends his time in solitude and meditation; the holy man who lives apart but acts as guide and adviser to people who take the trouble to seek him out in his wilderness home: this ideal seems to have gone out of fashion in tenth-century England. The reasons are not hard to see. First, the world had become a more dangerous place, with Viking attacks putting an end to the solitary life from a practical point of view. Second, the Benedictine revival – as we saw in unit 15 – had made the communal monastic life the ideal to which people aspired.

However, in the eleventh century, a number of Old English texts appear that are variously concerned with hermits and anchorites; they suggest that an interest in the way of the hermit was reviving. One of these texts is a recopying of the ninth-century *Old English Life of St Guthlac*, a story with a long history going back to the early 700s (see Reading below). Guthlac lived as a hermit on what was then the island of Crowland in the Fens of Lincolnshire. In the story, Guthlac is presented as having qualities of spiritual fortitude, closeness to nature and (more unusually) a sense of humour – as seen, for instance, in the episode of the thieving raven (**se hrefn**).

The first 'raven episode' from the OE prose *Life of Guthlac*:

 16.01

THE THIEVING RAVEN

Ðæt gelamp on sumere nihte þæt þær com sum man to þæs halgan weres spræce. Mid þy he þær dagas wunode, þa gelamp hit, þæt he sum gewrit awrat on cartan. Ða he hæfde þæt gewrit awriten, þa eode he ut. Ða com þær sum hrefn inn; sona swa he þa cartan geseah, þa genam he hig sona and gewat mid on þæne fenn. Sona swa se foresæda cuma ongean com, þa geseah he þone hrefen þa cartan beran, þa wæs he sona swyðe unbliþe.

It happened one night that there came a certain man for talk with the holy man. While he was staying there a few days, it happened that he wrote out a document on a piece of parchment. When he had written the document he went out. Then a raven came in; as soon as he saw the parchment he immediately took it and departed with it into the fen. As soon as the aforesaid guest came back again, then he saw the raven carrying the parchment, [and] then he was immediately very distraught.

ðæt gelamp	*it happened* 'yuh-LAMP' (a set phrase; present tense **gelimpeð**)	
mid þy	*while*	
dagas	*(a few) days* (irregular plural of **dæg** *day*)	
wunian	*remained* (from **wunian**, cf. German 'wohnen' to live, inhabit)	
awrat	*wrote* (past tense of **awritan** *to write*)	
awriten	*written* (past participle)	
ut	*out*	
inn	*in*	
sona swa	*as soon as*	
ongean	*back again*	
sona	*immediately*	
unbliþe	*unhappy* (**un** + **bliþe** *happy*)	

Language discovery

Look through the above text for examples of:

1 the third person pronoun and the definite article *the*

2 indefinite articles, i.e. words for *a* or *an*

3 other determiners, e.g. *some*, *this*

4 conjunctions, e.g. *when*, *as soon as* etc. What do you notice about word order and conjunctions?

For further assistance, see discussion below. In this section we will anticipate and explore various features of the language in the episode of Guthlac and the thieving raven, before presenting the full story.

1 COMPARING DEFINITE ARTICLE AND PERSONAL PRONOUN

The following phrases appear in the passages from the OE *Guthlac*.

	Definite article	pronoun
Masculine		
nominative	**se halga wer** *the holy man*	**hē**
accusative	**þone hrefn** *the raven* (direct object)	**hine**
genitive	**þæs halgan weres** *the holy man's*	**his**
dative	**on þam ylcan timan** *at the same time*	**him**
Neuter		
nominative	**þæt gewrit** *the document*	**hit**
accusative	**þæt gewrit** *the document* (object)	**hit**
genitive	**þæs huses** *of the house*	**his**
dative	**to þam yglande** *to the island*	**him**

Feminine		
nominative	**seo carta** *the parchment*	**hēo**
accusative	**þa cartan** *the parchment* (object)	**hig**
genitive	**þære cartan** *of the parchment*	**hire**
dative	**to þære cartan** *to the parchment*	**hire**

2 DETERMINERS

Determiners are words like *a, the, this, that, few*. A modern speaker of English will choose between determiners such as the articles (*a* or *the*), demonstrative pronouns (*this* or *that*) and quantifiers (*no, few, some, five* etc.). In modern English, we make a distinction between the indefinite article *a* and the definite article *the*. Although Old English did have a way of signalling definiteness using **se**, **seo**, **þæt** (as we have just seen in 1), the language did not as yet have an indefinite article. The adjectives **ān** *one* and **sum** *a certain* were used instead.

3 THE USE OF THE DETERMINER **SUM**

The phrase **sum man** often appears in Old English narratives as a way of introducing a new character at the beginning of a new episode. A strictly literal translation would be *a certain man* but quite often the phrase simply means *a man*. Frequently, then, **sum** corresponds to the modern English indefinite article *a, an*, although in some contexts its meaning can be more specific than simply *a*. The use of **sum** is illustrated here with extracts from the first of the two 'raven episodes' in the Old English prose *Life of St Guthlac*.

In *The Life of St Guthlac*, the first raven episode begins with the words:

Ðæt gelamp on sumere nihte þæt þær com sum man to þæs halgan weres spræce.

It happened one night that there came a certain man for the holy man's conversation [i.e. for talk with the holy man].

The storytelling formula *one night* is here **on sumere niht**, literally *on a certain night*. The man's name is not given, he remains identified simply as **sum man**, but the implication is that he will be referred to again in the rest of the episode. As in modern colloquial English, *some man came to see him*, the determiner is indefinite but specific. If his name were to be given here, it would no doubt follow the pattern found in the second 'raven's episode', which names a certain nobleman **þæs nama wæs Æþelbald** *whose name was Æthelbald*.

While he is staying a few days at Guthlac's fenland hermitage the man copies out a **gewrit** (*document*) on a leaf of parchment; then, having completed his task, he goes out:

Mid þy he þær dagas wunode, þa gelamp hit, þæt he sum gewrit awrat on cartan. Þa he hæfde þæt gewrit awriten, þa eode he ut.

While he was staying there a few days, it happened that he wrote a document on a piece of parchment. When he had written the document he went out.

Notice the change from the first mention of **sum gewrit** (a certain indefinite but specific document) to the second mention, **þæt gewrit** (any subsequent reference can refer to the document using the definite article).

Having introduced his human and inanimate protagonists, *some man* and *some document*, the narrator now introduces his third, an animate protagonist *some raven*:

Ða com þær sum hrefn inn; sona swa he þa cartan geseah, þa genam he hig sona and gewat mid on þæne fenn.

Two possible translations suggest themselves:

Either *Then some raven came in; as soon as he saw the parchment he immediately took it and departed with it into the fen.*

Or *Then there came in a raven; as soon as it saw the parchment it took it and departed with it into the fen.*

The translation affects the interpretation. It may not be correct to render the grammatical gender of **he** (referring back to the masculine noun **hrefn**) as *it*. (On natural and grammatical gender, look back to unit 5). Arguably the best translation is *a raven*; too much emphasis being placed on the animate agency of the bird if we translate *some raven came in*. But this may in fact be the very point of the story: the bird really is wilful, and Guthlac, who can communicate with other creatures, rebukes him for his cruelty. This is how the Old English narrator tells the story and (as you will see) he uses the determiner **sum** twice more in the episode, each time introducing – if briefly – a new agent in the plot: a lake and a reedbed.

> **LANGUAGE INSIGHT**
>
> In the later development of the English language, the determiner **sum** declined in use and was mostly replaced by **ān**, which subsequently divided into two words: the determiner *one* as in *one night* and the indefinite article *a* and *an*.

The endings on sum

Many examples of the form and use of **sum** can be found by looking through a text such as *The Life of St Guthlac* and noting examples, quite often at the beginning of new chapters or, as we have seen in this unit, at new turns in the story:

ch. 9 **þa com he to sumum mere**

then he came to a certain lake

ch. 12 **wæs on Eastenglalande sum man æþeles cynnes þæs nama wæs Hwætred**

there was in East Anglia a man of noble kin whose name was Hwætred

ch. 13 **swilce eac gelamp on sumne sæl …**

similarly also it happened at one time…

ch. 19 **wæs on sumre tíde þæt …**

it happened at one time that…

These endings have been encountered before, in various contexts and parts of speech:

- the common **-ne** ending marks masculine accusative

- the dative has **-um** in the masculine and neuter

- the feminine genitive and dative ending is **-re**.

In the expression **sum man æþeles cynnes** *a man of noble kindred*, the **-es** endings indicate the genitive *of*. The importance of the notion of **æþel cynn** *noble kindred* in Old English society is reflected in words like **cyning** *king*, **cynelic** *royal*, **Angelcynn** *the English*, **Wealhcynn** *the Welsh*. More general uses include **stancynn** *type of stone* (unit 5) and **gecynd** *nature*, modern English *kind*.

4 WORD ORDER AND CONJUNCTIONS

The fast-paced narrative of the Guthlac story affords a good opportunity to review word order after conjunctions of time.

In this passage, look out for the conjunctions **mid þy** *while* and **sona swa** *as soon as*; usually the verb goes to the end of the clause or towards the end of that part of the sentence (in contrast to the modern English equivalent):

mid þy he þær dagas wunode, þa gelamp hit þæt…

while he was staying there a few days, it happened that…

sona swa he þa cartan geseah, þa genam he hig sona

as soon as he saw the parchment, then he took it at once

Another example from later in the passage – worth studying as it marks a key moment in the story – is **efne swa** *even as if*, a conjunction which (like **swilce**) takes a subjunctive and sends the verb to the end of the clause:

efne swa hig mannes hand þær ahengce

even as if a man's hand had hung it there.

The same pattern is usually found after the temporal phrases *then it happened that …, it was not long afterwards that …* . Here the verb also tends to go near the end of the sentence:

Mid þy he þær dagas wunode, þa gelamp hit þæt he sum gewrit awrat on cartan.

While he was staying there a few days, it happened that he wrote out a document on a piece of parchment.

Perhaps for reasons of emphasis the writer chose to end with the word **cartan**. In the first sentence of the story, too, it looks as if the narrator avoids putting the verb at the end by using the 'empty subject' in the phrase *there came* and so allowing the sentence to conclude with a heavy emphasis on the hermit and the purpose of the visit:

Ðæt gelamp on sumere nihte þæt þær com sum man to þæs halgan weres spræce.

It happened one night that there came a certain man for talk with the holy man.

5 CORRELATION

A final point on style, syntax and sentence structure in this passage is the way the conjunction **sona swa** is recapitulated and echoed in the main clause by the adverbs **þa** *then* and **sona** *immediately*:

Ða com þær sum hrefn inn; <u>sona swa</u> he þa cartan geseah, <u>þa</u> genam he hig <u>sona</u> and gewat mid on þæne fenn.

<u>Then</u> there came a raven in; <u>as soon as</u> he saw the parchment <u>then</u> he took it <u>immediately</u> and departed with it into the fen.

<u>Sona swa</u> se foresæda cuma ongean com, <u>þa</u> geseah he þone hrefen þa cartan beran, þa wæs he <u>sona</u> swyðe unbliþe.

<u>As soon as</u> the aforesaid guest came back again, <u>then</u> he saw the raven carrying the parchment, [and] <u>then</u> he was <u>immediately</u> very distraught.

This is rather like the correlation of **þa… þa** meaning *when … then*, which also occurs in the passage (look back to unit 6 for more discussion):

Þa he hæfde þæt gewrit awriten, <u>þa</u> eode he ut.

<u>When</u> he had written the document, <u>then</u> he went out.

By such methods of correlation, the Old English narrative is held together and the connections between the various clauses of the sentence are made clearer and tighter.

One final example of correlation comes from the mouth of the hermit himself. This is the construction **swa… swa… þonne**… *as… so… then…* found in the advice which Guthlac gives to his guest on how to recover the stolen parchment:

'Ne beo þu broþor sarig, ac <u>swa</u> se hrefn þurh þa fennas upp afligeð, <u>swa</u> þu him æfter row; þonne metest þu þæt gewrit.'

'Do not be sad, brother, but <u>as</u> the raven flies up through the fens, <u>so</u> you row after him; then you will find the document.'

Guthlac, the raven, and the stolen parchment

Using the notes from Language discovery as a basis, study the whole of the story. Try listening and reading it out loud, at a lively pace.

16.02

Ðæt gelamp on sumere nihte

It happened one night

Ðæt gelamp on sumere nihte þæt þær com sum man to þæs halgan weres spræce. Mid þy he þær dagas wunode, þa gelamp hit, þæt he sum gewrit awrat on cartan. Þa he hæfde þæt gewrit awriten, þa eode he ut. Ða com þær sum hrefn inn; sona swa he þa cartan geseah, þa genam he hig sona and gewat mid on þæne fenn. Sona swa se foresæda cuma ongean com, þa geseah he þone hrefen þa cartan beran, þa wæs he sona swyðe unbliþe.

Ða wæs on þam ylcan timan, þæt se halga wer Guðlac ut of his cyrcan eode; þa geseah he þone broþor sarig. Þa frefrode he hine and him to cwæð, 'Ne beo þu broþor sarig, ac swa se hrefn þurh þa fennas upp afligeð, swa þu him æfter row; þonne metest þu þæt gewrit.'

Næs þa nænig hwil to þan, þæt he to scipe eode se ylca þe þæt gewrit wrat. Mid þy he þurh þa fenland reow þa com he to sumum mere, þe wel neah þam eglande wæs; þa wæs þær on middan þam mere sum hreodbed; þa hangode seo carte on þam hreode, efne swa hig mannes hand þær ahengce; and he sona þa bliþe feng to þære cartan, and he wundriende to þam Godes were brohte…

sarig	*sad*
frēfran	*to console*
mētan	*meet, find* (**mētt, mētte, mētton, gemēted**)
bliþe	*happy* (**unbliþe** *unhappy*)

Check your comprehension of the passage against the translation:

It happened one night that there came a certain man for talk with the holy man. While he was staying there a few days, it happened that he wrote out a document on a piece of parchment. When he had written the document he went out. Then a certain raven came in; as soon as he saw the parchment he immediately took it and departed with it into the fen. As soon as the aforesaid guest came back again, then he saw the raven carrying the parchment, [and] then he was immediately very distraught. Then it happened at the same time that the holy man Guthlac came out of his church; then he saw the brother sad. Whereupon he consoled him and said to him, 'Do not be sad, brother, but as the raven flies up through the fens, so you row after him; then you will find the document.'

It was not any time before he went to his ship – the same one who wrote the document. As he rowed through the fenlands he came to a certain lake, which was well near to the island; there was in the middle of the lake a certain reed-bed and there was the parchment hanging on the reed as if a man's hand had hung it there. And immediately he took the parchment, and marvelling he brought it to the man of God.

Cultural contexts

Part of the Guthlac prose narrative occurs in the form of a sermon in the tenth-century *Vercelli Book*, but the only full copy of the Old English prose *Life of Guthlac* appears in British Library manuscript Cotton Vespasian D. xxi, copied in the eleventh century. Although separated from its original binding, it looks – from the evidence of parchment and script – as if this story occurred originally as the final piece in a manuscript of the Old English *Hexateuch* translation, following the version of the biblical *Judges* by Ælfric, abbot of Eynsham, friend of Wulfstan and a prolific writer of sermons in the late Old English church.

Reading

The extracts below present other passages illustrating events in the biography of the Fenland hermit Guthlac, along with some related material.

1 FROM THE *ANGLO-SAXON CHRONICLE* AD 714

The first mention of Guthlac in Old English is a brief entry in the *Anglo-Saxon Chronicle* for the year 714, which may be translated as *Here the holy Guthlac departed*, where *the holy Guthlac* is the normal way of expressing Saint Guthlac in Old English, similar to the equivalent German phrase 'der heilige Guthlac'. The following is the text in the D Chronicle:

AN. .dccccxi.

AN. .dccccxii.

AN. .dccccxiii.

AN. .dccccxiiii. Her geferde Guðlac se halga.

For the preceding three years (711–13), the chronicler had apparently found nothing worth recording and the date of Guthlac's passing away thus stands out prominently on the manuscript page.

2 FINDING A VOCATION: FROM *THE LIFE OF GUTHLAC*

Historically, Guthlac was a famous Mercian nobleman of the late seventh century who became profoundly dissatisfied with his warrior lifestyle and converted first to the monastic life and then to the solitary isolation of an anchorite's cell in the wild fenland of Crowland near Peterborough.

Guthlac's Life was told first in Latin by the Mercian writer Felix and then in Old English by two anonymous poets (Guthlac A and Guthlac B in the *Exeter Book*). Probably during the reign of king Alfred in the ninth century, when Old English became a medium of education, the Latin life was translated into Old English prose. The following extract records the moment when Guthlac decides to follow his vocation:

Ða ymbe twa winter, þæs he his lif swa leofode under munuchade, þæt he þa ongan wilnian westenes and sundersetle. Mid þy he gehyrde secgan and he leornode be þam ancerum, þe geara on westene and on sundorsettlum for Godes naman wilnodon and heora life leofodon, ða wæs his heorte innan þurh godes gifu onbryrdod, þæt he westenes gewilnode.

After two winters when he had lived his life in monastic orders, he began to yearn for the wilderness and a solitary cell. And when he heard tell and learned of the anchorites who, for the name of God, for many years desired the desert and lived the life of seclusion, then his heart was inspired within by God's grace so that he desired the wilderness.

3 THE DESCRIPTION OF THE HERMIT FURSA, FROM THE OLD ENGLISH *BEDE*, III.19

The events in the life of Guthlac and its various retellings were inspired by the stories of St Antony and the other Desert Fathers, the first hermits who had inhabited the Egyptian desert in the early Christian centuries. The desire to live in the desert, or in northern European terms 'the wild', was taken up by Irish pilgrims and hermits. Felix wrote about Guthlac with the model of the Irish hermit, Fursey, in mind. For a comparison with Fursey, we may turn to the

Ecclesiastical History of the English Nation by Bede, the greatest writer and historian of the early Anglo-Saxon period. In the time of king Alfred, Bede's Latin text was translated into Old English.

Mid ðy ðe Sigeberht þa gyta rice hæfde, cwom of Hibernia Scotta ealonde halig wer sum, þæs noma wæs Furseus. Se wæs in wordum and dædum beorht and scinende, swelce he wæs in æðelum mægenum mære geworden. Wilnade he, þætte he swa hwær swa he gelimplice stowe findan meahte, þæt he wolde for Godes noman in elþeodignisse lifian. [ed. T. Miller, p. 210]

While Sigeberht was still on the throne, there came from Ireland, the island of the Scots, a holy man, Fursey by name. He was bright and shining in words and deeds, just as he had become famous for his noble virtues. He desired, wherever he might find a suitable place, that he would live, for the name of God, on pilgrimage.

This description of Fursa the saint may be compared with that of Guthlac in extract no. 7 below.

4 THE THREE IRISH PILGRIMS, FROM THE *ANGLO-SAXON CHRONICLE*

The following is a famous story of the visit of the three Irish pilgrims to king Alfred's court in the year 891. In the short passage given in Old English, compare Fursa's ideal of living *on pilgrimage* with the Irishmen's desire to be **on elþeodignesse**; the same wording is used in each case.

In this year the Viking army went to the east, and king Earnulf, with the East Franks, Saxons and Bavarians, fought against the mounted army and put them to flight before the ships had arrived.

[and þry Scottas comon to Ælfrede cynge on anum bate butan ælcum gereþrum of Hibernia, þanon hie bestælon for þon ðe hi woldon for Godes lufon on elþeodignesse beon, and hi ne rohton hwær.]

And three Scots in a boat without any oars came to king Alfred from Ireland, which they left because they wanted, for the love of God, to be on pilgrimage; and they did not care where.

The boat they travelled in was made of two and half hides; they took with them enough that they had food for seven nights, and after the seven nights they came to land in Cornwall, and they went from there to king Alfred. Their names were Dublasne, Machbethu and Maelmumin. And Swifneh died, the best teacher there was among the Scots. In the same year after Easter around Rogationtide, or earlier, the star appeared that is called, in Latin, a 'cometa'. Some men say in English that it is 'the long-haired star', because long beams of light come out of it on one side or the other.

5 GUTHLAC'S CELL

In the Old English prose *Life of Guthlac*, *the great barrow* (**mycel hlæw**) where Guthlac takes up his abode is associated with buried treasure plundered by robbers long ago and now the haunt of demons, with which he must do spiritual battle before he can make the place habitable and fit for visitors:

Wæs þær in þam sprecenan iglande sum mycel hlæw of eorðan geworht, þone ylcan hlæw men iu geara men bræcon and dulfon for feos þingum.

There was there in the above-mentioned island a certain great barrow made of earth, which same barrow in former years men broke into and dug up for the sake of its treasure.

(For another significant **hlæw**, see the reading texts in unit 19.)

6 *THE WIFE'S LAMENT*

In the *Exeter Book* poem *The Wife's Lament*, the speaker appears to have been exiled into the wilderness to an earthen cave rather like a mound or barrow. Situated under an oak-tree in a forest grove, this is a landscape with pagan associations (lines 27–32):

Heht mec mon wunian   on wuda bearwe,

under actreo   in þam eorðscræfe.

Eald is þes eorðsele,   eal ic eom oflongad,

sindon dena dimme,   duna uphea,

bitre burgtunas   brerum beweaxne,

wic wynna leas.

They ordered me to dwell in a forest grove,

under oak tree in the earth cave.

This earthen hall is old, I am all longing,

the valleys are dim, the hills up high,

the bitter town dwellings are grown over with briars,

the settlement joyless.

7 A DESCRIPTION OF THE SAINT, FROM THE OLD ENGLISH *GUTHLAC*

Wæs he on ansine mycel and on lichaman clæne, wynsum on his mode and wlitig on ansyne; he wæs liðe and gemetfæst on his worde, and he wæs geþyldig and eadmod; and á seo godcunde lufu on hys heortan hat and byrnende. [ed. Gonser, p. 111]

He was in appearance large, in body clean, cheerful in his mind and handsome of face; he was gentle and modest in his speech, and he was patient and humble; and ever the divine love hot and burning in his heart.

Test yourself

The second 'raven episode' from *The Life of St Guthlac*.

Read the text and answer the questions below.

Note the following words and phrases: **begytan æt** to *acquire from*, **forlætan** to *leave behind*, **gesegon** *saw*, **þæt nebb** *beak*, **þæt þæc** *thatch*, **þrean** to *rebuke*, **hyrsumode** *obeyed*, **fugel** *bird*, **westen** *wilderness*, **seo gyrd** *staff*, **seo hyð** *hithe*, i.e. *landing place*, **þæt tacen** *signal*, **se andwlita** *face*, **feng** to *began, took to*, **smerciende** *smiling*, **seo bletsung** *blessing*.

Þa wolde he [Æþelbald] to þæs halgan weres sprace cuman, beget þa æt Wilfride, þæt he hine to þam Godes were gelædde; and hi þa sona on scipe eodon and ferdon to þam yglande þær se halga wer Guthlac on wæs.

Ða hi þa to þam halgan were comon, þa hæfde Wilfrið forleten his glofan on þam scipe; and hi þa wið þone halgan wer spræcon. He þa se eadiga wer Guthlac acsode hi hwæðer hi ænig þinc æfter heom on þam scipe forleton, swa him God ealle þa diglan þingc cuð gedyde. Þa andswarode him Wilfrið and cwæð þæt he forlete his twa glofan on þam scipe.

Næs þa nænig hwil to þan, sona swa hi ut of þam in eodon þa gesegon hi þone hræfn mid þan sweartan nebbe þa glofe teran uppe on anes huses þæce. He þa sona se halga wer Guðlac þone hrefn mid his worde þreade for his reþnysse, and he þa his worda hyrsumode; swa fleah se fugel west ofer þæt westen. He þa Wilfrið mid gyrde of þæs huses hrofe þa glofe geræhte.

Swylce næs eac nænig hwil to þam, sona comon þær þry men to þære hyðe and þær tacn slogon. Þa sona eode se halga wer Guðlac út to þam mannum mid bliðum andwlite and gode mode; he þa spæc wið þam mannum. Mid þan þe hi faran woldon, þa brohton hi forð ane glofe, sædon þæt heo of anes hrefnes muðe feolle. He se halga wer Guþlac sona to smerciende feng, and heom his bletsunge sealde, and hi eft ferdon; and he eft ageaf þa glofe þam þe hi ær ahte.

1 How did the nobleman Æthelbald find his way to Guthlac's hermitage?

_____

2 What had Wilfrid done with his gloves? How did Guthlac know this?

_____

3 What did they realize had happened when they came out of the house?

_____

4 Why did the raven fly away?

_____

5 What did the three men do as soon as they arrived at the landing place?

_____

6 Why had they come to the hermitage?

_____

7 What words or phrases are used to describe Guthlac's state of mind?

_____

8 Review both raven episodes and make a list of nouns whose gender you can identify from the context. Pay careful attention to the endings of any definite articles or adjectives that occur with the nouns.

_____

_____

_____

_____

17

And Æþelnoð biscop for to Rome
And bishop Æthelnoth travelled to Rome

In this unit you will learn about:
▶ *the career of Archbishop Æthelnoth*
▶ *different types of adverb*
▶ *adverbial phrases*
▶ *travels to Rome*
▶ *complex syntax and word order*
▶ *the translation of St Alphege*
▶ *stylistic analysis of Old English prose*

You will read:
▶ *passages from the* Anglo-Saxon Chronicle *version D 1020–1023*
▶ *Cnut's writ to Canterbury of 1035 concerning archbishop Æthelnoth*

Ⓥ Vocabulary builder

MANNER

hraðe	*quickly*
eadmodlice	*humbly*
bliðelice	*happily*
eallunga	*completely*

LOCATION

hēr	*here*
þær	*there*

DIRECTION

hām	*home*
þider	*to there*
hider	*to here*
feorr	*far*
ut	*out*
norð	*northward*
suð	*southward*

MOVEMENT FROM

þonan	*from there*
heonan	*from here*
feorran	*from afar*
utan	*from outside*
norðan	*from the north*
suðan	*from the south*

Language discovery

In the following sentences identify the adverbials, either a single-word adverb, or a multi-word phrase functioning as an adverbial. For further discussion, see Grammar below.

1 **Æþelnoð biscop for to Rome.**

Bishop Æthelnoth travelled to Rome.

2 **He wæs þær underfangen mid mycclan weorðscype.**

He was received there with great honour.

3 **He ferde bliðelice ham to his earde.**

He travelled joyfully home to his own country.

The career of Archbishop Æthelnoth

Æthelnoth was archbishop of Canterbury from 1020 to 1038. Information about his career can be found in a number of charters and annals, including two entries in the D Chronicle that offer some rare biographical details about him.

In the annal D 1020, the Chronicler tells of events following Cnut's return to England after spending the winter in Denmark. The account here should be compared with the corresponding text of C 1020, in unit 5.

How do the two texts differ?

D 1020 Her com Cnut cyng eft to Englalande. And þa on Eastron wæs micel gemot æt Cyrenceastre, þa geutlagade man Æþelward ealdorman. And on þisan geare for se cyng and Þurkyl eorl to Assandune, and Wulfstan arcebiscop, and oðre biscopas, and eac abbodas and manege munecas, and gehalgodan þæt mynster æt Assandune. And Æðelnoð munuc, se þe wæs decanus æt Cristes cyrcan, wearð on þam ilcan geare on Idus Nouembris to biscope gehalgod into Cristes cyrcan.

The D annal adds the phrase **and eac abbodas and manege munecas** emphasizing that abbots and monks were also involved in the consecration of the church at Assandun (Ashdon in Essex). And in contrast to the C text it reports the consecration of the new archbishop, who happens also to be a monk:

And Æðelnoð munuc, se þe wæs decanus æt Cristes cyrcan, wearð on þam ilcan geare on Idus Nouembris to biscope gehalgod into Christes cyrcan.

And the monk Æthelnoth, who was prior at Christ Church, was in the same year, on the ides of November, consecrated as bishop into Christ Church [i.e. consecrated on November 13th as archbishop of Canterbury].

As various historians writing about the reign of Cnut have shown (see Bibliography), the fact that Æthelnoth was **munuc** and **decanus** is significant. Following the example set by Winchester and Worcester in the tenth century, Christ Church Canterbury had recently become monastic, i.e. it was run not by cathedral clergy but by monks, on the lines of a Benedictine monastery (see units 7 and 15). Daily business was now conducted by meetings of the monastic Chapter, presided over by the abbot (or in his absence on duty as archbishop, by the provost or prior). As usual in a Benedictine house, on the death or retirement of an abbot, it was the role of the Chapter to elect a replacement from among the members of their own community, and then to petition the king to ratify their decision. In the twelfth century, a riveting, almost novelistic account of the run-up to such an election at Bury St Edmunds is told by Joscelin of Brakelond, one of the monks of that monastery; his narrative includes the story of how the monks subsequently persuaded the king to accept the candidate of their choice (see Bibliography).

A similar sequence of events seems also to have happened in 1020: the monks duly elected their new spiritual father, Æthelnoth. But the problem was that in choosing their new abbot the monks also simultaneously chose the new archbishop of Canterbury, whereas previously such an appointment had been made by the king. As revealed in the next document, a letter to Cnut and Emma from Wulfstan archbishop of York, the king agreed to the appointment, for he seems to have sent a declaration to this effect. However, on the next occasion when the see became vacant, he would take greater care to appoint his own man, as we will see.

Grammar

1 BASIC ADVERBS

Adjectives describe a noun, whereas a major use of adverbs is to describe the verb, often giving the manner, degree, time or location of the action, for example:

He ferde bliðelice ham to his earde.

He travelled joyfully home to his own country.

Old English adverbs are formed from adjectives by adding **-e**, e.g. **hraðe** *quickly*; but they frequently end with **-lice** 'leecheh' instead, e.g. **eadmodlice** *humbly*, **bliðelice** *happily*, and sometimes also with the suffix **-unga**, e.g. **eallunga** *completely*. The **-lic** 'leech' ending appears on adjectives and takes an **-e** to give the adverb; originally the ending derives from a noun **þæt lic** meaning *body* (cf. modern *lychgate*); there is a corresponding adjective **gelic** *like*. The modern adverb ending *-ly*, the adverb *alike*, the adjective *like* and its derivative *likeness* all come from Old English **lic**.

The adverb **swiþe** from an adjective meaning *strong* is used as the intensifier *very:* **swiþe gōd** means *very good* while **swiþe arwurðlice** means *very honourably* (see text below).

2 OTHER ADVERBS

Some adverbs are formed from **þær** + preposition: **þæræfter** *after that*, **þærmid** *with that, immediately*. A few adverbs are formed by inflecting the noun. A genitive ending **-es** can turn a noun into an adverbial (which functions like an adverb):

dæges and nihtes *by day and by night*

Another conversion of this kind puts select nouns into the dative plural; the resulting word then functions as an adverb: **hwilum** *at times*. An adjective can also become an adverb in the same way:

micel → miclum ('mitch-lum')	*much*
lytel → lytlum ('lüt-lum')	*little*

There is also **furþum** *even*, from the adverb **forþ** *forth*.

3 SHORT ADVERBS AND WORD ORDER

Some adverbs are short monosyllabic words which behave rather like pronouns in that they can replace another word or phrase: **þa** *then*, **her** *here*, **þær** *there*. The adverb **þa** often appears at the beginning of the clause, with the verb in second place:

þa geseah he þone broþor sarig

[literally] *then saw-he the brother sad*

þa frefrode he hine

[literally] *then consoled-he him*

In the *Anglo-Saxon Chronicle*, the introductory clauses starting with **hēr** *here* tend to follow the same pattern:

her com Cnut cyng eft to Englalande

here came Cnut again to England

But subject–verb word order also occurs, as in modern English:

her Cnut kyning for ut mid his scypum to Wihtlande

[literally] *here Cnut king travelled out with his ships to Wight*

4 ADVERBS OF MOVEMENT

Adverbs expressing direction or movement towards something include: **hām** *home*, **þider** *to there*, **hider** *to here*, **feorr** *far*, **ut** *out*, **norð** *northward*, **suð** *southward*. A set of adverbs also express direction from: **þonan** *from there*, **heonan** *from here*, **feorran** *from afar*, **utan** *from outside*, **norðan** *from the north*, **suðan** *from the south*.

5 THE ADVERBIAL PHRASE

Adverbs can be one word, as most of the examples above; alternatively, several words can combine into an adverbial phrase, often with a preposition. So, for example, in the annal D 1022 below, the adverbial **mid mycclan weorðscype** is used to show how the archbishop was received in Rome with great honour; the phrase is very similar in function to the single-word adverb **arwurðlice** *honourably*, which occurs later in the same passage. Another adverbial of manner in the same text is **mid his agenum handum** describing how the pope performed the ceremony with his own hands, an adverbial phrase roughly corresponding to the modern adverb *personally*.

Because of their structure, these particular adverbials can also be described as prepositional phrases, as in the following table, where the determiner can be a pronoun like *his* or an article such as *the*:

preposition	+ determiner	+ adjective	+ noun
mid		mycclan	weorðscype
mid	his	agenum	handum
on	þam	sylfan	dæge

Travels to Rome

There were many reasons for contacts between England and Rome in the Anglo-Saxon period. For religious reasons, as a city of ancient churches, as the site of St Peter's bishopric and the residence of the head of the western Church, Rome was a magnet for pilgrims, and both king Alfred in the ninth century and king Cnut in the eleventh visited the city. In the year 597, it had been the mission from Rome that had brought about the conversion of the kings of Kent and southern England, and religious, intellectual and cultural contacts continued thereafter.

> **CULTURAL INSIGHT**
>
> From the eighth century, there was a custom of paying a religious tax to Rome, called in Old English **Rom-scot**, or *Rome penny*, later called *Peter's Pence*. This served to support the travellers' hospice especially built to accommodate the many English pilgrims, and it came to be known by its Latin name 'Schola Saxonum', the Saxon School.

Whenever a new archbishop of Canterbury was appointed, it was the custom for him to make the long journey to Rome to receive the pope's blessing and the **pallium**, a kind of scarf or band of white wool with six black crosses on it, which the pope bestowed on the archbishop as a sign of his authority. The archbishops would only wear the **pallium** on important solemn occasions, such as Christmas, Epiphany and Easter.

 17.00

And Æþelnoð biscop for to Rome

And Bishop Æthelnoth travelled to Rome

D 1022 Her Cnut kyning for ut mid his scypum to Wihtlande. And Æþelnoð biscop for to Rome, and wæs þær underfangen mid mycclan weorðscype fram Benedicte þam arwurðan papan, and he mid his agenum handum him pallium on asette, and to arcebiscope swiðe arwurðlice gehalgade and gebletsade on Nonas Octobris, and se arcebiscop sona þærmid mæssan sang on þam sylfan dæge, and syððan þæræfter

mid þam sylfan papan arwurðlice gereordade, and eac him seolf þone pallium genam on Sancte Petres weofode, and þa seoððan bliðelice ham to his earde ferde.

to Rome	pronounced 'to Roh-meh' (dative after **to**)
wæs underfangen	*was received* (**wæs** + past participle of **underfon**)
arwurð	*honourable* (**seo ar** *honour* + **wurð** *worthy*)
se weorðscipe	*honour*
arwurðlice	*honourably*
seo mæsse	*mass (i.e. communion, the eucharist)*
reordian	*to feast*
se pallium	*ceremonial scarf (see explanation above)*
bliðelice	*happily (cf. blithe)*

Practice

Reread the text of D 1022 and analyse the use of adverbials (either single-word adverbs or multi-word phrases); find the following types:

1 four adverbials of manner

_____

2 four adverbials of place or direction

_____

3 four adverbials of time

_____

WORD ORDER

The common pattern of word order in Old English is characterized by a sentence from *The Life of Guthlac* (see unit 16):

sona swa he þa cartan geseah, þa genam he hig sona

as soon as he saw the parchment, he took it at once

This pattern can be summed up by the following rule of thumb:

subordinate clause – verb goes to the end (**geseah**)

main clause – verb comes as second element (**genam**)

In the above annal D 1022, there are two events recorded, Cnut's foray to the Isle of Wight and Æthelnoth's journey to Rome. These two events are recounted in separate sentences, each being given a main-clause word order:

connector + subject	verb	adverbials
(1) Her Cnut kyning	for	**ut mid his scypum to Wihtlande**
(2a) And Æþelnoð biscop	for	**to Rome …**

A clause then follows with the same subject, Æthelnoth, with the auxiliary verb in second place and the main verb (the past participle) towards the end, but with a long emphatic prepositional phrase in final position:

(subject)	+ auxiliary verb	+ adverb	+ past participle	+ final elements
(2b) and	wæs	þær	underfangen	mid mycclan weorðscype

The remaining clauses in the annal each begin with the coordinating word **and**. Since they all have a main verb, some of them could be analysed as separate sentences, but the position of the verb in each case speaks against this. Although not, strictly speaking, subordinate, these clauses beginning with **and** behave like subordinate clauses in their word order because the verb tends to come towards the end:

subject	other elements	verb	final element
(2c) and he	mid his agenum handum him pallium on	asette	
(2d) and	to arcebiscope swiðe arwurðlice	gehalgade gebletsade	on Nonas Octobris

Here the verbs appear at the end or towards the end of the clause, with one emphatic adverbial phrase *on the nones of October* in final position. The pattern continues with the new subject the archbishop in (2e), and the effect of this is to make the series of clauses (2e)–(2h) effectively subordinate to the main clause (2a), with verbs postponed and the occasional emphatic element, always a prepositional phrase using **on** + noun, in final position (reading down and across):

connector	other elements	verb	final element
(2e) and se arcebiscop	sona þærmid mæssan	sang	on þam sylfan dæge
(2f) and	syððan þæræfter mid þam sylfan papan arwurðlice	gereordade	
(2g) and	eac him seolf þone pallium	genam	on Sancte Petres weofode
(2h) and	þa seoððan bliðelice ham to his earde	ferde	

Language and style

ST ALPHEGE (CHRONICLE D 1023)

The story of *The Translation of St Alphege* appears in D 1023. It is a typical account of the veneration of a new saint, whose mortal remains must be honoured by being 'translated' to a more suitable and worthy resting place, which then becomes a place of pilgrimage. A late eleventh-century account in Latin by Osbern of Canterbury tells of trouble at the ceremony, with some Londoners wanting their favourite martyr to remain within the city and clashing with the housecarls or royal guards. Probably there were political reasons for this, at a time when England was ruled by the Danish king Cnut (see Lawson in Bibliography). But the Old English version in D sets a wholly celebratory tone for the events of the day.

With regard to sentence structure, the narrative is longer and more complex than D 1022, with several relative clauses at (1c), (4a) and (4d). Largely, however, it follows a similar style and word order, with and-clauses usually taking verb-final order but allowing occasional prepositional phrases to follow the verb. Examples are clauses (1d), (2b), (2c), (3b) and (3c). It is, of course, likely that the two adjacent annals D 1022 and D1023 about Æthelnoth's role as archbishop were written by the same Chronicle author. But on stylistic grounds, arguably, this supposition is supported by the sentence structure.

Her Cnut kyning binnan Lundene on Sancte Paules mynstre

Here king Cnut in London at Saint Paul's

(1a) Her Cnut kyning binnan Lundene on Sancte Paules mynstre sealde fulle leafe Æðelnoðe arcebiscope and Bryhtwine biscope and eallon þam Godes þeowum (1b) þe heom mid wæron (1c) þæt hi moston nyman up of þam byrgene þone arcebiscop Sancte Ælfheah, (1d) and hi þa swa dydon on .vi. Idus Iunii.

seo leafe	*leave, permission*
se þeow	*servant*
moston	*were allowed*
nyman	*take*
se byrgen	*burying place, sepulchre*
dydon	*did (from **dōn**, see unit 15)*

(2a) And se brema cyng and se arcebiscop and leodbiscopas and eorlas and swiðe manege hadode and eac læwede feredon on scype his þone halgan lichaman ofer Temese to Suðgeweorke, (2b) and þær þone halgan martyr þan arcebiscope and his geferum betæhton, (2c) and hi þa mid weorðlican weorode and wynsaman dreame hine to Hrofesceastre feredan.

se brema cyng	*the glorious king (base form of the word is **brēme**)*
se lichaman	*body*
ofer Temese to Suðgeweorce	*over the Thames to Southwark*
se gefēra	*companion*
betæhton	*they entrusted 'beTÆHton' from **betæcan** entrust*
weorðlic	*worthy*
se weorod	*host, troop*
wynsam (also **wynsum**)	*delightful*
se dream	*joy*
to Hrofesceastre	*to Rochester*
feredan	*conveyed from **ferian***

(3a) Ða on þam þryddan dæge com Imma seo hlæfdie mid hire cynelican bearne Hardacnute, **(3b)** and hi þa ealle mid mycclan þrymme and blisse and lofsange þone halgan arcebiscop into Cantwarebyri feredon, **(3c)** and swa wurðlice into Cristes cyrcan brohton on .iii. Idus Iunii.

Imma seo hlæfdie	*Emma the Lady*, an honorific title for queen Emma
cynelic	*royal*
þæt bearn	*child*
se þrymm	*glory*
seo bliss	*happiness* (also spelt **bliþs**, from **bliþe** *happy*)
se lofsang	*song of praise*

(4) Eft syðð an on þam eahteoðan dæge, on .xvii. Kalendas Iulii, Æðelnoð arcebiscop and Ælfsie biscop and Bryhtwine biscop, and ealle **(4a)** þa þe mid heom wæron,

(4b) gelogodon Sancte Ælfeages halgan lichaman on norðhealfe Cristes weofodes, Gode to lofe, and þam halgan arcebiscope to wurðmynte, and eallon þam to ecere hælðe **(4c)** þe his halgan lichoman þær mid estfulre heortan and mid ealre eadmodnysse dæghwamlice seceað.

gelogodon	*placed* (from **gelōgian** *to lodge, place, arrange*)
lichoman	*body* (weak noun **se lichama** *body*)
Gode to lofe	*in praise of God* (**þæt lof** *praise*)
se wurðmynt	*honour* (also spelt **weorðmynd**)
seo hælð	*salvation, health*
ēstful	*devout*
seo heorte	*heart*
seo eadmodnys	*humility*

(5) God ælmihtig gemiltsie eallum Cristenum mannum þurh Sancte Ælfeges halgan gegearnunga.

gemiltsie	*have mercy (on)* (subjunctive) (**gemiltsian** + direct object in dative)
gegearnunga	*merits*

Archbishop Eadsige

After a long period of service, Æthelnoth was succeeded in 1038 by Eadsige, formerly a chaplain at Cnut's court. It looks as if the king was determined to have his own man in the archbishopric eventually, and Eadsige was first of all appointed bishop at St Martin's for the period 1035–38. During which time he appears to have acted as Æthelnoth's deputy administrator; for example, he helped to safeguard Canterbury from attempts by the king's reeve to levy excessive amounts of money on land owned by the cathedral (see text below). In the end, Cnut did make some concessions to the monastic establishment, in that Eadsige duly became a monk before he became archbishop. He held the see from 1038 to 1044, when he stood down for health reasons, but he served a second term as archbishop from 1048 to his death in 1050. It was Eadsige who crowned Edward (later called Edward the Confessor) as king at Easter in 1043 (see unit 1).

Test yourself

Cnut protects the archbishop against the reeve in a letter dated to the year 1035 (see Sawyer catalogue S 987 and Harmer no. 29).

Translate the following text:

Cnut cyngc gret Eadsige biscop and Ælfstan abbot and Ægelric and ealle mine þegnas on Cent freondlice. And ic cyþe eow þæt ic wylle þæt Æþelnoð arcebiscop werige his landare into his bisceoprice nu eal swa he dyde ær Ægelric wære gerefa and siððan he gerefa wæs forð oð þis, and ic nelle na geþafian þæt man þam bisceope ænige unlage beode beo gerefa se þe beo.

_____

_____

_____

_____

SELF-CHECK

I CAN ...
recognize various types of adverb
identify adverbial phrases
analyse complex syntax and word order
do stylistic analysis

18 *Wulfstan arcebiscop gret Cnut cyning*
Archbishop Wulfstan greets king Cnut

In this unit you will learn about:
▶ *the MacDurnan Gospels*
▶ *personal pronouns* I, we, you
▶ *the use of the dual* you
▶ *variant spellings of the definite article*
▶ *the declension of the strong adjective*

You will read:
▶ *various texts and documents added to the manuscript of the MacDurnan Gospels, including:*
  – *archbishop Wulfstan's letter to king Cnut and queen Emma*
  – *agreements between archbishop Æthelnoth and Toki*
  – *agreements between archbishop Eadsige and Toki*

V Vocabulary builder

ADMINISTRATION

gerefa	*reeve*
wicnere	*bailiff, officer*

CRIME

sacu	*conflict*
forsteall	*hindrance, assault*
þeof	*thief*
fyrmð	*harbouring*

CONFLICT RESOLUTION

þa forword	*the agreements*
freondscipe	*friendship*
þances kepan	*to show gratitude*
tiðian	*to permit, grant*
becweðan	*to bequeath, leave in a will*
cwyde	*a will*
grið	*truce, protection*
alysednes	*redemption*

AFFECTION

leof	*dear*
wyrþe	*worthy*
gerysenlic	*honourable*
mæþ	*reverence*

RELIGIOUS LIFE

biddan	*to pray*
bletsian	*to bless*
se halga	*saint*
had	*religious order*
ge gehadude ge læwede	*both clergy and laity*
for Godes lufon	*for the love of God*

The MacDurnan Gospels

Now in the archbishop's library as London, Lambeth Palace 1370, the MacDurnan gospel book is an attractive illuminated manuscript of the four gospels in Latin. It was written in Ireland in the ninth century, when each of the four gospels was furnished with an evangelist portrait and other elaborate decoration. Originally it belonged to **Mael Brigte mac Tornain** (*Maelbright MacDurnan*), abbot of Iona and *'head of the piety of all Ireland and of the greater part of Europe'* as an Irish chronicle puts it. The book later came into the possession of Æthelstan, king of England from 924 to 939, who presented it to Canterbury cathedral. Over time various texts were added to the manuscript, usually in blank spaces at the beginning or end of the four texts: a Latin poem commemorating the book's illustrious owners, a letter from Wulfstan to king Cnut and queen Emma, and two records of an agreement between successive archbishops of Canterbury and a certain Toki (a name of Scandinavian origin).

1 THE LATIN INSCRIPTION

The Latin poem appears on a blank page after the preface to Matthew. It is written in a rhythmical style with alliteration (a favourite English technique) and even contains an Old English genitive plural ending on the word **Anglosæxna** *of the Anglo-Saxons* in line three (in correct Latin this should be 'Anglosaxonum').

Try reading the passage out loud, for the rhythmic and alliterative effects:

> \+ MÆIELBRIÐUS MAC DURNANI
>
> ISTUM TEXTUM PER TRIQUADRUM
>
> DEO DIGNE DOGMATIZAT
>
> \+ AST AETHELSTANUS ANGLOSÆXNA
>
> REX ET RECTOR DORVERNENSI
>
> METROPOLI DAT PER ÆVUM.

Mælbright MacDurnan

this text – through the wide world

to the honour of God – proclaims

but Æthelstan, the Anglo-Saxons'

king and ruler, to the Canterbury

metropolitan see, gives it for ever.

2 WULFSTAN'S LETTER

 18.00

Wulfstan arcebiscop gret Cnut cyning

Archbishop Wulfstan greets king Cnut

This letter (S 1386) seems to have been sent to king Cnut and queen Emma shortly after Æthelnoth was appointed as archbishop (see unit 17); the copy here appears on folio 69v of the MacDurnan Gospels.

As you read, study carefully the personal pronouns used in the text (*I, you, he* etc.) and refer to the first part of the Grammar section.

Wulfstan arcebiscop gret Cnut cyning his hlaford and Ælfgyfe þa hlæfdian eadmodlice. And ic cyþe inc leof þæt we habbað gedon swa swa us swutelung fram eow com æt þam biscope Æþelnoþe, þæt we habbað hine nu gebletsod. Nu bidde ic for Godes lufon, and for eallan Godes halgan þæt ge witan on Gode þa mæþe, and on þam halgan hade, þæt he mote beon þære þinga wyrþe þe oþre beforan wæron – Dunstan þe god wæs and mænig oþer – þæt þes mote beon eall swa rihta and gerysna wyrðe, þæt inc byð bam þearflic for Gode, and eac gerysenlic for worolde.

Archbishop Wulfstan greets king Cnut his lord and Ælfgyfu the lady humbly. And I declare to you dear ones [i.e. affectionately] that we have done as the declaration came to us from you concerning bishop Æthelnoth, that we have now blessed him. Now I pray for the love of God and for all God's saints that you may know reverence to God and to the holy office, that he might be worthy of the things which others were before (Dunstan who was good and many another) that this man might be also worthy of rights and honours. So that it will be – for both of you – profitable before God and also honourable before the world.

inc	*you both* (dual, see Grammar)
se halga	*saint* (from **halig** *holy*; All Hallows = the feast of All Saints)
biddan	*to pray*
seo mæþ	*reverence*
mote	*might* (subjunctive of **moste**)
se had	*rank, order, status*
gerysna	*what is fitting, dignity, honour*
gerysenlic	*honourable*
bam	*both* ('bām'; dative of **begen**; see Grammar)

3 ÆTHELNOTH'S DECLARATION TO TOKI

Archbishop Æthelnoth and Toki (S 1464) (from the MacDurnan Gospels, folio 115r)

Her swuteliað on ðisse Cristes bec Æþelnoðes arcebisceopes forword and Tokiges embe þæt land æt Healtune; þæt wæs þæt Tokig com to Hrisbeorgan to ðam arcebisceope syððan Æðelflæd his wif forðfaren wæs, and cydde him Wulfnoðes cwyde þæt he þæt land becweden hæfde into Cristes cyrcean æfter his dæge and his wifes, and bæd þone arcebisceop þæt he þæt land habban moste his dæg, and æfter his dæge þæt hit lage into Cristes cyrcean mid eallum þingum þe he þæron getilian mihte unbesacen, and cwæð þæt he wolde þam bisceop þances kepan and his mannum, and se arcebisceop him þæs tiðude, and sæde þæt he riht wið hine gedon hæfde þæt he sylf him for þam cwyde secgean wolde, þeh he hit ær ful georne wiste. And ðises wæs to gewitnysse Æþelstan æt Bleddehlæwe, and Leofwine his sunu, and Leofric æt Eaningadene, and feala oðra godra cnihta, þeh we hi ealle ne nemnon, and eall ðæs arcebiscopes hired, ge gehadude ge læwede.

bec	books ('**baytch**', dative singular of **seo boc** book)
æt Healtune	at Halton (Buckinghamshire)
to Hrisbeorgan	to Risborough (Monks Risborough, Buckinghamshire)
cydde	declared (from **cyðan** to make known)
se cwyde	will (from **cweðan** to speak)
becweden	bequeathed (from **becweðan** to bequeath, leave in a will)
bæd	asked, from **biddan** to ask, pray (**bitt, bæd, bædon, gebeden**)
moste	be allowed
lage	past subjunctive from **licgan** to lie (lið, læg, lægon, gelegen)
getilian	to till, cultivate, produce
þances kepan	to show gratitude (**kepan = cepan** to show, observe)
se arcebiscop him þæs tiðude	the archbishop granted him this
tiðian	to permit, grant (followed by dative of the person and genitive of the thing granted)
secgean = secgan	to say
þeh = þeah	although
ær	previously
ær… wiste	had known (the adverb **ær** conveys the sense had happened)
ful georne	perfectly well
æt Bleddehlæwe	at Bledlow
æt Eaningadene	(location unidentified)
feala	many

4 THE PORTRAIT OF ST LUKE

A portrait of the evangelist Luke (from the MacDurnan Gospels, folio 115v)

5 EADSIGE'S DECLARATION TO TOKI

Archbishop Eadsige and Toki (S 1466) (added out of chronological sequence to folio 114r of the MacDurnan Gospels)

+ Eadsige arcebiscop cyþ on ðisse Cristes bec þæt Tokig sende to me to Hrisbeorgan his twegen cnihtas oðor hatte Seaxa oðor hatte Leofwine, and bæd me þæt þa forword moston standan þe Æðelnoð arcebishop and he geworht hæfdon ymbe þæt land æt Healtune þæt he his bruce his dæg, and eode æfter his dæge into cristes cyricean and ic him ðæs tiðude on manegra godra manna gewitnysse and ealles mines hiredes ge gehadudra ge læwedra.

Grammar 1

THE PERSONAL PRONOUNS *I* AND *YOU*

In the accusative and dative cases, the pronoun **ic** (pronounced to rhyme with 'rich') changes to **me** (pronounced 'may') meaning *me* and *to me*, whereas **ge**, the plural *you* (pronounced 'yay' to rhyme with 'may'), changes to **eow**:

me þuhte þæt we bundon sceafas on æcere

it seemed to me that we were binding sheaves in the field (unit 6)

ic cyðe eow þæt ic wylle beon hold hlaford

I make known to you (i.e. *I inform you*) *that I will be a gracious lord* (unit 7)

In the table below, the forms of the first and second person pronoun are arranged according to their grammatical case (the usual four cases) and number (singular, dual, or plural); for convenience, a length mark has been employed to indicate long vowels:

Personal Pronouns first person			
	singular	dual	plural
	I, me	*we-two*	*we, us*
nominative	**ic**	**wit**	**wē**
accusative	**mē**	**unc**	**ūs**
genitive	**mīn**	**uncer**	**ūre**
dative	**mē**	**unc**	**ūs**
second person			
	you	*you-two*	*you*
nominative	**þū**	**git**	**gē**
accusative	**þē**	**inc**	**ēow**
genitive	**þīn**	**incer**	**ēower**
dative	**þē**	**inc**	**ēow**

It is worth reviewing the patterns of pronunciation in the commoner forms: **ic** 'itch', **me** 'may', **þe** 'thay', **we** 'way' and **ge** 'yay', and the long vowels in **mīn** 'meen', **þīn** 'theen', **ūre** 'OOruh', and **ēower** 'Éo-wer'. The last four pronouns also function as the possessive and survive in modern English as *mine, thine, our* and *your*.

For examples in use, look at Wulfstan's letter above. The second sentence is particularly rich in personal pronouns, including a switch from **ic** (the writer of the letter) to **we** and **us** (who carried out the blessing), and a change from the dual **inc** (*you-two*, pronounced 'ink') to the general plural **eow**:

And ic cyþe inc leof

þæt we habbað gedon

swa swa us swutelung fram eow com

æt þam biscope Æþelnoþe,

þæt we habbað hine nu gebletsod.

And I declare to you-two dear ones

that we have done

as the declaration came to us from you

concerning bishop Æthelnoth,

that we have now blessed him.

Wulfstan's choices of pronoun in this letter are open to interpretation. He may have used **ic cyðe inc** and later **inc byð bam** as opening and closing formulas of direct address to the king and lady. But in the middle of the letter he switched to **eow** and **ge** because it was a more natural way of speaking for the main part of his message. Alternatively, he may have switched to **ge** for the main message because the whole court was intended to hear it rather than only the royal couple. In this respect, it should be remembered that letters, writs and declarations were almost certainly read out loud before the assembled gathering.

Variation in the definite article *the*

1 THE *ANGLO-SAXON CHRONICLES*

Take two versions of the *Chronicle* and you will find that for any annal that they have in common the two texts are not spelt exactly the same in each case. During Alfred's wars with the Danes in the ninth century, for example, the *Chronicle* reports on the movements of the Danish army as follows:

A 892 Here in this year the great army which we spoke about earlier travelled back from the East Kingdom (East Francia) to Boulogne, and there they were provided with ships…

The original text of the *A Chronicle* scribe can be compared with that of the later scribe who copied the annal into the *D Chronicle*; the differences are minor:

A 892 Her on þysum geare for se micla here þe we gefyrn ymbe spræcon eft of þæm eastrice westweard to Bunnan, & þær wurdon gescipode…

D 893 Her on þyssum geare for se mycla here þe we fyrn ær ymbe spræcon eft of þam eastrice westweard to Bunan, & þær wurdon gescipude…

As further perusal of the whole passage in the two versions would show, the later writer consistently prefers to write **þam** where the A scribe has **þæm**. This is one kind of scribal variation, probably based on the house style of a particular scriptorium that was in operation at the time of writing.

2 BYRHTFERTH

Another kind of variation occurs in a passage from Byrhtferth's *Handbook* (I.i.92), where **þæne** and its variant **þone** (masculine accusative) appear in close proximity even in the same sentence. Describing the creation of the heavens Byrhtferth writes:

God… gesceop sunnan and monan and tungla and steorran, and he gesette twegen sunnstedas, þæne ænne on .xii. kalendas Ianuarii and þone oþerne on .xii. kalendas Iulii.

God created sun and moon and planets and stars, and he established two solstices, the one on the twelfth of the kalends of January, the other on the twelfth of the kalends of July.

The relevant part of this sentence is structured as follows:

nominative	verb	accusative
God	gesceop	sunstedas: þæne ænne... þone oþerne
God	*created*	*solstices: the one... the other*

There may be several reasons for the contrast between the preferred form **þæne** and the here less frequent **þone**. But looking at the vowels in **þæne ænne... þone oþerne** (æ... æ, o... o) one might speculate that Byrhtferth – or perhaps the scribe who copied the text – enjoyed the way the sounds in each phrase echoed from one word to the next.

3 THE LADY EMMA

A further reason for spelling variation is the influence of the spoken language, particularly the way the inflected endings on Old English words could be pronounced less distinctly in the eleventh century. So a fairly common variant in some texts is **þan** instead of **þam**. This almost certainly reflects the pronunciation. The dative **þan** occurs in the following short document of king Edward's reign (S 1229), also written for safekeeping in a deluxe gospel book. Here Ælfgyfu the Lady (Emma) makes a declaration about a property transaction that took place during the reign of her husband Cnut:

 18.01

Ic Ælfgyfu seo hlæfdige, Eadweardes cyninges modor, geærndede æt Cnute cyninge minum hlaforde þæt land æt Niwantune and þæt þærto hyrð into Cristes cyrcean, þa Ælfric se þegen hit hæfde forworht þan cyninge to handan. And se cyning hit geaf þa into Cristes cyrcean þan hirede to fosterlande for uncre beigra sawle.

I Ælfgyfu the lady, king Edward's mother, acquired from king Cnut my lord the land at Newington and what pertains to it for Christ Church, when Ælfric the thegn had forfeited it to the king. And the king gave it then to Christ Church for the community to use as fosterland, for the benefit of both our souls.

To understand this passage it must be remembered that one legal sanction for serious crime was to deprive a man of his property, which then was taken over by the monarch. This had occurred in the case of a certain Ælfric, for crimes unspecified, or in Emma's words:

þa Ælfric se þegen hit hæfde forworht þan cyninge to handan

when Ælfric the thegn had forfeited it to the king into (his) hands

Here the idiomatic use of the definite article **þan** (for normal dative **þam**) has possessive meaning: **þan cyninge to handan** *into the king's hands*.

This forfeiture was not the end of the story. Not one to leave the matter entirely in the king's hands, Emma intervened with the request that the property be donated to Christ Church, the cathedral abbey in Canterbury, to be used as **fostorland**, literally *fosterland*, i.e. land that is granted to the recipients to use for food.

From the point of view of structure, the final sentence could be broken down as follows:

subject	object	verb	adverbials	of time	of place	of purpose	of reason
se cyning	hit	geaf		þa	into Cristes cyrcean	þan hirede to fosterlande	for uncre beigra sawle

The adverbial of purpose (which in classic Old English would have been **þam hirede to fosterlande**) could be explained as another 'possessive' use of the dative definite article **þan**, but meaning literally *to the community for fosterland.*

Grammar 2

Unit 14 gave an introduction to strong adjective endings and demonstrated in particular how to recognize the masculine accusative **-ne** in Old English poems. Here now is the full table for declining the strong adjective:

THE DECLENSION OF THE STRONG ADJECTIVE

In the table (or paradigm) below, the strong endings are presented for the adjective **gōd** *good* (pronounced 'goad' and sometimes written by the scribes as **gód**):

	Masculine	Neuter	Feminine
Singular			
nominative	gōd	gōd	gōdu
accusative	gōdne	gōd	gōde
genitive	gōdes	gōdes	gōdre
dative	gōdum	gōdum	gōdre
Plural			
nominative	gōde	gōdu	gōda
accusative	gōde	gōdu	gōda
genitive	gōdra	gōdra	gōdra
dative	gōdum	gōdum	gōdum

Variants include nominative and accusative plural in **-e** in all genders; in later Old English the **-um** ending is often replaced by the form **-an**. Possessive adjectives such as **mīn** and **þīn** decline like **gōd**. The adjectives **bisig** *busy* and **micel** *great* are uninflected in the nominative singular feminine.

Reading

CNUT GIVES ARCHBISHOP ÆTHELNOTH HIS LEGAL POWERS

In the following text, from folio 114v of the MacDurnan Gospels (S 986; Harmer no. 28), Cnut gives to Æthelnoth **sacu and socn** or *sake and soke*, i.e. *the right to hold a court and exact fines*, especially for such misdemeanours as **griðbryce** *breach of sanctuary*, **hamsocn** *attacking a man in his own home*, **forsteall** *ambush and assault*. He also grants him the right to fine thieves caught in his jurisdiction, i.e. **infangene-þeof**, and to exact penalties for **flymena fyrmð** *the harbouring of fugitives* (**flymena**: genitive plural of **flyma** *fugitive*).

Who are the intended recipients of the letter?

Cnut cyncg gret ealle mine biscopas and mine eorlas and mine gerefan on ælcere scire þe Æþelnoð arcebiscop and se hired æt Cristes cyrcean land inne habbað freondlice. And ic cyðe eow þæt ic hæbbe geunnen him þæt he beo his saca and socne wyrðe and griðbryces and hamsocne and forstealles and infangenes þeofes and flymena fyrmðe ofer his agene menn binnan byrig and butan and ofer Cristes cyrcean and ofer swa feala þegna swa ic him to lætan hæbbe. And ic nelle þæt ænig mann aht þær on teo buton he and his wicneras for þam ic hæbbe Criste þas gerihta forgyfen minre sawle to ecere alysednesse, and ic nelle þæt æfre ænig mann þis abrece be minum freondscipe.

se gerefa	*reeve*
seo sacu	*conflict, lawsuit, contention*
seo sōcn	*seeking, visit, attack; right to take fines; district where this right holds sway*
þæt grið	*truce, protection, sanctuary*
se forsteall, foresteall	*hindrance, assault, ambush*
se þeof	*thief*
infangene	*from* **fon** *to seize* (**fēhð, fēng, fēngon, ge-fangen**)
seo fyrmð	*harbouring*
lætan *also spelt* læten	*granted* (**lætan, lætt, lēt, læten**)
ic nelle	*I do not want*
aht	*anything*
þær on teo	*take from it:* **tēon** *to take, pull* (**tyhð, tēah, tugon, togen**)
se wicnere	*bailiff, officer*
seo sāwol, sāwel	*soul* (dative **sawle**)
seo ālysednes	*redemption* (**ālīesan** *to release*)
abrece	*break:* present subjunctive of **ābrecan** (**-bricð, bræc, bræcon, brocen**)
se freondscipe	*friendship*

? Test yourself

1 In the reading text, find and translate phrases containing strong adjectival endings, e.g. **on ælcere scire** *in every shire*.

_____

_____

_____

_____

2 Find phrases in the study texts with the meaning:
   a many other retainers _____
   b with the witnessing of many good men _____
   c after his lifetime _____
   d with all things _____
   e in this gospel book _____
   f I inform you both _____

SELF-CHECK

I CAN ...
○ decline personal pronouns: first and second person
○ recognize the use of the dual *you*
○ identify variant spellings of the definite article
○ recognize and understand the declension of the strong adjective

19
Hu Wynflæd gelædde hyre gewitnesse
How Wynflæd summoned her witnesses

In this unit you will learn about:
▶ *Wynflæd's lawsuit*
▶ *the Tironian* nota *as an abbreviation in texts*
▶ *the word* **gewitnes**
▶ *contemporary figures in the witness list*
▶ *women's names*
▶ *the use of oaths*
▶ *reported speech and the 'conjectural subjunctive'*
▶ *ancient sites along the Berkshire Ridgeway*

You will read:
▶ *the lawsuit heard during the Berkshire assembly at Cwichelm's Barrow in the year 991 (document S 1454)*
▶ *'Weland the smith': an extract from* The Old English Boethius
▶ *part of* Chronicle C 1006: the Vikings at Cwichelm's Barrow

Ⓥ Vocabulary builder

SHIRE LAWSUITS

scir	*shire*
scirgemot	*shire assembly*
þa witan	*the councillors* (i.e. members of the assembly)
sprecan	*to claim*
ontalu	*a claim*
geahnian	*to prove a claim of ownership*
swerian	*to swear*
cyþan	*to make known*
aþ	*oath*
aþ sellan	*to give an oath*
aþ aweg lætan	*to dispense with an oath*
aþ gebiorgan	*to protect the validity of an oath*
forgyldan	*pay compensation*

Wynflæd

The document for study in this unit provides a series of snapshots from a significant episode in a woman's life (S 1454 in Sawyer's catalogue and no. 66 in Robertson's *Anglo-Saxon*

Charters). Recorded as a **swutulung** or *declaration*, it tells how Wynflæd defended herself before the law against the man Leofwine, who had seized some disputed land from her in the years 990–92, during the reign of Æthelred the Unready (978–1016). The case concerned two estates in Berkshire, which had belonged originally to a certain Ælfric (a common name at the time – see below). This Ælfric had apparently given Hagbourne and Bradfield to Wynflæd in return for an estate in Buckinghamshire.

But now the dispute starts, for Leofwine, who must be Ælfric's son, questions all this during the proceedings of the court, perhaps because he is worried about some gold and silver that had belonged to his father which was now allegedly in Wynflæd's possession. How she may have acquired it is not stated. Did Leofwine also pay her some money? Or was the gold and silver somehow left on the property itself? This is certainly possible. Apart from the royal treasury, and monasteries in fortified places, there were few places in early medieval England where money could be deposited safely, and it was customary to provide for the future by concealing stores of silver coin as treasure hoard. Perhaps this money had been hidden away and so had remained somewhere on the two estates after the transaction. And even though Leofwine had temporarily seized the two estates, he had not found any money.

THE TIRONIAN *NOTA* AS AN ABBREVIATION IN TEXTS

In the text, note the use of the symbol 7. This is known as the Tironian *nota* after the Roman writer M. Tullius Tiro (assistant to the famous orator Cicero), who developed the form of shorthand from which it was taken. In Anglo-Saxon manuscripts written in Old English, the sign 7 represents the word **and** (sometimes also **ond**), which quite simply means *and*; most introductory textbooks of Old English expand this abbreviation for clarity's sake, but the Tironian *nota* is very common in the manuscripts and standard editions, and it is worth familiarizing yourself with its use, for it makes a difference to the appearance of the page, and perhaps to the way it was read. The Tironian *nota* certainly prevents the superfluous writing out of the word **and** or **ond**. Arguably also, it served as a kind of supplementary punctuation mark to distinguish items in lists.

 19.00

Hu Wynflæd gelædde hyre gewitnesse

How Wynflæd summoned her witnesses / presented her testimony (S 1454)

How many supporters can Wynflæd muster at the assembly?

Her cyþ on þysum gewrite hu Wynflæd gelædde hyre gewitnesse æt Wulfamere beforan Æþelrede cyninge: þæt wæs þonne Sigeric arcebiscop 7 Ordbyrht biscop 7 Ælfric ealderman 7 Ælfþryþ þæs cyninges modor, þæt hi wæron ealle to gewitnesse þæt Ælfric sealde Wynflæde þæt land æt Hacceburnan 7 æt Bradanfelda ongean þæt land æt Deccet. Þa sende se cyning þær rihte be þam arcebiscope 7 be þam þe þær mid him to gewitnesse wæron to Leofwine 7 cyþdon him þis. Þa nolde he butan hit man sceote to scirgemote. Þa dyde man swa.

gelædde	*led*, *presented* (**lædan** *to lead*)
æt Wulfamere	**at Woolmer** (perhaps *Woolmer Forest in Hampshire*)

beforan	*before, in the presence of*
æt Hacceburnan	*at Hagbourne* (Berkshire)
æt Bradanfelda	*at Bradfield* (Berkshire)
ongean	*against* (i.e. *in exchange for*)
æt Deccet	*at Dachet* (Buckinghamshire)
sende	*sent* (i.e. *sent a message*, from **sendan** *to send*)
þær rihte	*right away, straightaway*
butan	*except that*
butan hit man sceote	*except that it be referred to the shire assembly* (**sceote** 'sheet-e'
to scirgemote	from **scēotan**, literally **to shoot**)

LANGUAGE INSIGHT

The word gewitnes

In tracing the history of the word, the Oxford English Dictionary shows that *witness* has gradually changed in meaning from abstract to concrete, from an idea of knowledge to the more personal eye-witness. Derived from the verb **witan** *to know*, **gewitnes** at first meant *knowledge* and then later *testimony*, and it could be used in such expressions as modern English *to bear witness to* (*a fact or event*). In the Old English records of lawsuits and charters, it is often stated that the transaction or agreement was carried out **to gewitnesse**, *with the cognizance of those present* (see the example in unit 11). Accordingly **hu Wynflæd gelædde hyre gewitnesse** (accusative singular) should literally mean *how Wynflæd presented her testimony*, but in context this noun *testimony* refers to a collective group of important individuals, the *witnesses* to the original exchange of gifts.

 19.01

Þa sende se cyning be Æluere abbude his insegel

Then the king sent his seal by abbot Ælfhere

Þa sende se cyning be Æluere abbude his insegel to þam gemote æt Cwicelmeshlæwe 7 grette ealle þa witan þe þær gesomnode wæron: þæt wæs Æþelsige biscop 7 Æscwig biscop 7 Ælfric abbud 7 eal sio scir 7 bæd 7 het þæt hi scioldon Wynflæde 7 Leofwine swa rihtlice geseman swa him æfre rihtlicost þuhte. And Sigeric arcebiscop sende his swutelunga þærto 7 Ordbyrht biscop his. Þa getæhte man Wynflæde þæt hio moste hit hyre geahnian; þa gelædde hio þa ahnunga mid Ælfþryþe fultume þæs cyninges modor: þæt is þonne ærest Wulfgar abbud 7 Wulfstan priost 7 Æfic þara æþelinga discsten 7 Eadwine 7 Eadelm 7 Ælfelm 7 Ælfwine 7 Ælfweard 7 Eadwold 7 Eadric 7 Ælfgar 7 Eadgyfu abbudisse 7 Liofrun abbudisse 7 Æþelhild 7 Eadgyfu æt Leofecanoran 7 hyre swustor 7 hyre dohtor, 7 Ælfgyfu 7 hyre dohtor 7 Wulfwyn 7 Æþelgyfu 7 Ælfwaru 7 Ælfgyfu 7 Æþelflæd 7 menig god þegen 7 god wif þe we ealle atellan ne magon þæt [þær] forþ com eal se fulla ge on werum ge on wifum.

æt Cwicelmeslæwe	*at Cwichelm's Low* (pronounce the name 'Quick-helm')
sio scir	*shire*
rihtlice	*justly*
rihtlicost	*most just*
geseman	*reconcile*

getæhte	*instructed* (**tǣcan** *teach* 'tae-chan', **tǣcð**, **tǣhte**, **getǣht**)
moste	*was allowed*
geahnian	*prove ownership* (perfective **ge-** + verb **agnian**)
seo ahnung	*declaration of proof of ownership*
se fultum	*help, assistance*
abbud	*abbot*
abbudisse	*abbess*
æþeling	*prince*
se discten	*steward* (i.e. **disc-þegn** literally *dish servant*)
atellan	*recount* 'ahTELLan' (**ā-tellan**)
þegen	*thegn* (variant spelling)
se fulla	*fullness*
ge… ge …	*both… and …*

Cultural contexts

CONTEMPORARY FIGURES IN THE WITNESS LIST

Apart from king Æthelred and his mother Ælfthryth, the most important figure in the list of witnesses is Sigeric, archbishop of Canterbury from 990 to 995. Sigeric is known to have been a patron of religious literature and actively involved in politics, particularly (as the Chronicle accounts reveal) in devising peaceful ways of dealing with the Viking threat by buying off the invaders with tribute.

The name Ælfric ('Alfritch') was common in this period. Another man of the same name witnesses the first stage of the dispute; this Ælfric – the ealdorman of Hampshire – features in the dramatic Chronicle accounts of the 990s and early 1000s, chiefly for his notorious treachery. Two important churchmen of the time also shared the name Ælfric; one was to be consecrated as archbishop of Canterbury in 996 as archbishop Sigeric's successor. The other Ælfric, a monk and priest who lived at Cerne Abbas in Dorset, was the most prolific writer of the period. He composed the first volume of his renowned Catholic Homilies in the period 990–92 and sent a copy with a dedicatory preface to archbishop Sigeric.

WOMEN'S NAMES

Document S 1454 is remarkable for the number of women's names it contains. There seem to be political reasons for this, since Wynflæd was able to count on the assistance of **Ælfþryþ þæs cyninges modor**, *Ælfthryth the king's mother*, a powerful force in the early years of Æthelred's reign; this probably helped her to muster a strong contingent of female witnesses in support of her case. The names are the typical dithematic ones consisting of two parts (see unit 1), with the common naming elements **Wyn-** *joy*, **Ælf-** *elf*, **Ead-** *blessed*, **Liof-** *dear*, **Æþel-** *noble* and **Wulf-** *wolf* for the first part of the name and **-flæd** *beauty*, **-þryþ** *power*, **-gyfu** *gift* and **-run** *counsel* for the second part of the name, as well as the perhaps more surprising **-hild** *battle* and **-waru** *protection*. Many of these elements were still productive and meaningful words in their own right and reflect something of the values of the parents.

FAMILY CONNECTIONS

The use of particular names can also reveal family connections. As was discussed in unit 1, there were many kingly names beginning **Ead-** in the tenth century, and children sometimes shared one of their name elements with a parent. St Wulfstan, godson of archbishop Wulfstan, was born about this time (1008) but was not necessarily named after his baptismal sponsor, since his father was called Æthelstan and his mother Wulfgifu; as the Latin Life of St Wulfstan puts it, in the translation by M. Winterbottom and R. Thomson: 'He was given the name Wulfstan, made up of the first part of his mother's and the second of his father's. The child had fair hopes, and fair too the omen which gave him a name taken from both parents, considering that he was destined to pour into himself the sanctity of both, and perhaps to surpass it beyond all comparison.'

OATH HELPING

The so-called *oath helping* was a common legal practice in many early medieval societies. It required that a plaintiff in a dispute should gather together a number of supporters who then swore to his or her good character. This is what seems to be happening in the case of Wynflæd's lawsuit; there is a distinction between witnessing, i.e. to establish her **ontalu** *claim*, and oath helping, i.e. to act as **ahnung** *proof of ownership*. First, Wynflæd gathers her witnesses (archbishop Sigeric, bishop Ordbryht, ealdorman Ælfric and the dowager royal mother Ælfthryth), who all witness to the fact of the earlier land transaction. Next, Wynflæd summons her character witnesses (the longer list of names in the second paragraph), **eal se fulla ge on werum ge on wifum** *all the plenitude*, as the text states, *of both men and women, who are all prepared to undertake the oath helping*.

 19.02

Þa cwædon þa witan þe þær wæron

Then the counsellors who were there said

Þa cwædon þa witan þe þær wæron þæt betere wære þæt man þene aþ aweg lete þonne hine man sealde, forþan þær syþþan nan freondscype nære 7 man wolde biddan þæs reaflaces þæt he hit sciolde agyfan 7 forgyldan 7 þam cyninge his wer. Þa let he þone aþ aweg 7 sealde Æþelsige biscope unbesacen land on hand þæt he þanon forð syþþan þæron ne spræce.

[This part of the text is translated in the section on reported speech.]

wære	*was, would be* (subjunctive form of **wæs** *was*)
þene = þæne, þone	*the*
se āþ	*oath, judicial swearing* 'ahth'
lete	*subjunctive of* **lǣtan let**, *leave* (**lǣtt, lēt, lēton, lǣten**)
aþ aweg lætan	*dispense with the oath*
aþ sellan	*give* (i.e. swear) *an oath*
forþan	*because*
nære	*would not be* from **ne + wære** (subjunctive of **wæs**)

þær syþþan nan freondscype nære	*there would not be any friendship afterwards*
biddan	*ask, demand* (with genitive)
þæt rēaflāc	*robbery*
agyfan	*to give up*
forgyldan	*to compensate* (e.g. for loss of income from rents)
wer = wergild	*compensation* (see unit 7)
unbesacen	*undisputed*
þæt	*so that*
þanon forð	*thenceforth, from then on*
spræce	*lay claim to* (legal term), subjunctive of **sprecan** *speak*

 19.03

Þa tæhte man hyre þæt hio sciolde bringan his fæder gold 7 siolfor

Then they told her that she had to bring his father's gold and silver

Þa tæhte man hyre þæt hio sciolde bringan his fæder gold 7 siolfor eal þæt hio hæfde, þa dyde hio swa hio dorste hyre aþe gebiorgan. Þa næs he þagyt on þam gehealden butan hio sceolde swerian þæt his æhta þær ealle wæron. Þa cwæþ hio þæt hio ne mihte hyre dæles ne he his.

And þyses wæs Ælfgar þæs cyninges gerefa to gewitnesse 7 Byrhtric, 7 Leofric æt Hwitecyrcan, 7 menig god man toeacan him.

dorste	*dared* (see Grammar)
gebiorgan	*to protect*
þagyt	*still*
gehealden	*satisfied*
butan	*except that*
swerian	*swear*
æhta	*possessions*
hyre dæles ne he his	*for her part, nor he for his*
æt Hwitecyrcan	*at Whitchurch* (the name apparently refers to a church rendered with white plaster, a style of ecclesiastical architecture that had become common by the year 1000)

Practice

Answer these questions about the study text.

1 What happened at Woolmer? _____

2 How did Leofwine react to the message from the king? _____

3 Did the king attend the meeting at Cwichelm's Barrow? _____

4 Why did Leofwine dispense with the oath? _____

5 What was Wynflæd required to do at the settlement of the dispute? _____

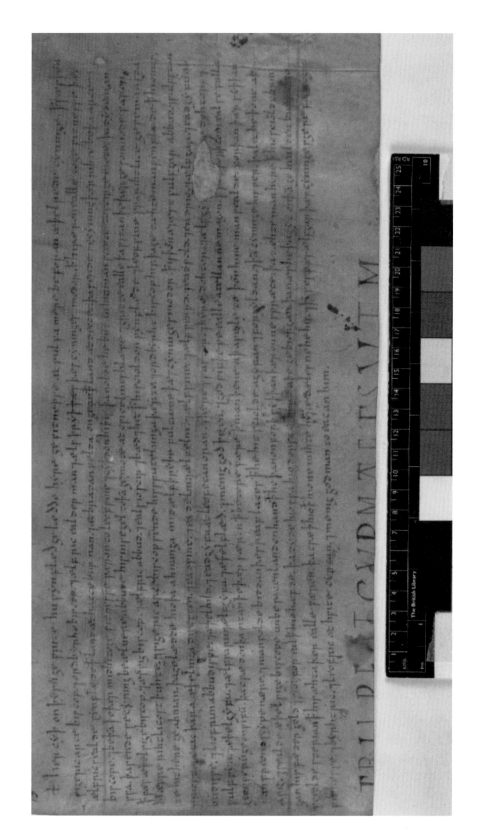

Grammar

REPORTED SPEECH

Reported speech, otherwise known as indirect speech or indirect discourse, is a grammatical term for dialogue which is reported indirectly by verbs of saying and speaking. In modern English, the direct utterance Edith said, '*I am well*' can be reported indirectly by a sentence such as *Edith said that she was well*. Here the present tense verb *is* becomes past tense *was*.

In similar contexts in Old English, instead of an agreement of tense, or sequence of the same tense, the verb usually goes into the subjunctive mood, which makes the words of the utterance more conjectural. This is hearsay, what was probably said.

The 'conjectural subjunctive'

In the Wynflæd dispute, for example, the counsellors' spoken decision is reported in the subjunctive:

Þa cwædon þa witan þe þær wæron þæt betere <u>wære</u> þæt man þene aþ aweg <u>lete</u> þonne hine man <u>sealde</u>, forþan þær syþþan nan freondscype <u>nære</u>, 7 man <u>wolde</u> biddan þæs reaflaces þæt he hit <u>sciolde</u> agyfan 7 forgyldan, 7 þam cyninge his wer.

Then the counsellors who were there said that it was better that one should dispense with the oath than give it because there would not be any friendship afterwards (between them) and people would ask of the stolen property that he should return it and pay compensation for it, and pay the king his wergild.

The verbs in the subjunctive in this passage are underlined. It will be seen that the basic principle of the 'subjunctive as conjecture' (see unit 13) applies also to reported speech. The facts of the narrative – that is, what was done – are given in the indicative, while the ephemeral words – what was said – are reported in the subjunctive.

HOW TO RECOGNIZE THE SUBJUNCTIVE

Particularly distinctive are the past subjunctive forms **nære**, which corresponds to the past indicative **næs**, and **lete**, which corresponds to the normal past *let*, as seen in the subsequent sentence:

Þa let he þone aþ aweg, 7 sealde Æþelsige biscope unbesacen land on hand þæt he þanon forð syþþan þæron ne spræce.

Then he dispensed with the oath, and gave the land undisputed into the hands of bishop Æthelsige (promising) that thenceforth thereafter he would make no other claim to it.

The subjunctive **spræce** (equivalent to indicative **spræc**) in the phrase **þæron ne spræce** is here translated as *would make no other claim to it*; it expresses conjecture and anticipation, and as reported speech, it implies that this is the substance of the words Leofwine used when he promised not to lay claim to the land thereafter.

SHORTCOMINGS OF THE SUBJUNCTIVE

It will be seen in the two sentences just quoted that **sealde** *gave* has the same form in both subjunctive and indicative. To see how this happens it is worth reviewing verb conjugation, taking the 3rd person singular and plural of **sellan** *to give* and **sprecan** *to speak*:

	weak	strong
present indicative	he selð, hi sellað	he spricð, hi sprecað
present subjunctive	he selle, hi sellen	he sprece, hi sprecen
past indicative	he sealde, hi sealdon	he spræc, hi spræcon
past subjunctive	he sealde, hi sealden	he spræce, hi spræcen

Comparing tenses, we see that the subjunctive is most distinctive in the present tense because of its **-e** or **-en** ending, which contrasts with the indicative '*th*' sound in its endings **-ð** or **-að**. In the past, it is the strong verb which has the most distinctive subjunctive (**spræce**) while the weak verb cannot as easily distinguish the two moods.

ANCIENT SITES ALONG THE RIDGEWAY

Cwichelm's Barrow

The Berkshire assembly took place regularly at the mound called Scutchamer Knob near the village of East Hendred. At a high point on the ridge, and now surrounded by trees, this barrow still commands a wide view of the surrounding countryside. In Old English texts the landmark was known as **Cwichelmeshlæwe** or **Cwichelm's Barrow**, after an early West Saxon king, and it served as a meeting place presumably because of its 'ancestral value' (Sarah Semple p. 87) and its archaic and ancient associations, of which there are many in this region.

Ashdown

Located near East Hendred, Cwichelm's Barrow stands beside the old green road known as the Ridgeway. As its name suggests this is a long high ridge; the bedrock is chalk, well drained and hence a good surface underfoot. It has been a highway since prehistoric times, with numerous archaeological sites along its route, as the 1:50 000 map for Newbury and Wantage testifies (Ordnance Survey sheet 174). Beginning south of Swindon at the earthwork of Liddington Castle, travellers on foot follow the high ground eastwards along Æscesdun or Ashdown, site of Alfred's pitched battle against the Danes in 871. As the Chronicle put it: **ond þæs ymb .iiii. niht gefeaht Æþered cyning 7 Ælfred his broþur wiþ alne þone here on Æcesdune**, *and after four nights king Æthelred and his brother Ælfred fought with all the Viking army at Ashdown.*

Wayland's Smithy and further sites

Passing further eastwards along the ridge, you come first to Wayland's Smithy, a chambered long cairn looking northwards to present-day Ashbury and Compton Beauchamp. You move then to the earthwork of Uffington Castle and the famous White Horse, a huge leaping figure of chalk cut out of the turf on the north-facing slope. From here the route continues eastwards to a large earthwork ring at Segsbury Down just south of Wantage, birthplace of king Alfred. The Ridgeway then passes various mounds and other sites before reaching Cwichelm's Barrow. Finally, after passing Grim's Ditch (perhaps associated with another legendary figure, the pagan god Woden) the Ridgeway divides near the site of an old Roman temple and makes for the Thames at Streatley by the southerly route and the Thames at Cholsey by the northerly path.

Clearly, as the recent researches of Sarah Semple also confirm (see Bibliography), many of these sites were seen as significant or symbolic places; they were known and re-named in Anglo-Saxon times.

Some related texts

1 *THE OLD ENGLISH BOETHIUS* ON WAYLAND SMITH

Wayland's Smithy is a prehistoric monument to which the Old English name Weland became attached. This legendary Germanic blacksmith is mentioned briefly in various texts, including the poems *Beowulf* (line 455) and *Deor* (lines 1–7). Notably his story features in the carved illustrations on the whale-bone artefact known as the Franks Casket. In the Old English version of Boethius's *Consolation of Philosophy*, his remains are associated with a great mound or barrow in the landscape. Here the Old English translator and adapter improvises and expands on Boethius's Latin text and introduces Weland into an elegiac passage in Metre 10 (*The Consolation* is a prosimetric work, divided into alternating passages of prose and poetry):

> **Hwær sint nu þæs wisan   Welandes ban,**
> **þæs gold-smiðes,   þe wæs geo mærost?**
> **Forðy ic cwæð þæs wisan   Welandes ban,**
> **forþy ængum ne mæg   eorð-buendra**
> **se cræft losian   þe him Crist onlænð.**
> **Ne mæg mon æfre þy eð   ænne wræccan**
> **his cræftes beniman,   þe mon oncerran mæg**
> **sunnan onswifan,   and ðisne swiftan rodor**
> **of his rihtryne   rinca ænig.**
> **Hwa wat nu þæs wisan   Welandes ban,**
> **on hwelcum hlæwa   hrusan þeccen?**

> *'Where now are the bones of the wise Weland,*
> *the goldsmith, who was previously very famous?*
> *I said the bones of wise Weland*
> *because the skill which Christ grants to*
> *any earth dweller cannot be lost by him.*
> *Nor can anyone ever deprive a wretch*
> *of his skill more easily than any man can divert*
> *and turn aside the sun and this swift firmament*
> *from its correct course.*
> *Who now knows in which mound the bones*
> *of wise Weland cover the earthen floor?'*

(*The Old English Boethius*, ed. and trans. Irvine and Godden, pp. 112–13)

2 CWICHELM'S BARROW AND THE VIKINGS

As we saw above, Cwichelm's Barrow was the site of the Berkshire assembly in the years 990–2; about fourteen years later it once again became a site of dramatic confrontation. The C version of the *Anglo-Saxon Chronicle* reports extensively on the Viking Wars of the years 991 to 1016; the narrative is one of almost constant defeat, peppered with touches of irony and indignation but told with great skill and command of rhetoric. Here is this chronicler's account of the movements of the Viking army in the winter of 1006, as it passed along the Ridgeway over Ashdown to Cwichelm's Barrow:

Þa hit winterlæhte, þa ferde seo fyrd ham. 7 se here com þa ofer þa Sancte Martines mæssan to his friðstole Wihtlande 7 tylode him þær æghwær þæs ðe hi behofedon, 7 þa to ðam middan wintran eodan him to heora gearwan feorme ut þuruh Hamtunscire into Bearrucscire to Readingon, 7 hi a dydon heora ealdan gewunan, atendon hiora herebeacen swa hi ferdon. Wendon þa to Wealingaforda and þæt eall forswældon, 7 wæron him þa ane niht æt Ceolesige, 7 wendon him þa andlang Æscesdune to Cwicelmeshlæwe, 7 þær onbidedon beotra gylpa, forðon oft man cwæþ, gif hi Cwicelmeshlæw gesohton, þæt hi næfre to sæ gan ne scoldon, wendon him þa oðres weges hamwerd. Þa wæs ðær fyrd gesomnod æt Cynetan, 7 hi þær togædere fengon, 7 sona þæt wered on fleame gebrohton 7 syþþan hiora herehyþe to sæ feredan, ac þær mihton geseon Wincester leode rancne here 7 unearhne ða hi be hiora gate to sæ eodon, 7 mete 7 madmas ofer .l. mila him fram sæ fetton.

When winter came the English army went home. And the Viking army came then at St Martin's Mass to its refuge on the Isle of Wight, and acquired there what it needed, and then at Midwinter they went to their ready feast out through Hampshire into Berkshire to Reading. And they practised their old custom and lighted their beacons as they travelled. They came to Wallingford and burned it all, and were then one night at Cholsey, and so moved along Ashdown to Cwichelm's Barrow. There they awaited the boasted threats, because it was often said that if they reached Cwichelm's Barrow, they would never get back to the sea, and they returned home by a different route. By this time the local levy was assembled at Kennet, and they came together, and at once they put the levy to flight, and afterwards they transported their plunder to the sea. So there the people of Winchester could see the proud bold army as they passed their gates towards the sea, and they had taken food and money over fifty miles from the sea.

? Test yourself

1 Read through the Wynflæd versus Leofwine narrative again and identify one more verb (other than those verbs discussed in the grammar section) which is unambiguously in the subjunctive both in its form and function in the sentence. Translate the sentence.

_____

2 Are there any verbs in the passage which could be either indicative or subjunctive according to their form and their use in the sentence? In each case translate the clause or sentence in question. What helps the reader to decide which mood is intended?

_____

_____

_____

_____

SELF-CHECK

I CAN ...
understand the typical language of Old English legal disputes
read texts containing the Tironian *nota*
recognize the use of the subjunctive in contexts of conjecture and reported speech

20 *Doð þegnlice, and wel abeodað mine ærende to þam gemote*

Act like thegns, and deliver my message to the assembly

In this unit you will learn about:
▶ *the changing English vocabulary*
▶ *Old Norse vocabulary in English*
▶ *the influence of French*
▶ *modal verbs*
▶ *'thegnly' behaviour*

You will read:
▶ *the account of the Herefordshire lawsuit*
▶ *an extract from Wulfstan's Promotion Law*
▶ *an extract from* The Battle of Maldon, *lines 286–94*

 20.00

Doð þegnlice, and wel abeodað mine ærende to þam gemote
Act like thegns, and deliver my message to the assembly

Ⅴ Vocabulary builder

THE CHANGING ENGLISH VOCABULARY

In the eleventh-century Herefordshire Lawsuit, the main text in this unit, three thegns are appointed to learn the details of an unnamed lady's claim to some land: **Leofwine æt Frome**, **Ægelsig þe Reada**, and **Winsig scægðman**. Their names throw light on the state of the Old English lexicon as society moved from the time of king Cnut to the reign of Edward the Confessor. Apart from the names of these thegns, some interesting insights can be also gained from two other names in the document, both of mixed origin: **Tofi Pruda** and **Eadwine Enneawnes sunu**.

TRADITIONAL NAMES AND NEW BYNAMES

Leofwine æt Frome *Leofwine of Frome*

The first of the three thegns is **Leofwine æt Frome**. **Leofwine** is a traditional Old English dithematic name; of its two elements **leof** *dear* was still in current use, whereas **wine** *friend* was otherwise confined to verse contexts, e.g. **goldwine** *gold-friend* i.e. lord or patron, a poetic compound akin to **beahgifa** *ring-giver* in line 288 of *The Battle of Maldon* (see extract below). In everyday prose, by contrast, the word for *friend* was **freond**. Leofwine's by-name

216

æt Frome indicates the location of his thegnly residence, perhaps a fortified place of the kind described in *Wulfstan's Promotion Law* (see below). Under later Norman and French influence, the preposition **æt** in such names was replaced by **de**.

Ægelsig þe Reada *Æthelsige the Red*

With hindsight, we can see that the name *Ægelsig þe Reada* (in traditional Old English **Æþelsige Reada** or perhaps **Æþelsige se Reada**) points to various ways in which the English language was changing at this time. Firstly, instead of using the definite article **se** – or indeed missing it out as with **Þurcil Hwita** or *Thorkell (the) White* – the name **Ægelsig þe Reada** demonstrates one of the first occurrences in the language of the definite article **þe**. This was to become the determiner *the* (i.e. the definite article) in Middle English and modern English. Another change is phonetic rather than grammatical: the name **Æþelsige** is simplified, dropping its 'th' sound and final syllable **-e** to become *Ægelsig*, probably pronounced roughly as 'Ael-see'. A similar loss of 'th' occurred in the name **Æðelræd**, which became *Ailred*; in the twelfth century a famous Latin religious writer signed his name *Ailred de Rivaulx*, his domicile being one of the great Yorkshire monasteries of the French-based Cistercian order. Such changes are more likely to occur first in personal names, which are on people's lips all the time, rather than in the phrases of formal writing. In the eleventh century the Old English written standard was taught alongside Latin in the monastic and cathedral schools; this was less common in the twelfth century, thus allowing such linguistic changes to continue more freely.

Old Norse vocabulary in English

Winsig scægðman *Winsig the Viking*

Of the three thegns delegated to hear the lady's claim at Fawley in the Herefordshire Lawsuit, the third – Winsig – has an interesting Old Norse byname **scægðman**, to be translated *ship-man* or even *Viking*. Old Norse was the language spoken by the Vikings, although with dialectal variants, throughout Scandinavia and in parts of England – especially the region known as the Danelaw. Cognate with Old English, Old Norse had many similar-sounding words but significantly different grammatical structures. *In king Cnut's day*, **be Cnutes dæge cinges**, Old Norse was heard at the royal court in Winchester, and the skalds performed their poems not far from the church where archbishop Wulfstan declaimed his Old English sermons and lawcodes. It is no surprise that in this context a number of words connected with Anglo-Danish rule were borrowed from Old Norse into Old English; for example:

MARITIME: liþ *fleet*, **æsc** *warship*, **barda** *beaked ship*, **cnear** *small warship*, **ha** *rowlock*, **hamele** *oarlock*, **hæfene** *haven*, **lænding** *landing-site*, **butsecarl** *sailor*, **steormann** *pilot*, **scegðmann** *Viking, shipman*

LEGAL: feolaga *fellow, formal treaty*, **grið** *truce* or *sanctuary*, **husting** *tribunal*, **lagu** *law*, **lahbryce** *breach of the law*, **lahmenn** *lawmen*, **mal** *law suit*, **niðing** *outlaw*, **sac** *guilty*, **sacleas** *innocent*, **utlaga** *outlaw*, **utlagian** *to outlaw* (see unit 4)

MILITARY: brynige *mailshirt*, **genge** *troop*, **targa** *small round shield*

POLITICS: eorl *earl*, **huscarl** *housecarl* or *member of king's guard*

MONETARY: gersum *treasure*

By the time Edward the Confessor came to the throne in 1042, most of these words were firmly entrenched in the language; they occur with increasing frequency in the later annals of the *Anglo-Saxon Chronicle* (especially manuscript E, which was copied in the twelfth century, probably from a Canterbury Chronicle, and which continues up to 1154).

The influence of French

TOFI PRUDA *TOFI THE PROUD*

Tofi (a Danish name) was a prominent figure in Cnut's England, known elsewhere as a witness to charters and as one of the main figures in a Latin history composed in the twelfth century known as the Waltham Chronicle. Tofi is also connected with a dramatic incident that took place shortly before the accession of Edward the Confessor: Cnut's son Harthacnut was taken seriously ill at the wedding feast of Tofi with Gytha, daughter of Osgod Clapa, a Danish landholder from the Eastern shires.

Interestingly, Tofi's name has cosmopolitan implications, for this important Anglo-Danish aristocrat Tofig Pruda has a French byname. Like **sott** *fool* (an insult cited by Byrhtferth), **prud** *proud* appears to derive from French, as do **tur** *tower*, **capun** *capon* and **castell** *castle* – signs of the wide cultural connections of late Old English society. This tendency to borrow from French increased enormously with the prestige of French in the later medieval period (see Bibliography).

Welsh

EDWINE ENNEAWNES SUNU

Little is known of this name other than these lines in the document. Since the dispute takes place in Herefordshire, in the border country, it is possible that Enneawn was a Welshman. It is a reminder that another language culture existed near at hand in Wales; its literature was to flourish under the Welsh princes in the twelfth century.

Grammar

MODAL VERBS

Modal verbs express the idea of ability, volition, obligation, necessity. The main group includes **cann** *know*, **dearr** *dare*, **mæg** *can*, **mōt** *must*, **sceal** *must*, **þearf** *need*. They are known in Old English grammar as preterite present verbs, preterite being the alternative name for the past tense. The distinguishing feature is that in the present tense these verbs resemble past tenses of strong verbs in their form.

modal verb present tense	strong verb (class III) past tense (preterite)
ic cann *I know*	**ic sang** *I sang*
þu cannst *you know*	**þu sunge** *you sang*
he cann *he knows*	**he sang** *he sang*
we cunnon *we know*	**we sungon** *we sang*

The historical development of these verbs is an interesting case of adaptation. Because of the past tense form but present tense meaning, these verbs were anomalous, and speakers eventually created new past tenses. The solution was to use a weak (consonantal) verb form, so that the past tense of **ic cann** is **ic cuðe** *I knew* and the plural form is **we cuðon** *we knew*.

MODAL VERBS **SCEAL** AND **MÆG** CONTRASTED WITH **WILLE** *WANT*

The modal verbs **sceal** and **mæg** are preterite present verbs. An exception to this pattern is **willan** *to want*; its forms are closer to those of an ordinary weak verb. For example:

cyning sceal rice healdan (unit 2) *a king must rule a country*

Ymbe þa feower timan we wyllað cyðan iungum preostum ma þinga, þæt hig magon þe ranclicor þas þing heora clericum geswutelian (unit 5)

About the four seasons we wish to proclaim to young priests more things, so that they can explain the more boldly these things to their clerics.

Present indicative		
ic sceal *I must*	**ic mæg** *I can*	**ic wille** *I want*
þu scealt *you must*	**þu meaht** *you can*	**þu wilt** *you want*
heo sceal *she must*	**heo mæg** *she can*	**heo wile** *she wants*
we sculon *we must*	**we magon** *we can*	**we willað** *we want*
Past indicative		
ic sciolde *I had to*	**ic mihte** *I could*	**ic wolde** *I wanted*
þu scioldest	**þu mihtest**	**þu woldest**
we scioldon	**we mihton**	**we woldon**

Other irregular verbs you should recognize are:

ic þearf, we þurfon *need*   **ic þorfte** *I needed*

ic dearr, we durron *dare*   **ic dorste** *I dared*

ic mōt, we mōton *am, are allowed*   **ic mōste** *I was allowed*

ic cann, we cunnon *know*   **ic cūðe** *I knew*

ic ann, we unnon *grant*   **ic ūðe** *I granted*

    ic hæbbe geunnen *I have granted*

THE HEREFORDSHIRE LAWSUIT (S 1462)

In the latter half of the reign of king Cnut, *a shire assembly* (**scirgemot**) gathered **æt Ægelnoðesstane** *'at Ailnothstan'* (now Aylton) in Herefordshire: Ailnoth's Stone was apparently a local landmark. The meeting was presided over by the local bishop, called Æthelstan, and attended by **ealle þa þegnas on Herefordscire**. Its purpose was to hear the pleading of a lawsuit by one Eadwine, son of Enneawn, against his own mother, not named, who lived at **Fæliglæh** i.e. Fawley, nine miles south west of Aylton. The following is the text (S 1462).

Notice the presence of the bishop at this gathering, but one question to bear in mind is: what was his role in the actual hearing?

Most of the vocabulary in the first section below will be familiar from previous units in this book, but note that **sceawian**, which normally means *to look at*, here takes on the idiomatic meaning *to appoint*.

 20.01

Be Cnutes dæge cinges *in the time of king Cnut*

Her swutelað on þissum gewrite þæt an scirgemot sæt æt Ægelnoðesstane be Cnutes dæge cinges. Þær sæton Æðelstan biscop, and Ranig ealdorman, and Edwine þæs ealdormannes sunu, and Leofwine Wulsiges sunu, and Ðurcil Hwita. And Tofig Pruda com þær on þæs cinges ærende. And þær wæs Bryning scirgerefa, and Ægelgeard æt Frome, and Leofwine æt Frome and Godric æt Stoce and ealle þa þegnas on Herefordscire. Ða com þær farende to þam gemote Edwine Enneawnes sunu, and spæc þær on his agene modor æfter sumon dæle landes, þæt wæs Weolintun and Cyrdesleah. Ða acsode þe bisceop hwa sceolde andswerian for his moder. Ða andsweorode Ðurcil Hwita and sæde þæt he sceolde, gif he þa talu cuðe. Þa he ða talu na ne cuðe, ða sceawode man þreo þegnas of þam gemote ðær þær heo wæs – and þæt wæs æt Fæliglæh – þæt wæs Leofwine æt Frome, and Ægelsig þe Reada, and Winsig scægðman.

 20.02

Þa acsoðon heo hwylce talu heo hæfde

Then they asked what claim she had

And þa þa heo to hire comon þa acsoðon heo hwylce talu heo hæfde ymbe þa land þe hire sunu æfter spæc. Ða sæde heo þæt heo nan land hæfde þe him aht to gebyrede, and gebealh heo swiðe eorlice wið hire sunu, and gecleopade ða Leoflæde hire magan to hire Ðurcilles wif and beforan heom to hire þus cwæð, 'Her sit Leoflæde min mage þe ic geann ægðer ge mines landes, ge mines goldes, ge rægles, ge reafes, ge ealles þe ic ah æfter minon dæge.' And heo syððan to þam þegnon cwæþ, 'Doð þegnlice, and wel abeodað mine ærende to þam gemote beforan eallum þam godan

mannum. And cyðaþ heom hwæm ic mines landes geunnen hæbbe, and ealre minre æhte – and minan agenan suna næfre nan þing! And biddað heom beon þisses to gewitnesse.'

gebyrian	*to belong*
gebelgan	*to become angry* (**gebelgan, belhð, bealh, bulgon, gebolgen**)
eorlice	*angrily* (cf. **ierlic** *angry*)
gecleopade	*past tense of* **cleopian** *to call*
þæt rægl = þæt hrægl	*clothing*
ic ah	*I own*
þegnlice	*in a thegnly manner* (adverb in suffix **-lice**)
abeodan	*announce* 'ah-BAIo-dan'
þæt ærende	*message* 'AIR-en-deh'
hwæm	*to whom* (dative)

 20.03

Ða astod Ðurcil hwita up on þam gemote

Then Thorkell the White stood up at the assembly

And heo ða swæ dydon; ridon to þam gemote and cyðdon eallon þam godan mannum hwæt heo on heom geled hæfde. Ða astod Ðurcil hwita up on þam gemote, and bæd ealle þa þægnas syllan his wife þa land clæne þe hire mage hire geuðe. And heo swa dydon. And Ðurcill rad ða to sancte Æþelberhtes mynstre, be ealles þæs folces leafe and gewitnesse, and let settan on ane Cristes boc.

ridon	*they rode* 'riddon' (**rīdan, rītt, rād, ridon, geriden**)
geled	'yuh-laid' from **lecgan** *to lay* (**legð, legde, legdon, gelegd**)
lecgan on	*to charge with*
astod	*stood up* 'a-STOHD' (**ā + standan, stent, stōd, stōdon, gestanden**)
clæne	*cleanly, completely*
seo mage	*kinswoman* 'mah-yuh'

'THEGNLY' BEHAVIOUR

In the Herefordshire Lawsuit, there is a rare occurrence of the adverb **þegnlice**, which connotes not only social status but also behaviour appropriate to that rank:

Doð þegnlice, and wel abeodað mine ærende to þam gemote beforan eallum þam godan mannum.

Act in a thegnly manner, and present my statement well at the Assembly, before all the good men.

What does 'thegnly' behaviour entail? Two Old English texts throw some light on the connotations of this word: the Promotion Law by Wulfstan archbishop of York yields information on the status of **þegenriht**, *the rights and privileges of a thegn*, while a line in the poem *The Battle of Maldon* gives information on the kind of actions or attitudes that 'thegnly' might imply.

1 *Wulfstan's* geþyncðo *promotion law*

The text by Wulfstan known as *Geþyncðo* (which means *Status* or the *Promotion Law*) is recorded in two manuscripts:

- the Corpus Wulfstan Anthology (Corpus Christi College, Cambridge manuscript 201), already mentioned earlier since it contains the Joseph story (see unit 14)

- the Textus Roffensis, an anthology of legal texts compiled at Rochester in the twelfth century. Compared with the Corpus Christi text, the Rochester version contains a few extra details on the legal requirements for thegnly status; this is the text given here.

The translation below poses a number of problems, in its attempt to represent the rhyme of **cheorl** and **eorl** and the alliteration of **thegn** and **theoden** (þeoden is a traditional poetic word for *prince*). Especially difficult is the question of how to translate **ceorl** ('cheorl'). Normally the word refers to a low-ranking landowner or freeman, but the modern English *churl* and *peasant* have the wrong connotations.

Hit wæs hwilum on Engla lagum þæt leod and lagu for be geþincðum; and þa wæron leodwitan weorðscipes wyrðe ælc be his mæðe, eorl and ceorl, þegen and þeoden. And gif ceorl geþeah þæt he hæfde fullice fif hida agenes landes, cirican and kycenan, bellhus and burhgeat, setl and sundernote on cynges healle, þonne wæs he þanon forð þegenrihtes weorðe.

Once it was in the laws of the English that nation and law proceeded by rank; and at that time counsellors were worthy of honour each according to his degree: earl and cheorl, thegn and theoden (prince). And if a freeman flourished so that he had five hides of his own land, a church and kitchen, a bell-house and a castle-gate, a seat and special office in the king's hall, then he was thenceforth worthy of thegnly legal status.

Here the key term is **þegenriht** *thegnly legal status*; this is something that can be acquired: a freeman can rise through the ranks, as long as he has the right prerequisites.

Recent archaeological research has confirmed the thegnly status of the criteria listed: it seems that by the eleventh century high-ranking nobility were living in fortified settlements, basically a manor house equipped with a stone castle-gate, a stone tower such as the one at Earls Barton in Northamptonshire, a kitchen, and – in contrast to earlier periods of communal minsters – with their own private chapel or church. It is not strictly correct to call this kind of **burh** a *castle*, since the word **castel** came into Old English in the eleventh century, usually to denote the particular motte and bailey as built by some of Edward the Confessor's continental supporters, and by the Normans after 1066. Nevertheless such accoutrements make the thegn seem very similar in status to the knight who was shortly to appear on the medieval English social scene (for further details see Bibliography).

2 From *The Battle of Maldon*

This passage (lines 288–94) comes from the end of the poem as the warriors each in turn declare their intentions to fight on despite the certainty of imminent defeat. In keeping with the warrior theme, there are a number of traditional poetic words and martial images, including three words for *battle*: **hild**, **here** and **wælstow**; three words for *lord*: **frea**, **beahgifa** and **þeoden**; and one word connected to the traditional relationship between lord and retainer: **beotian** *to make a formal vow of service*. Such passages are often cited to show the Anglo-Saxon adherence to an ancient Germanic type of heroic code, as celebrated in poems in an older style such as *Beowulf*, *The Wanderer* and (with a religious application) *The Dream of the Rood*. But *The Battle of Maldon* mixes the old and the new. In the light of the previous passage from *Wulfstan's Promotion Law* it is interesting to see here an evocation of riding **hale to hame**, *safely home* to the thegnly **burh**, a day-dream that is contrasted with the reality of the battle from which Offa will not return. Instead the thegn will lie next to his fallen **theoden** (note the same alliterative pattern as in Wulfstan); he will not desert his lord. Here the word **þegnlice** connotes *courage* and absolute *loyalty*, thegnly qualities.

> Raðe wearð æt hilde   Offa forheawen;
>
> he hæfde ðeah geforþod   þæt he his frean gehet,
>
> 290 swa he beotode ær   wið his beahgifan
>
> þæt hi sceoldon begen   on burh ridan,
>
> hale to hame,   oððe on here crincgan,
>
> on wælstowe   wundum sweltan:
>
> he læg ðegenlice   ðeodne gehende.

> *Quickly Offa was cut down at the battle;*
>
> *he had nevertheless accomplished what he promised his lord*
>
> *as he had vowed to his ring-giver*
>
> *that they would both ride into the castle,*
>
> *safely home, or else fall in the fighting,*
>
> *on the battlefield die of their wounds:*
>
> *he lay in a thegnly manner close to his theoden.*

? Test yourself

Translate the text of the Herefordshire Lawsuit into natural idiomatic English.

_____

_____

_____

_____

_____

_____

_____

_____

_____

_____

_____

_____

_____

_____

_____

_____

_____

_____

_____

_____

_____

_____

_____

_____

_____

_____

_____

SELF-CHECK

	I CAN ...
⬤	observe lexical and grammatical changes in Old English in the 11th century
⬤	recognize loanwords from Old Norse and French
⬤	understand Old English modal verbs
⬤	understand the connotations of the term **þegn** _thegn_

21 *Se flod ut gewat*
The tide went out

In this unit you will learn about:
▶ *specifically poetic vocabulary*
▶ *the rhythm of Old English poetry*
▶ *patterns of alliteration in an Old English poem*
▶ *occasional effects of rhyme and assonance*
▶ *problems of editing and interpreting manuscript texts*

You will read:
▶ *lines 55b–83 from* **The Battle of Maldon**
▶ *four contemporary annals from the* **Anglo-Saxon Chronicle version C**

The Battle of Maldon in August 991

During the reign of Æthelred the Unready, in the same year in which Wynflæd won her lawsuit at Cwichelm's Barrow (see unit 19), a battle was fought against Viking raiders at the Blackwater estuary near Maldon in Essex, the East Saxon region of England. The coast there is characterized by harbour towns at the heads of long, broad, winding inlets, accessible to sea trade but also open to Viking raiders. Already that summer a fleet of dragon ships had sailed up the Orwell estuary and attacked and plundered the rich trading settlement at Ipswich. They had then moved south and sailed up the Blackwater estuary, and apparently were now beached on Northey island a few miles from Maldon. The East Saxon **ealdorman**, i.e. *the prince or governor of the region*, whose name was Byrhtnoth, raised the greater **fyrd** (*the standing army of local levies*) to deal with the threat.

Some time after 991, the events of the day were revisited, and an anonymous poet composed an Old English poem on the battle in a traditional style, which we call *The Battle of Maldon*. This vivid and dramatic account of the battle, comparable in tone perhaps to Alfred Lord Tennyson's *Charge of the Light Brigade* (1854), has become one of the key texts of Old English literature. An extract from *The Battle of Maldon is* given below (for other passages from the poem, see units 6, 7 and 20).

THE ORIGINS OF MALDON

1 The place-name Maldon

The most likely interpretation of the name **Mældun** is *the hill marked with a cross* (see Reaney 1935). There is also Malden in Surrey, Maulden in Bedfordshire and Meldon in Northumberland, all of which have the same origin (Rumble 2006: 36).

The element **dūn** in the name means *a low, level-topped hill* suitable for a settlement-site; it is regarded by place-name specialists Gelling and Cole (2014: 164–5) as an early Old English name for what was already an ancient settlement. Central Essex has a cluster of such place-names: Ockendon, Basildon, Laindon and Horndon (Gelling and Cole, xix), and south of Maldon are Ashdon *Assa's Hill* and Canewdon *Cana's Hill* overlooking the River Crouch (Rodwell 1991:129–30).

The element **mæl** *sign, monument, cross* is found in other place-names in the descriptions of the boundaries of estates (for charter bounds see unit 10). In charter S 714, which records a gift of land at Washington in Sussex to an important bishop in the reign of Edgar (959–975) the word occurs as **ealdan cristesmæle** *the old Christ-cross*, **Cristes mæl** meaning literally *Christ's cross*. The cross in this document seems to be located on the slopes of the ancient Iron Age hill-fort of Chanctonbury Ring: the bounds of the estate follow a route that goes past Lidgeard's Barrow, Tatemann's Tomb and Hatheburg's Mound, landmarks perhaps named after men and women of the distant past (like Cwichelm's Barrow; see unit 19). Charter S 1546 records such a prominent cross at Shellingdon on the Ridgeway, between Faringdon and Wantage **andlang hrycgeweges to þam cristes mæle** *along the Ridgeway to the Christ-cross*. Another charter from the year 966 describes a similar landscape feature (S 738). The key phrasing here is **wearddune þær þæt cristelmæl stod**, which means literally *the guardian-hill* (or perhaps *beacon-hill*) *where the Christ-cross stood*.

Given these parallels, it is possible that **Mældun** in Essex was a similarly named place, with ancient associations.

2 A parallel in Bede

The historian Bede, writing his *Latin Ecclesiatical History of the English Nation* in the year 731, records the victory of the saintly Oswald, king of Northumbria from 634 to 642, over the 'heathen' Cadwalla at a place called Hefenfeld or Heavenly Field. Oswald's success is ascribed to his hands-on piety as he personally helps to construct a wooden cross on the eve of the battle. In the *Old English Bede*, a paraphrase of *Bede's Latin Ecclesiastical History* written around the year 900, this cross is called specifically **þæt Cristes mæl**, literally, *the Christ's cross*, which Oswald personally holds in his hands as his men set it in the ground:

Is þæt sægd, þæt he þæt Cristæs mæl hraðe weorce geworhte ond seað adulfe, in þæm hit stondan scolde. Ond he se cyning seolf wæs wallende in his geleafan; and þæt Cristes mæl genom and in þone seað sette ond mid his hondum bæm hit heold and hæfde, oð þæt his þegnas mid moldan hit bestryðed hæfdon ond gefæstnadan.

It is said that he constructed the Christ's cross quickly and dug out the pit in which it was to stand. And the king himself was fervent in his faith; he picked up the cross and set it in the pit and held it and had it in his two hands while his thegns covered it with earth and fixed it there.

Unlike this cross in Northumbria, we have no record of who placed the cross in the ground on the hill at Maldon, but it must have constituted a prominent feature in the Essex landscape. Evidently the local people who perpetuated the name remembered that a cross had once stood on this spot.

3 Fortress Maldon

The first actual written record of the name **Mældun** occurs about halfway through the reign of Edward the Elder, king Alfred's son and successor, in the records of the *Anglo-Saxon Chronicle*. In the annal for the year 912, we see the king residing temporarily at Maldon while his men are building fortresses, one six miles to the north at Witham, the other thirty-six miles to the west at Hertford. Edward's policy was to construct a network of defensive places across the southern part of the Danelaw in order to control the region. The policy was successful, and the mixed population – not only of Angles and East Saxons but also of Danes, i.e. descendants of Viking settlers from the 870s – was slowly but surely submitting to him and acknowledging him as king. It is interesting to note Edward's choice of the securely guarded hill at Maldon as the location for his temporary encampment, and it is significant that a little later, in the year 916, Maldon too was rebuilt as a fortress.

4 The Fight at Maldon in 917

Shortly afterwards, in the autumn of 917, as the Chronicle reports, a battle was fought at Maldon, in which the English emerged victorious. Ironically, given that this was to be the site of the famous defeat for the English some seventy-four years later in 991, the new **burh** proved its worth:

Þa æfter þam þa giet þæs ilcan hærfestes gegadorode micel here hine of Eastenglum ægþer ge þæs landheres ge þara wicinga þe hie him to fultume aspanen hæfdon 7 þohton þæt hie sceoldon gewrecan hira teonun 7 foron to Mældune 7 ymbsæton þa burg 7 fuhton þæron oþ þam burgwarum com mara fultum to utan to helpe, 7 forlet se here þa burg 7 for fram; 7 þa foron þa men æfter ut of þære byrig, 7 eac þa þe him utan comon to fultume, 7 gefliemdon þone here 7 ofslogon hira monig hund, ægþer ge æscmanna ge oþerra.

*Then yet again afterwards that same autumn, a great raiding-army [**here**] gathered from East Anglia, both from the land-army [**landhere**] and from the Vikings that they had enticed to assist them; and they thought that they would avenge their wrongs. They went to Maldon and besieged the city [**burh**] and fought against it until more help came to the citizens [**þam burgwarum**] from outside. And the raiding-army left the burh and departed, whereupon the men came out of the burh in pursuit, along with those who had come to help them from outside. And they put the host to flight and slew many hundreds of them, both the shipmen [**æscmanna**] and the others.*

The Chronicler has some very specific terminology to describe the Danes: there is the **landhere** *the land host*, no doubt composed of some veterans of the old wars from Alfred's day, but reinforced now with the support of younger men, many of whom must have been born in East Anglia. These are the Danes of the Danelaw, Anglo-Danish by birth, but still very firmly Danish by identity. But the Chronicler distinguishes them from another kind of

Dane, for the East Anglian Danes are ready and willing to join in alliance with a much worse enemy – the verb suggestively used is *to entice* – namely, an army of **wicinga**, *Vikings*. These men are referred to rather pointedly and figuratively as **æscmanna**, *shipmen*, the word **æsc** being a loanword in Old English from Old Norse **askr** meaning warship. Similar expressions are used to characterize the Viking enemy in the poem *The Battle of Maldon*.

Ⓥ Vocabulary builder

POETIC DICTION

Characteristic of *The Battle of Maldon* are the many poetic synonyms: for the term *warrior*, there are **beorn, hæleð, hyse, rinc, wiga**, while for *battle* there are the single nouns **guð, hild**, and the compounds **wæl-stow**, *battle-place* and **gar-ræs** (literally *spear-rush*). Sometimes the diction varies in register: for the humble **spere** *spear* we have also have the more heroic **daroð, franca, gar**, and for prosaic **hors** there are also the poetic words **eoh, mearh** and **wicg**. Such poetic expressions were handed down; they rarely or never appear in prose, except some which occur in traditional personal names, e.g. **Ead-gar** (*Blessed spear*), **Guð-lac** (*Battle-play*). Normally, to write a poem in Old English (at least before the eleventh century) meant to employ this deliberately archaic style, a special poetic diction.

LAND (LAND)
folde	*earth*
eþel	*homeland*
eard	*home country*

PEACE (SIBB)
frið	*peace, protection*
freod	*friendship, peace*
grið	*truce, peace*
gebeorg	*protection*

FIGHT (GEFEOHT)
guþ	*battle*
hild	*battle*
gefeoht	*fight*

WEAPONS (WÆPNU)
æsc	*spear*
flan	*arrow*
gar	*spear*
bord	*shield*
ecg	*sword*
ord	*spear*
rand	*shield*

THE EAST SAXONS (EAST-SEAXE)
leoda	*men*
beornas	*troops*

cniht	young man
frea	lord
ealdor	prince
werod	troop
heorðwerod	hearth-troop

THE VIKINGS (SÆMEN)

æsc-here	ship-army
wicing	Viking
ar	messenger
boda	messenger
brimliþend	sea-traveller
sælida	seafarer

THE BATTLE OF MALDON, LINES 55B–83

The Vikings have offered to take payment of *tribute* (spelt **gafol** or **gofol**) in return for **frið** *peace* (see unit 7 above) and **grið** *truce* (**grið** being a word of Old Norse origin). But Byrhtnoth indignantly rejects their offer:

55b ' […]   **To heanlic me þinceð**

    þæt ge mid urum sceattum   to scype gangon

    unbefohtene,   nu ge þus feor hider

    on urne eard   in becomon.

    Ne sceole ge swa softe   sinc gegangan;

60 **us sceal ord and ecg   ær geseman**

    grim guðplega,   ær we gofol syllon.'

56	**me þinceð** *it seems to me*; **to heanlic** *too shameful*; **ge** *you* (plural); **mid urum sceattum** *with our payments*; **unbefohtene** *unfought*; **nu** *now*; **hider** *here, hither*;
58	**ur-ne** *our*; **in becomon** *have come in*; **ne sceole ge** *nor should you*; **swa softe** *so agreeably*; **sinc** *treasure*;
60	**ord and ecg** *point and edge*; **ær** *first*; **geseman** *reconcile*; **guðplega** *battle-play*; **ær** *before*; **gofol** *tribute*;

    Het þa bord beran,   beornas gangan

    þæt hi on þam easteðe   ealle stodon

    ne mihte þær for wætere,   werod to þam oðrum.

65 **Þær com flowende   flod æfter ebban;**

    lucon lagustreamas.   To lang hit him þuhte

    hwænne hi togædere   garas beron.

62	þa *then;* **bord** *shields;* **beornas** *men;*
	hi *they;* **on þam easteðe** *on the river bank;*
64	**for wætere** *because of the water;*
	ne mihte … werod to þam oðrum *one troop could not (get) to the other;*
	flowende *flowing;* **æfter ebban** *after the ebb-tide;*
66	**lucon** *joined;* **lagustreamas** *streams of water;* **to lang** *too long;*
	hwænne *until the time when;* **beron** *they would bear*

Hi þær Pantan stream   mid prasse bestodon

Eastseaxena ord   and se æschere

70 ne mihte hyra ænig   oþrum derian

buton hwa þurh flanes flyht   fyl gename.

68	**mid prasse** *in great array;*
	se æschere: æsc *warship i.e. warship* + **here** *army*
70	**hyra ænig** *any of them;* **derian** *cause harm;*
	oþrum *to the others;*
	þurh flanes flyht *through the flight of an arrow;*
	fyl *fall;* **gename** *might take;*

72 Se flod ut gewat   þa flotan stodon gearowe

wicinga fela,   wiges georne.

72	**Se flod** *the flood-tide;* **þa flotan** *the seamen;*
	gearowe *ready*
73	**wicinga** *Vikings;* **fela** *many;* **wiges georne** *eager for battle.*

Het þa hæleða hleo   healdan þa bricge

75 wigan wigheardne se wæs   haten Wulfstan

cafne mid his cynne   þæt wæs Ceolan sunu

þe ðone forman man   mid his francan ofsceat

þe þær baldlicost   on þa bricge stop.

þær stodon mid Wulfstane   wigan unforhte,

80 Ælfere and Maccus   modige twegen,

þa noldon æt þam forda   fleam gewyrcan,

ac hi fæstlice   wið ða fynd weredon

þa hwile þe hi wæpna   wealdan moston.

💡 Language discovery

RHYTHM AND METRE

As we have seen, for example in unit 2, Old English poets wrote what is known as 'alliterative verse': they used an accentual alliterative metre for most of their verse-making. To create these metrical effects, they drew on the resources and rhythms of the spoken language, but formalized them into elaborate rules (not all of which will be covered in this book). Before thinking any further about metre in Old English poetry, therefore, you would do well to re read units 11 and 14, which deal in part with the basis: the rhythmical elements in Old English prose.

The next step is to listen to recordings of Old English poems, to develop your ear for poetic rhythm further, but it is useful to listen also to contemporary poetry, to go to modern English poetry readings, simply to hear poems being spoken out loud. Some poetry is intended for the eye as a visual shape or pattern on the page, but actually most poems should be heard to be appreciated. If you cultivate an ear for more recent poetry this will be an enormous aid to reading the poems of an earlier English.

The basic practice in Old English poetry is to work with a line of usually four beats – the emphatic syllables are known as lifts. The line should then be divided in the middle by a pause or caesura. In modern editions, the caesura is marked by a gap in the text, so that we, as readers, can see the shape of the line and perceive the varying rhythm of the verses. Here are lines 68–70, with the caesura marked by a gap, and the lifts underlined for further emphasis:

Hi þær <u>Pan</u>tan <u>stream</u>   mid <u>pras</u>se be<u>sto</u>don

<u>East</u>seaxena <u>ord</u>   and se <u>æsc</u>-here

70   **ne mihte hyra ænig   <u>o</u>þrum <u>der</u>ian**

buton hwa þurh <u>flanes</u> <u>flyht</u>   <u>fyl</u> ge<u>name</u>

There they stood in array along the river Panta,

the East Saxon force and the Viking horde:

none of them could harm the other

except when someone fell to the flight of an arrow.

When reading out loud, you should give special strength and prominence to the four lifts in each line and allow the unstressed syllables, which form the so-called dips in between, to trail along weakly before or after. This creates the varying rhythm of the line, which is used by a good poet to underline his intended meaning.

Various modern poets have tried their hand at alliterative verse. One famous case is the poem *The Age of Anxiety* (1947) by W.H. Auden, who was interested in Old English verse and its rhythmical effects. Here he describes a war-time ambush:

All <u>war's</u> <u>woes</u> I can <u>well</u> <u>im</u>agine.

<u>Gun</u>-barrels <u>glint</u>, <u>gath</u>ered in <u>am</u>bush,

<u>May</u>hem among <u>moun</u>tains, <u>min</u>erals <u>break</u>

<u>In</u> by <u>or</u>der on <u>in</u>timate <u>groups</u> of

<u>Ten</u>der <u>tis</u>sues, at their <u>tough</u> <u>vi</u>sit

<u>Flesh</u> <u>flus</u>ters that was so <u>flu</u>ent till <u>now</u>,

<u>Stam</u>mers some <u>non</u>sense, <u>stops</u> and sits <u>down</u>,

Apa<u>thet</u>ic to all <u>this</u>.

This alternation of strong heavy single lifts with weaker dips of shifting length (one, two, three or even four unstressed syllables) gives the line its varying force and rhythm.

Here again is the passage from *Battle of Maldon* with the weaker syllables marked by an 'x' and the lift or beat marked with a forward slash / (as in unit 11). It will be seen that the half-line (known in the terminology of metrical studies as a verse) is the basic unit of Old English metre, on the basis of which the poet creates a variety of rhythms:

```
    x   x   /   x   /       x   /   x x  /   x
```
Hi þær Pantan stream   mid prasse bestodon

```
    /   x   x x   /     x   x   /   / x
```
Eastseaxena ord   and se æsc-here

```
    x   x   x x x / x     / x   / x
```
70   **ne mihte hyra ænig   oþrum derian**

```
    x   x   x     x   / x   /     / x   / x
```
buton hwa þurh flanes flyht   fyl gename

This is unlike, say, the more constant and regular five-beat metre of a line from a Shakespearean sonnet:

```
    x       /   x   /   x   /   x   /   x   /
```
Rough winds do shake the darling buds of May
And summer's lease hath all too short a date
sometime too hot the eye of heaven shines,
And often is his gold complexion dimmed;

As you do more of this kind of analysis, however, you will start to hear that the various rhythms of the Old English line are not infinite in number (as will be shown in the next unit, there are five basic metrical rhythms). In the on-verse of 68 the first dip is shorter than in 71a, but the essential rhythm (dip, lift, dip, lift) is the same:

```
        x   x       /   x       /
```
Hi þær   Pantan stream

and
```
    x   x   x   x   /   x   /
```
buton hwa þurh flanes flyht

Another way of comparing these two verses and stating this principle is to say that **Hi þær Pantan stream** and **buton hwa þurh flanes flyht** can be spoken with a similar rising-rising rhythm.

Sometimes, for special effect, two lifts can be neighbours, with no intervening dip, creating what is called the clashing effect of:

```
    x   x   /   /   x         or        x   x       /   / x
```
and se æsc-here   *at their tough visit*

The clash in both cases seems appropriate. There is the sudden impact of the gun shots in the ambush in Auden's *Age of Anxiety*, while in Maldon, the invasive Viking horde has a suitably clashing name, literally *the warship-army*, that contrasts with the longer-sounding and arguably more euphonious name of the East Saxon force.

ALLITERATION

In Old English, the rules of this kind of poetry were strictly applied, and they were combined with patterns of alliteration, hence the term *alliterative verse* for this metre.

To gain an impression of the way the alliteration is used, we can consider one particular passage in detail (lines 62–7):

Sound

	b	Het þa <u>b</u>ord <u>b</u>eran <u>b</u>eornas <u>g</u>angan
	vowels	þæt hi on þam <u>ea</u>-<u>st</u>eðe <u>ealle</u> <u>st</u>odon
	w	ne mihte þær for <u>w</u>ætere, <u>w</u>erod to þam o<u>ð</u>rum
65	*f*	þær <u>c</u>om <u>f</u>lowende <u>f</u>lod æfter e<u>bb</u>an
	l	<u>l</u>ucon <u>l</u>agustreamas to <u>l</u>ang hit him <u>þ</u>uhte
	g	hwænne hi to<u>g</u>ædere <u>g</u>aras <u>b</u>eron

The alliterating sounds link usually two or three of the four lifts in the typical line. If there are two alliterating lifts in the on-verse this is called double alliteration, e.g. lines 62, 66, while one alliterating lift in the on-verse, e.g. lines 64, 65, 67, is known as single alliteration. Exceptionally, there is a special effect in the extra **st** alliteration in line 63, since the basic alliteration falls on the initial vowel sounds of **ea** and **ealle**.

RHYME

Old English readers and writers knew about end rhyme – it was heard in some kinds of Latin hymn – and those who had the right contacts abroad could have heard it in Old High German verse. In the rule-bound alliterative verse, however, rhyme was not part of the metrical form. It was not required, and whenever it does occur, it must be seen as an extra embellishment.

Rhyme, then, could be – and was – employed for special effects by the poets of the period, along with such features as assonance, when the vowel sound of the prominent syllables is repeated. In *The Battle of Maldon* we can hear such sound patterns in the descriptions of the tidal estuary, especially the repeated long **ō**-vowels of line 65:

> þær cōm flōwende   flōd æfter ebban
>
> *there came flowing the flood-tide after the ebb*

And here in lines 66 and 68, for instance, we have assonance on the short **a**-vowel:

> lucon l<u>a</u>gustreamas   to l<u>a</u>ng hit him þuhte
>
> Hi þær P<u>a</u>ntan stream   mid pr<u>a</u>sse bestodon

And for a final example, here is the internal rhyme in line 72, the description of the receding tide, with its **ō**-vowels recalling the flow of the rising flood in line 65:

> Se flōd ut gewat   þa flotan stōdon gearowe
>
> *The tide went out, the seamen stood ready*

CAPITALIZATION AND PUNCTUATION IN MANUSCRIPTS

The transcript

The only copy of the poem *The Battle of Maldon* is extant in an eighteenth-century transcript in the Bodleian Library in Oxford, the closest we can now come to what the scribe originally wrote. This is Oxford, Bodleian Library, Rawlinson B. 20, ff. 7r–12v (for a facsimile see Scragg 1991). The original Anglo-Saxon manuscript from which the transcript was made was part of the famous Cotton collection compiled by Sir Robert Cotton; notoriously, it was destroyed in the great fire at Ashburnham House on October 23rd, 1731 (Ashburnham House is a seventeenth-century building, now part of Westminster School). Fortunately the copyist had already completed his transcription. It was the work of a certain David Casley, who is known from other archival work: he appears to have transcribed accurately and to have kept closely to his model. The text here is therefore divided into sections according to the cues (large capital letters and punctuation) transcribed by Casley, presumably as he followed the text in the Anglo-Saxon manuscript.

On this page, you will see a representation of folio 8v of the Bodleian manuscript. The study of its layout is illuminating. Unlike many modern editions, the capitalisation and punctuation of the transcript appear to follow the manuscript, so that a letter in bold marks a new section, and the **punctus** or *point* marks a pause, while the **punctus versus** (here a colon) marks the end of a section. Oxford, Bodleian Library, manuscript Rawlinson B 203, folio 8r is set out as follows (for a facsimile reproduction, see Scragg 1991, p. 5). The three capital letters marking new sections are highlighted. The usual early medieval scribal abbreviations are found in this text:

7 = and

þ = þæt

ī = im, e.g. **grī = grim**

ā = am, e.g. **þā = þam**

ā = an, e.g. **francā = francan**

ū = um, e.g. **oþrū = oþrum**

--- --- ---

gangon unbe fohtene nuge þus feor hi-

der on urne eard inbecomon ne sceole

ge swa softe sinc ge gangan us sceal ord

7 ecg ærge seman grī guð plega ærþe

gofol syllon.

het þa bord beran beornas gangan þ

hi on þā ea steðe ealle stodon ne mihte

þærfor wætere. werod to þā oðrum þær

com flowende flod æfter ebban lucon

lagu streamas to lang hit him þuhte

hwænne hi to gædere garas beron

hi þær pantan stream mid prasse

be stodon eastseaxena ord 7 se æsc here

ne mihte hyra ænigoþrū derian buton

hwa þurh flanes flyht fylgename : **S**e

flod ut ge wat þa flotan stodon gearowe

wicinga fela wiges georne . **h**et þa hæle-

ða hleo healdan þa bricge wigan wig-

heardne se wæs haten wulfstan caf-

ne mid his cynne þ wæs ceolan sunu

þe ðone forman man mid his francā

of sceat þe þær baldlicost on þa

bricge stop. þær stodon mid wulfstāe

wigan unforhte. ælfere 7 maccus mo-

dige twegen. þa noldon æt þā forda [fleāge

SCRIBAL PRACTICE

As we saw in unit 20, Old English scribes copied prose texts using conventions of capitalization, punctuation, spacing and word-division that are very different to those of the present. Even more striking is the way in which Old English verse was recorded in writing. In all the manuscripts, the scribes copied the poems as though they were paragraphs of continuous prose – this despite the fact that Latin poetry in this period was laid out in clearly demarcated lines. Evidently the scribes were familiar with line-by-line layout when it came to Latin, but for Old English poetry the layout had to be different. Rather than see the lines on the page, the audience presumably had to hear them, with a skilful reader able to bring them to life in performance, probably in the hall of a **burh**, or in the refectory of a minster.

On the modern practice of adding commas and semi-colons in order to clarify the sentence structure, Edward B. Irving has written of how modern editors bear 'the burden of furnishing sometimes misleading modern punctuation to the text, simply because convention seems to demand it'. By departing from the editorial convention, going back as far as possible to the punctuation of the original Old English text and comparing it with that of modern editions, you will be able to explore different readings and interpretations of the language of the poems.

From the Chronicle of Æthelred's reign

Version C of the *Anglo-Saxon Chronicle* preserves the text of the 'Chronicle of Æthelred's Reign'. The author of this section of the Chronicle appears to have been writing with hindsight, perhaps during the early years of Cnut's reign, and very likely he was located in London, a city that is always treated with great respect in his work. His dominant theme is straightforwardly simple: that the years under Æthelred were a time of treachery and incompetence. But there is more to his writing than this, for he is a great stylist, with a sense of irony, a gift for the well-chosen anecdote or story and a liking for the occasional poetic turn of phrase.

His brief account of the battle at Maldon in 991 focusses on the aftermath, the decision to give the Vikings **gafol** *tribute*, an ongoing policy from this time onwards, of which, like Byrhtnoth in the *The Battle of Maldon*, the chronicler did not entirely approve.

How much was the gafol paid to the Vikings, and how quickly did the price increase?

THE YEAR 990

Her Sigeric wæs gehalgod to arcebisceope, and Eadwine abbod forðferde, and Wulfgar abbod feng to þam rice.

THE YEAR 991

Her wæs Gypeswic gehergod, and æfter þon swiðe raðe wæs Brihtnoð ealdorman ofslegen æt Mældune. And on þam geare man gerædde þæt man geald ærest gafol Denescum mannum for ðam miclan brogan þe hi worhton be ðam særiman, þæt wæs ærest .x. ðusend punda. Þæne ræd gerædde ærest Syric arcebisceop.

THE YEAR 992

Her Oswald se haliga arcebisceop forlet þis lif and geferde þæt heofenlice, and Æþelwine ealdorman gefor on þam ilcan geare. Þa gerædde se cyning and ealle his witan þæt man gegadrede ealle ða scipu þe ahtes wæron to Lundenbyrig, and se cyning þa betæhte þa fyrde to lædenne Ælfrice ealdormenn and Þorede eorle and Ælfstane bisceope and Æscwige bisceope, and sceoldon cunnian, meahton hy þone here ahwær utan betreppan. Þa sende se ealdorman Ælfric and het warnian ðone here, and þa on ðære nihte þe hy on ðone dæig togædere fon sceoldan, þa sceoc he on niht fram þære fyrde him sylfum to myclum bysmore, and se here ða ætbærst butan an scyp þær man ofsloh. And þa gemette se here ða scypu on Eastenglum and

of Lundene, and hi ðær ofgeslogan micel wæl and þæt scyp genaman eall gewæpnod and gewædod þæt se ealdorman on wæs. And ða æfter Oswaldes arcebisceopes forðsiþe feng Ealdulf abbod to Eoforwicstole and to Wigernaceastre, and Kenulf to ðam abbudrice æt Buruh.

THE YEAR 993

Her on þis geare wæs Bebbanburuh abrocen and mycel herehyþe ðær genumen, and æfter þam com to Humbran muþan se here and ðær mycel yfel worhton ægþer ge on Lindesige ge on Norðhymbran. Þa gegaderede man swiðe micle fyrde, and þa hi togædere gan sceoldon, þa onstealdan þa heretogan ærest þone fleam – þæt wæs Fræna and Godwine and Fryþegyst. On þyssum geare het se cyning ablendan Ælfgar, Ælfrices sunu ealdormannes.

THE YEAR 994

Her on ðissum geare com Anlaf and Swegen to Lundenbyrig on Natiuitas Sanctę Marię mid .iiii. and hundnigontigum scypum, and hi ða on þa buruh fæstlice feohtende wæron and eac hi mid fyre ontendon woldan, ac hi þær geferdon maran hearm and yfel þonne hi æfre wendon þæt him ænig buruhwaru gedon sceolde. Ac seo halige Godes modor on þam dæge hire mildheortnesse þære buruhware gecydde, and hi ahredde wið heora feondum. And hi þanone ferdon and worhton þæt mæste yfel ðe æfre æni here gedon meahte on bærnette and heregunge and on manslyhtum ægþer ge be ðam særiman and on Eastseaxum and on Kentlande and on Suðseaxum and on Hamtunscire, and æt neaxtan namon him hors and ridon him swa wide swa hi woldan and unasecgendlice yfel wyrcgende wæron. Þa gerædde se cyning and his witan þæt him man tosende and him behet gafol and metsunge wið þon ðe hi þære heregunge geswicon, and hi ða þæt underfengon, and com þa eall se here to Hamtune and ðær wintersetl namon, and hi mon þær fedde geond eall Westseaxena rice, and him mon geald feos .xvi. ðusend punda. Þa sende se cyning æfter Anlafe cynge Ælfeah bisceop and Æþelweard ealdorman, and man gislude þa hwile into þam scipum, and hi ða læddon Anlaf mid miclum wurðscipe to þam cyninge to Andeferan, and se cyning Æþelred his onfeng æt bisceopes handa and him cynelice gifode, and him þa Anlaf behet, swa he hit eac gelæste þæt he næfre eft to Angelcynne mid unfriðe cuman nolde.

THE YEAR 995

Her on þissum geare æteowde cometa se steorra, and Sigeric arcebisceop forðferde.

THE YEAR 990: **feng** *succeeded;*

THE YEAR 991: **Gypeswic** *Ipswich;* **wæs … gehergod** *was plundered;* **wæs … ofslegen** *was killed;* **man gerædde** *it was advised;* **worhton** *made, caused* (past tense of **wyrcan**); **broga** *terror;* **sæ-riman** *sea coast;*

THE YEAR 992: **þis lif** *this life;* **þæt heofenlice** *the heavenly one;*

þæt man gegadrede *that they should gather;* **ahtes** *of value;* **cunnian** *attempt;*

meahton hy … betreppan *whether they could ambush;*

ahwær *somewhere;* **utan** *outside;* **warnian** *warn;*

togædere fon *clash together;* **sceoc** *slipped away;* **bysmor** *disgrace;*

ætbærst *broke out;* **ofsloh** *destroyed;* **gemette** *encountered, met;* **wæl** *slaughter;* **gewæpnod and gewædod** *armed and equipped;* **Eoforwicstol** *the see of York (the archbishopric);* **abbudrice** *abbacy*

THE YEAR 993: **Bebbanburuh** *Bamburgh;* **abrocen** *captured, broken into;* **herehyþe** *plunder;* **genumen** *taken;*

togædere gan *to clash together;* **þa hi togædere gan sceoldon** *when they were meant to come to an engagement;* **þa heretogan** *the army-leaders;* **onstealdan … þone fleam** *initiated the flight;* **ablendan** *to blind*

THE YEAR 994: **Anlaf** *Olaf;* **buruh = burh** *city;* **ontendon** *to burn down;* **geferdon** *they experienced;* **seo buruhwaru** *the township* (collective noun for the citizens); **ahredde** *saved;* **þanone** *from there;* **bærnet** *burning;* **heregung** *plundering;* **manslyht** *manslaughter;* **swa wide swa hi woldan** *as widely as they wished;* **unasecgendlic** *unutterable;* **tosende** *sent a message;* **metsung** *provision;* **wið þon ðe** *in exchange for which;* **geswicon** *they ceased;* **underfengon** *complied;* **fedde** *fed;* **geald** *paid;* **feos** *in money* (from **feoh** *money);* **man gislude** *they gave hostages;* **gifode** *gave him gifts;* **Hamtun** *Southampton;* **Andeferan** *Andover*

THE YEAR 995: **æteowde** *appeared*

? Test yourself

Answer the questions on the passage from the Chronicle.

1 What happened to Wulfgar in the year 990?

_____

2 Which came first in the chronology, the plundering of Ipswich or the battle at Maldon?

_____

3 Whose idea was it to pay the Danes the tribute, and what was the reason given?

_____

4 Whose idea was it to appoint ealdorman Ælfric as leader of the English forces?

_____

5 How did the plan to ambush the Danish fleet come to nothing?

_____

6 What happened to ealdorman Ælfric's ship?

_____

7 Where was Oswald's benefice?

_____

8 What happened in Northumbria in 993?

_____

9 How does the Æthelred Chronicler show his partiality to the people of London?

_____

10 How did they put a stop to the ravaging of the Danish army in 994?

_____

SELF-CHECK	
I CAN ...	
●	recognize specifically poetic vocabulary
●	understand the rhythm of Old English poetry
●	identify patterns of alliteration in an Old English poem
●	observe occasional effects of rhyme and assonance
●	appreciate problems of editing and interpreting manuscript texts

22 *Dryhtsele dynede*
The hall resounded

In this unit you will learn about:
▶ *ellipsis of the definite article and the 'condensed style' of Old English poetry*
▶ *agency and ambiguity*
▶ *variation and parallelism*
▶ *patterns of repetition*
▶ *the five metrical types in Old English poems*
▶ *passive expressions*
▶ *pluperfects*

You will read:
▶ *'Beowulf's Fight with Grendel', Beowulf, lines 745–836*

The arrival at Heorot

The first half of the heroic poem *Beowulf* is all about the rise of the hero. The protagonist, a young kinsman of the Geatish king Higelac, risks everything on a new venture to prove his worth and make his name. Already he has established a reputation in his homeland, for the text tells us that *he was among mankind strongest in power on that day of this life* (lines 196–7):

> **se wæs moncynnes   mægenes strengest**
> **on þæm dæge   þysses lifes**

The expression is evidently significant, and is repeated with variation later (lines 789–90 and 806). Beowulf has heard the news of a monstrous cannibal called Grendel who has taken to attacking the Danish court and occupying the hall in the dark nights (line 167). So Beowulf sets out on his **siðfæt** or *venture* (line 202b) with his fourteen chosen companions, travelling from his home in Geatland (now part of central Sweden) to meet Hrothgar, king of the Danes, whose court is situated at the hall called Heorot (probably to be associated with Lejre in Zealand). Arriving in Denmark, Beowulf demonstrates his credentials first of all to the coastguard (229–300), who agrees to guide the travellers to Hrothgar's hall.

 Language discovery

Work through the passage from *Battle of Maldon* (lines 55–83) in unit 21. How many uses of the definite article can you identify?

ELLIPSIS OF THE DEFINITE ARTICLE AND THE 'CONDENSED STYLE' OF OLD ENGLISH POETRY

When in modern English do we use the indefinite article *a/an* or the definite article *the*? As David Crystal points out in his *Making Sense of Grammar* (p. 208), this depends on the context and the meaning we want to convey: 'Semantic factors govern the choice of the articles. They relate to whether a noun is to be interpreted as specific or generic, or as definite or indefinite.' The same is true of Old English literary prose. In the extracts from the *Chronicle* in unit 21 or from the prose romance *Apollonius of Tyre* in unit 23, the uses of the definite article correspond almost unfailingly to those of modern English. It seems that early Old English used the definite article rather like the demonstrative *this* or *that*, but the practice had changed by the ninth and tenth centuries (for determiners and the indefinite article *a/an*, reread unit 16).

The definite article is not always necessary. In certain types of modern English writing, the definite article may sometimes be omitted: in recipes (e.g. 'Beat egg lightly with fork'), headlines (FILMSTAR MARRIES PRESIDENT) and journals ('Met Susan yesterday at cinema'). The same is true for certain genres of Old English prose. For example, the definite article is sometimes omitted in the two charter bounds studied in unit 10.

As a rule, in contrast to the prose, the definite article is rare in Old English poetry. In *Maxims II*, to take an extreme case, there are only three definite articles in a poem of 66 lines. This is the generalizing tendency of the maxim or proverb:

Cyning sceal on healle beagas dælan

which is rendered literally as *king must deal out rings in hall*, though most modern translators feel a need to add articles to at least some of the nouns, as for instance:

The king must deal out rings in the hall

The ellipsis of the definite article is also quite prominent in *Beowulf*, in contrast to the late poem *Maldon* (which may in this respect be influenced by Old English prose); a good example is the scene of arrival at Heorot, lines 320–1 (for more of this passage see unit 10):

Strǣt wæs stanfah, stig wisode gumum ætgædere.

Street was paved with stone, path guided men together.

At first sight this is surprising. Surely we would expect the poet to mark as definite and specific the road on which these particular men travel, namely the fifteen men of Beowulf's expedition? Instead, the articles are omitted, and we have a condensed, generic, almost proverbial style of narration.

The condensed style is a constant feature of Old English verse, which needs to be borne in mind when reading and interpreting particular Old English poems.

V Vocabulary builder 1

OPPONENTS

rinc	*warrior*
feond	*enemy*
fyrena hyrde	*master of crimes*
mæg	*kinsman*
eoten	*giant*
eorl	*nobleman*
gram	*enemy*
se hearmscaþa	*the dangerous assailant*

ADVERBS OF MANNER

hraþe	*quickly*
inwitþancum	*with hostile intent*
fæste	*firmly*

ADVERBS OF PLACE

near	*nearer*
utweard	*outward*
furþur	*further forward*

MOVEMENT

ætstop	*stepped*
ræhte	*reached*
onfeng	*seized*
mette	*encountered*
fleon	*to flee*
secan	*to seek*
gesæt	*sat up*
astod	*stood up*
wiðfeng	*seized*
no þy ær fram meahte	*he could not get away any sooner*

HANDS/ARMS

mid handa	*with his hand*
mid folme	*with his hand*
mundgripe	*hand-grip*
geweald	*the power*
his fingra	*of his fingers*
grap	*grasp*

MENTAL PROCESSES

onfunde	*realized*
wolde	*wanted*
gemunde	*remembered*

mynte	*intended*
wiste	*knew*

MIND
on mode	*in [his] mind*
on ferhðe	*in spirit*

FEELINGS
forht	*afraid*
hinfus	*eager to be gone*

The start of the fight

The royal herald now admits Beowulf into Hrothgar's presence (lines 331–404). In a solemn vow to the king, Beowulf declares his purpose: to cleanse the hall (**Heorot fælsian**; line 432b) and rid it of the monster. After further exchanges with the suspicious Unferth, Hrothgar's right-hand man (499–606), the Danes celebrate their guest's arrival, and the king entrusts the hall to Beowulf and his men *to have and to hold* for the night (line 658a). Hrothgar then departs to other quarters with his company of men, leaving Beowulf and his companions to face the monster. Grendel duly arrives in the middle of the night, and begins his work of murderous destruction until, fatefully, he reaches out towards Beowulf, apparently asleep in one of the alcoves of the hall.

Forð near ætstop (lines 745b–66)

he stepped forward nearer

745   Forð near ætstop,
   nam þa mid handa   higeþihtigne
   rinc on ræste,   he him ræhte ongean
   feond mid folme;   he onfeng hraþe
   inwitþancum   ond wið earm gesæt.

750 Sona þæt onfunde   fyrena hyrde
   þæt he ne mette   middangeardes,
   eorþan sceata,   on elran men
   mundgripe maran,   he on mode wearð
   forht on ferhðe;   no þy ær fram meahte.

755 Hyge wæs him hinfus,   wolde on heolster fleon,
   secan deofla gedræg;   ne wæs his drohtoð þær
   swylce he on ealderdagum   ær gemette.
   Gemunde þa se modga,   mæg Higelaces,
   æfenspræce,   uplang astod

760 ond him fæste wiðfeng;   fingras burston;

eoten wæs utweard,   eorl furþur stop.

Mynte se mæra,   þær he meahte swa,

widre gewindan   ond on weg þanon

fleon on fenhopu;   wiste his fingra geweald

765 on grames grapum.   Þæt wæs geocor sið

þæt se hearmscaþa   to Heorute ateah.

	forð *forward;* **near** *nearer;* **ætstop** *stepped*
746	**nam** *took;* **þa** *then;* **mid handa** *with his hand*
	higeþihtigne *the strong-spirited, courageous* (acc.)
	rinc *warrior;* **on ræste** *in his sleep;* **ræhte** *reached;*
	ongean *towards*
748	**feond** *enemy;* **mid folme** *with his hand;* **onfeng** *seized;*
	hraþe *quickly*
	inwitþancum *with hostile intent;* **wið** *against;*
	wið earm *supported by his own arm;* **gesæt** *he sat up*
750	**onfunde** *realized;* **sona þæt onfunde** *immediately he realized this*
	hyrde *master;* **fyrena** *of crimes;*
751	**ne** *not;* **mette** *encountered;* **þæt he ne mette** *that he had never encountered* **middangeardes** *in the world*
752	**eorþan sceata** *in [all] the regions of the earth;* **on elran men** *in any man*
753	**maran** *greater;* **mundgripe** *hand-grip;* **on mode** *in [his] mind;* **wearð** *became*
754	**forht** *afraid;* **on ferhðe** *in spirit;* **no** *not;* **no þy ær** *not any sooner;* **fram** *away;* **meahte** *could;*
	no þy ær fram meahte *he could not get away any sooner*
755	**hyge** *his thought;* **hinfus** *eager to be gone;* **wolde** *wanted;* **fleon** *to flee;* **on heolster** *into the darkness*
756	**secan** *to seek;* **gedræg** *company;* **deofla** *of devils;* **ne wæs** *nor was;* **drohtoð** *experience;* **þær** *there*
757	**swylce** *one that;* **ær gemette** *had ever encountered;* **on ealderdagum** *in the days of his life*
758	**þa** *then;* **se** *the;* **modga** *brave;* **mæg** *kinsman;* **Higelaces** *of Higelac;* **gemunde** *remembered*
759	**æfenspræce** *evening-talk;* **astod** *stood;* **uplang** *up*
760	**wiðfeng** *seized;* **fæste** *firmly;* **fingras** *fingers;* **burston** *strained*

761	**eoten** *giant*; **utweard** *outward*; **eorl** *nobleman*; **stop** *stepped*; **furþur** *forward*
762	**mynte** *intended*; **se mæra** *the famous one*; **þær** *where*; **meahte** *could*; **swa þær he**; **meahte swa** *if he so could*
763	**gewindan** *to escape*; **widre** *further*; **on weg** *away*; **þanon** *from there*
764	**fleon** *to flee*; **on fenhopu** *into the fenland refuges*; **wiste** *knew*;
	geweald *the power*; **his fingra** *of his fingers*
765	**gram** *enemy*; **grap** *grasp*; **on grames grapum** *in the adversary's grasp* (from the adjective **gram** *hostile*); **geocor** *bitter*; **sið** *journey*
766	**se hearmscaþa** *the dangerous assailant*; **ateah** *had undertaken*

AGENCY AND AMBIGUITY

This passage presents a lively narrative because of its sudden shifts in narrative perspective: the point of view moving from external narrator to monster, to hero and then back to monster, with the narrator providing the summarizing final comment (line 766: *that was a bitter journey*). The poet seems to aim for deliberate ambiguity as the fight begins in the darkened hall (presumably the only light is the glow of the logs in the central hearth). The narrative obscures the reference of the pronoun **he** so that it is sometimes unclear who is initiating the various actions. For example, who actually seized whom first? And since the poet also likes to begin a new sentence with the verb, it is unclear at first who is the agent: who *realized* in line 750 and who *remembered* at 758a? A little later, at 762, who *intended*? And who is **se mæra** *the famous one* anyway? It is even worth asking who is *the dangerous assailant* (766a)?

Check your comprehension of this passage against the following translation:

He stepped forward nearer, took then in his hands the strong-spirited warrior in his sleep, he reached towards the enemy with his hand, he quickly seized with hostile intent and sat up leaning on his own arm. Immediately the master of crimes realized this: that he had never encountered – in the world, in all the regions of the earth – in any man – a greater handgrip, in his mind and in his spirit he was afraid, he could not get away any sooner. His thought was eager to be gone, he wanted to flee into the darkness, seek the company of devils; nor was his experience there one that he had ever encountered in all the days of his life. Then he remembered – the brave kinsman of Higelac – his evening-talk, stood up, and seized him firmly, fingers strained: the giant moved outwards, the warrior stepped forwards. The famous one intended, if he so could, to escape further and to flee away from there into the fenland refuges; he knew the power of his fingers was in the enemy's grasp. That was a bitter venture that the dangerous assailant had undertaken to Heorot!

Language and style

VARIATION AND PARALLELISM

Variation is a traditional technique in Old English poetry, defined by Brodeur (p. 40) as 'a double or multiple statement of the same concept or idea in different words'. The *Beowulf* poet uses it in this traditional way: for instance, the two expressions in lines 751b–52a describing the world first as *the middle enclosure* and then as *the regions of the earth* are similar to the variations on the same concept in Riddle 66 (see unit 2). Variation becomes parallelism when the same syntax is used for both ideas:

he on mode wearð / forht on ferhðe

literally *he in mind became afraid [and] in spirit*

Grendel feels the fear both in mind and in spirit, and in each case the parallel structure is preposition + noun, preposition + noun.

In this scene the poet also manages some rather special effects with the same basic technique. Appropriate to a wrestling bout of this nature, there is variation throughout the passage on different synonyms for *hand*: **mid handa** *with his hand* (745); **mid folme** *with his hand*; **mundgripe** *hand-grip* – the latter two nouns **folm** and **mund** appearing mostly in poetry, while **hand** remains the neutral everyday term of either prose or verse. Later it is said that **his fingra geweald** *the power of his fingers* (and this presumably refers to Grendel) is now **on grames grapum** *in the adversary's grasp*, a phrase referring in hostile, negative terms to the hero Beowulf. Here the meaning varies, or crosses over, as it were, from monster to hero.

The next section revisits ironically the motif of music and song, a theme that has been presented already in the poem with the song of creation in Hrothgar's hall performed by the bard or poet-musician known as the **scop** (literally *the maker*), who accompanies his poem to **hearpan sweg** (line 89b) *the music of the harp* (for the passage see unit 23). This time it is the monster Grendel's lament that creates the music, along with the rhythm and crashing of the benches as the two assailants wrestle together. The Danes, who had departed from the hall with Hrothgar before night fell, now come out of their out-buildings and sleeping quarters: they can hear the noise inside the walls of the great hall, but in the darkness they do not know what is happening.

Practice

A useful method for appreciating the lexical patterns in a passage in *Beowulf* is to look for variation in keywords and synonyms.

Read through the passage below, lines 767–90, using the vocabulary notes provided, and see if you can identify variations on each of the following themes:

SOUND

1 _____

2 _____

3 _____

4 _____

5 _____

HALL

1 _____　　　4 _____

2 _____　　　5 _____

3 _____

FEELINGS AND EMOTIONS

1 _____

2 _____

Dryhtsele dynede

Royal hall resounded

Beowulf, 767–90

       Dryhtsele dynede;　Denum eallum wearð,
    ceasterbuendum,　cenra gehwylcum,
    eorlum ealuscerwen.　Yrre wæron begen,
770　reþe renweardas.　Reced hlynsode.
      Þa wæs wundor micel　þæt se winsele
    wiðhæfde heaþodeorum,　þæt he on hrusan ne feol,
    fæger foldbold;　ac he þæs fæste wæs
    innan ond utan　irenbendum
775a　searoþoncum besmiþod.
775b　 Þær fram sylle abeag
    medubenc monig,　mine gefræge,
    golde geregnad,　þær þa graman wunnon.
    Þæs ne wendon ær　witan Scyldinga
    þæt hit a mid gemete　manna ænig,
780　betlic ond banfag,　tobrecan meahte,
    listum tolucan,　nymþe liges fæþm
    swulge on swaþule.
          Sweg up astag
    niwe geneahhe;　Norðdenum stod
    atelic egesa,　anra gehwylcum

785 þara þe of wealle   wop gehyrdon,

gryreleoð galan   Godes ondsacan,

sigeleasne sang,   sar wanigean

helle hæfton.   Heold hine fæste

se þe manna wæs   mægene strengest

790 on þæm dæge   þysses lifes.

---

767   **dryhtsele** *royal hall* (**dryht** *royal, lordly* cf. **dryhten** *lord*); **Denum eallum** *to all the Danes* (dat. pl.)

768   **ceasterbuend** *fortress-dweller* (for **ceaster** see unit 2); **gehwylc** *each*; **cenra** *of the brave*; **ealuscerwen** *terror* (perhaps literally *dispensation of ale*); **yrre** *angry*; **begen** *both*

770   **reþe** *fierce*; **renweardas** *hall-guardians*; **reced** *hall*; **hlynsode** *resounded*; **se winsele** *wine-hall*

772   **wiðhæfde** *withstood, stood up to*; **heaþodeorum** *battle-brave ones* (i.e. the two fighting assailants Beowulf and Grendel); **þæt he ... ne feol** *so that it* [**he** refers back to the masculine noun **se winsele** *the hall*] *did not fall*

773   **fæger** *beautiful*; **foldbold** *earth-building* (i.e. *hall*; possibly a metaphorical expression); **ac** *but*; **he** *it* [**he** refers back to **se winsele** *the hall*]; **þæs** *so*; **fæste** *firmly*

774   **innan ond utan** *within and without* (cf. the phrase **binnan byrig** and **butan** in documents, see unit 10 above); **irenbendum** *with iron bonds* (dat. pl.)

775   **searoþoncum** *skilfully* (dat. pl.; lit. *with skilful designs*; **searo** *skill, contrivance, engineering*; **þonc** *thought*) **besmiþod** *forged* (cf. **smiþ** *smith*); **syll** *floor*; **abeag** *turned away, started away*

776   **medubenc monig** *many a mead-bench* **mine gefræge** *to my knowledge* (used as an epic formula: *as I have heard*)

777   **golde** *with gold* (dative of **gold**); **geregnad** (from **regnian** *to adorn*); **þær** *where*; **þa graman** *the adversaries* (cf. **gram**, line 765)

778   **þæs** *this*; **ne wendon ær** *they had not supposed*; **witan** *counsellors* (literally *the wise men*; cf. the institution of the **witan** *the assembly*, see unit 19); **Scyldinga** (genitive) *the Shieldings*, descendants of Scyld, the founder of the Danish dynasty at the beginning of the poem)

779	**manna ænig** *any man* (subject of the verb **meahte**); **a** *ever*; **hit** *it* (neuter pronoun referring to **fold**; **mid gemete** *by any means*)
780	**betlic** *excellent*; **ban-fag** *adorned with bone or ivory* (cf. **fag**, **fah** *coloured*); **meahte** *would be able to*; **tobrecan** *to break, shatter*
781	**tolucan** *to destroy*; **nymþe** *unless*; **liges** *of fire*; **fæþm** *embrace*
782	**swulge** *would swallow* (subjunctive); **swaþul** *flame*; **sweg** *music* (cf. **hearpan sweg** in *Beowulf*, line 89b); **astag** *rose up*
783	**niwe** *new*; **geneahhe** *often*; **stod** *there was* (literally *stood*); **Norðdenum** *for the Danes* (dative plural cf. *Denum eallum* line 767b)
784	**atelic** *terrible*; **egesa** *fear*; **anra gehylcum** *for each one*
785	**þara þe** *for those who*; **gehyrdon** *heard*; **wop** *lamentation*; **of wealle** *from the wall*
786	**Godes andsacan** *God's adversary*; **galan** *chanting* (infinitive; cf. **galdor** *enchantment*, line 3052); **gryre-leoð** *terror-song* (**leoð** is cognate with German 'Lied' *song*, as in 'Liederabend', an evening concert of 'Lieder')
787	**sige-leas sang** literally *victory-less*, i.e. *a song of defeat* (**-ne** in **sigeleasne** is the masculine accusative ending, the object of the verb **galan**); **sar** *wound*
787-8	**sar wanigean / helle hæfton** *the captive of hell lamenting [his] wound*
789 **mægene**	**se þe** *he who*; **manna** *of men* (genitive in **-a**); *in power*; from **þæt mægen** *power, virtue* (cf. **þa feower mægna** *the four virtues* in unit 12); **on þæm dæge** *on that day*; **þysses lifes** *of this life*

Language and style

PATTERNS OF REPETITION

In lines 767a and 770b, there are two subject-verb combinations in parallel, both meaning *the hall resounded*:

Subject	Verb
dryhtsele	dynede
reced	hlynsode

These form the outsides of a so-called 'envelope' pattern. Within this envelope, we have the description of the terror of the Danes and the anger of the contending assailants. The terror is **ealuscerwen**, *a dispensing of ale* (evidently a metaphor for something to be feared) which came to the Danes – this notion is expressed by four variations, with the idea of *to* or *for* rendered by the dative **-um** endings:

Nominative	Dative
Dene *Danes*	**Denum eallum** *to all the Danes*
ceasterbuend *fortress-dweller(s)*	**ceasterbuendum** *to the fortress-dwellers*
gehwylc *each*	**gehwylcum** *to each*
eorlas *warriors*	**eorlum** *to the warriors*

Later, at lines 783–4, the idea that terrible fear then came to the Danes (**Norðdenum** *to the North-Danes*, **anra gehwylcum** *to each of them*) is repeated, providing yet another envelope structure, within which is heard the sound of the fighting and the terrifying musical lament from Grendel. The Danes are on the outside listening in, and this intensifies their fear.

Finally, at the end of the passage, which is also the end of Fitt XI (the fitts are scribal or authorial divisions numbered in the original manuscript), we have the narrator's summarizing comment (788b–90):

Heold hine fæste

se þe manna wæs   mægene strengest

on þæm dæge   þysses lifes.

This echoes the earlier statement when Beowulf was first introduced (lines 196–7; see above) and serves to praise Beowulf's achievement as well as locating him in a time and place back then, on that day of this life and so arguably also relativizing his success. (A little later, at 806, the line is used to describe Grendel too.) The emphasis on *that* and *this* is authorial – I will return to that point shortly; first we need to look further at the basic patterns of rhythm and metre.

Ⓥ Vocabulary builder 2

PRINCE

freadrihten	*princely lord*
eorla hleo	*protector of warriors*
mæra þeoden	*famous prince*
se modega mæg Hygelaces	*the brave kinsman of Higelac*

WARRIOR

eorl, **hildemecg**	*warrior*

GRENDEL

þone cwealmcuman	*the killer-guest (masc. acc.)*
þone synscaðan	*the sinful assailant, doer of sin (masc. acc.)*
se ellorgast	*the alien spirit*
se þe fela æror ... fyrene gefremede	*he who had committed many crimes*

WEAPONS

irenna cyst	*best of irons*
sigewæpen	*victory weapon*
guðbill	*war-sword*
ecg	*sword (lit. edge)*

NEGATIVES

nolde	*he did not want (negative of **wolde** wanted)*
nolde ænige þinga	*he did not by any means want*
ne... tealde	*he did not reckon*
hie þæt ne wiston	*they did not know that*
guðbilla nan gretan nolde	*no weapon would affect (him)*
him se lichoma læstan nolde	*his physical strength would not help him*

Nolde eorla hleo *The protector of heroes did not wish*

Beowulf, 791–815a

Nolde eorla hleo ænige þinga
þone cwealmcuman cwicne forlætan,
ne his lifdagas leoda ænigum
nytte tealde.
Þær genehost brægd

795 eorl Beowulfes ealde lafe,
wolde freadrihtnes feorh ealgian,
mæres þeodnes, ðær hie meahton swa.
Hie þæt ne wiston, þa hie gewin drugon,
heardhicgende hildemecgas,

800 ond on healfa gehwone heawan þohton,
sawle secan: þone synscaðan
ænig ofer eorþan irenna cyst,
guðbilla nan, gretan nolde,
ac he sigewæpnum forsworen hæfde,

805 ecga gehwylcre. Scolde his aldorgedal
on ðæm dæge þysses lifes

earmlic wurðan,   ond se ellorgast

on feonda geweald   feor siðian.

Ða þæt onfunde   se þe fela æror

810 modes myrðe   manna cynne,

fyrene gefremede   – he wæs fag wið God –

þæt him se lichoma   læstan nolde,

ac hine se modega   mæg Hygelaces

hæfde be honda;   wæs gehwæþer oðrum

815 lifigende lað.

791	**nolde** *did not want;* **eorla** *of warrriors;* **hleo** *protector;* **ænige þinga** *by any means*
792	**forlætan** *leave;* **þone cwealmcuman** *the killer-guest* (masc. acc.); **cwicne** *alive* (masc. acc.)
793	**ne… tealde** *he did not reckon;* **his lifdagas** *the days of his life;* **nytte** *of use;* **leoda ænigum** *to any man*
794	**þær** *there;* **genehost** *most swiftly;* **brægd** *drew*
795	**eorl Beowulfes** *Beowulf's man* (i.e. one of Beowulf's men); **ealde lafe** *ancient heirloom,* i.e. sword (a circumlocution)
796	**wolde** *wanted* (contrasts with **nolde** at line 792); **ealgian** *protect;* **freadrihtnes feorh** *[his] noble lord's life*
797	**mæres þeodnes** *[his] famous prince's [life]* (two phrases in parallel); **ðær hie meahton swa** *if they so could* (cf. line 762)
798	**hie þæt ne wiston** *they (i.e. Beowulf's men) did not know this* (the syntax looks forward to **þone synscaðan** *the evil enemy,* in line 800, (i.e. they did not know this … that no sword … would affect the evil enemy); **þa hie gewin drugon** *when they undertook the fight*
799	**heardhicgende** *brave-hearted;* **hildemecgas** *warriors*
800	**ond on healfa gehwone** *and on every side;* **heawan þohton** *thought to strike;* **sawle secan** *to seek out his soul;* (after **sawle secan** the conjunction *that* should be supplied to follow *they did not know* in line 800); **þone synscaðan** *the evil assailant* (**syn** *evil* + **scaða** *causer of harm*)
802	**ænig** *any* (i.e. any sword); **ofer eorþan** *in all the earth;* **irenna cyst** *best of irons*
803	**guðbilla nān** *none of the war-swords;* **gretan nolde** *would not affect*
804	**ac** *but rather;* **he** *Beowulf or Grendel?;* **sigewæpnum** *victory weapons;*

805   **ecga gehwylcre** *every weapon;* **scolde** *was to;* **his aldorgedal** *his tally of life*

806   **on ðæm dæge** *on that day;* **þysses lifes** *of this life* (cf. lines 197, 790)

807   **earmlic wurðan** *to become pitiable* (**wurðan** = **weorðan** *to become*)

807–8   **ond se ellorgast** *and the alien spirit [was to]* **feor siðian** *journey far;* **on feonda geweald** *into the power of enemies;* **ða þæt onfunde** *when he realized this;* **se þe** *he who*

809/811 **se þe fela æror ... fyrene gefremede** *he who had committed many crimes*

810   **modes myrðe** *affliction of mind* (Tolkien translates *grief of heart*); **manna cynne** *on humankind, against humanity*

811   **he wæs fag wið God** *he was in a feud against God;* **þæt him se lichoma** *that his body;* **læstan nolde** *would not help him*

812   **ac hine se modega mæg Hygelaces** *the brave kinsman of Higelac;* **hæfde be honda** *had [him] by the hand*

814   **wæs** *was;* **gehwæþer** *each;* **oðrum** *to the other*

815   **lifigende** *while alive;* **lað** *hostile*

The five metrical types

In unit 21, we noted that Old English poets used recurring patterns of rising, falling and clashing rhythms to create their metrical effects. The Old English line is divided into two verses with a clear break or caesura between them: the on-verse and off-verse. This verse is the unit of Old English metre. Each verse normally contains two lifts, a lift being a stressed syllable or beat (*Beowulf*, lines 791–796):

     Nolde <u>eor</u>la <u>hleo</u>   ænige þinga

     þone <u>cwealm</u>-<u>cuman</u>   <u>cwic</u>ne forlætan,

     ne his <u>lif</u>-<u>dagas</u>   <u>leo</u>da ænigum

     <u>nyt</u>te <u>teal</u>de.   þær gen<u>e</u>host <u>brægd</u>

795 **<u>eorl</u> <u>Beo</u>wulfes   <u>eal</u>de <u>la</u>fe,**

     wolde <u>frea</u><u>driht</u>nes   <u>feorh</u> <u>eal</u>gian,

The protector of heroes did not wish by any means to leave the killer-guest alive, he did not reckon the days of his life of use to any man. There one of Beowulf's men most swiftly drew his ancient heirloom [i.e. sword]: he wanted to protect his noble lord's life [...]

The alliteration on two or three of the lifts acts as the link between the on-verse and the off-verse:

Alliteration

on vowels	**Nolde <u>eo</u>rla <u>h</u>leo**	**<u>æ</u>nige þinga**
on **c**	**þone <u>c</u>wealm-<u>c</u>uman**	**<u>c</u>wicne forlætan,**
on **l**	**ne his <u>l</u>if-dagas**	**<u>l</u>eoda ænigum**
on **n**	**<u>n</u>ytte tealde.**	**þær ge<u>n</u>ehost <u>b</u>rægd**
on vowels	**<u>eo</u>rl <u>B</u>eowulfes**	**<u>ea</u>lde <u>l</u>afe,**
on **f**	**wolde <u>f</u>rea-drihtnes**	**<u>f</u>eorh ealgian,**

The lifts are stressed syllables and these normally are placed on the significant, weighty lexical words: the nouns, adjectives, and infinitives, rather than on the lesser grammatical linking words such as determiners (e.g. *the, this, that*), prepositions (e.g. *in, on, for, with* etc.), or pronouns (*he, she, his, her*).

Each verse normally conforms to one of five metrical types (A to E), as devised originally by the German philologist and phonetician Eduard Sievers in the latter two decades of the nineteenth century. Here are these rhythms expressed in modern English examples, using mnemonics suggested by the writings on Old English of scholars Bruce Mitchell, D.G. Scragg and J.R.R. Tolkien (see Bibliography):

Type	Mnemonic	Rhythm	Description
A	Tyger tyger	/ x / x	falling
B	the tides of time	x / x /	rising
C	on high mountains	x / / x	clashing

Types D and E are heavier verses containing a secondary stress marked with a backward slash \ to distinguish it from the main stress / of the two lifts; this gives the following patterns:

Type	Mnemonic	Rhythm	Description
Da	díng dówn stròngly	/ / \ x	falling in stages
Db	bóld brázenfàced	/ / x \	broken fall
E	híghcrèsted hélms	/ \ x /	fall and rise

We can find all of these rhythms employed in J.R.R. Tolkien's modern English narrative poem *The Fall of Arthur*, edited by his son Christopher Tolkien and published in 2013. Since Tolkien was a specialist in the field, this poem obeys all the classic rules of the Old English alliterative metre. In the following short sample, we can identify the metrical type used in each verse as follows:

A	<u>Dark</u> wind came <u>dr</u>iving over <u>deep</u> <u>w</u>ater;	C
C	from the <u>South</u> <u>sw</u>eeping <u>surf</u> upon the <u>bea</u>ches,	A
B	a <u>r</u>oaring <u>s</u>ea <u>r</u>olling <u>e</u>ndless	A
Da	<u>Huge</u> <u>h</u>oarcrested <u>h</u>ills of <u>th</u>under.	A
C	The <u>w</u>orld <u>d</u>arkened.	

It will be seen that the A-verses predominate in this passage, but the metre always changes from the on-verse to the off-verse, imparting a crafted quality to the line.

A similar analysis can be applied to our passage from *Beowulf* (791–96):

B	**Nolde <u>eorla</u> <u>hleo</u> ænige þinga**	A
C	**þone <u>cwealm</u>-<u>cuman</u> <u>cwicne</u> forlætan,**	A
C	**ne his <u>lif</u>-<u>dagas</u> <u>leoda</u> ænigum**	A
A	**<u>nytte</u> <u>tealde</u> Þær <u>genehost</u> <u>brægd</u>**	B
Da	**<u>eorl</u> <u>Beowulfes</u> <u>ealde</u> <u>lafe</u>,**	A
C	**wolde <u>frea</u>-<u>drihtnes</u> <u>feorh</u> ealgian,**	Db

Again, we see the predominance of type-A verses in this metre, but again the rhythm always shifts from on-verse to off-verse within the line. One feature to be observed at lines 792–3 is the pattern C A / C A. This is a kind of parallelism by which the poet creates a semantic contrast between the two type-C verses **þone cwealm-cuman** *that killer-guest* and **his lif-dagas** *the days of his life*. In this way, the verses are shaped to mirror the rhetoric and to contribute to the meaning.

> **CULTURAL INSIGHT**
>
> J.R.R. Tolkien (1892–1973), poet and author of *The Lord of Rings* (1954–5), was primarily a scholar of Old English at the University of Oxford: in his long career he served as Rawlinson and Bosworth Professor of Anglo-Saxon (1925–1945) and Merton Professor of English Language (1945–1959). His best known scholarly work is his lecture *Beowulf: The Monsters and the Critics;* his translation of *Beowulf* has also been published, along with his useful commentary on the poem.

Finally, while we are on the subject of the days of his life, we should recall the unusual patterning in the lines that the narrator employs, on different occasions, to comment on the figures of both Beowulf and Grendel (788b–90):

	<u>Heold</u> hine <u>fæste</u>	A
B	**se þe <u>manna</u> wæs <u>mægene</u> <u>strengest</u>**	A
C	**on <u>þæm</u> <u>dæge</u> <u>þysses</u> <u>lifes</u>.**	A

> *He held him firmly:*
>
> *he who was among men strongest in power*
>
> *on <u>that</u> day of <u>this</u> life.*

In these two-and-a-half lines (five verses), there are five instances of assonance of the **æ**-vowel, which adds an embellishing effect, but it is the departure from the rhythmical norm that really stands out. As well as using the natural word stress of life and day to create his rhythm, the poet chooses also to place his alliteration and emphasis on the determiners *that* and *this*, which as we noted above do not normally serve as lifts in a line of alliterative poetry.

> **LANGUAGE INSIGHT**
>
> Normally there is a two-stress rule. There are two lifts per verse (i.e. four lifts per line), and lifts are confined to nouns, adjectives and infinitives. Finite verbs, especially auxiliary verbs like **hæfde** *had* or **mihte** *could* are not usually stressed. But this means that in *Maldon* lines 64a and 70a and in *Beowulf* 825a (see below) there is only one lift. Here, then, the normal two stress-rule for an on-verse is waived. In *The Battle of Maldon* line 64a, for example, the single lift is on the first syllable of the noun **wætere**, and this type of verse is regularly classified as type A3.

Licsar gebad *he endured a wound*

Beowulf, 815–36

815   Licsar gebad

atol æglæca;   him on eaxle wearð

syndolh sweotol,   seonowe onsprungon,

burston banlocan.   Beowulfe wearð

guðhreð gyfeþe.   Scolde Grendel þonan

820 feorhseoc fleon   under fenhleoðu,

secean wynleas wic;   wiste þe geornor

þæt his aldres wæs   ende gegongen,

dogera dægrim.

                    Denum eallum wearð

æfter þam wælræse   willa gelumpen:

825 hæfde þa gefælsod   se þe ær feorran com,

snotor ond swyðferhð,   sele Hroðgares,

genered wið niðe.   Nihtweorce gefeh,

ellenmærþum: hæfde Eastdenum

Geatmecga leod   gilp gelæsted,

830 oncyþðe   ealle gebette,

inwidsorge,   þe hie ær drugon

ond for þreanydum   þolian scoldon,

torn unlytel.

                    Þæt wæs tacen sweotol,

syþðan hildedeor   hond alegde,

835 earm ond eaxle   – þær wæs eal geador

Grendles grape   – under geapne hrof.

815	**licsar** body-wound; **gebad** he endured, experienced; **atol** terrible; **æglæca** assailant; **on eaxle** on his shoulder
817	**syndolh** a great wound (**sin-** great + **dolh** wound); **sweotol** clear (i.e. clearly seen); **seonowe** sinews; **onsprungon** sprang away
818	**burston** burst; **banlocan** joints; **Beowulfe** to Beowulf (dative)
820	**guðhreð** battle-triumph; **wearð… gyfeþe** was granted; **scolde** was to, had to; **feorhseoc** life-sick; **fleon** flee; **under fenhleoðu** under marshy slopes

821	**secean** *to seek;* **wyn-leas** *joyless;* **wic** *dwelling-place;* **wiste** *he knew;* **þe geornor** *all the more certainly* (**georn** *normally = eager*)
822	**his aldres.... ende** *the end of his life;* **wæs... gegongen** *had come* (lit. *gone*)
823	**dogera** *of days;* **dæg-rim** *day-count, number of days;* **Denum eallum** *to all the Danes;* **wearð... gelumpen** *was come about*
824	**æfter þam wælræse** *after the battle-rush;* **willa** *(their) desire*
825	**se þe** *he who...;* **ær** *previously;* **feorran** *from afar;* **com** *came;* **se þe ær feorran com** *he who had come from afar;* **þa** *then, now;* **hæfde þa gefælsod** *had now cleansed*
826	**snotor** *wide, prudent;* **swyð-ferhð** *strong-hearted* (i.e courageous); **sele** *hall;* **sele Hroðgares** *Hrothgar's hall*
827a	**genered** *saved;* **wið niðe** *against enmity;* **gefeh** *rejoiced;* **niht-weorc** *night-work;* **nihtweorce** *in the work of the night;* **ellen** *courage;* **ellen-mærþum** *in the glories of his courage* (dat. pl.)
829a	**leod** *leader;* **Geat-mecga** *of the Geatish men* (gen. pl.); **gilp** *vow;* **gelæsted** *fulfilled*
830	**swylce** *also;* **oncyþðe ealle** *all the distress;* **gebette** *made good;* **inwit, inwid** *evil, malice* + **sorg** *sorrow =* **inwidsorge** *evil sorrow*
831b	**þe** *which;* **hie** *they;* **ær drugon** *had endured;* **for þrea-nydum** *for sad necessity;* **þolian** *suffer;* **scoldon** *had to*
833	**torn** *bitterness;* **unlytel** *great;* **tacen** *sign;* **hilde-deor** *battle-bold* (adj. implies the battle-bold one, i.e. Beowulf); **alegde** *placed*
835	**geador** *together;* **Grendles grape** *of Grendel's grasp* (irregular genitive); **geap** *steep;* **hrof** *roof*

The end of the fight

The narrative reaches a high point in this passage as Beowulf gains the upper hand (lines 815–36). Two themes and patterns, both in fact grammatical devices, serve to underline the hero's triumph: the switch to the passive voice and the heavy use of the pluperfect in the aftermath of victory.

PASSIVE EXPRESSIONS

The Old English passive voice consists of the verb *was* or *became* + past participle; in practice, this means usually the past tense singular **wearð** *became* (sometimes plural

wurdon) followed by the past participle e.g **gifen** *given* or by an adjective with a sense of completion e.g. the poetic adjective **gifeþe** or **gyfeþe** *granted*. A speaker or writer uses the passive when the agent (the cause of the action) is unknown or unnecessary. In *The Battle of Maldon*, for example, a cluster of such passives suddenly appear in the text as the main fighting begins, and they reflect something of the confusion of the scene. Examples include:

hream wearð ahafen *a clamour was raised* (*Maldon*, line 106)

wund wearð Wulfmær ... (113) *Wulfmær was wounded*

Since the passive is often used when the agent – the person actively responsible for the action – is unknown, e.g. *he was wounded*, this suitably fits with the initial stages of the narrative as the fighting starts, when it is difficult to be sure who is doing what to whom. Similarly in *Beowulf* at the end of the fight, two passives appear in which the agent is kept vague or uncertain: **wearð gyfeþe** *was granted* (*Beowulf*, 818–19) and **wearð gelumpen** *was come about* (823–4). The first is translated in Klaeber's glossary as *was granted by fate*, but the text reads:

> **Beowulfe wearð guðhreð gyfeþe**
>
> *To Beowulf was granted triumph in battle*

There is no mention of any agent, and the poet leaves us wondering whether this is fate or providence. Or, alternatively, should we see it as actual divine intervention, which is how Hrothgar regards it when, later in the next Fitt XIV, he thanks the Almighty for the victory (928)?

PLUPERFECTS (I.E. WHAT *HAD HAPPENED* BEFORE)

In Old English, there was no separate form for a pluperfect tense referring to the pre-past before the main action, i.e. what *had happened* before. Instead writers used the little adverb **ær** *before, previously*, which often does not need to be translated if we use the auxiliary *had*. So when the poet names Beowulf as **se þe ær feorran com** (825) this means in modern English: *he who had travelled from afar* (825).

But like modern English, the language could also allow *had* + past participle, used in the final summary of our passage to show what Beowulf had achieved at the end of his fight, just as he had promised:

hæfde þa gefælsod ... sele Hroðgares (825–6) *he had now cleansed Hrothgar's hall.*

In the next sentence, these statements are reiterated, using both types of expression for conveying the pluperfect pre-past meaning:

hæfde ... gilp gelæsted (828–9) *he had fulfilled his vow*

hæfde ... ealle gebette (830–1) *he had completely made good*

inwidsorge þe hie ær drugon (831) *the sorrow which they had endured.*

The Danes celebrate in the next section (fitt XIII) with horse-racing and story-telling, and here there is yet another expression in the passive (lines 856–7):

ðær wæs Beowulfes / mærðo mæned *there Beowulf's fame was told.*

Test yourself

Identify the metrical type (choosing from A to E) for each of the verses in the following passage from *Beowulf* (lines 823b–829). (NB In one of the verses you will find there are two interpretations possible.)

<blockquote>

               Denum eallum wearð

æfter þam wælræse   willa gelumpen.

Hæfde þa gefælsod   se þe ær feorran com,

snotor ond swyðferhð,   sele Hroðgares,

genered wið niðe;   nihtweorce gefeh,

ellenmærþum.   Hæfde Eastdenum

Geatmecga leod   gilp gelæsted…

</blockquote>

For all the Danes after the battle their desire was come about. He had now cleansed – he who had come from afar, wise and courageous – Hrothgar's hall, redeemed it from malice; he rejoiced in the night's work, the glorious deeds of courage. The prince of the Geats had fulfilled his vow to the Danes…

SELF-CHECK

	I CAN …
○	appreciate the ellipsis of the definite article and the 'condensed style' of Old English poetry
○	interpret examples of agency and ambiguity
○	identify variation and parallelism
○	analyse patterns of repetition
○	categorize the five metrical types in Old English poems
○	observe passive expressions
○	identify pluperfects

23 þare hearpan sweg

the music of the harp (Apollonius of Tyre, chs XVI–XIX)

In this unit you will learn to:
▶ *read and translate passages from the Old English* Apollonius of Tyre
▶ *compare similar motifs in* Beowulf *and* The Wanderer
▶ *explore cultural contexts in documents from Anglo-Saxon Winchester*

The Old English *Apollonius of Tyre*

With *Apollonius of Tyre*, a new kind of literature reached the shores of Anglo-Saxon England. Set in another maritime world, that of the Mediterranean, this is a courtly adventure and a love story, and is often assigned to the genre of the romance, but it does not have the chivalry and tournaments of the later chivalric and Arthurian romances. Instead this is a family romance in which the members of a noble kindred are separated through ill chance but are then reunited at the end. It is also a quest in which a young man achieves good fortune, loses it all, but then regains it. An analogy can be drawn with Shakespeare's *A Comedy of Errors*, *The Winter's Tale*, and *The Tempest*, which draw on similar Classical sources in the ancient novel, and indeed *Pericles Prince of Tyre* tells the same story as the Old English *Apollonius* (the Middle English writer John Gower also wrote a version; see Archibald in Bibliography).

The manuscript into which the story has been copied is the Corpus Wulfstan anthology, a manuscript associated probably with Winchester. This is the very same collection of Wulfstan's writings in which the laws and sermons of the archbishop and statesman are supplemented with other narratives such as the *Story of Joseph*. *Apollonius* is another Old English reworking of an old tale in which, by demonstrating his wisdom and discernment, the protagonist rises through the ranks to a position of power and authority in the kingdom (see unit 14). It seems, then, that the narrative also had political messages about rank, status and rulership to interest and attract its contemporary readers.

As a translator or paraphraser of an earlier Latin story, the anonymous author of the OE *Apollonius* is in full control of his or her medium, Old English literary prose, and adapts and transforms the Classical subject matter so that, despite the outlandish names, this fictional world becomes the world of the mead hall and royal court, and the new boroughs and market towns of eleventh-century England. And in literary terms there is the courtliness and formality, the love of riddle and song, the elegiac tone, the theme of exile and loss that we find also in *Beowulf* and *The Wanderer*. But there is also a new interest in realistic dialogue and in touches of comedy, features it shares with *The Life of Guthlac* (see unit 16).
(For convenience each chapter of the text is divided into individual paragraphs numbered in square brackets; this numbering is not part of the original manuscript.)

APOLLONIUS ÞA SOÐLICE HYRE AREHTE EALLE HIS GELYMP *SO APOLLONIUS THEN TOLD HER ALL HIS STORY*

Apollonius of Tyre, chapter XVI

Why does Apollonius remain silent after the king's daughter has played the harp?

Apollonius þa soðlice hyre arehte ealle his gelymp and æt þare spræcan ende him feollon tearas of ðam eagum. [1]

Mid þy þe se cyngc þæt geseah, he bewænde hine ða to ðare dohtor and cwæð: 'Leofa dohtor, þu gesingodest – mid þy þe þu woldest witan his naman and his gelimp, þu hafast nu geedniwod his ealde sar. Ac ic bidde þe þæt þu gife him swa hwæt swa ðu wille.' [2]

Ða ða þæt mæden gehirde þæt hire wæs alyfed fram hire fæder þæt heo ær hyre silf gedon wolde, ða cwæð heo to Apollonio: 'Apolloni, soðlice þu eart ure. Forlæt þine murcnunge, and nu ic mines fæder leafe habbe, ic gedo ðe weligne.' [3]

Apollonius hire þæs þancode, and se cyngc blissode on his dohtor welwillendnesse, and hyre to cwæð. 'Leofa dohtor, hat feccan þine hearpan, and gecig ðe to þine frynd, and afirsa fram þam iungan his sarnesse.' [4]

Ða eode heo ut and het feccan hire hearpan, and sona swa heo hearpian ongan, heo mid winsumum sange gemægnde þare hearpan sweg. Ða ongunnon ealle þa men hi herian on hyre swegcræft, and Apollonius ana swigode. [5]

Ða cwæð se cyningc: 'Apolloni, nu ðu dest yfele, forðam þe ealle men heriað mine dohtor on hyre swegcræfte, and þu ana hi swigende tælst.' [6]

Apollonius cwæð: 'Eala ðu goda cyngc, gif ðu me gelifst, ic secge þæt ic ongite þæt soðlice þin dohtor gefeol on swegcræft, ac heo næfð hine na wel geleornod. Ac hat me nu sillan þa hearpan – þonne wast þu nu þæt þu git nast.' [7]

Arcestrates se cyning cwæð: 'Apolloni, ic oncnawe soðlice þæt þu eart on eallum þingum wel gelæred.' [8]

Ða het se cyng sillan Apollonige þa hearpan. Apollonius þa ut eode and hine scridde and sette ænne cynehelm uppon his heafod, and nam þa hearpan on his hand and in eode and swa stod, þæt se cyngc and ealle þa ymbsittendan wendon þæt he nære Apollonius ac þæt he wære Apollines ðara hæðenra god. [9]

Ða wearð stilnes and swige geworden innon ðare healle. And Apollonius his hearpenægl genam, and he þa hearpestrengas mid cræfte astirian ongan, and þare hearpan sweg mid winsumum sange gemægnde. And se cyngc silf and ealle þe þar andwearde wæron micelre stæfne cliopodon and hine heredon. [10]

Æfter þisum forlet Apollonius þa hearpan and plegode and fela fægera þinga þar forð teah þe þam folce ungecnawen wæs and ungewunelic, and heom eallum þearle licode ælc þara þinga ðe he forð teah. [11]

[1]	**þa** *then*; **arehte** *related*; **gelymp** *story* (in the sense of events that had happened to him); **æt þare spræcan ende** *at the end of the speech*; **tearas** *tears*
[2]	**Mid þy þe** *when*; **bewænde hine** *turned*; **leofa dohtor** *my dear daughter*; **þu gesingodest** *you did wrong*; **witan** *to know*; **þu hafast nu geedniwod** *you have now renewed*; **his ealde sar** *his old wound*; **ic bidde þe** *I ask you*
[3]	**Ða ða … ða** *when … then* (for correlation see unit 16); **þæt mæden** *the girl, young (unmarried) woman*; **hire wæs alyfed** *she was permitted*; **þu eart ure** *you are one of us* (literally *you are ours*; cf. translation by Elaine Treharne, see Bibliography); **seo murcnung** *grief*; **nu** *now that*; **mines fæder leafe** *my father's permission*; **ic gedo ðe** *I will make you*; **welig** *wealthy*
[4]	**blissode** *rejoiced*; **welwillendnes** *kindness* (literally *the quality of wanting well*); **hat feccan** *have them fetch*; **seo hearpa** *harp*; **and gecig ðe to** *and invite* (literally *and call to you*); **frynd** *friends*; **afirsa** *drive away*; **se iunga** *the young man* (adjectival noun); **sarnes** *pain*
[5]	**feccan** *fetch*; **hearpian** *to play the harp*; **winsum** *beautiful*; **gemægnde** *blended*; **herian** *admire*; **swegcræft** *musicianship*; **ana** *alone*; **swigode** *was silent*
[6]	**nu ðu dest yfele** *now you are doing wrong*; **þu … hi tælst** *you reproach her*; **swigende** *in silence*
[7]	**Eala, ðu goda cyngc**: the word **eala** is a vocative, *O king*; the whole phrase could be translated *Good king, …*; **gif ðu me gelifst** *if you believe me*; **ic ongite** *I perceive*; **gefeol** *fell* (the word is used later, at the beginning of ch. 17); **on** *into* (i.e. she fell into music-making); **geleornod** *learned*; **sillan** *give*; **þonne wast þu nu þæt þu git nast** *then you will come to know now what you do not know*; **wast** from **witan** *to know*; (**ne + wast = nast** *do not know*)
[8]	**ic oncnawe** *I acknowledge*; **gelæred** *educated*
[9]	**hine scridde** *clothed himself*; **se cynehelm** *royal crown* (the Latin has 'corona', which means *garland* in this context, but **cynehelm** in Old English means *royal head-cover*, i.e. *crown*); **ealle þa ymbsittendan** *all the ones sitting around there* (the idea of sitting around, presumably on benches and chairs at a board or trellis table, is Anglo-Saxon, wheras the Latin text has 'discumbentes' i.e. people reclining on couches in the Roman manner); **wendon** from **wenan** *to think, suppose*; **wære / nære** subjunctive of **wæs** *was*, negative form **næs**; **Apollines** *Apollo*; **ðara hæðenra god** *the god of the heathen*

[10]   **stilness and swige** *stillness and silence;* **wearð …
geworden** *had become, had come about;* **innon ðare
healle** *inside the hall* (**seo healle** *the hall* translates
Latin 'triclinium' and 'domum'; this process of translation
is one of acculturation and domestication; in other
words making the scene familiar to the Anglo-Saxon
audience and readership)

[11]   **plegode** lit. *played,* i.e. entertained; **forð teah**
performed (from **teon**); **ungecnawen** *unknown;*
ungewunelic *unusual;* **heom eallum þearle licode** *it
was very pleasing to them all* (i.e. they all enjoyed it very
much)

AC ÞÆT MÆDEN HÆFDE UNSTILLE NIHT *BUT THE YOUNG WOMAN HAD A RESTLESS NIGHT*

Apollonius of Tyre, ch. XVIII

In the intervening time after the feast, as told in chapter XVII, the princess has arranged with the king to provide accommodation for their unexpected guest. Furnished with gifts of money and servants, and grateful for the lavish hospitality he has received, Apollonius takes his leave of the king and the princess and retires to his lodgings for the night.

In chapter XVIII, how does the princess contrive further to prolong Apollonius's residence in Pentapolis?

Ac þæt mæden hæfde unstille niht, mid þare lufe onæled þara worda and sanga þe heo gehyrde æt Apollonige, and na leng heo ne gebad ðonne hit dæg wæs, ac eode sona swa hit leoht wæs and gesæt beforan hire fæder bedde. [1]

Ða cwæð se cyngc: 'Leofa dohtor, for hwi eart ðu þus ær wacol?' [2]

Ðæt mæden cwæð: 'Me awehton þa gecnerdnessan þe ic girstandæg gehyrde. Nu bidde ic ðe forðam þæt þu befæste me urum cuman Apollonige to lare.' [3]

Ða wearð se cyningc þearle geblissod, and het feccan Apollonium and him to cwæð: 'Min dohtor girnð þæt heo mote leornian æt ðe ða gesæligan lare ðe þu canst, and gif ðu wilt þisum þingum gehyrsum beon, ic swerige ðe þurh mines rices mægna þæt swa hwæt swa ðu on sæ forlure ic ðe þæt on lande gestaðelige.' [4]

Ða ða Apollonius þæt gehyrde, he onfengc þam mædenne to lare and hire tæhte swa wel swa he silf geleornode. [5]

[1]	mid þare lufe, from **seo lufu** *love*; **onæled** *burning, ignited*; **æt** *from*; **na leng heo ne gebad** *she couldn't wait any longer*; **ðonne** *when*; **ac** *but*; **beforan** *before, in front of, at the end of*; **þæt bedd** *bed*
[2]	**þus ær** *so early*; **wacol** *awake*
[3]	**þa gecnerdnessan** *displays of learning* (**seo gecneordnes** *diligence, study*); **me awehton** *kept me awake*; **girstandæg** *yesterday*; **befæste me** *entrust me, commend me*; **urum** *to our* **cuma** *guest*; **to lare** *for tuition*
[4]	**þearle** *greatly*; **geblissod** *pleased*, past participle from **blissian** *to rejoice*; **æt ðe** *from you*; **gesælig** *superior* (see Goolden 1958, p. 57); **ðe þu canst** *which you know*; **þisum þingum** *in these matters*; **gehyrsum** *agreeable*; **ic swerige ðe** *I swear to you*; **mægen** *power*; **swa hwæt swa** *whatever*; **ic ðe þæt gestaðelige** *I will restore that to you*
[5]	**onfengc** *received* (w dat. as obj.); **swa wel swa** *as well as*; **he silf** *he himself*; **geleornode** *had learned*

HYT GELAMP ÐA ÆFTER ÞISUM BINNON FEAWUM TIDUM *AND SO IT HAPPENED A FEW HOURS AFTER THIS*

Apollonius of Tyre, ch. XIX

The Old English text at this point differs in content from the Latin version (edited by Archibald), which has the young woman falling ill with love-sickness at the end of chapter XVIII, and the doctors unable to diagnose the complaint. The Latin story resumes in chapter XIX a few days later, with the king taking a stroll with Apollonius in the forum of Pentapolis. The Old English version, by contrast, makes no mention of any love-sickness, and has the two men a few hours later (Goolden 1958: 57) strolling arm in arm **on ðare ceastre stræte** *in the main street of the town* when they encounter the three comic suitors.

Why is the king amused at the behaviour of the three suitors?

Hyt gelamp ða æfter þisum binnon feawum tidum þæt Arcestrates se cyngc heold Apollonius hand on handa and eodon swa ut on ðare ceastre stræte. Þa æt nyhstan comon ðar gan ongean hy þry gelærede weras and æþelborene, þa lange ær girndon þæs cyninges dohtor. [1]

Hi ða ealle þry togædere anre stæfne gretton þone cyngc. [2]

Ða smercode se cyng and heom to beseah and þus cwæð: 'Hwæt is þæt þæt ge me anre stæfne gretton?' [3]

Ða andswerode heora an and cwæð: 'We bædon gefirn þynre dohtor, and þu us oft rædlice mid elcunge geswænctest. Forðam we comon hider to dæg þus togædere. We syndon þyne ceastergewaran, of æðelum gebyrdum geborene. Nu bidde we þe þæt þu geceose þe ænne of us þrym hwilcne þu wille þe to aðume habban.' [4]

Ða cwæð se cyngc: 'Nabbe ge na godne timan aredodne. Min dohtor is nu swiðe bisy ymbe hyre leornunga, ac þe læs þe ic eow a leng slæce, awritað eowre naman on gewrite and hire morgengife, þonne asænde ic þa gewrita minre dohtor þæt heo sylf geceose hwilcne eowerne heo wille.' [5]

Ða didon ða cnihtas swa, and se cyngc nam ða gewrita and geinseglode hi mid his ringe and sealde Apollonio, þus cweðende: 'Nim nu, lareow Apolloni, swa hit þe ne mislicyge, and bryng þinum lærincgmædene.' [6]

[1]	**tid** *hour* (cf. unit 5); **æt nyhstan** *next*; **comon ðar gan ongean hy** *there came walking towards them*; **æþelborene** *noble-born* (pl.)
[2]	**anre stæfne** *with one voice*; **gretton** *past tense of* **gretan** *to greet*
[3]	**smercode** *smiled* (cf. *Life of Guthlac* in unit 16); **him to beseah** *looked at them* (phrasal verb); **hwæt is þæt þæt** *why is it that…?* (colloquial register)
[4]	**heora an** *one of them*; **we bædon** *we have asked for* (w. dat.); **gefirn** *in the past*; **rædlice** *immediately*; **mid elcunge** *with delay*; **geswænctest** *oppressed* (i.e. gave us a difficult reception); **forðam** *that's why* (in more formal contexts *therefore*); **to dæg** *today* (everyday speech, found also in homilies and sermons); **of æðelum gebyrdum** *of noble origins* (of the best families); **nu bidde we þe** *now we ask you* (colloquial equivalent of more formal **biddaþ**); **geceose** *choose* (subjunctive); **ænne of us þrym** *one of us three*; **hwilcne** *which* (accusative); **to aðume habban** *to have as son-in-law*
[5]	**nabbe ge** *you haven't*; **aredod** *arranged*; **bisy** *busy*; **slæce** *delay* (subjunctive); **awritað** *write down* (imperative); **hwilcne eowerne** *which of you*
[6]	**ða cnihtas** *the young men*; **Ða didon … swa** *then they did so*, i.e. *acted accordingly* (cf. Herefordshire Lawsuit, unit 20, and **heo ða swæ dydon**); **geinseglode hi** *sealed them*; **swa hit þe ne mislicyge** *if it doesn't displease you*

Literary and cultural contexts

1 THE MUSIC OF THE HARP

The courtly interest in the skilful playing of the harp is a feature that links the court of Arcestrate in Apollonius with the court of Hrothgar in *Beowulf*:

1 a from *Beowulf*, 86–90

Ða se ellengæst   earfoðlice
þrage geþolode,   se þe in þystrum bad,
þæt he dogora gehwam   dream gehyrde
hludne in healle: þær wæs hearpan sweg,
swutol sang scopes.

Then the powerful spirit impatiently
suffered for a time – he who waited in dark places –
that every day he heard the joy
loud in the hall: there was the music of the harp,
the clear song of the poet.

1 b from *Beowulf*, 2105–10 (Hrothgar plays the harp)

Þær wæs gidd ond gleo.   Gomela Scilding,
felafricgende,   feorran rehte;
hwilum hildedeor   hearpan wynne,
gomenwudu grette,   hwilum gyd awræc
soð ond sarlic,   hwilum syllic spell
rehte æfter rihte   rumheort cyning.

There was singing and music. The old Scylding
recalled the stories he had learned from long ago.
At times the brave warrior would play the harp with joy,
songs from the wood, at times he would perform a lay,
true and sorrowful, at times tell a tale of wonder
as was fitting – the magnanimous king.

2 THE THEME OF SORROW RENEWED

from *The Wanderer*, 45–57

In terms of character, the parallel with the poem of exile *The Wanderer* is instructive: both the **anhaga** (*the solitary man*) in *The Wanderer* and also the former ealdorman in *Apollonius of Tyre* find that their sorrow is renewed as they recall past joys and lost friends.

45   Ðonne onwæcneð eft   wineleas guma
gesihð him biforan   fealwe wegas,
baþian brimfuglas,   brædan feþra,

hreosan hrim ond snaw   hagle gemenged.

Þonne beoð þy hefigran   heortan benne,

50   sare æfter swæsne.   Sorg bið geniwad

þonne maga gemynd   mod geondhweorfeð;

greteð gliwstafum,   georne geondsceawað

secga geseldan;   swimmað oft on weg

fleotendra ferð   no þær fela bringeð

55   cuðra cwidegiedda.   Cearo bið geniwad

þam þe sendan sceal   swiþe geneahhe

ofer waþema gebind   werigne sefan.

45   *Then the friendless man wakes up again: –*

sees in front of him the dark waves,

the seabirds bathing, spreading their wings,

the ice and snow falling mingled with hail.

Then the wounds of the heart are all the heavier,

50   *painfully yearning for the beloved. Sorrow is renewed*

when the memory of kinsmen passes through the mind;

he greets them with joy, eagerly he watches them,

the companions of men: they float away again,

the fleeting figures do not bring there

55   *many familiar counsels. Trouble is renewed*

for the one who must send – very frequently –

over the binding of the waves – his weary spirit.

3 DOCUMENTS FROM WINCHESTER

Winchester, formerly a Roman city, had been thoroughly rebuilt by the West Saxons under Alfred and his successors. By the time of Æthelred and Cnut it had long been a royal city with a new grid of Anglo-Saxon streets laid differently to the Roman plan, the exception being the main street from west to east. You can still enter the city through the medieval West Gate, once Roman (cf. the mention of **þare ceastre geate** *the city gate* in Apollonius, ch. XXI), and then walk down the High Street, which in medieval times was the market street.

3a from Lantfred, *The Translation and Miracles of St Swithun* (written c. 970)

In a unique street scene, the smith encounters a tenant-farmer from Winchcombe passing through the market street in Winchester, described in Latin as the 'forum':

Tandem eodem die, dum peragraret forum, repperit quondam commemorate inquilinum canonici, qui causa necessariae coemptionis Wintoniniam uenerat.

Afterwards, on the very same day, while he was passing through the market street, he came across a certain tenant of the canon in question, who had come to Winchester to make some necessary purchases (trans. M. Lapidge).

3b A charter from the year 996 (Sawyer S 889; Rumble 2002, no. 26)

This charter concerns a property which had been bequeathed in a lady's will to the Old Minster in Winchester. The bounds of the property are thoroughly urban, unlike the typically rural settings of the usual boundary clause (as seen in unit 10) and the document is an early witness to the developing street-names of the city. Here the old 'forum', as it was called in Latin, has become **cyp-stræt**, *the purchase-street* or *Market Street* in Old English, reflective of the changes that had taken place over the six centuries since the Romans. Such changes are reflected in the way the Latin story of *Apollonius* is reworked in the Old English version. It seems appropriate that the manuscript of the *OE Apollonius* – the Corpus Wulfstan Anthology – may have been compiled at Winchester itself (for the relevant reading on this issue see Bibliography).

What names of streets are given in the text?

_____

_____

Ærest fram Leofan hagan west andlang cypstræte oð hit cymð to flæsmangere stræte; andlang flæscmangara stræte ðet it cymð to scyldwyrhtana stræte; andlang scyldwyrhtana stræte east eft ðæt hit cymð to Leofan hagan.

? Test yourself

Using the word index at the back of the book and any other resources available (see Bibliography), translate chapter XVII of the Old English *Apollonius of Tyre*.

XVII

Soðlice, mid þy þe þæs cynges dohtor geseah þæt Apollonius on eallum godum cræftum swa wel wæs getogen, þa gefeol hyre mod on his lufe. [1]

Ða æfter þæs beorscipes geendunge, cwæð þæt mæden to ðam cynge: 'Leofa fæder, þu lyfdest me litle ær þæt ic moste gifan Apollonio swa hwæt swa ic wolde of þinum goldhorde. [2]

Arcestrates se cyng cwæð to hyre: 'Gif him swa hwæt swa ðu wille. [3]

Heo ða sweoðe bliðe ut eode and cwæð: 'Lareow Apolloni, ic gife þe, be mines fæder leafe, twa hund punda goldes, and feower hund punda gewihte seolfres, and þone mæstan dæl deorwurðan reafes, and twentig ðeowa manna.' [4]

And heo þa þus cwæð to ðam þeowum mannum: 'Berað þas þingc mid eow þe ic behet Apollonio, minum lareowe, and lecgað innon bure beforan minum freondum.' [5]

Þis wearð þa þus gedon æfter þare cwene hæse, and ealle þa men hire gife heredon ðe hig gesawon. Da soðlice geendode þe gebeorscipe, and þa men ealle arison and gretton þone cyngc and ða cwene, and bædon hig gesunde beon, and ham gewændon. [6]

Eac swilce Apollonius cwæð: 'Ðu goda cyngc and earmra gemiltsigend, and þu cwen, lare lufigend, beon ge gesunde.' He beseah eac to ðam þeowum mannum þe þæt mæden him forgifen hæfde, and heom cwæð to: 'Nimað þas þing mid eow þe me seo cwen forgeaf, and gan we secan ure gesthus þæt we magon us gerestan.' [7]

Ða adred þæt mæden þæt heo næfre eft Apollonium ne gesawe swa raðe swa heo wolde, and eode þa to hire fæder and cwæð: 'Ðu goda cyningc, licað ðe wel þæt Apollonius, þe þurh us todæg gegodod is, þus heonon fare, and cuman yfele men and bereafian hine?' [8]

Se cyngc cwæð: 'Wel þu cwæde. Hat him findan hwar he hine mæge wurðlicost gerestan.' [9]

Ða dide þæt mæden swa hyre beboden wæs, and Apollonius onfeng þare wununge ðe hym getæht wæs, and ðar in eode, Gode þancigende ðe him ne forwyrnde cynelices wurðscipes and frofre. [10]

SELF-CHECK

I CAN ...
read and translate passages from the Old English *Apollonius of Tyre*
compare similar motifs in *Beowulf* and *The Wanderer*
explore cultural contexts in documents from Anglo-Saxon Winchester

24 *Soðlice hi ledon forð heora lac*
So they brought out their gifts

In this unit you will learn how to:
▶ *read and transcribe texts from their original manuscript or a manuscript facsimile*

You will read:
▶ **the Story of Joseph 5:** *a direct transcription from the facsimile of the manuscript of the Old English Illustrated* **Hexateuch**
▶ *two riddles from the* **Exeter Book** *in their original manuscript layout*
▶ *the King's Promise, from the manuscript Cotton Cleopara B xiii*

 Language discovery

READING A MANUSCRIPT IN FACSIMILE

Compared with later periods up to and including the Renaissance, the handwriting of Old English scribes is relatively easy to read. For practice, it is recommended that you begin with a text you already know. For our purposes here we will use the Old English *Hexateuch*. This has already been the focus of several units in this book, and its text is written in a clear late Old English scribal hand. For those who wish to read the text in its original script, the facsimile of the manuscript is available in good research libraries and also online (see Bibliography). Folio 63v is the relevant page, showing Joseph's second meeting and feast with his brothers. Some guidance on text and script will be given shortly; but to start, try reading the first line:

Soþlice hiledon forð heoralac ongean þæt iosep ineode . 7 feollon

PRACTISING TRANSCRIPTION

Use the old method of look and listen: in order to familiarize yourself with the scribal conventions, turn to the online facsimile (see Bibliography) and at the same time listen to the recording once, following the text with your finger. Next, try to transcribe the text. Then compare your text with the transcription here. Letters that are difficult to make out at first are **d**, which curls back on itself (see **ledon** in line 1), **f** and **r**, which extend below the line (e.g. **forð**). Note the shape of **g** in **ongean** and the alternative form of the letter **s** (a little like the modern letter 'r') as it appears in **iosep** (*Joseph*). The Tironian *nota* represents the Old English conjunction **and**, which means quite simply *and*. Apart from this, the main punctuation mark in the text is a point. Capital letters are used sparingly: the initial **S** marks a new section, but **Iosep** is written with lower case **i** in line 1 and upper case **I** in line 2. One interesting feature is word division by phrase: smaller words tend to be written together with the larger stressed word that follows (e.g. **ineode**). Watch out, in particular, for the round 'w' rune (called **wynn**, which means *joy*), e.g. **wiþ hine** in the middle of line 2.

THE *STORY OF JOSEPH* 5

The passage selected presents the brothers' second meeting with their as yet unrecognized brother, Joseph, and the beginning of the protracted and hard-won reconciliation between them.

 24.00

Soðlice hi ledon forð heora lac

So they brought out their gifts

Line-by-line transcription

Soðlice hiledon forð heoralac ongean þæt iosep ineode. 7 feollon

onþa eorðan. 7geeaðmeddon wiþhine. Iosep hioncneowða arful

lice. 7axode hi hwæðer heora fæder wære hal. Þehihim fore sædon

oþþehwæðer heleofode. Þacwædon hi gesund isþin þeow urefæder

gyt he leofaþ. Ðaiosep geseah hisge meddredan broþor beniamin.

þacwæþ he. isþis secnapa þegeme foresædon. 7eft hecwæþ godgemilt

sige þe sunu min. 7hewearð swaswiðe astyrod þæthim feollon tearas

for his broþor þingon. 7he eode into his bed cleofan 7weop. 7 þahe

þæs geswac. þa eode he ut tohim 7hiæton. Onsundron. þaegyptiscean.

hit næs na alifed þæthiætgædere æton. 7 himan oferdrencte.

Edited text

Soðlice hi ledon forð heora lac ongean þæt Iosep in eode, and feollon on þa eorðan, and geeaðmeddon wiþ hine. Iosep hi oncneow þa arfullice, and axode hi hwæðer heora fæder wære hal, þe hi him foresædon oþþe hwæðer he leofode.

Þa cwædon hi: Gesund is þin þeow ure fæder gyt he leofaþ.

Ða Iosep geseah his gemeddredan broþor Beniamin, þa cwæþ he, is þis se cnapa þe ge me foresædon. And eft he cwæþ: God gemiltsige þe sunu min.

And he wearð swa swiðe astyrod þæt him feollon tearas for his broþor þingon, and he eode into his bedcleofan 7 weop. And Þa he þæs geswac, þa eode he ut to him and hi æton. Onsundron þa egyptiscean: hit næs na alifed þæt hi ætgædere æton. And hi man oferdrencte.

So they brought out their gifts as Joseph came in, and fell on the ground and prostrated themselves before him. Joseph acknowledged them graciously, and asked them whether their father was well, whom they had mentioned before, or whether he lived.

Then they said, 'Your servant our father is well, he is still living.'

When Joseph saw his maternal brother Benjamin, then he said, 'Is this the boy you mentioned to me?' And again he said, 'God protect you, my son.'

And he was so deeply moved that his tears fell for the sake of his brother, and he went to his bedchamber and wept. And when he had stopped, he went out to them and they ate. The Egyptians separately. It was not allowed that they should eat together. And they gave them too much to drink.

MANUSCRIPT ILLUSTRATIONS

It is possible with some caution to use manuscript illustrations as a source of information on the material culture of the period. In the illustration accompanying the text of Joseph and his brothers, the figures of the men wear tunics of varying colours and 'flat, black ankle shoes, with a white strip down the front' (Gale Owen-Crocker, *Dress in Anglo-Saxon England*, p. 259; see Bibliography). Many of the men wear cloaks fastened with a round brooch at the shoulder. They eat with large prominent knives (the Saxon type known as a **seax**) and take their wine in drinking horns and beaker cups – the Egyptians with forked beards form a group in the chamber in the lower left of the picture, while on the right are the Hebrews, who appear to be drinking more prominently.

In the upper picture, the brothers bring gifts to the man they call the **landhlaford** *lord of the land* (their unrecognized brother Joseph); the picture shows as their collective gift an assemblage of goods: a money bag, a tall jar with a lid, a cup, a golden goblet, a drinking horn and a bowl. Such assemblages appear in other manuscript illustrations, where they clearly represent the concept of treasure. In contrast to the brothers, Joseph carries a sword with a trilobed pommel, a symbol of his authority. On the far right of the picture he departs with cloak held to his eyes to weep unseen in his chamber. The location of the meeting is a hall with tiled roof and carved columns. Like the assemblage of rich goods, this is, of course, a kind of icon rather than a realistic depiction; it represents the concept of the **heall** *hall* or – as the text calls it in Genesis 44: 13 – the **burh** (*stronghold* or *castle*) where the **landhlaford**, like Byrhtnoth in the poem *The Battle of Maldon*, has his residence.

Reading

This section presents – for further reading and interpretation – three short texts taken from two books owned by Leofric of Exeter, the continental cleric of English origins who rose to prominence in England during the reign of Edward the Confessor (see chapter 3):

from Exeter Cathedral Library, the *Exeter Book*:

- Riddle 30b **Ic eom ligbysig** *I am beset with flames* (for title see Treharne in Bibliography)

- Riddle 60 **Ic wæs be sonde** *I was by the shore*

from London, British Library, Cotton, Cleopatra B xiii:

Ic þreo þing behate *I promise three things*, the Old English coronation oath, as perhaps used by Edward when he was consecrated at Winchester in 1043 (see unit 1).

For the manuscript contexts and related historical texts, and for further discussion, see the Bibliography.

TWO RIDDLES FROM THE *EXETER BOOK*

Ic eom ligbysig

I am beset with flames

Riddle 30b (manuscript layout):

Ic eom lig bysig lace mid winde [...fire damage in the manuscript]

dre ge somnad fus forð weges fyre gemylted [...]

blowende byrnende gled ful oft mec gesiþas sendað

æfter hondū þærmec weras 7wif wlonce gecyssað þōn

ic mec onhæbbe hion hnigað tome modge miltsum

swa ic mongum sceal ycan up cyme eadignesse :7

Riddle 30 (text edited with readings from Riddle 30A):

Ic eom ligbysig   lace mid winde

wuldre bewunden   wedre gesomnad

fus forðweges   fyre gemylted

bearu blowende   byrnende gled

5   **ful oft mec gesiþas   sendað æfter hondum**

þær mec weras ond wif   wlonce gecyssað

þonne ic mec onhæbbe   hi onhnigað to me

modge miltsum   swa ic mongum sceal

ycan upcyme   eadignesse :7

ic wæs be sonde

I was by the shore

Riddle 60 (manuscript layout):

Ic wæs besonde sæ wealle neah æt mere

faroþe minum gewunade frum staþole fæst. fea

ænig wæs. monna cynnes þæt minne þær on an æde

eard be heolde. ac mec uhtna gehwam yð sio brune

lagu fæðme beleolc lyt icwende þ ic ær oþþe sið.

æfre scolde ofer meodu muð leas sprecan wordum wrix

lan þ is wundres dæl onsefan searolic þā þe swylc ne

conn. humec seaxeð ord 7seo swiþre hond eorles inge

þonc 7ord somod þingum geþydan þæt ic wiþþe sceolde

for unc anum twan ærend spræce abeodan bealdlice
swa hit beorna ma uncre word cwidas widdor ne
mænden :7

Riddle 60 (lightly edited text):

Ic wæs be sonde   sæwealle neah
æt merefaroþe   minum gewunade
frumstaþole fæst.   fea ænig wæs.
monna cynnes   þæt minne þær
5   on anæde   eard beheolde.
ac mec uhtna gehwam   yð sio brune
lagufæðme beleolc   lyt ic wende
þæt ic ær oþþe sið.   æfre scolde
ofer meodu   muðleas sprecan
10   wordum wrixlan   þæt is wundres dæl
on sefan searolic   þam þe swylc ne conn.
hu mec seaxes ord   ond seo swiþre hond
eorles ingeþonc   ond ord somod
þingum geþydan   þæt ic wiþ þe sceolde
15   for unc anum twan   ærendspræce
abeodan bealdlice   swa hit beorna ma
uncre wordcwidas   widdor ne mænden :7

Practice

Read the following text from the *Exeter Book* in the illustration below. Using an anthology of Old English poems (see Bibliography), identify the title of the poem.

The Old English Coronation Oath

Entitled in Latin PROMISSIO REGIS, The king's promise, this was copied into a manuscript belonging to Leofric bishop of Exeter in the reign of Edward the Confessor. The text gives us the English words of the oath sworn by Edward's father Æthelred the Unready when he was consecrated king by St Dunstan at Kingston in 978. In the intervening reigns, it is likely that king Cnut and his sons had used another crowning ceremony, but we may speculate that Edward the Confessor – listening to archbishop Eadsige and repeating after him – spoke these actual words for his consecration at Winchester in 1043 (for Edward's coronation see unit 1).

 24.01

Ic þreo þing behate *I promise three things*

Þis gewrit is gewriten be stæfe be þam gewrite þe Dunstan arcebisceop sealde urum hlaforde æt Cingestune, þa on dæg þa hine man halgode to cinge, and forbead him ælc wedd to syllanne butan þysan wedde þe he up on Cristes weofod léde, swa se bisceop him dihte:

On þære halgan þrinnesse naman ic þreo þing behate Cristenum folce and me underðeoddum: án ærest, þæt Godes cyrice and eall Cristen folc minra gewealda soðe sibbe healde; oðer is, þæt ic reaflac and ealle unrihte þing eallum hádum forbeode; þridde, þæt ic beháte and bebeode on eallum dómum riht and mildheortnisse, þæt us eallum arfæst and mildheort God þurh his ecean miltse forgife, se lifað and rixað.

This document is written according to the letter from the document that archbishop Dunstan gave to our lord at Kingston on the day when he consecrated him as king and forbade him from giving any oath except the oath which he laid on Christ's altar, as the bishop dictated to him:

In the name of the Holy Trinity, I promise three things to my Christian people and subjects: first, that God's church and all Christian people of my domains should keep true peace; the second is that I forbid robbery and all unjust acts to all orders of society; third, that I promise and command in all the laws justice and mercy, which gracious and merciful God may grant us all through his eternal favour, who liveth and reigneth.

Bibliography

General Bibliography

KEY REFERENCE WORKS

Kenneth Cameron, *English Place Names*, new edition (London, 1996)

Malcolm Godden and Michael Lapidge (eds.), *The Cambridge Companion to Old English Literature*, 2nd edition (Cambridge, 2013)

David Hill, *An Atlas of Anglo-Saxon England* (Oxford,1981)

Catherine E. Karkov, *The Art of Anglo-Saxon England* (Cambridge, 2011)

Michael Lapidge, John Blair, Simon Keynes and Donald Scragg (eds.), *The Wiley Blackwell Encyclopedia of Anglo-Saxon England* (Oxford, 2014)

Peter H. Sawyer, *Anglo-Saxon Charters: An Annotated List and Bibliography* (London, 1968); available online as the Electronic Sawyer

Frank M. Stenton, *Anglo-Saxon England*, 3rd edition (Oxford, 1998)

INTRODUCTIONS

Mark Atherton, *The Making of England: A New History of the Anglo-Saxon World* (London, 2017)

John Blair, *Anglo-Saxon England: A Very Short Introduction* (Oxford, 2000)

David Crystal, *The Stories of English* (London, 2004)

Barbara Raw, *The Art and Background of Old English Poetry* (London, 1978)

Andrew Reynolds, *Later Anglo-Saxon England: Life and Landscape* (Stroud, 1999)

Michael Wood, *In Search of England: Journeys into the English Past* (London, 2000)

Barbara Yorke, *The Anglo-Saxons* (Stroud, 1999)

TRANSLATIONS

S.A.J. Bradley, *Anglo-Saxon Poetry* (London, 1995)

Kevin Crossley Holland, *The Anglo-Saxon World*, new edition (Woodbridge, 2002)

Seamus Heaney, *Beowulf* (London, 1999)

Michael J. Swanton, *Anglo-Saxon Prose* (London, 1975)

Tolkien, J.R.R., *Beowulf: A Translation and Commentary, together with Sellic Spell*, ed. Christopher Tolkien (London, 2014)

ANTHOLOGIES WITH OLD ENGLISH–MODERN ENGLISH PARALLEL TEXTS

Greg Delanty and Michael Matto (eds.), *The Word Exchange: Anglo-Saxon Poems in Translation* (London, 2011)

Richard Hamer (ed. and trans.), *A Choice of Anglo-Saxon Verse* (London, 1970)

Elaine Treharne (ed. and trans.), *Old and Middle English c.890–c.1450: An Anthology*, 3rd edition (Oxford, 2009)

EDITIONS OF SPECIFIC TEXTS

Robert E. Bjork (ed.), *Old English Shorter Poems, Volume II: Wisdom and Lyric* (Cambridge MA and London, 2014)

Christopher Jones (ed.), *Old English Shorter Poems, Volume I: Religious and Didactic* (Cambridge MA and London, 2013)

Bernard J. Muir (ed.), *The Exeter Anthology of Old English Poetry: An Edition of Exeter Dean and Chapter MS 3501*, 2nd edition (Exeter, 2000)

Florence E. Harmer (ed.), *Anglo-Saxon Writs*, 2nd edition (Stamford, 1989)

A.J. Robertson (ed. and trans.), *Anglo-Saxon Charters* (Cambridge, 1939)

APPROACHES TO LANGUAGE LEARNING

Two good guides are Stella Hurd and Linda Murphy (eds.) *Success with Languages* (London, 2005) and Vivian Cook, *Second Language Learning and Language Teaching*, 4th edition (London, 2008). The challenge to purely grammar-based methods is taken up by Michael Lewis, *The Lexical Approach. The State of ELT and a Way Forward* (Andover, 2008). On different types of language learner see the specialist study by P. Skehan, *Individual Differences in Second-Language Learning* (London, 1989). Still worth reading are the surveys by H.H. Stern *Fundamental Concepts of Language Teaching* (Oxford, 1983) and by W.F. Mackey, *Language Teaching Analysis* (London, 1965).

LANGUAGE LEARNING AND OLD ENGLISH

The now classic work on the subject *The Practical Study of Languages* (London, 1899) was written by the phonetician and Old English specialist Henry Sweet, author of *An Anglo-Saxon Reader*, 1st edition (Oxford: Clarendon Press, 1876), 15th edition (Oxford: Clarendon Press, 1967). Sweet's insightful, context-based approach to language learning was lost sight of by twentieth-century Anglo-Saxon studies. For discussion, see two articles by M. Atherton, 'Henry Sweet's Psychology of Language Learning', in Klaus D. Dutz and Hans-J. Niederehe (eds.), *Theorie und Rekonstruction* (Münster, 1996), pp. 149–168; and 'Priming the Poets: The Making of Henry Sweet's *Anglo-Saxon Reader*' in David Clark and Nicholas Perkins (eds.), *Anglo-Saxon Culture and the Modern Imagination* (Woodbridge, 2010).

FOLLOW-UP READING TO THE CHAPTERS

Old English (Anglo-Saxon)

The poem 'Bone Dreams' is found in Seamus Heaney, *North* (London, 1975) and Seamus Heaney, *Opened Ground: Poems 1966–1996* (London, 1998). Another approach to Old English poetry is outlined in J.R.R. Tolkien, *The Monsters and the Critics and Other Essays* (London, 1983), particularly in his essay 'On Translating *Beowulf*'. For the development of the language see David Crystal, *The Stories of English* (London, 2004) and Melvyn Bragg, *The Adventure of English 500 AD–2000: The Biography of a Language* (London, 2003).

1 Here Edward was consecrated as king

Frank Barlow, *Edward the Confessor*, new edition (London, 1997); Katherine O'Brien O'Keeffe (ed.), *The Anglo-Saxon Chronicle: A Collaborative Edition Vol. 5: Manuscript C* (Woodbridge, 2001). For an illustration of Harold's coronation and portraits of Edward the Confessor, see David M. Wilson, *The Bayeux Tapestry* (London, 2004), with discussion in Catherine Karkov, *The Ruler Portraits of Anglo-Saxon England* (Woodbridge, 2004).

2 A king must hold a kingdom

Paul Cavill, *Maxims in Old English* (Cambridge, 1999). For a text and translation of the poem *Maxims II*, see Greg Delanty and Michael Matto (eds.), *The Word Exchange: Anglo-Saxon Poems in Translation* (London, 2011) and T.A. Shippey, *Poems of Wisdom and Learning in Old English* (Totowa NJ and London, 1976). The other poem in the manuscript, *Menologium*, is edited by Kazutomo Kurasawa (Woodbridge, 2016). For place-names based on **burh, ceaster, tun**, see Victor Watts (ed.), *The Cambridge Dictionary of English Place-Names* (Cambridge, 2004).The standard edition of version D of the *Chronicle* is: G. P. Cubbin (ed.) *The Anglo-Saxon Chronicle: A Collaborative Edition Vol. 6: MS D* (Woodbridge, 1996).

3 Say what I am called

Frank Barlow, *Leofric of Exeter: Essays in Commemoration of the Foundation of Exeter Cathedral Library in AD 1072* (Exeter, 1972). A convenient text and translation is John Porter (ed. and trans.), *Anglo-Saxon Riddles* (Hockwold-cum-Wilton, 2003). For discussions, see Jonathan Wilcox ' "Tell Me What I Am": the Old English Riddles,' in David Johnson and Elaine Treharne (eds.) *Readings in Medieval Texts: Interpreting Old and Middle English Literature* (Oxford, 2005), pp. 46–59; Andy Orchard, 'Enigma Variations: The Anglo-Saxon Riddle-tradition', in Katherine O'Brien O'Keeffe and Andy Orchard (eds.), *Latin Learning and English Lore: Studies in Anglo-Saxon Literature for Michael Lapidge* (Toronto, 2005), pp. 284–304. There is a forthcoming edition of all the Anglo-Saxon riddles by Andy Orchard.

4 Here in this year

M.K. Lawson, *Cnut: England's Viking King* (Stroud, 2004); Katherine O'Brien O'Keeffe (ed.), *The Anglo-Saxon Chronicle: A Collaborative Edition Vol. 5: Manuscript C* (Cambridge, 2001); A.R. Rumble, *The Reign of Cnut: King of England, Denmark and Norway* (London, 1994); Michael J. Swanton (trans.), *The Anglo-Saxon Chronicles* (London, 2000).

5 About the four seasons

P.S. Baker and M. Lapidge (eds.), *Byrhtferth's Enchiridion*, Early English Text Society, supplementary series vol. 15 (Oxford, 1995). Earl R. Anderson, 'The Seasons of the Year in Old English', in the journal *Anglo-Saxon England* 26 (1997), pp. 231–63.

6 I saw in a dream

The biblical text of the Joseph story is found in Genesis, chapters 37–50. The standard edition of the illustrated Old English *Hexateuch* is Samuel J. Crawford (ed.), *The Old English Version of the Heptateuch*, Early English Text Society vol. 160 (London, 1969). For discussion of dream vision in *The Dream of the Rood* see Andrew Galloway, 'Dream Theory in *The Dream of the Rood* and *The Wanderer*', *Review of English Studies* 45 (1994), 475–85; C. B. Hieatt, 'Dream Frame and Verbal Echo in *The Dream of the Rood*', *Neuphilologische Mitteilungen* 72 (1971), 251–63; R.C. Payne, 'Convention and Originality in the Vision Framework of *The Dream of the Rood*', *Modern Philology* 73 (1976), 329–41; Antonina Harbus, 'Dream and Symbol in *The Dream of the Rood*', *Nottingham Medieval Studies* 40 (1996), 1–15.

7 King Cnut greets his archbishops

The full text of Cnut's Proclamation of 1020 is printed in Elaine Treharne, *Old and Middle English: An Anthology* (2009). There is general discussion in Richard Sharpe, 'The Use of Writs in the Eleventh Century', *Anglo-Saxon England* 32 (2003), pp. 247–91. N.P. Brooks, *The Early History of the Church of Canterbury. Christ Church from 597 to 1066* (Leicester, 1984), pp. 288–90, discusses archbishop Lyfing. Cnut's writ to Lyfing in the the Royal Gospel Book (Royal 1 D. ix) can also be examined online in the manuscript viewer at the British Library website. For a photograph of a **friþstol** and some background to the reigns of Cnut and Edward the Confessor, read Richard A. Fletcher, *Bloodfeud: Murder and Revenge in Anglo-Saxon England* (London, 2003).

8 He promised her the land at Orleton

Christine Fell, *Women in Anglo-Saxon England* (London, 1984); Andreas Fischer, *Engagement, Wedding and Marriage in Old English* (Heidelberg, 1986); A.J. Robertson, *Anglo-Saxon Charters*, no. 76.

9 I seek my brothers, where they are keeping their herds

The economic and cultural life of the period is presented in Robert Lacy and Danny Danziger, *The Year 1000. What Life was Like at the Turn of the First Millennium* (London, 2000). For an image of the manuscript illustration on folio 53v, the scene where the man shows Joseph the way to Dothaim, consult Bibliography to unit 14. The place-name **leah** *pasture* is explored in some detail in Margaret Gelling and Ann Cole, *The Landscape of Place-Names* (Donington, 2014), pp. 237–42.

10 These are the bounds of the pasture at Hazelhurst

On charter bounds and literature: Nicholas Howe, 'Writing the Boundaries', ch.1 of his book *Writing the Map of Anglo-Saxon England. Essays In Cultural Geography* (New Haven and London, 2008). On topography: John Blair, *Anglo-Saxon Oxfordshire* (Thrupp, 1994), p. xxv; on boundaries and meeting places: Margaret Gelling, *Signposts to the Past: Place-Names and the History of England* (London, 1978), pp. 191–214. For reflections on this theme see Robert Macfarlane, *The Old Ways: A Journey on Foot* (London, 2013). T.G. Allen describes the excavation of a Roman villa at Fawler in the journal *Oxoniensia* liii (1988), pp. 293–315. For discussion of the name **denn**, see Kenneth Cameron, *English Place Names*, p. 204 and Gelling and Cole, *Landscape of Place-Names*, p. 267; Gelling and Cole also study the element **ersc** (as in **Hæselersc** *Hazelhurst*) at pp. 267–9. Sarah Semple's work is published in the monograph *Perceptions of the Prehistoric in Anglo-Saxon England. Religion, Ritual and Rulership in the Landscape* (Oxford, 2013). For the scribe Eadwig Basan see N.P. Brooks, *Early History of the Church of Canterbury*, pp. 257–60, 267–70, 289–90. His work as an artist is surveyed by Michelle P. Brown, *Manuscripts from the Anglo-Saxon Age* (London: British Library, 2007), p. 132; this book prints a colour facsimile of Eadwig's calligraphic script and signature at p. 155 and examples of his splendid manuscript illumination pp. 154–9, including his own self-portrait as a monk kneeling at the feet of St Benedict. The poem *The Ruin* is printed with parallel translation in Richard Hamer, *A Choice of Anglo-Saxon Verse*. For a map of the charter bounds of a typical estate, Stanton St Bernard in Wiltshire, see Andrew Reynolds, *Later Anglo-Saxon England: Life and Landscape* (Stroud, 1999), pp. 82–83, figure 28 with photographs of the area in colour plates 2, 3, 4 and 5.

11 Here it declares in this document

The Godwine Charter, produced at Canterbury, was acquired by the Canterbury Cathedral Archives in 2013. https://www.canterbury-cathedral.org/whats-on/news/2013/04/26/an-ancient-manuscript-comes-home/ [accessed 5.6.18] On declarations, see Ann Williams, *Kingship and Government in Pre-Conquest England c. 500–1066* (London, 1999), especially pp. 109–15. On the formulaic phrase **her swutelað**, see Benjamin C. Withers, *The Illustrated Old English Hexateuch, Cotton Claudius B.iv. The Frontier of Seeing and Reading In Anglo-Saxon England* (London, and Toronto, 2007), pp. 191–5.

12 word-hoard

The Fuller Brooch can be viewed in the British Museum. http://www.britishmuseum.org/research/collection_online/collection_object_details.aspx?objectId=87155&partId=1 [accessed 28.7.18]. For further vocabulary work consult Stephen Pollington, *Wordcraft: Concise Dictionary and Thesaurus. Modern English–Old English* (Pinner, 1993). There is a discussion of the landscape and the seabirds of the poems *The Wanderer* and *The Seafarer* in Nicole Guenther Discenza, *Inhabited Spaces: Anglo-Saxon Constructions of Place* (Toronto, 2017), pp. 169–74.

13 And they put him into the waterless well

Text in S.J. Crawford, *The Old English Version of the Heptateuch*. Randolph Quirk and C. L. Wrenn, *An Old English Grammar*, 2nd edition (London, 1957) has a very useful section on prefixes. For approaches to metaphorical language, try George Lakoff and Mark Johnson, *Metaphors we Live by* (London, 2003); Peter Stockwell, *Cognitive Poetics* (London, 2002). On the plot and characters of the original Joseph story, see Robert Alter, *The Art of Biblical Narrative* (London, 1981) and Laurence A. Turner, *Genesis* (Sheffield, 2000). For the narratives on the murder of Edward the Martyr, see Catherine A.M. Clarke, 'Sites of Economy: Power and

Reckoning in the Poetic Epitaphs of the Anglo-Saxon Chronicle', in her *Writing Power in Anglo-Saxon England: Texts, Hierarchies, Economies* (Cambridge, 2012), pp. 44–79, at 59–61.

14 The boy is not here

Double negation in English is described by James Milroy and Lesley Milroy, *Authority in Language. Investigating Standard English*, 3rd edition (London, 1999), pp. 53–4. For the text of the Joseph Story, see the edition cited in the bibliography for unit 6. For black-and-white reproductions of the manuscript text and illustrations of the Joseph story, consult C.R. Dodwell and P.A.M. Clemoes (eds.), *The Old English Illustrated Hexateuch*, Early English Manuscripts in Facsimile vol. 18 (Copenhagen, 1974). For a colour facsimile see the CD attached to the book by Benjamin C. Withers, *The Illustrated Old English Hexateuch, Cotton Claudius B.iv. The Frontier of Seeing and Reading In Anglo-Saxon England* (London and Toronto, 2007).The whole manuscript of Cotton Claudius B iv can be viewed in the Manuscript Viewer on the British Library website: http://www.bl.uk/manuscripts/FullDisplay.aspx?ref=Cotton_MS_Claudius_B_IV [accessed 27.8.18]; the illustrations relating to Joseph's betrayal by his brothers can be seen at folios 53v-55r. Literary approaches to the Old English Joseph story are found in Mary Richards, 'Fragmentary Versions of Genesis in Old English Prose: Context and Function', in Rebecca Barnhouse and Benjamin C. Withers, *The Old English Hexateuch. Aspects and Approaches* (Kalamazoo, 2000), pp. 145–64; Benjamin C. Withers, 'Unfulfilled Promise: the Rubrics of the Old English Prose Genesis', *Anglo-Saxon England* 28 (1999), 111–39; and Daniel Anlezark, 'Reading "The Story of Joseph" in MS Cambridge, Corpus Christi College 201', in Hugh Magennis and Jonathan Wilcox (eds.) *The Power of Words: Anglo-Saxon Studies Presented to Donald G. Scragg on his Seventieth birthday* (Morgantown, 2006), pp. 61–94.

15 I always wanted to convert to the monastic life

Debby Banham (ed.), *Monasteriales Indicia: The Anglo-Saxon Monastic Sign Language* (Pinner, 1991). Two monks appear to be communicating in sign language in an illustration drawn in a Latin book of the Psalms (London, British Library, Arundel 155, folio 10r); for a photograph see Francis Wormald, *English Drawings of the Tenth and Eleventh Centuries* (London, 1952), plate 24(b) (I owe this reference to Barbara Raw). The anonymous *Life of Euphrosyne*, which appears in a manuscript of Ælfric's *Lives of the Saints*, is edited by W.W. Skeat, *Ælfric's Lives of Saints*, Early English Text Society original series 76, 82, 94, 114 (Oxford, 1881–1900). Fred C. Robinson, 'European Clothing Names and the Etymology of *Girl*', in his *The Tomb of Beowulf and other Essays on Old English* (Oxford, 1993), pp. 175–81. Richard Gameson, 'The Origin of the Exeter Book of Old English Poetry', *Anglo-Saxon England* 25 (1996), 135–85.

16 It happened one night

The Prose *Life of Guthlac* is edited by P. Gonser, *Das angelsächsische Prosa-Leben des heiligen Guthlac* (Heidelberg, 1909) and discussed by Jane Roberts, 'The Old English Prose Translation of Felix's *Vita Sancti Guthlaci*', in Paul E. Szarmach, *Studies in Earlier Old English Prose* (Albany, 1986). See also Mary Clayton, 'Hermits and the Contemplative Life in Anglo-Saxon England' in Paul E. Szarmach (ed.) *Holy Men and Holy Women: Old English Prose Saints' Lives and their Contexts* (Albany, 1996). For the Old English story of Fursey see the edition with parallel translation by Thomas Miller (ed.), *The Old English Version of Bede's Ecclesiastical History of the*

English People, Early English Text Society original series 95 and 96 (Millwood, 1990). *Guthlac A*, the *Exeter Book* poem on the life of the hermit in his fenland retreat, is discussed by Catherine A.M. Clarke, *Literary Landscapes and the Idea of England, 700–1400* (Cambridge, 2006). pp. 36–66.

17 And bishop Æthelnoth travelled to Rome

Æthelnoth's predecessors also travelled to Rome; in one case the itinerary has been preserved; it is discussed by Veronica Ortenberg, 'Archbishop Sigeric's Journey to Rome in 990', *Anglo-Saxon England* 19 (1990), 197–246; see also her *The English Church and the Continent in the Tenth and Eleventh Centuries: Cultural, Spiritual, and Artistic Exchanges* (Oxford, 1992). For Æthelnoth's career see N.P. Brooks, *The Early History of the Church of Canterbury. Christ Church from 597 to 1066* (Leicester, 1984), pp. 257–60, 273, 291–2; M.K. Lawson, *Cnut: England's Viking King* (Stroud, 2004). For the election of an abbot, read H.E. Butler (ed. and trans.), *The Chronicle of Joscelin of Brakelond* (London, 1949).

18 Archbishop Wulfstan greets king Cnut

J. Armitage Robinson, *The Times of St Dunstan* (Oxford, 1923); Simon Keynes, 'King Athelstan's Books', in Michael Lapidge and Helmut Gneuss (eds.), *Learning and Literature in Anglo-Saxon England* (Cambridge, 1985), pp. 143–201.

19 How Wynflæd summoned her witnesses

Images of Cwichelm's Barrow can be found by searching online for Scutchamer Knob or Cuckhamsley Barrow. The text of the dispute is printed in A.J. Robertson, *Anglo-Saxon Charters*, no. 66. For a general explanation of the judicial process and oath-swearing, see Andrew Reynolds, *Later Anglo-Saxon England: Life and Landscape* (Stroud, 1999), pp. 99–100. The Wynflæd–Leofwine case is discussed by Ann Williams, *Kingship and Government in Pre-Conquest England c. 500–1066* (London, 1999), pp. 11–12. See also Sarah Semple, *Perceptions of the Prehistoric in Anglo-Saxon England. Religion, Ritual and Rulership in the Landscape* (Oxford, 2013).The *Life of St Wulfstan* is the principal piece in M. Winterbottom and R.M. Thomson (eds. and trans.), *William of Malmesbury: Saints' Lives* (Oxford, 2002). For allusions to the story of Welund, see Leslie Webster, *The Franks Casket* (London, 2012) and Susan Irvine and Malcolm R. Godden (eds. and trans.), *The Old English Boethius: With Verse Prologues and Epilogues Associated with King Alfred* (Cambridge MA and London, 2012).

20 Act like thegns, and deliver my message to the assembly

The Herefordshire Lawsuit occurs on folios 134r and 134v of a Latin gospel book (shelfmark P. I. 2) at Hereford Cathedral Library; the original text is edited by Robinson, *Anglo-Saxon Charters*, no. 78 and by Dorothy Whitelock in Sweet's *Anglo-Saxon Reader* (Oxford, 1966); for a literary-critical approach, see Daniel Donoghue, *Old English Literature: A Short Introduction* (Oxford, 2004), pp. 1–5 and a photograph of the actual document at p. 3. The case is discussed at length by Clare A. Lees and Gillian R. Overing, *Double Agents: Women and Clerical Culture in Anglo-Saxon England* (Philadelphia, 2001), pp. 72–89.

ANGLO-SAXON THEGNS

On the lifestyle of later Old English thegns, see *Later Anglo-Saxon England: Life and Landscape* (Stroud, 1999) in which Andrew Reynolds discusses the Promotion Law at p. 60, the place-name Yatesbury corresponding to **burhgeat** at p. 93, and the tower at Earl's Barton Northamptonshire at p. 96 and colour plate 8. See also Ann Williams, 'A Bell-House and a Burh-Geat: the Lordly Residences in England before the Norman Conquest', in C. Harper-Bill and R. Harvey (eds.), *Medieval Knighthood IV* (Woodbridge, 1992), pp. 241–40. For bynames with **æt** such as **Leofwine æt Frome** see Gösta Tengvik, *Old English Bynames* (Uppsala, 1938), pp. 31–6.

OLD NORSE AND OLD FRENCH

Old Norse developed into various modern languages in mainland Scandinavia, but modern Icelandic is essentially the same language. A starting point for learning Old Norse, therefore, is basic Icelandic; see Hildur Jónsdóttir, *Teach Yourself Icelandic* (London, 2004). For Old French, consult E. Einhorn, *Old French: A Concise Handbook* (Cambridge, 1974) and Jane Bliss, *An Anglo-Norman Reader* (2018). For an example of Old Norse–Old English communication see Robert McCrum, Robert MacNeil and William Cran, *The Story of English*, 3rd edition (London, 2002), p. 69. Borrowings from Old Norse and Old French are discussed in David Crystal, *The Stories of English* and Dennis Freeborn, *From Old English to Standard English*, 2nd edition (Basingstoke, 1998). Melvyn Bragg's television series *The Adventure of English* showed some interesting survivals of Norse in the English dialects of Cumbria and Yorkshire; see his *The Adventure of English 500 AD–2000: The Biography of a Language* (London, 2003).

OLD NORSE POETRY IN ENGLAND

Roberta Frank, 'Cnut and his Skalds', in Alexander Rumble (ed.), *The Reign of Cnut*, pp. 106–24; also Matthew Townend, 'Contextualizing the *Knútsdrápur*: Skaldic Praise-Poetry at the Court of Cnut', *Anglo-Saxon England* 30 (2001), 145–79.

21 The tide went out

For the name Maldon, see P.H. Reaney, *The Place-Names of Essex*, English Place-Name Society, XII (Cambridge, 1935); Watts, *Cambridge Dictionary of English Place-Names*, p. 393; Alexander R. Rumble, 'The Cross in English Place-Names: Vocabulary and Usage', in Catherine E., Karkov, Sarah Larratt Keefer, and Karen Louise Jolly (eds.), *The Place of the Cross in Anglo-Saxon England* (Woodbridge, 2006), pp. 29–40.

THE REIGN OF EDWARD THE ELDER

Michael Swanton, *The Anglo-Saxon Chronicles* (London, 2000). Ryan Lavelle, 'Geographies of Power in the Anglo-Saxon Chronicle', in Alice Jorgensen, ed., *Reading the Anglo-Saxon Chronicle: Language, Literature, History* (Turnhout, 2010), pp. 187–219, at 204–5. David Hill and Alexander R. Rumble (eds.) *The Defence of Wessex: The Burghal Hidage and Anglo-Saxon Fortifications* (Manchester, 1996).

DISCUSSIONS OF *THE BATTLE OF MALDON*

D.G. Scragg (ed.), *The Battle of Maldon AD 991* (Oxford, 1991); Janet Cooper (ed.) *The Battle of Maldon: Fiction and Fact* (London, 1993). There is a forthcoming monograph by Mark Atherton, *The Battle of Maldon: War and Peace in Anglo-Saxon England*. See also Alice Jorgensen, 'Power, Poetry and Violence: *The Battle of Maldon*', in *Aspects of Power and Authority in the Middle Ages*, ed. Brenda Bolton and Christine Meek (Turnhout, 2007), pp. 235–49. For the historical background, see Ann Williams, *Æthelred the Unready: The Ill-Counselled King* (London, 2003); Levi Roach, *Æthelred the Unready* (New Haven and London, 2016). On the 'foreign accent' of the Viking messenger, see Fred C. Robinson, 'Some Aspects of the *Maldon* Poet's Artistry', *Journal of English and Germanic Philology* 75 (1976), 435–46; reprinted in his *The Tomb of Beowulf and Other Essays*. On the decision to fight the battle away from the city see Ryan Lavelle, *Alfred's Wars: Sources and Interpretations of Anglo-Saxon Warfare in the Viking Age* (Woodbridge, 2010), p. 251.

EDITIONS OF *THE BATTLE OF MALDON*

D.G. Scragg (ed.), *The Battle of Maldon* (Manchester: Manchester University Press, 1981); E.V.K. Dobbie, *The Anglo-Saxon Minor Poems* (New York, 1942); E. V. Gordon, *The Battle of Maldon* (London, 1937); Richard Marsden, *The Cambridge Anglo-Saxon Reader* (Cambridge, 2004); B.J. Muir, *Leoð: Six Old English Poems* (New York, 1990); J.C. Pope, *Seven Old English Poems* (Indianapolis, 1966); D. Whitelock, *Sweet's Anglo-Saxon Reader* (London, 1970).

METRE AND POETIC FORM

Pure stress metres are discussed in general by G.S. Fraser, *Metre, Rhyme and Free Verse* (London, 1970), pp. 13–25. Other profitable discussions can be found in Phil Roberts, *How Poetry Works* (London, 2000), pp. 18–37, and Philip Hobsbaum, *Metre, Rhythm and Verse Form* (London, 1996), pp. 53–70. For a slightly different discussion of Auden's *The Age of Anxiety*, see Fraser, pp. 19–20. Auden's interest in Old English is explored in Chris Jones, *Strange Likeness: The Use of Old English in Twentieth-Century Poetry* (Oxford, 2006), pp. 68–121.

EDITING ISSUES AND PUNCTUATION

Many of the problems are discussed in Bruce Mitchell's article 'The Dangers of Disguise: Old English Texts in Modern Punctuation', published in the journal *Review of English Studies* new series 31 (1980), 385–413. See also Sarah Larratt Keefer and Katherine O'Brien O'Keeffe (eds.), *New Approaches to Editing Old English Verse* (Cambridge, 1998). For the eighteenth-century copying of this text, see H.L. Rogers, '*The Battle of Maldon*: David Casley's Transcript', in the journal *Notes & Queries*, new series, vol. 32 (1985), 147–55.

22 The hall resounded

On the determiners *a* and *the*, consult David Crystal, *Making Sense of Grammar* (Harlow, 2004), p. 208. For the basic study of *Beowulf* the introductory edition to use is George Jack (ed.), *Beowulf: A Student Edition* (Oxford, 1994). Thereafter the standard edition is Fulk, R.D., Robert E. Bjork, and John D. Niles (eds.), *Klaeber's Beowulf and the Fight at Finnsburg* (Toronto,

2008). A new edition of *Beowulf* by Andy Orchard is in hand (the passages printed here are based on the text of his forthcoming edition). For a translation you might compare R.D. Fulk, *The Beowulf Manuscript* (Cambridge MA, 2010) with J.R.R. Tolkien, *Beowulf: A Translation and Commentary*, ed. Christopher Tolkien (London, 2014), but be aware that the line numbers in Tolkien's translation do not correspond to those of the standard editions of *Beowulf*.

DISCUSSIONS OF *BEOWULF*

Andy Orchard, '*Beowulf*', in Richard North (ed.) *Beowulf and Other Stories*. Andy Orchard, *A Critical Companion to Beowulf* (Cambridge, 2003). J.R.R. Tolkien, '*Beowulf*: the Monsters and the Critics', *Proceedings of the British Academy* 22 (1936), 245–95. Reprinted in his *The Monsters and the Critics and Other Essays*, and also in Lewis E. Nicholson, *An Anthology of Beowulf Criticism*. On variation and parallelism, see A.G. Brodeur, *The Art of Beowulf* (Berkeley CA: University of California Press, 1959).

METRE

On metre, good introductions are: Bruce Mitchell and Fred C. Robinson, *A Guide to Old English*, 7th edition (Oxford: Blackwell, 2007), Appendix C, pp. 161–7; D.G. Scragg, 'The Nature of Old English Verse', in *The Cambridge Companion to Old English Literature*; J.R.R. Tolkien, 'On Translating *Beowulf*', in *The Monsters and the Critics and Other Essays* (London, 1983 and reprinted many times). Thereafter, for more detail, see Jun Terasawa, *Old English Metre: An Introduction* (Toronto and London, 2011) and John C. Pope, 'Old English Versification', in his edition *Eight Old English Poems*, 3rd edition, revised by R.D. Fulk (New York and London, 2001), pp. 129–58.

23 The music of the harp

For the full OE text of *Apollonius of Tyre* see Elaine Treharne (ed.), *Old and Middle English c.890–c.1400: An Anthology*, and the critical edition (now out of print) of text and source in P. Goolden (ed.) *The Old English 'Apollonius of Tyre'* (Oxford, 1958). The Latin text, with a full translation, is edited by Elisabeth Archibald, *Apollonius of Tyre: Medieval and Renaissance Themes and Variations* (Cambridge, 1991). The political context is discussed in Mark Atherton, 'Cambridge, Corpus Christi College 201 as a Mirror for a Prince: *Apollonius of Tyre*, Archbishop Wulfstan and King Cnut', *English Studies*, 97:5 (2016), 451–472; and Melanie Heyworth, '*Apollonius of Tyre* in its manuscript context: an issue of marriage', *Philological Quarterly* 86 (2007), 1–26. See also Anlezark on the Joseph Story (above, unit 14). On the process of domestication in translation, see Susan Bassnett, *Translation* (London, 2014). There is a study of this translator's approach to domesticating his text in Anita R. Riedinger, 'The Englishing of Arcestrate: Women in *Apollonius of Tyre*', in Helen Damico and Alexandra Hennessey Olsen, *New Readings on Women in Old English Literature* (Bloomington, 1990), pp. 292–306, with the discussion of **ymbsittendum** and the hall at p. 294 and the omission of the love-sickness motif at p. 298. The style of the prose is discussed by Hiroshi Ogawa, 'Stylistic features of the Old English *Apollonius of Tyre*', in his *Studies in the History of Old English Prose* (Tokyo, 2000), pp. 181–204. For the documents from Winchester, see Michael Lapidge (ed. and trans.), *The Cult* *of St Swithun* (Oxford, 2003) and Alexander R. Rumble (ed. and trans.), *Property and Piety in Early Medieval Winchester* (Oxford, 2002).

24 So they brought out their gifts

For the facsimile of the Illustrated *Hexateuch,* see the Manuscript Viewer on the British Library website: http://www.bl.uk/manuscripts/FullDisplay.aspx?ref=Cotton_MS_Claudius_B_IV [accessed 27.8.18]; the relevant page for this transcription exercise is folio 63v.

TEXTUAL IMAGE AND ARCHAEOLOGY

Gale Owen-Crocker, *Dress in Anglo-Saxon England* (Woodbridge, 2010).

ART AND MANUSCRIPT ILLUMINATION

Janet Backhouse, D.H. Turner and Leslie Webster, *The Golden Age of Anglo-Saxon Art 966–1066* (London, 1984); Richard Gameson, *The Role of Art in the Late Anglo-Saxon Church* (Oxford, 1995); D.M. Wilson, *Anglo-Saxon Art from the Seventh Century to the Norman Conquest* (London, 1984); Catherine E. Karkov, *The Art of Anglo-Saxon England* (Woodbridge, 2011).

THE TEXTS OF THE *EXETER BOOK*

At some stage in the course of his career, Leofric acquired the tenth-century anthology of traditional poetry now known as the *Exeter Book*, which he left in his will to Exeter cathedral in 1072 (Exeter, Cathedral Library, 3501). The two poems are to be found on folio 122v and 123r of the manuscript. For a full edition see Bernard J. Muir (ed.), *The Exeter Anthology of Old English Poetry*, 2 vols. (Exeter, 1994). For a discussion of Riddles 30a and 30b see the article by A.N. Doane, 'Spacing, Placing and Effacing: Scribal textuality and Exeter Riddle 30a/b', in Keefer and O'Keeffe, *New Approaches to Editing Old English Verse*, pp. 45–65; and Roy M. Liuzza, 'The Texts of Old English *Riddle 30*', in *Journal of English and Germanic Philology* 87 (1988), 1–15. For facsimile plates of Riddle 30b, Riddle 60 and *The Husband's Message*, consult Anne L. Klinck, *The Old English Elegies: A Critical Edition and Genre Study* (Montreal, 1992). On the riddles, see Mercedes Salvador-Bello, *Isidorean Perceptions of Order: The Exeter Book Riddles and Medieval Latin Enigmata* (Morgantown: West Virginia University Press, 1995).

THE CORONATION OATH

The Old English coronation oath text was copied in the eleventh-century manuscript London, British Library, Cotton Cleopatra B xiii, the book that belonged to bishop Leofric. The text is also found in Oxford, Bodleian Library Junius 60, a copy of the lost manuscript Cotton Vitellius A vii. There is an edition and translation in A.J. Robertson, *The Laws of the Kings of England: From Edmund to Henry I* (Cambridge, 1925) and a critical edition and discussion in Mary Clayton, 'The Old English *Promissio regis*', in *Anglo-Saxon England* 37 (2008), 91–150. For more discussion of Leofric and his books, see Elaine M. Treharne, 'The Bishop's Book: Leofric's Homiliary and Eleventh-Century Exeter', in Stephen Baxter, Catherine Karkov, Janet Nelson, and David Pelteret (eds.), *Early Medieval Studies in Memory of Patrick Wormald* (London, 2009), pp. 521–37.

MANUSCRIPTS

A good introduction is Michelle Brown, *Anglo-Saxon Manuscripts* (London, 1991). Basic reference works are: Helmut Gneuss, *Handlist of Anglo-Saxon Manuscripts: A List of Manuscripts and Manuscript Fragments Written or Owned in England up to 1100* (Tempe, 2001); N.R. Ker, *Catalogue of Manuscripts Containing Anglo-Saxon* (Oxford, 1990); Elzbieta Temple, *Anglo-Saxon Manuscripts 900–1066* (London, 1976). See also the catalogue of the British Library exhibition: Claire Breay and Joanna Story (eds.), *Anglo-Saxon Kingdoms: Art, Word, War* (London, 2018).

INTERPRETING OLD ENGLISH LITERATURE

John Hines, *Voices in the Past: English Literature and Archaeology* (Cambridge, 2004); David F. Johnson and Elaine Treharne, *Readings in Medieval Texts: Interpreting Old and Middle English Literature* (Oxford, 2005); Clare A. Lees, *Tradition and Belief: Religious Writing in Late Anglo-Saxon England* (London, 1999); Katherine O'Brien O'Keeffe, *Reading Old English Texts* (Cambridge, 1997); Phillip Pulsiano and Elaine Treharne, *A Companion to Anglo-Saxon Literature* (Oxford: *Blackwell*, 2001); T.A. Shippey, *Old English Verse* (London, 1972).

FURTHER STUDY OF OLD ENGLISH LANGUAGE

Apart from books on Old English already mentioned, the following two textbooks are recommended: the first, Chris McCully and Sharon Hilles, *The Earliest English: An Introduction to Old English* (Harlow, 2005), presents pronunciation, phonology, metre and grammar in interesting and accessible ways. The second, Peter S. Baker, *Introduction to Old English* (Oxford, 2012), contains a grammar followed by a good selection of poems and prose. A portable paperback dictionary is J.R. Clark Hall, *A Concise Anglo-Saxon Dictionary* (Toronto and London, 2000). A standard survey and reference work for Old English, with full bibliography, is Richard M. Hogg, *The Cambridge History of the English Language. Volume I. The Beginnings to 1066* (Cambridge, 1992).

Answer key

UNIT 1

Practice 1

1a (literal translation) Eadsige archbishop him hallowed and before all the people him well taught, and to his own need and of-all people well admonished. **1b** (idiomatic) Archbishop Eadige consecrated him and instructed him before all the people and admonished him well for his own need and that of all the people. **1c** (pronunciation) þam 'tham', lærde 'LAIRdeh', arcebiscop 'AR-chuh-bi-shop', agenre 'AH-yun-reh'. **1d** (suggested answer) the preposition *to his own need*; note the **-de** ending on the past tenses; note also that hine, the word for him, precedes the three verbs … consecrated, … taught, … admonished. **1e** (modernized, with some endings omitted) Eadsie archebishop him halwade, and tofor all tha folk him wel lærde, and to his awen neod and all folks wel manude. **2a** And Stigant priest was blessed to bishop to East Angles. **2b** And the priest Stigant was consecrated as bishop of East Anglia **2c** biscop 'BIshop'. **2d** Note the preposition to after *blessed* and, on word order, the way the word for a rank or profession comes after the name to which it refers, e.g. Eadsige arcebiscop, Stigant preost. **2e** (suggested modernization) And Stigant preost was i-bletsad to bishop to East-englum.

Practice 2

Some famous men: Ælfræd (Alfred the Great), Æþelstan (Æthelstan the tenth-century king), Eadgar (Edgar the Peaceable, king of England 959–75), Æþelræd (Æthelred the Unready), Eadweard (Edward the Confessor), Wulfstan (archbishop of York), Godwine (father of Harold II)

Some famous women: Æþelþryþ (St Æthelthryth, also St Etheldreda in Bede's *Ecclesiastical History*, later form of name was Audrey), Queen Eadgifu (tenth century, king Edgar's grandmother), Eadgyð (St Edith, daughter of king Edgar), Queen Ælfþryþ (Ælfthryth, mother of Æthelred), Queen Ælfgifu (also called Emma, married first to Æthelred and then to Cnut), Godgifu (Lady Godiva, wife of the earl of Mercia), Eadgyð (Edith, wife of Edward the Confessor and sister of Harold Godwineson, i.e. king Harold II)

Practice 3

a cinges tun or cynges tun *king's estate* **b** sumor *summer* **c** norð *north* **d** suð *south* **e** ac *oak* **f** mere *lake* **g** scip *ship* or sceap *sheep* **h** oxena ford *ford of the oxen* **i** here *army* **j** heort *hart* i.e. *stag* (cf. the common English pub name The White Hart) **k** niw *new* and brycg *bridge*

Test yourself

1 4 mycel *great*, **b**6 ælf *elf*, **c**2 wæs *was*, **d**5 forma *first*, **e**7 ræd *advice*, **f**1 dæg *day*, **g**3 wine *friend*
2 a forman **b** halgade **c** biscope **d** cynge

UNIT 2

The king in hall: **1** the king is placed in parallel with a bear and a river **2** the river

The army rides together **1** a company of glorious men **2** both are described as on the earth **3** a dweller in the heavens, a judge of deeds

Practice

beagas, bera; eald, egesfull, ea; flodgræg feran fyrd; tirfæstra ge-trum treow; wisdom were wudu; blædum blowan beorh; grene God; dæda demend

Test yourself

a Bera sceal on hæðe, eald and egesfull. **b** Ea of dune sceal flodgræg feran. **c** Wudu sceal on foldan blædum blowan. **d** Beorh sceal on eorþan grene standan.

UNIT 3

Vocabulary builder 1

earth, heaven, sky, moon, star

More riddles (suggested solutions only): **a** ice **b** dog **c** hen

Test yourself

1 a þu eart **b** þu dearst **c** mona and sunne **d** Engle, Wealas, Scottas **e** git **f** sæ, mere **g** garsecg
2 a wearð **b** leohtre **c** ic **d** wiht

UNIT 4

The year 1019: Cnut spent the winter in Denmark, since travel was diffcult in winter, and he needed to secure matters there before returning to England in the spring.

The year 1020: Cnut needed to remove any political opposition and build a memorial church on the site of his victory at Assandun.

The years 1021 to 1027: 1 Thorkell was outlawed by king Cnut. 2 Cnut must have ordered a naval sortie to the Isle of Wight, while Athelnoth's visit to Rome involved a papal ceremony of inauguration as archbishop of Canterbury. 3 Cnut had Thorkell's son at his court to ensure Thorkell's loyalty. 4 Cnut had the relics taken from London to Canterbury.

Practice

1 D 1026 Here bishop Ælfric went to Rome, and received the pallium from Pope John on the second of the ides of November (12th November).

D 1031 Here king Cnut went to Rome. And as soon as he returned home, he then went to Scotland, and the king of the Scots submitted to him and became his man, but kept it only for a little while.
2 The C version emphasizes Olaf's sanctity after his death, while D sounds more secular in its insistence that Olaf died in battle. The D version explicitly explains Cnut's active involvement in Norway and his driving out of Olaf, while C omits or assumes this information. C mentions the loss at sea of earl Hakon.

Test yourself

1 a gewunode, gewunade **b** nam **c** forðferde **d** let **e** gehalgode **f** betæhte **2 a** for **b** geseah
c geutlagode **d** gehalgodon

UNIT 5

About the four seasons: spring – wet and warm, summer – warm and dry, autumn – dry and cold, winter – cold and wet

Language discovery

1 a byð **b** hæfð **c** gæð **d** springað **e** greniað **2 a** cyning **b** Cnut cyng **3 a** se dæg – masculine **b** seo tid – feminine **c** seo todælednys – feminine

Test yourself

1 a wyllað **b** gæð **c** hæfð **d** springað **e** weaxað **f** ripiað **g** byð **2 a** Concerning the sun we speak thus. When it rises it makes (the) day. When it is gone down then it brings the night. **3 a** is called, it, can, it **b** touch, burns **c** it, wanes **d** is

UNIT 6

1 Joseph's first dream **a** cwæð **b** ðuhte **c** bundon **d** stodon **e** abugon **f** cwædon **g** hatedon **h** hæfdon

2 Joseph's second dream: In the dream the sun and moon and eleven stars represent Joseph's family, who take exception to the idea that their upstart brother has dreamed of lording it over them.

Comparison with Shakespeare: 'walk' from wealcan *to roll*; 'tell' from tellan *to count* (cf. modern English 'teller' *bank clerk, counter of votes in Parliament*); 'tumble' from tumbian *to leap, dance*; 'main' from mægen *power*; 'fear' from fær *danger*; 'wedge' from wecg *piece of money*

Test yourself

1 me þuhte means *it seemed to* me whereas ic þohte means *I thought*. **2 a** So because of his dream they hated him. **b** When his brothers saw this, that his father loved him more than his other sons, they shunned him.

UNIT 7

Language discovery

1 plurals: arcebiscopas, leodbiscopas, eorlas, gewritu, word

2 prominent alliteration falls on <u>C</u>nut <u>c</u>yning, <u>e</u>alle his <u>e</u>orlas, <u>tw</u>elf<u>h</u>ynde and <u>tw</u>y<u>h</u>ynde, <u>h</u>old <u>h</u>laford, Godes ge-<u>r</u>ihtum and to <u>r</u>ihtre woroldlage, ic nam <u>m</u>e to ge-<u>m</u>ynde þa ge-<u>w</u>ritu and þa <u>w</u>ord, <u>f</u>ull <u>f</u>rið

3 Antonyms include twelfhynde and twyhynde *rich and poor*, gehadode and læwede *clergy and laity*, aræran *raise up* alecgan *put down*; the opposite of hold *loyal* is implied in the swicende *deceitful* of unswicende; divine and secular spheres of law are suggested by the phrases to Godes gerihtum and to woroldlage.

Practice

1 Lyfing's grievance was that Christ Church did not seem to enjoy as much freedom (e.g. exemption from rent payments) as it had once had. **2** Cnut offered Lyfing a new royal charter of freedom.
3 Realizing that the old charters needed to be renewed and made effective, Cnut placed them with his own hands on the altar of the cathedral.

Test yourself

se biscop, þone biscop *the bishop*, þæs biscopes *of the bishop*, þam biscope *to the bishop*, þa biscopas, þa biscopas *the bishops*, þara biscopa *of the bishops*, þam biscopum *to the bishops*

UNIT 8

The marriage agreement: Archbishop Wulfstan is negotiating the marriage of his sister.

Practice

a hyne **b** hi **c** hyne **d** hym or hyne **e** hi

From *The Life of Euphrosyne*: **a** Euphrosyne was famed for her wisdom and learning and virtuous living. **b** The father's words 'God's will be done' are a polite form of refusal to the young suitors, at the same time they suggest that he believes St Euphrosyne must follow the divine vocation ordained for her. **c** The father only changed his mind when approached by a man of the thegnly class who was wealthier than the other suitors and could pledge a larger sum of money.

Test yourself

a hire **b** his **c** him **d** him

UNIT 9

Practice

1 Their father was worried about why his brothers were delayed and sent Joseph to see whether it was well with them and then to report back to him. **2** When he meets the man Joseph appears to be wandering aimlessly on Shechem. **3** The man has overheard his brothers talking about going to Dothaim.

Test yourself

1 ic blissie, þu blissast, heo blissaþ, we, ge, hi blissiaþ; blissiende; ic blissode, þu blissodest, heo blissode, we, ge, hi blissodon; geblissod **2 a** hit gelamp **b** ic swamm **c** we druncon **d** þu hit funde

UNIT 10

Practice 1

a þone **b** þære **c** þære **d** þære **e** þære **f** þam **g** þa

Practice 2

From the ditch end into the stream. From the stream into the sandy road; along the road northwards onto the bishop's measure of land, over the bishop's land to the innermost flax field path. From the flax field into the hedge; along the hedge onto badger hole way. From badger hole way into the croft. From the croft by the enclosure into Leofsunu's croft.

Test yourself

a ðæs **b** fearnleges burnan **c** Holan beames **d** Holan beames **e** þære **f** þam **g** þam **h** þæne **i** þæne **j** þæs

UNIT 11

Practice

1 a gret **b** mine **c** freondlice **d** cyðe **e** birig, byrig **f** wuda **g** forð

2 I Thored grant the land at Horsley to the community at Christ Church for the sake of my soul as fully and completely as I myself owned it. **3** These are the lands which Thorketel grants to God and St Mary and St Edmund: that is, the land at Culford that was his own, as it stands, with food and labour provision, and with jurisdiction, and all the land at Wordwell, and the land at Ixworth as it stands with food and labour provision.

Test yourself

a þes ceorl **b** he hatað þisne cyning **c** he lufað þas cwen **d** þyses cynges land **e** he hit geaf þyssum ceorle **f** þas eorlas **g** he hit geaf þyssum eorlum

UNIT 12

Practice 1

Riddle 36, numbers: four feet below the stomach, eight feet on its back, two wings, twelve eyes, six heads; proposed solution: a ship with four oars, four rowers and two sails; the six heads are the four seamen and the two figureheads of the ship (see Porter, *Anglo-Saxon Riddles*, p. 135). Riddle 86: one eye, two ears, two feet, twelve hundred heads, one neck, two sides; proposed solution: a one-eyed seller of garlic

Practice 2

1 The annus solaris (solar year) has three hundred and sixty-five days, and fifty-two weeks, and in fact the year has eight thousand and sixty-six hours. **2 a** feower and twentig **b** eahta and feowertig **c** twa and hundseofontig **d** an hund tida and twentig tida

Test yourself

1 woodland pasture for cows; seo cu **2** dairy farm for sheep; se sceap **3** ford for goats; se gat **4** eagle clearing; se earn **5** crane ford; se cran **6** horse ford; þæt hors **7** woodland pasture for sheep; þæt scip **8** stream for stags; se heort **9** wolf clearing; se wulf **10** dairy farm for herds; seo heord **11** island of the calves; þæt cealf **12** estate with dogs; se hund **13** boar wood; se eofor **14** sheep stream; se scip

UNIT 13

When they saw him from afar The brothers intend to murder Joseph and throw him into the dry well.

Test yourself

1 The brothers deprived Joseph of his coat. **2** They were about to eat when they saw the traders.
3 Ruben presents his motivation to his brothers as one of propriety; it is better to keep their hands clean of bloodshed. In fact he wants to rescue Joseph from the well and return him to his father. Judah, contrariwise, has no wish to return Joseph to their father. He agrees with Ruben about the impropriety of murdering their own brother, a member of their own kin, but instead proposes selling Joseph as a slave. **4** The thirty pieces of silver would recall the Gospel narrative of how Judas betrayed Jesus for the same amount of money.

UNIT 14

Reading 1

1 The brothers killed a goat kid and dipped the tunic in its blood. **2** Ruben and Jacob both tear their clothes as an expression of grief; in both illustrations this action is clearly indicated to the right of the picture. **3** The Midianites sold Joseph to Potiphar, captain of the guard.

Practice

1 a Alliteration on the stressed syllables of <u>wi</u>tan, ge-<u>wea</u>rð, <u>wu</u>rðe **b** full rhyme in gesealde, sealde, gewealde **c** understande se ðe wille **2 a** <u>ma</u>re and <u>mæ</u>nigfealdre … <u>ma</u>nige, for<u>sw</u>orene and <u>sw</u>iðe **b** forsworene, forlogone, tobrocene **c** oft and gelome **3** MAnige sind forSWOrene, and swiðe forLOgene, and WED synd toBROcene, OFT and geLOme.

Test yourself

strong adjective endings on oþer<u>ne</u>, fremd<u>um</u>, micel<u>e</u>, egeslic<u>e</u>, forsworen<u>e</u>, forlogon<u>e</u>, tobrocen<u>e</u>

UNIT 15

The Life of Euphrosyne: Euphrosyne decides to run away to a monastery.

1 Her father will look for her in the women's convent and then take her away to marry her bridegroom.
2 Euphrosyne disguises herself in men's clothing and waits until evening. **3** The visitor falls at the abbot's feet to receive a blessing. **4** The visitor has heard of the reputation of the monastery and claims to have been at the king's court but says there is no possibility of leading a monk's life in the city.

Riddle 47 The usual solution is *bookworm*.

Riddle 48 The solution is probably *chalice*.

Test yourself

1 a magistres **b** teacher's **2 a** syxes **b** knife **3 a** briwes **b** briw **c** soup **d** soup **4 a** sealt **b** seltan **c** salt **d** to salt

UNIT 16

Test yourself

The second 'raven episode' **1** Æthelbald asked the man Wilfrid to lead him to the hermitage. **2** Wilfrid had left his gloves in the ship; Guthlac knew by divine inspiration: God made known to him all secret things. **3** They realized that the gloves had been stolen by ravens. **4** The raven obeyed Guthlac's command. **5** The three men struck the signal – presumably a bell – to announce their arrival at the landing place. **6** They also wanted a period of conversation with the hermit. **7** mid bliðum andwlite and gode mode *with happy countenance and good disposition;* smerciende *smiling* **8** first episode: on sumere nihte (feminine), þæt gewrit (neuter), þa cartan (feminine accusative), on þæne fenn (masculine accusative), se foresæda cuma (masculine) þone hrefen (masculine accusative), se halga wer (masculine), þone broðor (masculine accusative), se hrefn (masculine), þa fennas (masculine plural), þa fenland (neuter plural), seo carte (feminine), to þære cartan (feminine), second episode: wið þone halgan wer (masculine accusative), ealle þa diglan þingc (neuter plural), se fugel (masculine), þæt westen (neuter), þa glofe (feminine accusative), to þære hyðe (feminine dative), ane glofe (feminine accusative), his bletsunge (feminine accusative)

UNIT 17

Practice

1 four adverbials of manner: mid mycclan weorðscype, mid his agenum handum, arwurðlice, bliðelice **2** four adverbials of place or direction: ut, to Rome, on Sancte Petres weofode, ham to his earde **3** four adverbials of time: on Nonas Octobris, sona þærmid, on þam sylfan dæge, syððan þæræfter

Test yourself

King Cnut sends friendly greetings to bishop Eadsige and abbot Ælfstan and Æthelric and all my thegns in Kent. And I inform you that I wish that Æthelnoth shall keep his landed property in his episcopal see now just as he did before Æthelric was reeve and after he was reeve until the present time, and I will not allow any wrong to be done to the bishop, whoever the reeve may be.

UNIT 18

Test yourself

1 swa feala þegna *so many thegns*, minre sawle to ecere alysednesse *to the eternal salvation of my soul*, be minum freondscipe *by my friendship*

2 a feala oðra godra cnihta **b** on manegra godra manna gewitnysse **c** æfter his dæge **d** mid eallum þingum **e** on ðisse Cristes bec **f** ic cyþe inc

UNIT 19

Practice

1 Wynflæd presented her witnesses at Woolmer before the king, and they confirmed that Ælfric had given Wynflæd the land at Hagbourne and at Bradfield in return for the estate at Datchet. **2** Leofwine refused to accept the decision and insisted that the case should be referred to the shire court. **3** The king sent abbot Ælfhere (Æluere) to the assembly with his message of greetings and an instruction to work out a just agreement between the two parties. **4** When he saw that Wynflæd's claim was supported by a formidable array of oath helpers, Leofwine must have realized that his counterclaim would fail. The counsellors at the meeting advised him not to take an oath as this would spoil the chance of an amicable agreement. If the verdict had then been against him, Leofwine would have had to pay not only compensation to Wynflæd, for holding her estates illegally, but also his wergild to the king, as punishment for his theft of the property. **5** Wynflæd was instructed to give back any of Leofwine's father's gold and silver that she still had; in fact she gave back as much as she could.

Test yourself

1 Þa nolde he butan hit man sceote to scirgemote. *He would not do this except if it was referred to the shire court.* **2** Þa getæhte man Wynflæde þæt hio moste hit hyre geahnian *Then they instructed Wynflæd that she should prove her ownership;* þa tæhte man hyre þæt hio sciolde bringan his fæder gold and siolfor eal þæt hio hæfde *then they instructed her that she should bring his father's gold and silver, all that she had* (or *all that she might have* – if subjunctive); Þa næs he þagyt on þam gehealden butan hio sceolde swerian þæt his æhta þær ealle wæron *then he was still not satisfied until she would swear that all his possessions were there* (*butan* governs the subjunctive earlier in the text); Þa cwæþ hio þæt hio ne mihte *then she said that she could not…*

UNIT 20

Test yourself

Here is declared in this document that a shire assembly sat at Æthelnoth's Stone in the time of king Cnut. Bishop Æthelstan and ealdorman Ranig sat there, and Edwine the ealdorman's son and Leofwine Wulfsige's son, and Thorkell the White. And Tofi the Proud came there on the king's business. Bryning the shire-reeve was there, and Æthelgeard of Frome, Godric of Stoke, and all the thegns of Herefordshire. Then Edwine Enneawn's son travelled to the assembly and sued his own mother there for a certain portion of land, which was Wellington and Crawley. Then the bishop asked who would answer for the mother, and Thorkell the White answered that he would if he knew the claim. Since he did not know the claim, they appointed three thegns from the assembly (to go) where she was, which was at Fawley, and these were Leofwine of Frome, and Æthelsige the Red, and Wynsige the Shipman. When they came to her, they asked what claim she had to the land for which her son was suing. But she said that she did not have any land that belonged to him in any way. And she became extremely angry with her son; and she called her kinswoman Leofflæd to her – Thorkell's wife – and in their presence spoke to her as follows: 'Here sits Leofflæd my kinswoman to whom I grant both my land and also my gold, clothing and garments and all I possess, after my lifetime.' And after that she spoke to the thegns: 'Act in a thegnly way and present my statement well at the assembly, before all the good men. And have them know who I have granted my land to, and all my possessions, and to my own son never a thing! And let them be witness to this.' And they did so. They rode to the assembly and made known to all the good men what she had charged them with. Then Thorkell the White stood up at the assembly and petitioned all the thegns to give cleanly to his wife the lands which her kinswoman had granted to her. And they did so. And Thorkell then rode to Saint Æthelberht's Minster, with the consent and witness of all the people, and had it recorded in a Gospel Book.

UNIT 21

Test yourself

The first tribute amounted to 10,000 pounds in 991, but this rose to 16,000 pounds in 994. **1** Wulfgar succeeded to the abbacy after Edwin had died (though the text is not explicit, we know from other sources that Wulfgar became abbot of Abingdon). **2** First Ipswich was plundered, then the battle was fought at Maldon. **3** The idea of paying tribute is attributed to archbishop Sigeric, because of the terror the Vikings were causing along the coast. **4** Ealdorman Ælfric was appointed as one of the leaders of the army by the king. **5** Ealdorman Ælfric apparently warned the Viking army of the attack and then took flight from the English army. **6** The wording of the text *they took the ealdorman's ship all equipped and armed* seems to suggest that it was the Vikings who took his ship. **7** Oswald was bishop of Worcester and archbishop of York. **8** The fortress at Bamburgh was taken and plundered. **9** The Chronicler describes the stout resistance of the Londoners, greater than anything the Vikings had ever experienced. He also says that the people of London were under the protection of St Mary, who showed them her favour and saved them from their enemies. **10** The king and his council sent messages to the Vikings offering them tribute and food, in return for which they would stop their raiding and plundering.

UNIT 22

Language discovery

The definite article occurs nine times in the passage from *Maldon* (55–83): on þam easteðe *on the river shore* (63), to þam oðrum *to the other* (64), se æschere *the Viking army* (69), se flod *the flood-tide* (72), þa flotan *the seamen* (72), þa bricge *the bridge* (74, 78), æt þam forda *at the ford* (81), wið ða fynd *against the enemies* (82)

Practice

In the semantic field of ' SOUND' there are the verbs dynede *resounded*, hlynsode *resounded*, galan *to chant*, wanigean *to bewail*, and the nouns sweg *sound, music*, sang *song*, and wop *weeping*; for 'HALL': reced *hall*, foldbold *earth-dwelling*, winsele *wine-hall*, dryhtsele *princely hall*, renweardas *hall guardians*; 'FEELINGS' include ealuscerwen *dispensation of ale, distress, terror*, and egesa *awe, terror*.

Test yourself

823 b either Db or E, 824 C A, 825 A3 B, 826 A Da, 827 A E, 828 A C, 829 E A

UNIT 23

The Old English *Apollonius of Tyre*

Ch. XVI Apollonius remains silent because in all honesty he does not admire her style of playing; he is a much more experienced musician than the princess and feels that she has 'fallen into' playing the harp, rather than being taught the proper techniques. Ch. XVIII The princess cannot sleep, and goes to see her father in the middle of the night, saying that the visitor's accomplishments have set her thinking. She would like the king to secure the young man as her tutor (apparently for music and, as the story unfolds later, for literacy and writing, the scribal art being a separate skill in the middle ages – apparently the time when this narrative is now set). Ch. XIX The three suitors all make their request at the same moment, as it were with one voice, with an inevitably comic effect on the king as he walks with Apollonius in the street.

A charter from Winchester

The streets are named: cypstræt *Market Street*, flæsmangere stræt *Butcher Street*, scyldwyrhtana stræt *Shield-makers' Street*.

Test yourself

So when the king's daughter saw that Apollonius was so well versed in all the best arts, she fell in love with him [lit. her mind fell into love of him]. [2] Now after the end of the feast the girl said to the king: 'Father dear, a little while ago you allowed me to give Apollonius whatever he wished from your treasury.' [3] King Arcestrates said to her: 'Give him whatever you want!' [4] Very happy now, she went outside and said: 'Magister Apollonius, with my father's permission I am giving you two hundred pounds of gold and four hundred pounds in weight of silver and a large amount of costly clothing, and twenty serving men.' [5] This was then done at the queen's [i.e. the daughter's] behest, and all the people who saw her praised her generosity. [6] So now the feast ended, and all the people rose and took their leave of the king, and of the queen, and bid them fare well, and turned homewards. [7] Likewise also Apollonius said, 'Good king and benefactor of the poor, and O queen, lover of learning, I bid you fare well.' He turned to the serving men that the girl had given him, and said to them, 'Take these things with you that the queen has given me, and let's go and look for an inn where we can rest.' [8] At this the young woman became anxious that she would never again see Apollonius as quickly as she wanted to, and so she went to her father and said, 'Good king, is it acceptable to you that Apollonius, who today has been restored to wealth by us, should depart, and maybe evil men will come and rob him?' [9] The king replied, 'Well said. Have them find a place where he can stay most comfortably.' [10] So the girl did as she had been commanded, and Apollonius accepted the lodgings that were offered him, and he went in thanking God, who had not denied him the royal honour and respite.

UNIT 24

Practice

The title of the poem is *Widsith*.

Old English–English word index

The index covers words and phrases occurring in the practice exercises and the study texts. Different meanings of a word are listed separately:

þær *there* (adv.) 4

þær *where* (conj.) 15

The number indicates the unit in this book in which the word or phrase occurs prominently. You should refer back to that unit to study the word in context and find further information on grammar, usage, pronunciation, etymology, and word formation.

Each word is translated briefly, according to its meaning in context. Occasionally, where it is necessary to be clear, grammatical information is given; e.g. '**agen** *own* (adj.) 1' shows that *own* here is an adjective.

Abbreviations used are: acc. accusative, adj. adjective, adv. adverb, comp. comparative, conj. conjunction, dat. dative, fem. feminine, gen. genitive, imp. imperative, masc. masculine, past part. past participle, pl. plural, subj. subjunctive.

The arrangement is alphabetical, but following normal practice in dictionaries of Old English, you will see that the unstressed **ge-** prefix is not regarded as fully part of the word. The letters **ð** and **þ** should be treated as interchangeable, so that **ðeow** and **þeow** are seen to be the same word, and they follow **t** in the alphabetical arrangement. Otherwise you should be able to find the different forms and spellings of a word listed separately, e.g. '**gif** *if* 15' and '**gyf** *if* 7'.

When learning a language it is important that you acquire words, phrases and patterns as they appear in context. Use this word index also as a review or revision tool, to recall the original context in which your learning took place.

A

ā *ever, always* 4, 22

abbod *abbot* 17

abbodas *abbots* 17

abbud *abbot* 19

abbudisse *abbess* 19

abeag *started away* 22

abeodan *announce* 20, 24

abrece *break* (subj.) 18

abrocen *captured, broken into (past part.)* 21

abugan *bow down* 6

abugon *they bowed* 6

ac *but* 15, 21, 22

āc *oak* 2

acsode *asked* 20

acsodon *asked (pl.)* 20

adraf *drove out* 4

adred *feared* 23

astod *stood* 22

æcer *field* 6

æfen *evening* 5

æfen-spræce *evening-talk* 22

æfentid *evening time* 15

æfre *ever* 19

æfter *after; along* 10

Ægelnoðesstan *Aylton* 20

æglæca *assailant* 22

ægðer ge… ge *both… and* 8

æht *possessions* 10

æhta *possessions* 19

ælc *each, every* 18

ælf *elf* 1

Ælfere *Ælfhere* 21

Ælfþryþ *Ælfthryth (mother of Æthelred)* 19

ænig *any* 11, 21

ænige þinga *by any means* 22

ær *earlier*

ær ðam *before that* 4

ær ðam ðe *before (conj.)* 13

ær *previously (used for pluperfect)* 22

ær com *had come* 22

ær drugon *had endured* 22

ær gemette *had ever encountered* 22

ær wiste *had known* 18

ærende *message, errand* 20

ærendspræc *message* 24

ærest *first* 10

ge-ærndede æt *acquired from* 18

ærnemerigen *early morning* 5

æror *earlier (pluperfect)* 22

se þe fela æror … fyrene gefremede *he who had committed many crimes* 2

æsc *ash-tree* 9

æsc *warship* 21

æschere *Viking army* 21

æt *at* 4

æt *from;* **onfeng æt** *received from* 4

æt: Godric æt Stoce *Godric of Stoke* 20

ætbærst *broke out* 21

æteowde *appeared* 21

ætgædere *together* 20

æt Hatabaþum *At the Hot Baths (Bath)* 1

æton *they ate* 20

ætsomne *together* 2

ætstop *stepped* 22

ætwitan *reproach* 21

æþelborene *noble-born (pl.)* 23

æþeling *prince* 19

Æþelnoð biscop *bishop Æthelnoth* 17

Æþelred *king Æthelred the Unready* 19, 21

afirsa *drive away* 23

afleogan *fly away* 16

afligeð *flies away* 16

afysan *drive away* 6, 14

agan *have, own* 11

agen *own (adj.)* 1

agenre *see* **agen**

ageotan *spill, pour out* 13, 14

agyfan *deliver, give over to* 13, 19

ageaf *gave back* 16

ah: ic ah *I own* 20

ahengce *hung (subj.)* 16

(ge)ahnian *possess* 4, 19

ahnunga *proofs of ownership* 19

ahredde *saved* 21

ahrinest *you touch* 5

aht *anything* 18

ahte *owned* 11, 16

ahtes *of value* 21

ahwær *somewhere* 21

Akemannesceaster *Bath* 1

aldor *life* 22

aldorgedal *tally of life* 22

his aldres… ende *the end of his life* 22

alecgan *put down, lay down* 7

alegde *placed* 22

alifed *permitted* 20

alysednes *release* 18

amber *pitcher, measure, amber* 11

an *one* 3, 4

ana *alone* 23

anæd *solitude* 24

anda *enmity* 6

Andeferen *Andover* 21

andland = andlang

andlang *along* 10

andsaca *adversary* 22

andswarode *answered* 9

andwlita *face* 16

ane *alone (fem.)* 3

Angelcynn *the English nation* 3, 4

ann: ic geann *I grant* 11

annus solaris (Latin) *the solar year* 12

anra gehwylcum *for each one* 22

anræd *of single counsel, of one mind* 4

anre stæfne *with one voice* 23

Apollines *Apollo* 23

Apollonius *Apollonius* 23

ar *messenger* 21

aræran *raise* 7

arcebiscop *archbishop* 1, 4

aredod *arranged* 23

arehte *related* 23

arfæst *gracious* 24

arfullice *graciously* 20

arison *they rose* 23

arwurð *venerable* 17

arwurðlice *honourably* 17

asette *put, placed* 17

asprang *sprang forth* 8

Assandun   *Ashdon, Essex* 4
astag   *rose up* 22
astigen   *descended* 5
astod   *stood up* 20
astyrod   *moved* 20
ateah   *had undertaken* 22
atelic   *terrible* 22
atellan   *recount* 19
atiht: manige wurdon atihte   *many were attracted* 8
atol   *terrible* 22
aþ   *oath* 19
aþreatode   *rebuked* 6
aðum   *son-in-law* 23
Augustin: æt sancte Augustine   *at St Augustine's* 10
aþel   *noble* 1
aðreatode   *rebuked* 6
aweg   *away* 19
aweg lætan   *dispense with* 19
awehton   *kept awake* 23
awrat   *wrote down* 16
awriten   *written* 7, 16
axode   *asked* 9
ge-axode ic   *I have heard of* 15

B

bæd   *asked, requested* 18
bærnet   *burning* 21
baldlicost   *most boldly* 21
bam   *both* (dat.) 18
bana   *killer* 13
ban-fag   *adorned with bone or ivory* 22
banlocan   *joints* 22
bar   *boar* 12
Baþanceaster   *Bath* 1, 10
baþu   *baths* 10
be   *about, by, concerning* 5, 10
bead   *commanded* 7
beagas   *rings* 2
beah = beag   *arm-ring* 8
beahwriða   *arm-ring* 8
bealdlice   *boldly* 24
beam   *tree* 6, 10
beam   *beam (of light)* 6
bearm   *lap* 3
bearn   *child, son* 17
bearn   *sons* (pl.) 14

bearu   *grove, wood* 24
Bebbanburuh   *Bamburgh* 21
bebeodan   *command* 20
beboden   *commanded* (past part.) 23
bec   *book* (dat.) 18
becomon   *came* 21
becweden   *bequeathed* (past part.) 18
becweðan   *bequeath* 18
bedd   *bed* 23
befæste me   *entrust me, commend me* 23
befeng   *embraced* 10
befer   *beaver* 9
beforan   *before* 18, 19
begeat   *received* 8
begen   *both* 22
begytan   *acquire, receive* 8
behatan   *promise* 8
beheolde   *saw, beheld* 24
behet   *promised* 8
beleolc   *enclosed* 24
(ge)belgan   *become angry* 20
belle   *bell* 15
beo   *be* (imperative) 16
beodan   *command* 11
beon   *to be* 3
beon ge (subj.)   *may you be* 23
beorg   *mound, heap* 10
beorh   *mound* 2
beorht   *bright* 1
beorhtost   *brightest* 6
beornas   *men* 21
beorscipe   *feast* 23
beotian   *to vow* 20
beoð   *are* 3
Beowulf   *Beowulf* 22
bera   *bear (type of animal)* 2
beran   *carry* 16
berað   *carry (imp.)* 23
bereafian   *deprive* 13
bereafian   *rob* (subj.) 23
beron   *they would bear* (subj.) 21
besmiþod   *forged* (cf. **smiþ** *smith*) 22
bestodon   *stood along* 21
betæcan   *entrust* 4, 17
betæhte   *entrusted* 4
betere   *better* 19
betlic   *excellent* 22
betreppan   *to ambush* 21
betwux   *among* 5

betwux þysum   *meanwhile* 15
betwynan   *between, among* 13
beþencan   *ponder* 13, 15
bewænde hine   *he turned* 23
bewunden   *surrounded* 6, 24
biddan   *to ask* 19
bidde ic   *I pray* 18
binnan   *within* 11
(ge)biorgan   *protect* 19
bisceop   *bishop* 1
bitter   *bitter* 5
blæd-um   *with fruits* 2
Bleddehlæw   *Bledlow* 18
(ge)bletsad   *blessed* 1
bletsian   *to bless* 18
(ge)bletsod   *blessed (past part.)* 18
bletsung   *blessing* 16
bliss   *happiness* 17
blissian   *to rejoice* 9, 23
(ge)blissod   *pleased (past part.)* 23
bliðe   *happy* 16
bliðelice   *happily* 17
blowan   *to flourish* 2
blowende   *flourishing* 24
boc   *book, charter* 10
bocere   *scholar* 5
bord   *shield* 21
brad   *broad* 10, 21
æt Bradanfelda   *at Bradfield* 19
brægd   *drew* 22
breme   *famous* 17
bricg   *bridge* 21
bringan   *bring* 19
Britenland   *Britain* 13
brocc   *badger* 10
(ge)brocen   *broken* 10
brohte   *brought* 16
broðor   *brother* 6
broðru   *brothers* 6
broðrum   *(with his) brothers (dat.)* 6
bruce   *enjoy* 8, 18
brun   *dark, shining* 24
brycg   *bridge* 2, 10
brydguma   *bridegroom* 15
bufan   *above* 10
bur   *chamber* 23
bugan   *to bend* 8
burg = burh
burh   *city, stronghold* 1

burhgeat   *castle-gate* 20
burna   *burn, stream* 10
burston   *strained* 22
burston   *burst* 22
buruhwaru   *citizens* 21
butan   *without* 11
butan   *except that* 19
buton   *unless* 21
(ge)byrd   *birth* 23
byre   *youth(s)* 8
byrgen   *grave* 17
byrht   *bright* 1, 5
Byrhtferð   *Byrhtferth of Ramsey* 5, 12
Byrhtnoð   *ealdorman Byrhtnoth* 21
(ge)byrian   *belong* 20
byrig   *city, stronghold (dat.)* 11
(ge)byrigde   *buried* 13
byrnende   *burning* 16, 24
bysig   *busy* 24
bysmor   *disgrace* 21
byst ðu?   *are you?* 6

C
caf   *brave* 21
canst   *you know* 23
carta   *parchment* 16
ceald   *cold* 5
cealdost   *coldest* 5
cealf   *calf* 12
ceap   *price, transaction* 13
ceaster   *city* 1
ceasterbuend   *fortress-dweller* 22
cempena: cempena ealdor   *captain of soldiers* 14
cenra   *of the brave* 22
Cent   *Kent* 7
ceorl   *free peasant* 4, 20
ceosan   *choose* 23
(ge)cig   *call* 23
(ge)ciged   *called* 5
cild   *child, young nobleman* 11
cing   *king* 1
cirice   *church* 20
clæne   *cleanly, completely* 20
claðas   *clothes* 14
(ge)cleopian   *call* 20
cleric   *clerk, cleric* 5
cnapa   *boy* 14

gecneordnes *diligence, learning* 23
cniht *retainer* 11
cnihtas *young men* 23
Cnut *Cnut (king Canute)* 4, 5, 7, 10, 17, 18
com *came* 4, 22
conn: ne conn *does not know* 24
cræft *art, skill* 23
cran *crane, heron* 12
crawa *crow* 12
cringan *to fall* 10
cristen *Christian* 7
Cristes boc *gospel book* 20
Cristes cyrice *Christ Church* 7
croft *croft* 10
(ge)crong *fell* 10
cu *cow* 12
Culeford *Culford* 11
cum *come* (imp.) 9
cuma *guest* 16
cuman *come* 13
cuman *may come* (subj.) 23
cunnian *attempt* 21
cuð *known* 7
cuðe *knew* 19, 20
cwædon *(they) said* 6
cwæð *(he) said* 6
(ge)cweden *called* (past part.) 5
cwealmcuma *killer-guest* 22
cwen *queen, consort* 8
cweðað *(they) say* 5
cweðende *saying* (present part.) 15
cweðe *we we say* 5
æt Cwichelmeshlæwe *at Cwichelm's Barrow* 19
cwicne *alive* (masc. acc.) 22
cwyde *will, testament* 18
cwomon *they came* 10
cydde *proclaimed* 18
cynelic *royal* 17
cyng *king* 4
cyning *king* 2
cynn *kin, kindred* 2, 3, 16, 21
manna cynne *humankind* 22
(ge)cynd *nature* 16
cynehelm *crown* 23
cypa *merchant* 13
cyp-stræt *market street* 23
cyrcean: cyrice *church* 7
Cyrdesleah *Cradley* 20

cyrice, cirice *church* 7
(ge)cyrran *turn, convert* 15
(ge)cyssað *kiss* 24
cyst: irenna cyst *best of irons* 22
cyst: swefna cyst *best of dreams* 6
cyð *tell* (imp.) 9
(ge)cyðan *proclaim, make known* 5
cyta *kite (the bird)* 12

D
dæd *deed* 2, 13
dæg *day* 5
on þæm dæge *on that day* 22
to dæg *today* 23
dæg-rim *day-count, number of days* 22
dæl *part* 5
dæl: hyre dæles *for her part* 19
dælan *share out* 2
daga *of days* 5
decanus *dean, prior* 17
Deccet *Dachet (Buckinghamshire)* 19
demend *judge* 2
dene: denu *valley* 9
Dene-mearc *Denmark* 4
denn *woodland pasture* 10
Denum eallum *to all the Danes* (dat.pl.) 22
deofla *of devils* 22
deor *animal* 12
deor *dear, costly* 5
derian *harm, damage* 14, 21
deþ *(he, it) does* 15
dic *ditch* 10
digel *secret* 15
dihtan *dictate* 24
discten = discþegn
discþegn *steward, seneschal* 19
dogera *of days* (gen.) 22
dohtig *excellent* 4
dohtor *daughter* 19
dom: on eallum domum *in all the laws* 24
dom: on hyra sylfra dom *at their own judgement* 7
don *to do* 15
don *to put* 13
deorwurð *costly* 23
dorste *dared* 19
dream *joy* 17
drigge *dry* 5

Drihten *Lord, God* 1, 7
drohtnung *way of life* 15
drohtoð *experience* 22
drugon *undertook, endured* 22
dryhtsele *royal hall* (**dryht** *royal, lordly* cf.
  dryhten *lord*) 22
dun *hill* 2, 23
dyde *did* 15
dydon *they put* 13
dydon (didon) *they did* 17, 23

E

ea *river* 2
eac *also* 16
ead, eadig *blessed* 1, 16
ead *prosperity* 10
Eadgar *Edgar* 1
eadignesse *blessedness* 24
eadmodlice *humbly* 13
eadmodnys *humility* 17
Eadsige *archbishop Eadsige* 1, 17, 18
Eadward *Edward the Confessor* 1
Eadward *Edward the Martyr* 13
Eadwig *Eadui Basan* 7, 10
eagan *eyes* 12
eage *eye* 12
eahta *eight* 12
eahteoð *eighth* 17
eala *O* (vocative) 23
eald *old* 2
on ealderdagum *in the days of his life* 22
ealdor *captain, chief* 14
ealdorman *nobleman, prince* 4
ealgian *protect* 22
eall *all* 4
eall-es *of all* 1
eall-um *all* 1
eal-ne *all* 2
ealuscerwen *terror (perhaps literally
  dispensation of ale)* 22
earan *ears* 12
eard *region, land* 3
eardian *to live* 15
earmcearig *wretched* 5
earmlic wurðan *to become pitiable* 22
earmra *of the poor (gen. pl.)* 23
earn *eagle* 12
eart *you are (sing.)* 3

east *east* 2
Eastenglas *East Angles, East Anglia* 1
to Eastenglum *to the East Angles* 1
Easterdæig *Easter Day* 1
ea-steð *river-bank* 21
Eastseaxe *East Saxons, Essex* 4, 21
eaxl *shoulder* 12
ebba *ebb-tide* 21
ece *eternal* 11
ecg *edge, sword* 21
ecga gehwylcre *every weapon* 22
(ge)edniwod *renewed* 23
eft *again, back again* 4, 10
eg *island* 12
ege *fear* 2
egesa *fear* 22
egesfull *terrible* 2
egeslic *terrible* 14
egland *island* 16
Egypta land *Egypt, land of the Egyptians* 13
ehtuwe *eight* 12
mid elcunge *with delay* 23
ellen *courage* 22
ellen-mærþum *in the glories of his courage
  (dat. pl.)* 22
elles *else* 7
ellorgast *alien spirit* 22
elran: on elran men *in any man* 22
embe *about* 18
emniht *equinox* 5
endleofan *eleven* 6
(ge)endode *ended* 23
(ge)endung *end* 23
engla *of angels* 3
Engla *of the English* 4, 20
Englaland *England* 4
englisc *English* 3
eode *went* 4
eofor *wild boar* 12
Eoforwic *York* 21
eoh *horse* 12
eom *(I) am* 3
eorl *nobleman, earl* 2, 4
eorl Beowulfes *Beowulf's man (i.e. one of
  Beowulf's men)* 22
eorla *of warrriors* 22
eorlice *angrily* 20
eorþe *earth* 2
eorþan sceata *in [all] the regions of the earth* 22

ofer eorþan   *in all the earth* 22

eow   *(to) you* 7

eower   *your* (pl.) 9, 15

engel   *angel* 3

ersc   *stubble field* 10

estful   *devout* 17

eþel   *homeland* 3

Eufrosina   *Euphrosyne* 8, 15

eunuchus   *eunuch* 15

F

fæder   *father* 6

fæger   *beautiful* 22

Fæliglæh   *Fawley* 20

fæmne   *maid, woman* 15

fæmnena   *of women* 15

fæst   *firm* 24

fæste   *firmly* 22

fæstlice   *firmly* 15, 21

fæðm   *embrace* 3, 22

fag (fah)   *coloured, paved* 10

fag: he wæs fag wið God   *he was in a feud against God* 22

far   *go* (imperative) 9

faran   *to go, travel* 4

fare   *may go* (subj.) 23

farende   *travelling* 20

fea   *few* 24

gefea   *joy* 13

(ge)feaht   *fought* 19

feala   *many* 18

fearn   *fern* 10

feccan   *fetch* 23

fedde   *fed* 21

fela   *many* 21

feld   *field* 11

feng to   *took* 16

feng   *succeeded* 21

under fenhleoðu   *under marshy slope* 22

on fenhopu   *into the fenland refuges* 22

fenn   *fenland* 16

feoh   *money, cattle* 7, 12

feohtan   *to fight* 2

feoll   *fell* 15

(ge)feol   *fell* 23

feond   *enemy* 10, 22

feonda (gen.)   *of enemies* 22

feor siðian   *journey far* 22

feorh   *life* 22

feorhseoc   *life-sick* 22

feorran   *from afar* 13, 17, 22

feos   *in money* 21

feower   *four* 5, 12

feowertig   *forty* 11

(ge)fera   *companion* 4, 17

feran   *to depart, travel* 2, 12

(ge)ferdon   *they experienced* 21

on ferhðe   *in spirit* 22

ferian   *convey* 4, 17

fet   *feet* 12

fif   *five* 11

fiftig   *fifty* 3

fingras   *fingers* 15, 22

fisc   *fish* 15

fiþru   *wings* 7

flæsc   *flesh* 13

flæsmangere (flæsc-mangere)   *butcher* 23

flan: flanes   *of an arrow* (gen.) 21

fleah   *flew* 5, 16

fleam   *flight* 21

fleon   *to flee* 22

flet   *hall* 8

flod   *tide* 21

flodas   *floods* 3

flod-græg   *flood-grey* 2

flot   *sea* 7, 21

flotan   *seamen, Vikings* 21

flowende   *flowing* 21

flyht   *flight* 21

folc   *people* 1

folca   *of nations* 8

folces: ealles folces   *of all the people* 1

foldan: on foldan   *on the earth* 2

foldbold   *earth-building* (i.e. *hall*; metaphorical expression) 22

folde   *land, earth* 2

folm   *hand* 22

for   *went*, from **faran** *go* 4

for: for wætere   *because of the water* 21

forbead   *forbade* 20

forbeodan   *forbid* 20

ford   *ford, river-crossing* 2, 21

foresæd   *aforesaid* (past part.) 16

foresædon   *they mentioned* 20

forferde = forðferde   *departed* 4

forgeaf   *granted* 23

forgenga, foregenga   *predecessor* 11

forgife   *grant* 24

forgyfen   *granted* (past part.) 18

forgyldan   *compensate* 19

forgyldon   *(you) might buy off* (subj.) 21

forht   *afraid* 22

forlætan   *leave* 22

forleton   *they left behind* 16

forma   *first* 1, 21

forsteall   *ambush* 18

forstodan   *were worth, stood for* 7

forsworen hæfde   *had foresworn* or *had put a spell on* 22

for þam ðe   *because* 6

forð   *forward* 22

forð com   *came forth* 19

forðferde   *passed away* 4

forð teah   *performed* 23

forðweg   *onward journey* 24

for-ðam   *that is why, therefore* 23

forþan = forðam   *because* 19

forun   *they went* 13

for ut   *set out to sea* 4

forwerda   *terms of agreement* 8

forword   *agreement* 18

forworht   *forfeited* (past part.) 18

forwyrnde: him ne forwyrnde   *did not deny him* 23

fostorland   *land given to recipients to use for food* 18

fot   *foot* 12

fræton   *devoured, ate* 13

(ge)frætwod   *adorned* (past part.) 8

fram   *away* 22

no þy ær fram meahte   *he could not get away any sooner* 22

franca   *spear* 21

Frankland   *France* 4

frea   *lord* 20

freadrihten   *noble lord* 22

frefrode   *consoled* 16

(ge)frefrodon   *(they) consoled* 14

frefrung   *consolation* 14

fremd   *foreign* 11

fremdan   *to strangers* 11

fremdum   *to strangers* 14

fremian   *to benefit* 13

freode   *peace* 7

freols   *immunity, privilege* 7

freond   *friend* 6, 20, 23

freondlice   *in a friendly manner* 7

freondræden   *friendship* 6

freondscipe   *friendship* 18

frið   *peace* 7

friðusibb   *peace-pledge* 8

frod   *wise* 5

frofre   *comfort* (fem. acc.) (from **frofor**) 23

frumstaðol   *foundation, first state* 24

frynd   *friends* 23

fugel   *bird* 16

fuhton   *fought* (pl.) 4

ful georne   *very well* 18

fulla   *fullness* 19

full   *full* 7

full   *fully* 11

fultum   *help* 19

funde: ne funde   *could not find* 14

fundon   *(they) found* 14

furþur   *forward* 22

fus   *eager* 24

fyl   *fall* 21

(ge)fylle   *I fill* 3

fynd   *enemies* 6, 21

fyr   *fire* 24

fyrd   *army, militia* 2, 21

fyrena   *of crimes* 22

G

ga   *(I) go* 14

gaderung   *the gathering in, harvest* 5

gæð   *goes* 5

gafol   *tribute* 21

galan   *to chant* (inf.) 22

gan   *go* 5

gangan, gongan   *walk* 7, 12, 21

gangon   *they went* 21

gegangan   *obtain* 21

ganwe   *let us go* 23

gar   *spear* 1

garas   *spears* 21

gastlic   *spiritual* 7

gat   *goat* 12

ge   *you* (plural) 3, 18

ge… ge…   *both… and…* 19

geac   *cuckoo* 5

geador   *together* 22

geaf   *gave* from **gifan** 18

geat   *gate, castle* 13, 20

ge-ahnian   *take possession* 4

ge-ahnian   *prove possession* 19

ge-ahnade him eall þæt land *claimed all the land as his* 4

ge-ann (I) *grant* 11

geap *steep* 22

geard *enclosure* 10

gear *year* 4

geare: on þissum geare *in this year* 4

gearowe *ready* (pl.) 21

geat *gate* 10

Geat-mecga *of the Geatish men* (gen.pl.) 22

geatweard *gatekeeper* 15

ge-axode *he heard of* 15

ge-ærndede æt Cnute *acquired from Cnut* 18

gebad *he endured, experienced* 22

ge-bealh *she became angry* 20

ge-beorscipe *feast* 23

gebette *made good* 22

gebideð *experiences* 5

ge-biorgan *protect* 19

ge-bletsad *blessed* (past part.) 1

ge-bletsade *he blessed* 17

ge-bletsod *blessed* (past part.) 18

ge-blissod *pleased* (past part.) 23

ge-bohte *bought* 11

ge-brocen *broken* 10

ge-broðru *(group of) brothers* 4, 6

ge-byrd *birth* 23

ge-byrede *belonged* 20

ge-byrigde *buried* 13

ge-cig *call* 23

ge-ciged *called* (past part.) 5

ge-cleopade *called, summoned* 20

ge-cneow *he recognized* 14

ge-crong *fell* 10

ge-cweden *called* (past part.) 5

ge-cynd *nature* 16

ge-cyrran *turn, convert* 15

ge-cyssað *kiss* 24

ge-don *done* (past part.) 18

ge-dræg *company* 22

ge-dwola *error, wandering* 9

ge-earnunga *favours* 21

ge-eaðmeddon *they humbled themselves* 20

ge-edniwod *renewed* (past part.) 23

ge-endode *ended* 23

ge-endung *end* 23

ge-fælsod *cleansed* 22

ge-feaht *fought* 19

ge-feh *rejoiced* 22

ge-feoht *battle* 21

ge-fera *companion* 4

ge-firn *in the past* 23

ge-frætwod *adorned* (past part.) 8, 10

ge-frefrodon *(they) comforted* 14

ge-fremede *committed, performed* 22

ge-fylle *I fill* 3

ge-ga *go* (subj.) 11

ge-gaderian *gather* 5

gegangan *to obtain* 21

ge-gearnunga *merits* 17

ge-gierwed *equipped, clothed* (past part.) 12

ge-godod *enriched* (past part.) 23

wæs… gegongen *had come* (lit. gone) 22

ge-gyrla *garment, dress* 15

ge-hadod *ordained* (past part.) 7

ge-hadud *ordained* (past part.) 18

ge-halgian *consecrate* 4

ge-halgod *consecrated* (past part.) 1

ge-healden *satisfied* 19

ge-hergod *plundered* (past part.) 21

ge-hwam *to each* 5

ge-hwæde *little* 15

ge-hwæþer *each* 22

ge-hwone: on healfa gehwone *on every side* 22

ge-hwylc *each* 22

ecga gehwylcre *every weapon* 22

ge-hydde *hid* 15

ge-hyrde *heard* 9

ge-hyrdon *heard* 22

ge-hyrsum *agreeable* 23

ge-lamp *happened* 6

ge-lædde *led* 19

ge-læred *educated* 23

ge-lærednys *learning, skill* 8

ge-læsted *fulfilled* 22

geldan *pay* 11

ge-led *charged with* 20

ge-lede *laid* 7

ge-lede *lead* 16

ge-leornian *to learn* 23

ge-limpan *to happen* 9

ge-logodon *(they) placed* 17

ge-lome *frequently* 14

ge-lumpen: wearð… gelumpen *was come about* 22

ge-lymp *what had happened* 23

ge-meddred *maternal* 20

ge-met *way, means, manner* 15
ge-metfæst *moderate* 16
ge-metgung *moderation* 5
ge-mette *encountered* 22
ær gemette *had ever encountered* 22
ge-miltsige *have mercy* (subj.) 20
ge-miltsigend *pitier* 23
ge-mittan *meet, find* 9
ge-mot *assembly, meeting* 4
ge-munde *remembered* 22
ge-mylted *consumed* 24
ge-mynd *mind, memory* 7
ge-neahhe *often* 22
ge-nam *took* 16
ge-name *might take* (subj.) 21
ge-nehost *most swiftly* 22
ge-nemned *named* (past part.) 5
ge-nered *saved* 22
ge-nerian *save, rescue* 13
ge-nog, genuh *enough* 4, 7
ge-numen *taken* 21
geocor *bitter* 22
geomor *mournful* 5
geondhwearf *processed* 8
geong *young* 8
geong *went* 8
georn *eager* 21
georne *eagerly* 14
ger *year* 4
ger: þæs geres ær ðam *earlier in the year* 4
ge-rædest *you advise* 7
ge-ræhte *reached* 16
ge-refa *reeve* 17
ge-regnad (from **regnian** *to adorn*) 22
ge-reordade *feasted* 17
ge-riht *right, justice, obligation* 4
ge-riht: on geriht *straight on* 10
ge-rysna *what is fitting, dignity, honour* 18
ge-rysenlic *honourable* 18
ge-sæde *said* 13, 18, 20
ge-sælig *prosperous, fortunate* 23
ge-sæt *he sat up* 22
ge-sæton (they) *sat* 15
ge-samnodan (they) *gathered* 14
ge-sawe *would see* (subj.) 23
ge-sawon (they) *saw* 3, 6, 13
ge-scrydde (she) *clothed* 15
ge-seah (he) *saw* 6
ge-sealde *gave* 14

ge-seman *reconcile* 19, 21
ge-siðas *companions* 24
ge-sohton *they sought out* 13, 19
ge-somnod *gathered* (past part.) 19
ge-specen *spoken* 11
gesthus *lodging* 23
ge-sunde (pl. adj.) *prosperous* 23
ge-swac *ceased* 20
ge-swænctest *oppressed* 23
ge-swutelian *clarify* 5
ge-syne *seen* 13
ge-synscipe *marriage* 8
ge-tæhte *instructed* 19
ge-tæle *counting* 12
ge-tilian *produce* 18
ge-togen *educated* (past part.) 23
ge-trahtniað (they) *explain, expound* 5
ge-þafian *allow* 17
ge-þeah *flourished* 20
ge-þyncðo, geþincðo *rank, degree* 20
ge-unnan *grant* 11
ge-utlagian *to outlaw* 4
ge-wændon *returned* 23
ge-wæpnod *armed* 21
ge-wat *departed, went* 15, 21
(ge)weald *power* 14, 22
(ge)weald *dominion* 24
ge-wearð *occurred* 14
ge-wendan *to turn, return* 4
ge-wihte *weight* 23
ge-win *fight* 22
ge-windan *to escape* 22
ge-winnan *strive* 9
ge-witnes *witness, cognisance* 7, 11
ge-worht *made* 8
ge-wregan *to accuse* 6
ge-writ *letter, writ, document* 7
ge-writen *written* (past part.) 20
ge-wunelic *usual* 15
ge-wunian *remain* 2, 4
ge-wurþe Godes willa *God's will be done* 8
gif *give* (imp.) 23
gif *if* 15
gife *gift* (acc.) 23
gifode *gave gifts* 21
gifu *gift* 1
gilp *vow* 22
gim (gimm) *jewel* 2, 10
girnan (gyrnan) *to desire* 23

girstandæg   *yesterday* 23
man gislude   *they gave hostages* 21
glæd-mod   *glad of mind* 10
gled   *ember, flame* 24
glof   *glove* 2, 16
God   *God* 5, 8, 11, 13, 15
gōd   *good* 1, 11, 20
goda   *good* 22
godes   *well-being* (gen.) 21
goddra manna   *of good men* 7
Godwine   *earl Godwine* 10
Godwine   *Godwine (a Kentishman)* 11
gofol = gafol   *tribute* 21
gold   *gold* 11
goldhord   *treasury* 23
gongan   *walk, walking* 12
græg   *grey* 2
graf   *grove* 10
gram   *enemy* 22
on grames grapum   *in the adversary's grasp* 22
þa graman   *the adversaries* 22
grap   *grasp* 22
Grendles grape   *Grendel's grasp* 22
grene   *green* 2
greniað   *become green* 5
gret   *greets* 7
gretan   *greet* 7
gretan nolde   *would not affect* 22
grette   *greeted* 19, 23
gretton   *they took their leave of* 23
grim   *fierce* 21
grið   *truce, protection* 18, 20, 21
grið-bryce   *breach of protection* 18
grund   *depth, ground* 3
gryre-geatwe   *fear-inspiring wargear* 10
gryre-leoð   *terror-song* 22
gumena   *of men* (gen.) 5
gumum   *to the men* (dat.) 10
guð   *battle* 21
guð-billa nan   *none of the war-swords* 22
guð-hreð   *battle-triumph* 22
Guðlac   *Guthlac (Lincolnshire hermit)* 16
guð-plega   *battle-play* 21
gyf   *if* 7
gyfan, to gyfene   *to give* 8
gyfeþe   *granted* 22
gyrd   *staff* 16
gyrnan (girnan)   *to desire* 8
gyt   *still, yet* 20

Gypeswic   *Ipswich* 21
Gyxeweorðe   *Ixworth (Surrey)* 11

H

habban   *to have* 6
habbað   *(we) have* 18
æt Hacceburnan   *at Hagbourne (Berkshire)* 19
(ge)hadode   *ordained clergy* 7
(ge)hadude   *ordained clergy* 18
hæbbe   *I have* 11
hæfde   *had* 4, 7, 11
hæfð   *has* 5
hægl   *hail* 5
hælð   *health, salvation* 17
hæleða   *of warriors* (gen.) 21
hæleðum   *to men* (dat.) 5
hære   *sack cloth, hair-shirt* 14
hæsel   *hazel* 10
Hæselersc   *Hazelhurst* 10
hæð   *heath* 2
hæðen   *heathen* 23
ðara hæðenra god   *a god of the heathen* 23
hafuc   *hawk* 2, 12
haga   *homestead, enclosure* 23
hal   *safe, healthy* 20
halga   *saint* 18
halgade   *consecrated* 1
(ge)halgod   *consecrated* (past part.) 1
halig   *holy* 4
hām *home:* ham com   *came home* 4
Hamtun   *Southampton* 21
hamsocn   *attack at home* 18
hand   *hand* 4, 12, 13
hand: mid handa   *with his hand* 22
hand: on hand   *into his hands* 19
hangiende   *hanging* 15
hangode   *hung, was hanging* 16
hāt   *hot* (adj.) 5
hāt   *command* (imp.) 23
hatan   *to call, to command* 3, 6
haten   *called* (past part.) 5, 21
hatian   *to hate* 6
ic hatte   *I am called* 3, 12
he   *he or it* (masc.) 5
heafda   *of heads* (gen.pl.) 12
heafdu: siex heafdu   *six heads* 12
heafod   *head* 12
healdan   *hold, rule* 2
to healdenne   *to rule* 4

healf   *half, side* 4, 21
on healfa gehwone   *on every side* 22
heall   *hall:* **on healle** *in the hall* 2
Healtun   *Halton (Buckinghamshire)* 18
heanlic   *shameful* 21
heardhicgende   *brave-hearted* 22
hearm   *harm* 21
se hearmscaþa   *the dangerous assailant* 22
hearpa   *harp* 23
hearpian   *to play the harp* 23
heaþodeorum   *battle-brave ones* 22
heawan   *to strike* 22
hege   *hedge* 10
helle hæfton   *the captive of hell* 22
heo, hio   *she or it (fem.)* 5, 16
heofenas   *heavens* 2
on heofenum   *in the heavens* 2
heold   *held, kept* (from **healdan**) 4
on heolster   *into the darkness* 22
heom   *them* 4
heonon   *from here* 23
heora   *their* 9
heora an   *one of them* 23
heorde   *herds* 6
heort   *hart, stag* 2
heorte   *heart* 17
her   *here* 4
her on ðissum geare   *here in this year* 4
here   *army* 2
heregung   *plundering* 21
here-toga   *army-leader* 21
(ge)hergod   *plundered* (past part.) 21
herian   *to praise* 23
het   *commanded* 6
hie   *they* 22
Higelaces   *of Higelac* 22
hi, hig   *they* 3
hid   *hide (of land)* 10
hider   *here, hither* 15
hige-þihtigne   *the strong-spirited, courageous* (acc.) 22
hilde-deor   *battle-bold* 22
hilde-mecgas   *warriors* 22
him   *to him* (dat.) *or to them* (dat.) 8
hine   *him* (acc.) 1, 8
hin-fus   *eager to be gone* 22
hio, heo   *she or it (fem.)* 5, 16
hira   *their* 8, 9
hire   *her* 8, 9

hired   *community* 8
hired   *household, court* 15
hit   *it* 5
hlæfdie   *lady* 17
hlæfdige   *lady* 10
hlaford   *lord* 7
hleo   *protector* 21, 22
hlisa   *fame* 8
hlynsode   *resounded* 22
hnigan   *drop, incline* 3
hol   *hollow* 10
hol   *hole, cave* 10
hold   *gracious, loyal* 7
holt   *wood* 12
hond: æfter hondum   *from hand to hand* 24
hæfde be honda   *had [him] by the hand* 22
hors   *horse* 12
Horslege   *Horsley* 11
hrædlice   *quickly* 13
hraþe   *quickly* 22
hrefn   *raven* 16
hreod   *reed* 16
hreodbedd   *reed-bed* 16
hreðer   *heart* 10
hrimgicel   *icicle* 5
hrimig   *frosty* 5
hrine: ic hrine   *I touch* 3
hring   *ring* 6, 8
hring-iren   *ring-iron, chainmail* 10
Hrisbeorga   *Risborough* 18
hrof   *roof* 22
Hrofesceaster   *Rochester* 17
hrycg   *back* 12
hryre   *fall* 10
hu   *how* 5, 9
hund   *hundred* 12
hund   *dog* 12
hundseofontig   *seventy* 5
hundnigontig   *ninety* 5
hunig   *honey* 15
hwa   *who* 20
hwæm   *to whom* 20
hwæne   *each* 6
hwænne   *until* 21
hwæt   *what* 3
hwæt   *listen!* 6
hwæðer   *whether* 9
hwar   *where* 14
hwil   *while, period of time* 4

hwilc *which* 23
hwilum *at times* 8
hwita: Þurkil hwita *Thorkell the White* 20
æt Hwitecyrcan *at Whitchurch* 19
hwy *why* 23
hwyder *where to* 14
hy *them* 7
hyge *his thought* 22
hyne *him* 6, 8
(ge)hyran *hear* 9
(ge)hyrað *hear* 6
hyre *her* 19
hyrmen *servants* 6
(ge)hyrsum *agreeable* 23
hyrsumode *obeyed* 16
hyrð *belongs to* 18
hyrde *master* 22
hys *his* 6
hyt *it* 6

I
ic *I* 3
ides *lady* 3
idus (Latin) *ides (in Roman calendar)* 4, 5
ieg *island* 12
ilca *the same* 17
Imma seo hlæfdie *Emma the Lady (queen Emma)* 4, 17, 18
inc *you both* (dual) 18
infangene-þeof *the right to take and fine a thief caught in one's area of jurisdiction* 18
ingeþonc *thought* 24
innan *into* 10
innan ond utan *within and without* 22
inne *inside, within* 18
innmæst, innemest *inmost, deep* 10
innon *within* 23
insegel *wax seal on documents* 19
insegl = insegel *wax seal* 7
ge-inseglode *sealed* (past) 23
inwid-sorge *evil sorrow* 22
inwit-þancum *with hostile intent* 22
iren-bendum *with iron bonds* (dat.pl.) 22
irenna cyst *best of irons* 22
īs-ceald *ice-cold* 5
Ismahelitisc *Ismaelite* 6
iu *formerly* 10

iung *young* 5
se iunga *the young man* 23

K
kepan: þances kepan *to show gratitude* 18
kyning = cyning *king* 17

L
lac *present, gift* 15
laf: ealde lafe *ancient heirloom, i.e. sword (a circumlocution)* 22
lædan *to lead, carry* 6, 13
(ge)lædde *presented, led* 19
læddon *carried* 13
læg *lay* 18
lærde *taught* 1
(ge)læred *educated* 23
(ge)lærednys *learning, skill* 8
lærincgmæden *woman student* 23
læs *pasture* 9
læssa *smaller* 3
læstan *to help* 22
læswum: on læswum *in the pastures* 9
lætan = læten *granted* (past part.) 18
lætan *order, command* 4
lætan *leave, let* 19
læwede *lay people* 7
lace *leap, fly, play* 24
lage *would lie* (subj.) 18
lagon *(they) lay* 18
lagu *law* 7
lagu-fæðm *sea-embrace* 24
lagu-stream *sea-current, water* 21
land *land* 10
land-ar *landed property* 11
landgemæru *charter bounds* 10
lange *long:* **to lange** *too long* 9
lange tide *for a long time* 14
lar *teaching* 23
lare lufigend *lover of learning* 23
lað *hostile* 22
leafe *leave, permission* 17, 23
leah *ley, clearing* 9
leawede *lay people* 8, 11
lecgan *put, lay* 7
lecgað *put* (imp.) 23

(ge)led   laid, charged (past part.) 20

(ge)lede   laid 7, 24

leng   longer 23

lengest   longest 5

lengten-tima   spring season 5

leod   nation 20

leod   leader 22

leoda   people 7

leoda ænigum   to any of the men 22

leod-biscop   suffragan bishop 7

leod-wita   counsellor 20

leof   dear, beloved 18

leofaþ   lives, liveth 24

æt Leofecanoran   of Lewknor 19

leofest   dearest 8

Leofric   Leofric, Bishop of Exeter 3

Leofwine reada   Leofwine the Red 11

leoht   light 3

leornode   learned 23

let   ordered 4

lete   should leave (subj.) 19

lichoma   body 17, 22

licað   pleases 23

licode   was pleasing 23

(ge)licost   most like 10

lic-sar   body-wound 22

lif   life 4, 15

lifað   lives, liveth 24

lifigende   while alive 22

lig   fire, flame 10, 24

liges   of fire 22

lin   flax, linseed 10

lið   lies, is lying 18

loca   look, see 9

lof   praise 17

lof-sang   hymn 17

lucon   joined, enclosed 21

lufian   love 6

lufu   love 23

lufode   loved 6

Lunden   London 17

lyfde   granted 7

lyfdest   you granted 23

Lyfing   Lyfing, Archbishop of Canterbury 4, 11

lyft   air 6

lysan   ransom 7

lyt   little 24

litle ær   a little before 23

lytle hwile   for a short while 4

M

ma   more (comp. adv.) 4

Maccus   Maccus 21

mæg   can 19

mæg   kinsman 22

mæge   may (subj.) 23

mægen   power, virtue 23

mægene   in power 22

þa feower mægna   the four virtues 12

gemægnde   blended 23

mænden   declared 24

mænig   many 11, 18

mænigfeald   manifold, numerous 12

(ge)mære   boundary 10

se mæra   the famous one 22

mære   famous, great 15, 22

mærsode   glorified, made famous 13

mæru   famous, great (fem.) 8

mæssan: to Martins mæssan   on the feast of St Martin 4

mæssan = mæsse   holy mass 17

mæst   greatest, very great 6, 23

mætte: me mætte   I dreamed 6

mæð   measure, degree 20

mæþ   reverence 18

mage   kinswoman 20

magas   kinsmen 13

magon   they can 5

man   they, one 4

mancus   one eighth of a pound 8

mancsas   plural of **mancus** 16

manega   many 4

manig   many a 11

manna   of men (gen.) 22

manna ænig   any man 22

manna cynne   on humankind, against humanity 22

mannum   men, people (dat.) 5

manude   admonished 1

mara   greater 3

maran   greater 21, 22

martyr   martyr 17

meahte   could 22

no þy ær fram meahte   he could not get away any sooner 22

meahton   could 22

ðær hie meahton swa   if they so could 22

mearc   border 10

medubenc   mead-bench 22

menig   *many a* 19
meodu   *mead* 24
mere   *sea, lake* 3
mere-faroþ   *surging of the waves* 24
mere-stream   *sea water* 3
mergen   *morning* 15
mete   *food, provision* 11
metest   *you'll find* 16
ge-met: mid gemete   *by any means* 22
ge-met-fæst   *moderate* 16
metsung   *provision* 21
mette   *encountered* 10, 22
þæt he ne mette   *that he had never encountered* 22
mette: me mette   *I dreamed* 6
micel   *great, big* 3, 4
mid   *with* 4
middan: on middan   *in the midst* 6
middangeard   *world* 3
mid handa   *with his hand* 22
mid heom   *with them* 4
mid him   *with him* 4
mid mannum   *with provision of labour* 11
mid mete   *with food provision* 11
mid þan þe   *when* 16
mid þy þe   *when* 23
Mierce   *Mercia* 4
miht   *power* 7
mihte   *it could* 13
mihton   *they could* 6
mild-heort   *merciful* 20
miltse   *mercy, favour* 20
(ge)miltsie   *have mercy* 17
(ge)miltsigend   *pitier* 23
miltsum   *with favour, with humility* 24
min   *my, mine* 6,9, 15, 18
mine gefræge   *as I have heard* (epic formula) 22
mislicyge   *displease* (subj.) 23
mod *mind:*   **mode snottre** *with a wise mind* 12
on mode   *in [his] mind* 22
modega   *brave* 22
modes myrðe   *affliction of mind* 22
modige   *brave* (pl.) 21
modge   *proud* (pl.) 24
modor   *mother* 6
mona   *moon* 3
monað   *month* 5
monað (manað)   *gives warning* 5
monðas   *months* 5

mongum   *for many* 24
monige   *many* 3
morgen-gifu   *morning gift* 23
(ge)mot   *assembly, meeting* 4
moste   *be allowed* 7, *was allowed* 19, 23
moston   *they were allowed* 17
mote   *might* (subj.) 18
mund   *security, protection* 7
mund-gripe   *hand-grip* 22
munuc   *monk* 17
munucas   *monks* 17
munuclic   *monastic* 15
murcnung   *grief* 23
muðleas   *mouthless* 24
myccel, mycel   *great* 1
(ge)mylted   *consumed* 24
(ge)mynd   *mind, memory* 7, 13
mynster   *church, minster* 4
mynte   *intended* 22
myrðe: modes myrðe   *affliction of mind* 22

N
na   *not at all* 17, 20
nabbe ge   *you haven't* 23
nænig   *none* 16
næfre   *never* 20
nære   *would not be* (subj.) 19
næs   *was not* 20
nam   *took* 4, 22
(ge)nam   *took* 16
nama   *name* 5, 17
(ge)name   *might take* (subj.) 21
namon   *they took* 14
nan   *none* 14, 19
nast   *you do not know* 23
ne   *not* 14
neadunga   *forcibly* 15
neah   *near* 16
near   *nearer* 22
nebb   *face* 16
nelle   *(I) do not want* 18
nemnan   *to name* 18
(ge)nemned   *named* (past part.) 5
neod   *need* 1
nerian   *save* 12
niht   *night* 6
niht-weorc   *night-work* 22
nihtweorce   *in the work of the night* 22

niman   take 7, 15, 16, 21
nimað   take (imp.) 23
nið   enmity 22
niðer   down 10
niw   new 7
Niwantun   Newington 18
no   not 22
no þy ær   not any sooner 22
no þy ær fram meahte   he could not get away any sooner 22
nolde   did not want 19, 22
nonas   the nones (calendar) 5, 17
norð   north 2
Norðdenum   for the Danes (dat. pl.) 22
nosu   nose 12
nu   now 10
(ge)numen   taken 21
nyðer   down 5
nyhstan: æt nyhstan   at last 8, next 23
nyman   to take 17
nymþe   unless 22
nys   is not 14
nytte   of use 22

O
of   from, off 2
ofdyde   took off 15
ofer   over 3
oferstigan   climb over 3
of-myrþredon   murdered 13
ofsceat   shot down 21
ofslagen, ofslægen   slain, killed 4
ofslægen: he wearð… ofslægen   he was slain 4
ofslean: to ofsleane   to slay, kill 13
ofslegen   slain 21
ofsloh   destroyed 21
oft   often 14
oftalu   counter-claim 7
olfenda   camel 13
onæled   burning, ignited 23
onbyrnende   burning 5
ic oncnawe   I acknowledge 23
oncneow   acknowledged, recognized 20
oncyþðe   distress 22
ond = and   and 12
onfeng   received 4, 23
onfeng   seized 22

onfunde   realized 22
ongean   in exchange for 19
ongean   against 13, 21
ongean   back 16, 21
ongean   towards 22
onginnan   begin 7
ongite   perceive 23
onhæbbe: mec onhæbbe   raise myself 24
onhnigað   (they) bow 24
onriht   justly 7
onsprungon   sprang away 22
onscunian   shun 6
ontalu   claim 7
ontendon   to burn down 21
ord   point, spear 21
ord   vanguard 21
os-   (in names) a god 1
oð   until 10
oððæt   until 7
oðer   second 5
oðer   other, another 6, 21
oðer… oðer   the one… the other 8
oððæt   until 7, 21
oððe, oþþe   or (conjunction) 4, 24
oðrum   to the other (dat.) 21, 22
oxa   ox 2
oxena   of oxen (gen. pl.) 2

P
pallium   pallium, ceremonial scarf 4, 17
Pantan stream   river Panta 21
papa   pope 17
peneg   penny 11, 13
plegie   I play 4
plegode   played 4, 23
prass   military array 21
preost   priest 1
priost   priest 19
prud   proud 20
pund   pound 11
pytt   pit 13

R
rad   rode 20
ræce   reach, extend 3
ræd   advice 1
rædas   plans, advice 13

þu ... gerædest   *you advise* 7
man gerædde   *it was advised* 21
rædlice   *immediately* 23
rægl = hrægl   *clothing* 20
(ge)rǣhte   *reached* 16, 22
ræst: on ræste   *in his sleep* 22
Ramesige   *Ramsey* 5
ranclicor   *more boldly* 5
raðe, raþe   *quickly* 20, 21
read, reod   *red* 11
reaf   *clothing* 14, 20, 23
reaflac   *robbery* 19, 24
reced   *hall* 22
ge-regnad: from **regnian** *to adorn* 22
rehte   *told* 6
reliquias   *relics* 4
ren-weardas   *hall-guardians* 22
reord   *speech* 5
reord-berend   *speech-bearers, human beings* 6
reordian   *to feast* 17
reow   *rowed* 16
gerestan   *to rest* 23
reþe   *fierce* 22
reþnys   *cruelty* 16
ric   *powerful* 1
rice   *kingdom, authority* 2
ridon   *they rode* 20
(ge)riht   *right, privilege, obligation* 7
rihte   *right away* 19
rihte   *properly, correctly* 21
rihtlice   *justly* 19
rihtlicost   *most just* 19
rihtwisnys   *righteousness* 12
rinc   *warrior* 22
ring (hring)   *ring* 23
ripiað   *ripen* 5
ripung   *ripening* 5
rixað   *reigns, reigneth* 20
ruh   *rough* 10

S

sæ   *sea* 3
(ge)sæde   *said* (from **secgan**) 18
(ge)sælig   *prosperous* 23
sæ-riman   *sea coast* 21
sæton   *sat* (pl.) (from **sittan**) 4
sacu and socn   *jurisdiction* 18
saga   *say* (imp.) 3

(ge)samnodon   *they gathered* 14
sanct   *saint* 11, 13
sandiht   *sandy* 10
sang   *sang* 10
sar   *wound* 22
sarig   *sad* 16
sarnes   *pain* 23
sawle: sawol   *soul* 11, 22
(ge)sawon   *they saw* 6
scægðman   *shipman* 20
scan   *shone* 10
sceaf   *sheaf* 6
sceal   *must* 2
sceap   *sheep* 2
sceatt   *coin, price* 11
sceat: eorþan sceata   *in [all] the regions of the earth* 22
sceawa   *look* (imp.) 14
sceawian   *to look at, appoint* 20
sceoc   *slipped away* 21
sceolde   *should, would* 19
sceoldon   *had to* 20
sceole: ne sceole ge   *you should not* 21
sceolon   *must* 6
sceotan   *to shoot, appeal to* 19
scep   *sheep* 9, 12
scinan   *shine* 4
scioldon = sceoldon   *they should* 19
scip = scep   *sheep* 12
scip   *ship* 7
scipon: mid his scipon   *with his ships* 4
scipum: mid fiftig scipum   *with fifty ships* 4
scir   *bright* 10
scir   *shire* 18
scirgemot   *shire-court* 19
scirman   *shire-governor* 7
scirgerefa   *shire-reeve, sheriff* 20
scolde, sceolde   *must, should, had to* 7, 22
scoldon   *had to* 22
Scotta: Scotta cyng   *king of the Scots* 4
Scottas   *the Scots* 3
scridde: hine scridde   *clothed himself* 23
scrydde hyne   *clothed himself* 14
(ge)scrydde   *clothed* 15
Scyldinga   *of the Shieldings* (gen.) 22
scyld   *shield* 23
scyp   *ship* 21
se   *the* (masc.) 5
se þe   *he who* 22

se þe ær feorran com   *he who had come from afar* 22

(ge)seah   *saw* 2, 10

sealde   *gave* 8

sealde wið   *sold for* 13

searo   *intricately made*

searo   *skill, contrivance, engineering* 22

searolic   *ingenious* 24

searo-þoncum   *skilfully* 22

seax, syx   *knife* 15, 20, 24

secan   *look for, seek* 9, 22

sece   *I'm looking for* 9

secean   *to seek* 22

secgan   *say, tell* 6, 13

secgean = secgan   *say* 18

secð   *is looking for* 15

sefa   *mind* 24

sele   *hall* 22

sele Hroðgares   *Hrothgar's hall* 22

sellan   *to give, sell* 11

selre   *better* 13

(ge)seman   *to reconcile* 19, 21

sendan   *are* 11

sende   *sent* 8

seo   *the* (fem.) 5

seofon   *seven* 5

seolf   *self* 17

seolfor   *silver* 11

seolfres   *of silver* (gen.) 23

seonowe   *sinews* 22

seoððan   *afterwards* 17

setl   *seat* 8

settan   *compose, place* 11, 15

se þe   *who* 7, 17

sibb   *peace* 24

sibban   *to relatives* (dat.) 11

sida twa   *two sides* 7

side   *widely* 3

siex   *six* 12

sige   *victory* 1

sige-leas   *victory-less* 22

Sigeric   *archbishop Sigeric* 19

sige-wæpnum   *victory weapons* 22

sihter   *drain, ditch* 10

silf   *self* 23

sillan   *give* 23

sinc   *treasure* 10, 21

(ge)singodest   *you did wrong* 23

siolfor   *silver* 19

sið   *journey* 22

sið: ær oþþe sið   *before or after* 24

ge-siðas   *companions* 24

siðon   *times, multiplied by* 5

slæce   *delay* (subj.) 23

slogon   *struck* 16

smeagunga   *thoughts, meditations* 13

smercian   *to smile* 16

smerciende   *smiling* 16

smercode   *smiled* 23

smiþðe   *forge, smithy* 10

snoter, snotor   *prudent* 12

snoternys   *wisdom* 5

snotor   *wide, prudent* 22

socn   *see* **sacu**

softe   *softly, easily* 21

sohte   *sought* (from **secan**) 9, 13

(ge)sohton   *(they) sought* 13, 19

(ge)somnad   *gathered, united* 24

(ge)somnode   *gathered* 19

somod   *together* 24

sona   *immediately* 5

sona swa   *as soon as* 16

sond   *shore, sand* 24

sorg   *sorrow* 5

soð   *true* 24

soðlice   *truly, indeed* 5, 6

spæc   *spoke* 7

(ge)specen   *spoken* 11

spræc   *claim* 7

spræce   *should lay claim to* (subj.) 19

sprecan   *speak* 7, 19

springað   *spring up* 5

stæf   *letter* 24

anre stæfne   *with one voice* 23

stænt   *stands* 11

stan   *stone* 1

standan   *to stand* 2

stanfah   *stone-paved* 10

ic ðe þæt gestaðelige   *I will confirm that to you* 23

stent   *stands* 5

steorra   *star* 6

stig   *path* 10

stilnes   *quiet* 23

stod   *there was* (literally *stood*) 22

stode   *stood* (subj.) 6

stodon   *they stood* 21

stop   *advanced* 21

stow *place* 10

stræt *road, highway* 10

stream *river* 21

strengð *strength* 5

strynan *to gain, beget* 6

sum *a certain* 16

sumor *summer* 5

(ge)sunde *prosperous* (pl. adj.) 23

sunne *sun* 5

sunstede *solstice* 5

sunu *son* 4

suð *south* 2

swa *so, as* 16, 22

swa hwæt swa *whatever* 23

swa wel swa *as well as* 23

(ge)swænctest *oppressed* 23

swaþu: on swaþe *on the track* 3

swaþul *flame* 22

sweart *black* 16

swefn *dream* 6

swefniend *dreamer* 13

sweg *music* 22, 23

swegcræft *musicianship* 23

sweotol *clear,* i.e. *clearly seen* 22

sweora *neck* 12

swerian *swear* 19

ic swerige ðe *I swear to you* 23

geswicon *they ceased* 21

swift *swift* 3

swige *silence* 23

swigende *in silence* 23

swigode *was silent* 23

swilce *as if* (conj.)16

swilce *similarly* (adv.) 16

swincan *toil, labour* 9

swiðe *greatly, very* 6

swiðor *more* 6

Swiðrædingdænn *Southernden, Kent* 11

swiþre *stronger* 24

swustor *sister* 19

swulge *would swallow* (subj.) 22

(ge)swutelian *clarify, declare* 5

swutelað *declares, is declared* 11

swutelung *declaration* 11

swylc *such* 24

swylce *as it were* 6

swylce *also* 22

swymð *swims* 15

swyðe *very* 16

swyð-ferhð *strong-hearted,* i.e *courageous* 22

sy *is* (subj.) 8, 9, 11, 13

sylf (silf) *self* 3

sylf *the same* 17

sylfra *their own* 7

syllan, sellan *give* 13

syllan *pay* 7

syllan to ceape *sell* 13

syllene, to syllene *to give* 8

syllic *marvellous* 6

symle *always* 15

syndan *are* 10

syndolh *a great wound* 22

synscaða *evil assailant* 22

syððan *afterwards* 4

syðþan *after* 6

syx *six* 12

syxtig *sixty* 12

T

tacen *sign* 15, 22

(ge)tacnian *to signify* 5

(ge)tæhte *instructed* 19, 23

(ge)tæhte *shown* (past part., fem.) 23

(ge)tæle *counting* 12

tælst: þu hi tælst *you reproach her* 23

tær *tore* 14

talu *claim* 7, 20

tearas *tears* 23

teo *take* (subj. from **teon**) 18

tid *hour* 5

tida *of hours* (gen.) 12

(ge)tilian *till, cultivate, produce* 18

tima *time, season* 5

tir *glory* 2

tirfæst *glorious* 2

tiðude *granted* 18

to *to* 1

tobræd *spread widely* 13

tobrecan *to break, shatter* 22

todælednys *division* 5

toeacan *in addition to* 8

toforan *before* 1

togædere gan *to clash together* 21

togædere gesæton *they sat together* 15

togeanes: him togeanes *against him* 4

Toki *Toki* (a Kentish thegn) 18

tolucan *to destroy* 22

torn *bitterness* 22

tosende *sent a message* 21

totær: totær his reaf *tore his clothing* 14

(ge)togen *educated* 23

(ge)trahtniað *(they) explain, expound* 5

treddode *trod* 10

treow *loyalty:* **treow on eorle** *loyalty in a man* 2

treow *tree* 6

tu *two* (fem. and neuter) 7

tugon *pulled* (from **teon**) 13

tun *estate, farm* 1

tunece *coat* 6, 13

tunge *tongue* 12

tungol *star* 3

twa *two* (fem. and neuter) 3, 12

twan *two* 24

twegen *two* (masc.) 3, 12, 21

twelf *twelve* 12

twelfhynde *high-ranking* 7

twentig *twenty* 5

twihynde *low-ranking* 7

tyrwa *resin* 13

þ

þa, ða *then, at that time* 1, 4

þa… þa *when… then* 6, 22

þa *the* (fem. acc.) 6, 10

þa *the* (plural) 7

geþafian *allow* 17

þæc *thatch, roof* 16

þæne *the* (masc. acc.) 10

þær *there* (adv.) 4

þær *where* (conj.) 15

þær *if:* **þær he meahte swa** *if he so could* 22

þære *of the* (fem.) 7, 10

þære *to the* (fem.) 10

þæron: þæron getilian *produce on it, cultivate from it* 18

þær rihte *straightaway* 19

þærto: þærto hyrð *belongs to it* 11

þærto *to it, to that place* 19

þæs *of the* (masc. or neuter) 7, 10

þæs *this* (def. art. gen.) 22

þæt *the* (neuter) 5, 10

þæt *that, so that* 5, 22

þagyt *still, yet* 19

þam *to the* (masc.) 10

ðam ðe *to the one who* 11

þam þe hi ær ahte *to the one who owned it before* 16

þan = þam 10

þancigende *thanking* 23

þanon *from there* 22

þanon forð *from then on* 19

þar (ðar) *there* 23

þara þe *for those who* 22

þas þing *these things* 5

þas *these* 11

þe *to you* 18

þe *the* 20

þe *which, who* (relative pronoun) 4, 6, 7, 22

þe *or* 14

þe geornor *all the more certainly* (**georn** normally = *eager*) 22

þeah *though* 18

ge-þeah *flourished* 20

geðeaht *counsel, design, providence* 13

þearf *need* 19

þearflic *profitable* 18

þearle *greatly* 23

þeawas *virtues* 8

þegenas *thegns* 7

ðegenlice *in a thegnly manner* 20

þegenriht *thegnly legal status* 20

þegnas *thegns* 7

þegnlice *in a thegnly manner* 20

þeh, þeah *although* 18

þencan *think; intend* 13

þene = þæne *the* 19

þeode: þeod *nation* 14

þeoden *prince* 20

þeodscipe *nation, people* 7

þeow *servant* 13

þes *this* (masc.) 11

þin *your* (sing.) 9, 23

þing *thing or things* 5

þingum: for hwilcum þingum *for what reason* 15

þisum þingum *in these matters* 23

þiss, þis *this* (neuter) 11

þohte *thought, intended* 6, 13

þolian *suffer* 22

þone *the* (masc. acc.) 7, 10

þonne: swiftre þonne *swifter than* 3

þonne *then* 12, 16

þonne *when* (conj.) 5

þonne… þonne   *when… then (see þa… þa)* 6
þragum   *sometimes* 5
þrea-nyd: for þrea-nydum   *for sad necessity* 22
þreo hund   *three hundred* 12
þrinnes   *Trinity* 24
þritig   *thirty* 12
þrydda   *third* 17
þrymm   *glory* 5, 17
þryþ   *power* (used with personal names) 1
þu   *you* (sing.) 18
þuhte   *seemed* 6
þunar   *thunder* 5
þurh   *through* 6
Þurcil   *earl Thorkel the Tall* 4
þus, þus   *thus* 8
þusend   *thousand* 12
ge-þydan   *associate* 24
þyllic   *such a* 15
þyncan   *seem* 6
þysses lifes   *of this life* 22

U

ufon   *up above* 12
uhtna gehwam   *every morning* 24
unasecgendlic   *unutterable* 21
unbefohten   *without a fight* 21
unbesacan   *uncontested* 11
unbesacen   *uncontested* 19
unbesmiten   *untarnished* 13
unbliþe   *unhappy* 16
unc   *the two of us* (dual) 24
uncer, uncre   *our* (dual) 18, 24
under   *under* 3
underfangen   *received* (past part.) 17
underfengon   *complied* 21
underhnigan   *sink under* 3
unfæger   *ugly* 10
unforboden   *unforbidden* 11
unforhte   *fearless* 21
ungecnawen   *unknown* 23
ungewunelic   *unusual* 23
unlagu   *injustice, wrong* 17
unlytel   *great* 22
unnan   *grant* 11
unnendre heortan   *with a willing heart* 11
unriht *injustice:* **unriht alecgan**   *put down injustice* 7
unswicende   *faithful, undeceitful* 7

up   *up* 20
uparist   *rises* 5
upcyme   *ascendancy* 24
uplang   *up* 22
upp: upp afligeð   *flies up* 16
ura *our:* **ura leofa hlaford**   *our dear lord* 7
ure cyning   *our king* 6
ure Drihten   *our Lord* 1
ure gastlica broðor   *our spiritual brother* 7
urne *our* (masc. acc.): **ðeah we urne broðor ofslean**   *if we kill our brother* 13
urum   *our:* **in urum life** *in our life* (dat.) 1, 20, 21
ut   *out* 4
geutlagode man   *they outlawed* 4
uton   *let us* 13
utweard   *outward* 22

W

wacol   *wakeful* 23
wæg, weg   *wave* 3
wæl   *slaughter* 21
wælle   *stream* 10
wæl-ræs   *battle-rush* 22
(ge)wændon   *returned* 23
wæpna   *weapons* (genitive) 21
(ge)wæpnod   *armed* 21
wære   *was* (subj.) 7, 12
wæron, wæran   *were* (from **wesan**) 4
wæs   *was* 1
wæstm-as   *fruits* (plural) 5
wæt   *wet* 5
wæter   *water* 21
wæterleas   *waterless* 13
wanað   *wanes* 5
wang   *site, field* 10
wanigean   *to lament* 22
warnian   *warn* 21
wast   *you know* 23
wat   *know* 4
ge-wat   *departed, went* 18, 21
we   *we* 3
(ge)weald   *power* 22
(ge)weald   *dominion* 24
wealdan   *wield, control* 21
weall   *wall* 10, 22, 24
weard   *ward, guardian* 1
wearm   *warm* 5
wearð   *became* 4, 22

(ge)wearð   *occurred* 14

wearð... gelumpen   *was come about* 22

wearð ... geworden   *had become* 23

wearð... gyfeþe   *was granted* 22

wearð... ofslægen   *he was slain* 4

weaxað   *grows, waxeth* 5

wedd   *pledge* 8

weder   *weather, storm* 24

weg   *way* 10: **on weg** *away* 22

weg, wæg: on wege   *on the wave* 12

wegfarend   *wayfaring* 13

wege þu   *wave (imperative)* 15

wel: hine wel lærde   *instructed him well* 1

swa wel swa   *as well as* 23

welig   *wealthy* 8

welwillendnes   *kindness* 23

wēnan   *expect, suppose* 15

wēnde   *supposed* 24

(ge)wende   *returned, went* 4

wendon   *they went* 19

wēndon   *they supposed* 21, 23

weofod   *altar* 7

weold   *ruled,* from **wealdan** 11

Weolintun   *Wellington* 20

weop   *wept* 20

weorod   17

werod   *troop*

weorð   *worth, worthy* 20

weorðan   *become* 12

weorðlic   *worthy:* **mid weorðlican weorode**
   with a worthy retinue 17

weorðscipe   *honour* 17

wepan   *to weep* 20

wepende   *weeping* 14

wer   *man* 16, 24

wer wergild   *compensation* 19

wera   *of men* 15

weras   *men* 12

weredon   *they defended* 21

werige   *keep* 17

werlic   *masculine* 15

werod   *troop, force* 12, 21

wesan   *to be* 3

west   *west* 10, 16

west riht   *westwards* 10

west weard   *westwards* 18

wexseð and wanað   *waxes and wanes* 5

wic   *trading centre; dairy farm* 12

wic   *dwelling-place* 22

wicg   *horse* 12

wicinga   *of the Vikings* 21

wicneras   *bailiffs* 18

widdor   *more widely* 24

widre   *further* 22

wif   *woman, wife* 6, 8, 10, 18

wif   *women* 24

wiflic   *feminine* 15

wig   *battle* 1, 21

wig, wih   *sacred place, image* 10

wiga: wigan   *warriors* 21

wigheard   *battle-hard* 21

wihaga   *battle-wall (of shields)* 21

wiht   *creature* 3, 12

Wiht   *Isle of Wight* 4

(ge)wihte   *weight* 23

Wihtland   *Isle of Wight* 17

wildeor, wilddeor   *wild beast* 13

willa   *will:* **eower willa** *your wish* 15

willa   *(their) desire* 22

willan   *to want, to wish* 15, 21

wille (wylle)   *want (subj.)* 23

ðu wilt   *you will, want* 23

wilnode: ic symle wilnode   *I always wanted* 15

(ge)win   *fight* 22

wine   *friend* 1, 20

wīn-gāl   *inebriated with wine* 10

wīn-sele   *wine-hall* 22

winsum   *beautiful* 23

winter   *winter* 5

winterlæhte   *it became winter* 19

wis   *wise* 19

wisdom   *wisdom* 2

wisian   *to guide* 10

wiste   *knew* 18, 22: **þeh he hit ær wiste**
   though he had known it before 18

wiste   *he knew* 22

wiston   *they knew* 22

hie þæt ne wiston   *they did not know this* 22

witan   *counsellors* 4, 13, 19, 22

wið   *against:* **wið earm** *supported by his own
   arm* 22

wið   *against:* **wið niðe** *against enmity* 22

wið   *against:* **god wið yfele** *good against evil* 4

wið   *in exchange for:* **feoh wið freode** *money in
   exchange for peace* 7

wið   *in exchange for:* **wið ðrittigum penegum**
   in exchange for thirty pennies 13

wið þon ðe   *in exchange for which* 21

wið   near: **wið Deorhyrste** near Deerhurst 4

wið   with: **freondræden wið** friendship with 6

wiðfeng   seized 22

wiðhæfde   withstood, stood up to 22

witnys, witnes   knowledge, witness 7

ge-witnes: to gewitnesse   as witness 19

witodlice   indeed, so 6

wlonc   proud 10, 24

wolde   would 19

wolde   wanted 22

womb, wamb   stomach 12

wong, wang   field (uncultivated) 3, 10

wop   lamentation 22

word   word 7

wordcwidas   words, sayings 24

worhton   made 21

worold   world 7

woruld   world 1, 4

wræc   exile 5

wrætlice   wondrously 12

wrat   wrote 16

(ge)wrecan   avenge 13

wrecend   avenger 13

(ge)wregde   accused 6

Wridewellan   Wordwell 11

(ge)writ   letter, writ, document 7

(ge)writen   written (past part.) 16

wrixlan   exchange 24

wucena   of weeks 12

wudu   wood 2

wuldor   glory 3

wuldre   with glory 24

wulf   wolf 1

æt Wulfamere   at Woolmer 19

Wulfstan   archbishop Wulfstan 4, 7, 8, 14, 18

Wulfstan   Wulfstan (one of Byrhtnoth's **thegns**) 21

wunade   remained 5

wundor   wonder, miracle 3

wundriende   marvelling 16

wundrum   with wonders 12

(ge)wunian   remain 4

wununge   lodging (fem. acc.) (from **wunung**) 23

wurdon   they became 8

wurð   price 14

wurðlice   honourably 17

wurþmynt   honour 17

wurþra   richer 8

wurðscipe   honour 13

wyllað   we want 5

wylle   I want: **ic wylle beon** I wish to be 7

wylle: þu…wylle   you want 15

wylm (wielm)   surge 10

wyn-leas   joyless 22

wynn   joy 7, 20

wynsam   delightful 17

(ge)wyrcan   construct, make 2, 5, 6

(ge)wyrcean   construct, make 6

wyrcð   makes 5

wyrd   fate, events 5

wyrhta   maker, craftsman 23

wyrhtana   of the makers (gen.pl.) 23

wyrs   worse 13

wyrtgemang   spice mixture 13

wyrð   becomes 5

wyrðscype   honour 1, 17

Y

ycan   increase 24

yfel   evil 2

ylc: se ylca   the same person 16

yld: on his ylde   in his old age 6

ymbe   about: **ymbe þa feower timan** about the four seasons 5

þa ymbsittendan   all the ones sitting around there 23

ymbutan   round about 6

yrfe: on ece yrfe   as a permanent inheritance 11

yrmð   misery, crime 14

yrre   angry 22

yrremod   angry in mind 10

ys   is 13

ytemest   last 5

yð   wave 24

Appendices

Appendix I

THE SEVEN CLASSES OF OLD ENGLISH STRONG VERBS

In dictionaries of Old English, strong verbs are identified by the class number to which they belong:

Infinitive Plural Participle	Class	Present	Past singular	Past plural	Past participle
drīfan	I	drīfð	drāf	drifon	(ge)drifen
cēosan	II	cȳst	cēas	curon	(ge)coren
singan	III	singð	sang	sungon	(ge)sungen
cuman	IV	cymð	cōm	cōmon	(ge)cumen
gifan	V	gifð	geaf	gēafon	(ge)gifen
swerian	VI	swereð	swōr	swōron	(ge)sworen
cnāwan	VII	cnǣwð	cnēow	cnēowon	(ge)cnāwen

It may be helpful to compare the modern English equivalents:

Class I	*drive, drove, driven*
Class II	*choose, chose, chosen*
Class III	*sing, sang, sung*
Class IV	*come, came, come*
Class V	*give, gave, given*
Class VI	*swear, swore, sworn*
Class VII	*know, knew, known*

Image credits